The Inheritance of Genius

Why hide his faults? Why conceal his weaknesses in a cloud of periphrases? Why not show him, like him as he is, not robed in a marble toga, and draped and polished in a heroic attitude, but with inked ruffles, and claret stains on his tarnished laced coat, and on his manly face the marks of good fellowship, of illness, of kindness, of care, and wine.

William Makepeace Thackeray on Henry Fielding
The English Humourists of the Eighteenth Century (1853)

The Inheritance of Genius

*A Thackeray Family Biography,
1798-1875*

John Aplin

The Lutterworth Press

The Lutterworth Press
P.O. Box 60
Cambridge
CB1 2NT
United Kingdom

www.lutterworth.com
publishing@lutterworth.com

ISBN: 978 0 7188 9224 1

British Library Cataloguing in Publication Data
A record is available from the British Library

Copyright © John Aplin, 2010

First Published, 2010

All rights reserved. No part of this edition may be reproduced,
stored electronically or in any retrieval system,
or transmitted in any form or by any means,
electronic, mechanical, photocopying, recording, or otherwise,
without prior written permission from the Publisher
(permissions@lutterworth.com).

For

Belinda Margaret Thackeray Norman-Butler
(10 December 1908 - 26 December 2008)

If you could have seen her <u>talking</u> with her eyes to James yesterday after they had been parted. Sunshine Jimps said 'me too' & climbed up into the Perambulator & away they went through the other sunshine waving & waving goodbye.

Anne Thackeray Ritchie
On her grandchildren James and Belinda, 6 May 1910

CONTENTS

List of Illustrations	ix
Prelude and Acknowledgements	xi
Chapter One: Scenes of All Sorts (1798-1839)	1
Chapter Two: Not Yet Actors in the Play (1839-1846)	34
Chapter Three: Our Street (1847-1852)	63
Chapter Four: A Little Rain of Dollars (1852-1855)	91
Chapter Five: Towards the Unknown Ocean (1855-1862)	120
Chapter Six: Here is Night and Rest (1860-1863)	142
Chapter Seven: All This Endless Year (1863-1865)	168
Chapter Eight: A Woman's Cares and Joys (1865-1867)	185
Chapter Nine: A Great Enormous Half Grown Place (1867-1868)	205
Chapter Ten: The Shabby Tide of Progress (1869-1873)	234
Chapter Eleven: The Inscrutable Design (1873-1875)	253

Notes	275
Thackeray and Ritchie Family Tree	294
Abbreviations and Sources	296
Select Bibliography	299
Index	301

List of Illustrations

George Chinnery's portrait of Richmond and Anne Thackeray with their son, William Makepeace Thackeray, painted in Calcutta about 1813-14. Courtesy of the estate of Belinda Norman-Butler. *Front cover*

++++

Pages from Richmond Thackeray's 1798 journal. Courtesy of Juliet Murray.
Page 4

Anne Becher, artist unknown. Courtesy of Juliet Murray. *Page 9*

Title page from Thackeray's school copy of Horace. Courtesy of Juliet Murray.
Page 14

Page with Thackeray drawing, from school copy of Horace. Courtesy of Juliet Murray. *Page 15*

Pastel illustrations in a letter from Thackeray to his mother, written from Weimar in 1830. Courtesy of Juliet Murray. *Page 19*

Page from an album of Thackeray sketches (Houghton MS Eng 853). Courtesy of the Houghton Library, Harvard University. *Page 22*

Isabella Thackeray, pastel by Thackeray. Courtesy of the estate of Belinda Norman-Butler. *Page 26*

William and Isabella Out Walking. Courtesy of Juliet Murray. *Page 29*

Earliest surviving letter from Thackeray to Annie, written from Ireland in 1842. Courtesy of Juliet Murray. *Page 52*

Watercolour of Annie, by Thackeray. Courtesy of Juliet Murray. *Page 56*

Autograph pages from *Pendennis*. Courtesy of Juliet Murray. *Pages 74-5*

Thackeray's initial letter to chapter thirty-six of *Pendennis*. Photograph supplied by the author. *Page 81*

Thackeray's letter to Annie and Minny, with sketch of slaves, written from Savannah 1853. Courtesy of Juliet Murray. *Page 99*

Page of *The Newcomes* in Minny's hand, with Thackeray's annotations. Courtesy of Juliet Murray. *Page 105*

Annie in a studio photograph taken about 1854. Courtesy of the Provost and Fellows of Eton College. *Page 114*

Minny in a studio photograph taken about 1854. Courtesy of the Provost and Fellows of Eton College. *Page 115*

Sketch by Thackeray. Courtesy of Juliet Murray. *Page 130*

Page of the *Roundabout Paper* 'On Ribbons' in Minny's hand, with Thackeray's annotations. Courtesy of Juliet Murray. *Page 137*

Sketch by Thackeray. Courtesy of Juliet Murray. *Page 153*

Letter from Minny Thackeray to Annie Thackeray, 1862. Courtesy of Juliet Murray. *Page 156*

Young Street and Thackeray's house, second on the left-hand side, photographed by John Jones Merriman, 1868. Courtesy of Local Studies Department, Royal Borough of Kensington and Chelsea. *Page 163*

Sketch of Thackeray, by Frederick Walker. Courtesy of the estate of Belinda Norman-Butler. *Page 166*

Sketch by Thackeray. Courtesy of Juliet Murray. *Page 170*

Locket of Thackeray's hair taken after death. Courtesy of Juliet Murray. *Page 178*

Sketch by Thackeray. Courtesy of Juliet Murray. *Page 190*

Watercolour by Thackeray. Courtesy of Juliet Murray. *Page 201*

Sketch by Thackeray. Courtesy of Juliet Murray. *Page 209*

Sketch by Thackeray. Courtesy of Juliet Murray. *Page 219*

Minny and Laura with Leslie's dog Troy. Courtesy of the Provost and Fellows of Eton College. *Page 243*

Pages from Annie's journal, describing Minny's death in 1875. Courtesy of the estate of Belinda Norman-Butler. *Page 271*

Minny's grave at Kensal Green, part of the Stephen family plot. Photograph supplied by the author. *Page 274*

Prelude and Acknowledgements

At the start of 1862, William Makepeace Thackeray prepared to move into his new house in Palace Green, close to Kensington Palace. Here he hoped at last to find the time and energy to write a history of the reign of Queen Anne. As the builders finished their work, rehearsals were in progress for the private theatricals that would precede the transfer of the author and his two daughters from Onslow Square. Thackeray's younger daughter Minny was one of the acting company, while Annie, not pretty and more awkward, stood captivated as the rehearsals unfolded before her, watching, recording, remembering. It would be important for Annie to recall the happiness and hopefulness of this moment in later times, of her father standing in the house which had turned out to cost far more than at first imagined.

The first months at Palace Green passed contentedly. Thackeray's twice-widowed mother returned from Paris in March to join them in time for the move, and during the summer of 1862 Annie and Minny became caught up in the excitement of the engagement of Amy Crowe to their father's cousin, Edward Thackeray, which would be followed by the couple's departure for India, well-trodden territory for the Thackerays. After Amy's death, her two young children would be sent back to England to live with Annie and Minny, who created a role for themselves as step-aunts.

By then, the loss of Amy was just one more sadness to be endured by Thackeray's daughters who had already lost so much, and so quickly. The writer had not been well for years, and had several times contemplated surgery for a debilitating stricture of the urethra which caused him periodic agonies. In the end, he never went through with the treatment. When death came to him at the end of 1863, alone in his room in the early hours, it was as the consequence of a massive seizure, a stroke which distorted his features according to those who found his body as the household woke on Christmas eve morning. He was fifty-two.

A year later, the sisters lost their grandmother, whose death was as peaceful as their father's had been grotesque. This second death brought a kind of completion. Already aged twenty-eight and twenty-five, for the first time in their adult lives the sisters had to find their own way forwards even as their instincts seemed always to pull them back to the past, to their memories of life with an adored father. They had been his 'dearest women', his constant companions. Thackeray's friends were their friends, and only in a limited sense can they said to have had independent lives at all. Neither was yet married.

The silent member in this family roll-call is their mother Isabella. Since her daughters' early years she had lived away from them, cared for in a variety of institutions and private homes after symptoms of post-natal depression – probably linked with intermittent schizophrenia – overwhelmed her following Minny's birth in 1840. Isabella is still not infrequently described as Thackeray's 'mad wife', an unattractive shorthand that accepts without challenge the harsh language of the time and ignores any more nuanced diagnosis. The marriage was regarded by those who knew Thackeray as the great tragedy of his life, Isabella's looming absence making him cling with an almost desperate fondness to the company of his daughters, who returned his love in kind. They were the demonstrable evidence that, though his marriage may have been foolhardy it was very far from being a mistake. He treated them with an informality and spontaneous affection that was strikingly enlightened for the time.

When their father died, the sisters instinctively drew ever closer. During his lifetime, they had needed no-one else. With him gone, there *was* no-one else. Their exceptional bond never weakened, though it did change. Annie had already started to establish her own reputation as a writer, a first short novel having appeared before Thackeray's death. Minny chose a different path. In marrying Leslie Stephen she left Annie free to fulfil the great expectations already being placed upon her as 'Thackeray's daughter'. Marriage gave Minny happiness and real fulfilment, but it was undoubtedly a sacrificial act too, for she chose to create a home for the three of them, and with courage and intelligence provided the security and support which permitted husband and sister to pursue their different and more selfish ambitions. Leslie Stephen knew what he owed Minny in saving him from a crusty donnishness. He was never more lively and good-humoured than during the years of this, his first marriage. Minny loved Leslie, but her marriage was prompted by affections and loyalties of a more complex kind. By reaching outside the familiar certainties and forging new ties, she compelled Annie to find a meaning for herself within an independent life.

'When I drop, there is no life to be written of me; *mind this* and consider it as my last testament and desire.' Any biographer who decides to write about Thackeray begins by overruling the novelist's explicit proscription, which haunted his elder daughter and yet which eventually she managed to circumvent. This book, the first of two volumes, sets out to place the daughters, mother and wife of this remarkable man as central figures in a family history which continued beyond his death. As such, it is not primarily a study of Thackeray the writer, or of his better-known public, clubbable persona; instead, it foregrounds his domestic circle, and the effect that his life, death and legacy had on those closest to him. Gordon Ray, still his finest biographer, was right to suggest that Thackeray was someone for our own times, 'a big man, a ripe man, and a complete man', a writer of great technical strength if one uneven in his achievements, occasionally prickly in character, but usually charming and endearing, whose all too evident weaknesses were balanced by a genuine humanity. It is sad that he died before either of his adult daughters had really stepped out into the world, for he would have been proud of their accomplishments. Like him, they reveal themselves in their letters as intelligent observers of their rich environment, delighting in the comic absurdities of everyday living.

Not since Ray's classic biography, written fifty years ago, has it been possible to employ so much previously unused and largely unseen material. This book draws continuously on the letters, diaries, journals and notebooks of the Thackerays and their circle, as does its sequel, *Memory and Legacy*. For Thackeray's own letters I am indebted to Ray's four-volume collected edition, and to the two-volume supplement edited by Edgar Harden, and for some Anne Thackeray Ritchie materials to Lillian Shankman's collection. Virtually all of the remaining source material is newly transcribed. I have drawn on many archives, but three collections stand out. Early in my researches I was fortunate to meet Thackeray's great-granddaughter, Belinda Norman-Butler, who from the outset encouraged my work and maintained a lively interest until her death on Boxing Day of 2008, aged 100. She made freely available to me papers still in her possession, including her grandmother's (Annie's) journal and diaries, and permitted me to photograph Thackeray's pictures and drawings hanging on her walls. Her daughter, Catherine Wilson, has continued to encourage me in my work during its closing stages. Juliet Murray, another Thackeray great-great-granddaughter, has also been a wonderfully generous and hospitable friend, allowing me to use anything that I needed from her rich collection of letters, journals, drawings and other family papers. She witnessed my excitement in discovering amongst them more than eighty of George Smith's letters to Thackeray, written during the early years of the *Cornhill*. The opportunity to talk to her and to her aunt Belinda about people whose stories live on in the family memory has been a unique pleasure. Much from their collections has not previously been known to Thackeray scholars.

The third archive is the most extensive single collection of Anne Thackeray Ritchie papers, and was given by Belinda Norman-Butler to Eton College Library. It consists not just of Annie's letters, but also of many of Minny's, a large number of letters from Thackeray's mother to her granddaughters, as well as correspondence from many family members and friends. I have spent seven years reading all of this material, and find it hard adequately to thank the Eton library staff for their generous assistance during this period. I want especially to credit Nick Baker, Rachel Bond, Linda Fowler and Michael Meredith. Michael's interest in my work has been generous and constant. He has freely shared his expert knowledge of the Victorians with me, and I value his friendship.

For this first volume, I am most grateful to the following for permitting me to quote from materials in their collections: Beinecke Library, Yale University; the Syndics of Cambridge University Library; Duke University, Durham, North Carolina; the Provost and Fellows of Eton College; Harry Ransom Humanities Research Center, University of Texas at Austin; Houghton Library, Harvard University; Huntington Library, San Marino, California; Local Studies Department, Kensington Central Library; John Murray Archive, National Library of Scotland; Michael Millgate (private collection); Department of Rare Books and Special Collections, Princeton University Library; the Master and Fellows of Trinity College, Cambridge; Tennyson Research Centre, Lincolnshire County Council.

I am indebted to the late Belinda Norman-Butler, Catherine Wilson and Juliet Murray for the right to use Thackeray and Ritchie family materials, and to the following individuals and organisations for allowing me to quote from items for which they hold the copyright: Harvard University (for Oliver Wendell Holmes Sr), The Society of Authors (for Leslie Stephen, © 2010 the Estate of Leslie Stephen), the Tennyson Research Centre (for Tennyson family materials), and Sir Anthony Trollope (for Anthony Trollope). I have endeavoured to trace all copyright owners, and apologise for any inadvertent oversights.

My thanks are also due for the many and various kindnesses shown me by a number of people: Richard Aplin, Ian Brown (National Library of Scotland), Richard Childs (county archivist, West Sussex Record Office), Vanessa Curtis, Marion Dell, Colin Ford, Veronica Franklin Gould, M. E. Griffiths (Archivist, Sedbergh School), Susan Halpert (Harvard College Library), Fr Kenneth Havey, Lucinda Hawksley, Martin Hayes (Local Studies, West Sussex County Council), Sue Hodson (Huntington Library), John Hopson (archivist, British Library), Elisabeth Jay, Carol Hanbery Mackay, Jane Martineau, Michael Millgate, Leslie Morris (Harvard College Library), Maureen Moran, Xenia Murray, Christine Nelson (Morgan Library and Museum), Hilary Newman, Christina Rathbone, Simon Reynolds, the late Bryan Rhodes, Gayle Richardson (Huntington Library), William Ritchie, Aaron Schmidt (Boston Public Library), Carrie Starren (Leighton House Museum), John Sutherland, David Sutton (Reading University Library), Grace Timmins (Tennyson Research Centre), Ann Wheeler (archivist, Charterhouse) and Derek Wood. I also thank the ever-courteous staff of the London Library. At the Lutterworth Press I have appreciated the interest of Adrian Brink and Aidan Van de Weyer, and benefited from the thoughtful advice of my editor, Ian Bignall. To Peter Collister, who has lived with this project over the years, advised on drafts and steered me away from many of the crasser solecisms, I am more than grateful. He is not to blame for the faults that undoubtedly remain.

One or two explanatory notes are necessary. Thackeray's eldest daughter I have chosen to call 'Annie', even though Thackeray himself wrote 'Anny'. This may seem perverse, but after the death of her sister in 1875 the only person regularly to spell it like that was Leslie Stephen, as did the children of his second marriage (including Virginia and Vanessa). Everyone else – husband, other family members and friends – tended to keep with 'Annie'. However, I have not changed spellings of names in quoted letters. This means that in my own text I can reserve the name 'Anny Thackeray' for the daughter of Edward and Amy Thackeray, one of the two little girls who came to live with Annie and Minny after their mother's death. In my quotations from original manuscripts I have tended not to amend spelling errors or supply missing punctuation; full stops have occasionally been silently added to assist meaning.

One

SCENES OF ALL SORTS
(1798-1839)

There are scenes of all sorts: some dreadful combats, some grand and lofty horse-riding, some scenes of high life, and some of very middling indeed; some love-making for the sentimental, and some light comic business; the whole accompanied by appropriate scenery and brilliantly illuminated with the Author's own candles.

'Before the Curtain', *Vanity Fair*

A boy of sixteen prepares for a journey. On the last day of May in 1798, accompanied by his father, he travels to Portsmouth from his birthplace in Hadley, Middlesex. He is to board the *Thetis*, the ship that will soon start on the 5,000-mile voyage to Calcutta, where a job in the great East India Company awaits him. In his luggage is a large notebook in which he has promised to keep a record of his journey for his mother. Such a long voyage is not an unfamiliar one in his family. His father had gone out more than thirty years earlier; a brother has already preceded him, and four more brothers will later make the same passage to India.

Father and son arrive in Portsmouth with some days to spare, and there is an opportunity to explore the town before it is time for farewells, for the boy will sail alone. He will never return to England, nor see his parents again.

Not until some weeks into the voyage does he reach for the notebook and start to honour his promise.

> My Dear Mater
>
> You desired me to keep and at the end of this Long voyage to send you a journal of all the Little occurrences which may happen on Board: my dear Father gave me a

small book in which I write the Heads and afterwards enter them in this. R:T

Imp: you know on the 31st of May (98.) I left you and the family & with my father set out for Portsmouth. on the 1st of June we arrived there. we saw every thing of <u>note</u>. we staid there till the 7. when I left my very excellent father and sailed to St Helens where we arrived that afternoon & on the following day we left it & sailed slowly on. On the 10th we were off Plymouth & on the 11th lost sight of old England. the 12th our Convoy chased some unknown Ship also entered the Bay of Biscay so famous for storms the ship rocks very much. there has been very little or no sea sickness none but the Ladies complaining. the 14th we passed the Bay of Biscay a little rain & squally. real[l]y the Journal of a sea voyage cannot possibly be entertaining & very often I think of leaving it off & if you had not desired particularly I certainly should.[1]

The great adventure is being undertaken by Richmond Thackeray, father of the future novelist, and his rediscovered journal, incomplete as it is, is the earliest of the few surviving examples of his writing. He had been sent to school at Eton, but after securing a training position as a 'writer' or clerk for the East India Company he left to learn book-keeping skills, just as his father, the first William Makepeace Thackeray, had done before him.

His journal gives an engaging sketch of life on board the *Thetis* and its leading role in the small convoy that set out together for mutual protection, and he is full of admiration for Captain Henry Bullock, 'a very great man'. He is sanguine about the hardships and dangers of such a voyage; early in July two deaths are noted in the convoy, one on them on the *Thetis*. Resilience and good humour see him through the rough treatment of the traditional rites to Neptune as the ship crosses the line, and the sore throat which follows, but his mother must have read these details with alarm.

23 [June] out of the Lat of Madeira.... We have seen great plenty of flying fish & Porpoises. 26 was a remarkable fine day indeed we have had very fine weather upon the whole ... on the 2^d [July] Capt Makintosh a Passenger in the Osterly died & in the afternoon was buried (that is launched to the deep) with Military Honors & minute guns for Half an Hour. the sea is quite calm ... 4 we made a great many signals this morning particularly to the Osterly & Berington who would

not answer & we fired a gun. it was so dark in the Cabin that we could not write. at 12 oclock my servant who is a soldier was tried & flog[g]ed by a court Martial so that I am deprived of his services.... On the 7 a poor man died that is the first in our ship. 9th we expect to Cut the Line in about 4 days.... On 12th we passed the Line so celebrated for the Rites of Neptune. there were about 60 victims I among the number & immediately after the Procession which I suppose you must have seen we were dragged out by Constable & shaved & ducked. the Lather was made of Tar Pitch Oil of Old Lamps Grease & other various dirty Articles after which we had about 40 Pails of Water thrown over each of us not to forget the razor [which] was made out of an old Iron Hoop which made holes in my face. I caught a bad sore throat by the ducking which was the Greatest inconvenience of any & all the Cloathes I had on were total[l]y spoilt. 13th (still a sore throat) the Girls all went into fits at least pretended to be so & a great noise was made about it Note not on account of my ill health.... 17: throat Better but not well. we were very near sunk this afternoon by the Helm being left to go round before the wind which made us turn our side before the head of the Rockingham (she going at 7 miles per hour) being in Close order of sailing & in passing it was a miracle her bowsprit had not entangled us & she run over us for I might have thrown a biscuit on her Forcastle. 18 throat most well very fine wind. I never care what weather it is so as we go fast therefore of course I hate a calm.

The ship's company consisted of 'the wife of a captain in the Bengal Artillery; five young ladies; some thirty officers, writers, cadets, and surgeons; and eighty odd recruits to the Indian army',[2] a typical cargo of civil and military personnel required to sustain the needs of a burgeoning Empire. Once they had crossed the equator there was dancing, but Richmond shyly sat this out, 'for I did not nor do I intend to dance once during the whole voyage tho I hear it is to be evry night'. He did not take long to identify the personalities on board, discovering in himself the natural gift for caricature which his son would one day make his own. His awkwardness makes him dismiss most of the girls as plain or stupid, judging them with all the wisdom of his sixteen years as still in need of their schoolmistress. But the 'saucy' ones probably had the measure of him.

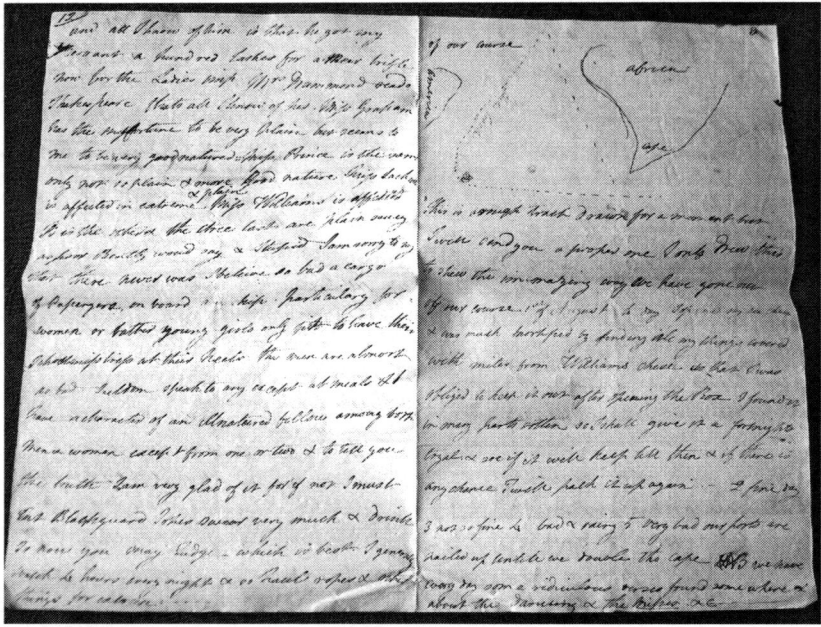

Pages from Richmond Thackeray's 1798 Journal

I wish I had some anecdotes to send you but really never was such a ship so crowded & at the same time so few Gentlemen really. I take my list & look over their characters & cannot find one I like at all. my dear father saw Mr Brisco and Blunt at Portsmouth and I am sure was much mistaken in them for Brisco is a complete wine drinker & card player & Blunt immitates [*sic*] him. the first mate Mr Jenkins took in every body for he has all the smiles & duplicity of a scotchman. he pretended to be so polite but now he is known throughout the Ship in fact I seldom or ever speak to him or indeed very few on board. I sometimes amuse myself with drawing caracatures [*sic*] & letting them come out without being known to be the drawer: but they never are offensive.... I have said little or nothing of the Ladies: by & by for them...

 the second mate of this ship is a very gentlelike man & much liked by every one on board ev'n M^r. Bathurst the Cynic likes him. When he arrives in England shew him any little civility for my sake. I intend god be willing to send by him some trifle or another by him [*sic*] & Perhaps this invaluable manuscript... now for the Ladies.... M^{rs}

One: Scenes of All Sorts 5

> Drummond reads Shakespeare that's all I know of her. Miss Graham has the misfortune to be very plain but seems to me to be very goodnatured: Miss Prince is the same only not so plain & more Good nature[d]. Miss Jackson is affected in extreme & plain. Miss Williams is affected as is the other & the three last are plain saucy as poor Bently would say & Stupid. I am sorry to say that there never was I believe so bad a cargo of Passengers on board any ship, particularly for women or rather young girls only fit to have their Schoolmistress at their heels. the men are almost as bad, [I] seldom speak to any except at meals & I have a character of an illnatured fellow among both Men & women except from one or two & to tell you the truth I am very glad of it for if not I must cut Blackguard Jokes swear very much & drink so now you may judge – which is best.

On 17 August Richmond recorded being off the Cape, believing that 'the Greater Part of our long voyage is over'; they were more than two months from their destination and some difficult conditions lay ahead. About a month later the vessel sprang 'a very dreadful leak' with all male passengers involved in pumping out the water, the women transferring to the companion ship, the *Osterly*. There was a threatened mutiny, the captain logging the harsh measures taken to enforce discipline and ensure the safety of the vessel, which was at last secured. 'The passengers exert themselves in an uncommon degree,' Bullock recorded. 'I am confident without their aid and example we shou'd not succeed in keeping her afloat.'[3] Richmond did not shrink from playing his part here, 'indeed it is very hard work', the captain having won his admiration from the start. 'Capt. Bullock seems very low. I now am glad I can swim for I am afraid there will be occasion.' Emergency repairs were made at Ceylon (now Sri Lanka) and the *Thetis* continued north. Having set sail in early June, the ship at last anchored at the mouth of the Hooghly river off Calcutta on 23 October after a journey of more than five months.

The most engaging journal entry was made soon after the travellers had experienced heavy weather, in early September. So far from home and family, with the dangers attendant on such a long sea-voyage much in his mind, he thinks fondly ahead to his eventual meeting with William, the brother who has preceded him to India, but he is already contemplating the idea of return.

> 1st Septr a day well remembered by my dear Fathers being taken so ill. you my dear Mater will never forget it. God grant that he may never more feel the effects of it. I remember it

as well as if it happened yesterday indeed it is the greatest [aid] to melancholy pleasure to think of past times. I read the notes you have written in the books you gave me over & over & the letters my dear Pater gave & sent me from Port & if there is any time Youngs night thoughts are to be read none can be so good as the present seperated from all we love by an immence space. however I have two things to look forward to returning & finding you all well & seeing dear William. I often figure to myself the family at home. my place is vacant no more I have your conversation after dinner no more Emily plays. Francis never smiles I never hear the rough stamp of St John. when I return or they come out the difference will be wonderful.

But for Richmond Thackeray there was a career to be forged, and he never would make that return passage and breach the 'immence space'.

Eleven years after Richmond's arrival in Calcutta, the girl whom he would marry made the same hard voyage out, but with ambitions very different from his own. Her family hoped that India would help to put aside troubling memories. In fact, the past eventually caught up with her, but not before she had married Richmond and given birth to a future novelist. Anne Becher's family had roots in India at least as strong as those of the Thackerays. John Harman Becher had also been a writer in the East India Company, and had married Harriet Cowper in Calcutta where Anne was born in 1792. Like most Anglo-India children she was sent home to England during her early years, so for her this passage was itself a return trip. For someone usually characterised by a set of inflexible religious convictions in later life, against which her son and her granddaughters were to come into conflict, Anne Becher's family circumstances were far from conventional, and her own wilful temperament seems to have been inherited through the female line.

John Becher died in Calcutta in 1800, but his widow, Harriet, is nowhere mentioned in his will, family tradition holding that she had already left him by then.[4] In his last years, Becher lost his job and became a bankrupt, although whether this was brought on by or caused his wife's departure is unknown. In 1802, just two years after Becher's death, Harriet is named in the will of Captain Charles Christie as his wife, although they may never have married. She might even have been living with Christie whilst Becher was still alive, the relationship never having subsequently been formalised. After Christie's own death in 1805, Harriet moved to Barrackpore and in October 1806 married for a third (or second) time another military man, Captain Edward Butler of the Bengal Artillery. That she was a woman of determination would be borne out when as a frail old lady she lived for a time in Kensington with Thackeray, her grandson, his daughters Annie and Minny being urged by his mother to 'take care of poor GM'.[5] Fifty years earlier, it appears that she had been more than capable of taking care of herself.

When Anne Becher and her sisters had been sent from India to be looked after by their grandmother and aunt at Fareham, near Portsmouth, they were leaving behind their mother's eventful first marriage. In England they encountered a rather severe household in which their grandmother called her own daughter Miss Becher and addressed each of them in like manner – Anne was 'Miss Nancy'. Miss Becher, Anne's aunt (also an Anne), was the real force for good in this female household, as Thackeray later acknowledged. 'This good old lady was a mother to my mother in her youth.'[6] During the winter of 1807-8 the young Anne, now aged fifteen, accompanied her grandmother to Bath, and in circumstances reminiscent of a Jane Austen novel became a centre of attention. She met the twenty-seven-year-old Lieutenant Henry Carmichael-Smyth of the Bengal Engineers, whose ancient Scottish lineage and recent distinguished record of Indian service lent him glamour. His was a charming personality, and therefore considered dangerous by Anne's grandmother; she took her duties *in loco parentis* seriously and disapproved of a man who, as a younger son, had uncertain prospects. Lieutenant Carmichael-Smyth pursued Anne to Fareham, and although Mrs Becher forbade an engagement they met in secret, until Anne was confined to her locked room. A sympathetic maid smuggled letters between the lovers.

It is very likely that some of the details of the complete story, repeated and embroidered as part of Thackeray family tradition, are apocryphal. Its themes of deception, an invented death and a denouement reached by means of chance encounters in foreign parts, make for a scarcely creditable sequence of events. Even the detail of love notes being passed through the convenient agency of a maid suggest the clichés of sensational fiction and drama. The old lady's role as dispenser of fate is played to perfection, and with an unhesitating ruthlessness, as Thackeray's granddaughter, Hester Ritchie, recounted more than a century later when she repeated (and perhaps reworked) the memories passed on to her. She told how those secret letters suddenly ceased: 'one day old Mrs. Becher hobbled into her granddaughter's room and told her to muster all her courage to bear a great blow; the

Ensign had died of a sudden fever and on his death-bed had sent her messages of his undying love. Anne pined and mourned in silence. After a time a family council decided that the broken-hearted young woman should be sent out to India as soon as possible to stay with her Becher relations.'[7]

And so in April 1809, Captain and Mrs Butler started out on their return journey to Calcutta after a long leave, accompanied by Anne, a sister, and her new step-sister. This passage took even longer than Richmond Thackeray's eleven years before, and they did not disembark until 24 October.

In the years since his arrival in India Richmond had done well and was now working for the Board of Revenue in Calcutta. His sisters Emily and Augusta had come out from England to join him, in the hope that they would find marriage opportunities in India – a conventional pattern for its time. He seems to have developed from a shy but optimistic boy into a rather priggish young man, fearing for Augusta's prospects as she was less good-looking than her sisters, 'whom nature has been kinder in forming'.[8] In due course, Emily married John Shakespear; Augusta continued to live with him, passed over as her brother had confidently expected, though she was eventually twice married.

A year younger than Henry Carmichael-Smyth, in 1809 Richmond was himself still unmarried, though not childless. As was common and acceptable in Anglo-Indian society, with its shortage of European women – a fact which made Augusta's apparent difficulties in winning a husband the more humiliating – he had taken an Indian mistress. Strictly speaking, she was probably of mixed race. Charlotte Sophia Judd, by whom Richmond had a daughter, Sarah, would subsequently marry James Blechynden.[9] Richmond acknowledged his daughter, and made provision for her in his will. In later years his son would also be meticulous in observing the rights of his half-sister, exhibiting the scrupulous fairness which characterised all his money dealings with other people, even though he tended towards extravagance and to spend beyond his income.

Richmond met Anne, now aged seventeen, during the winter of 1809, cutting a dash as he visited on his white horse. He must have found her as attractive as Lieutenant Carmichael-Smyth had done. On the rebound, and willing herself to put unhappiness behind her, she accepted his marriage proposal. Within a year of her return to India, on 13 October 1810, they married in St John's Church, Calcutta. Her only child was born prematurely, after just seven months, on 18 July 1811, and they called him William Makepeace after his grandfather, the

One: Scenes of All Sorts

Portrait of Anne Becher, artist unknown

first of the Thackerays in India. It had been a difficult birth. Anne was told that further pregnancies could not be contemplated, and that had William been a full-term baby she might not have survived. Scarcely anything is known of his infant years, though there is a charming family portrait by George Chinnery executed about 1813-14, reproduced on the present book's cover. The scene hints at more than it can show, and probably more than the artist himself realised. Richmond sits sideways, distracted, his long legs casually crossed, whilst Anne, standing and supporting her son who leans against her, looks dreamily upwards and out of the left of the picture, a dark-haired and strikingly handsome rather than a conventionally beautiful woman. Only the boy, perched on a pile of improbably big books, looks out of the picture and fixes the viewer in a clear unbroken gaze from his 'large-large eyes',[10] with something like a quizzical smile. The child is alert and, somehow, knowing.

Since his marriage, Richmond's status and income had both increased. Once he had completed twelve years in the service of the East India Company, at the end of 1811 he became eligible for positions attracting an annual income of over £4,000. By 1813 he was simultaneously Collector of the Twenty-four Pergunnahs (a large district south of Calcutta) and Collector of the House Tax at Calcutta. He probably commissioned the Chinnery watercolour as being something appropriate for a man of his position in Calcutta society. But by then an unsettling incident had disturbed the tranquillity of his home life, with a theme invoking little less than death and resurrection: Anne's former dead suitor was not only returned to life, but was coming to dinner. Henry Carmichael-Smyth, now a Captain, had returned to India, and in fact had been in the country since December 1810. The romance of their former history made somehow inevitable the irony not only that he and Anne should meet again, but that the innocent agent for their meeting would be Richmond. In her telling of the story Thackeray's granddaughter manages to translate the moment into an operatic *scena*.

> Returning from his club in Calcutta one day, Richmond Thackeray said to his wife: 'I have just made the acquaintance of a most delightful and interesting Engineer officer; he only arrived yesterday morning, knows no one, and I have invited him to dine with us to-night so that we can introduce him to our friends.'
>
> The hour of the dinner party arrived, the guests assembled, and the last to come was the stranger. The servant announce in a loud voice, 'Captain Carmichael-Smyth,' and in walked Anne's long-lost lover!
>
> What that dinner was like no words can describe. After what seemed an eternity, Anne and Captain Carmichael-Smyth had a moment to themselves, and in a low trembling voice she exclaimed: 'I was told you had died of a sudden fever.' And with bitter reproach he replied, 'I was informed

by your grandmother that you no longer cared for me and had broken our engagement. As a proof, all my letters to you were returned unopened. And when in despair I wrote again and again begging for an interview, you never gave me an answer or a sign.'

After a while the situation became so impossible that Richmond Thackeray had to be told; he listened gravely, said little, but was never the same to Anne again.[11]

If Chinnery's portrait makes husband and wife seem detached and lost in their separate thoughts, there was much to ponder. Carmichael-Smyth returned to Agra where he was based, and the marriage was not threatened, but in 1815 Richmond succumbed to fever. It was impossible to escape from the baking Calcutta heat, so he was transferred to a ship on the Ganges in search of cooling breezes, dying on 13 September, aged thirty-four. Many years later, Thackeray attended his aunt Augusta's final days in Paris. As she drifted in and out of consciousness, she imagined herself at her brother's death scene, 'fancying she was in the boat with my father dying – it affected me'.[12]

++++

The young man's life is just beginning: the boy's leading-strings are cut, and he has all the novel delights and dignities of freedom. He has no ideas of cares yet, or of bad health, or of roguery, or poverty, or to-morrow's disappointment. The play has not been acted so often as to make him tired.

Pendennis

The time was approaching when Richmond's boy needed to be sent for schooling in England. As she mourned her husband's loss, his mother could also entertain the prospect of an ultimate reunion with her first love: she promised to marry Henry Carmichael-Smyth after an eighteen-month period of mourning. It prevented her returning to England with her son, but his journey at least could not be delayed. She managed to book William a passage at the end of 1816 in the company of a former colleague of Richmond's who was returning on leave. With them went Thackeray's cousin, Richmond Shakespear, a year his junior. As the *Prince Regent* set sail, the five-year-old child left behind everything that was familiar. His father was dead, his mother would soon be taking a new name, and a stepfather was standing in the wings.

This was a final farewell to the country of his birth, for just as his father had never returned to England, on 17 December William Makepeace Thackeray left India behind for ever. It is scarcely surprising that with such painful and persistent memories of separation and loss, in circumstances barely understandable for a child of five, the adult Thackeray would devise strategies to avoid formal partings at the outset of long journeys. He was likely to slip away without warning, in an attempt to suppress the trauma of separation from loved ones and from an environment where he felt comfortable – 'the pain of parting is much greater than the pleasure of meeting – at least to my ill-regulated mind'.[13] For a child who had lost one parent, to be sent away from the other may well have carried with it a burden of guilt. Once in England, at first living with relatives and then at school, it was his absent mother he longed for. It explains the close bond he forged with her for the remainder of his life, and may also help account for the exceptional frankness with which he discussed intimate details of his interior life with her. It was the key relationship of his life, but also the most complex, informing the way in which as a single parent he chose to bring up his own children.

Under the charge of his Becher great-grandmother and great-aunt at Fareham, he was put into a small school at Southampton, and then, a year later, transferred to another at Chiswick, some of the details of which re-surface in the opening chapters of *Vanity Fair*. He was miserable in the first school, remembering later 'kneeling by my little bed of a night, and saying, "Pray God, I may dream of my mother!"'[14] His Chiswick experience was not much better, but he survived it, and his lot was probably no different from the many who endured the casual brutalities and deprivations of a pre-Victorian education. The main hardship was separation from his mother, but in that too his was not a unique plight, for most sons of the British administrators in India were sent home to be schooled, enduring sustained periods without seeing their families. Holidays were spent at Fareham. 'I have lost my Cough and am quite well, strong, saucy, & hearty; & can eat Granmamas Goosberry pyes famously after which I drink yours & my Papa's Good health & a speedy return.'[15] The tone of those first childish letters to his mother are affectionate and longing, but also faintly accusatory in dwelling on her absence. He would not see her again for more than three years, when the Carmichael-Smyths returned to England on what was intended to be a long leave, but which turned out to be their own final departure from India. Mrs Carmichael-Smyth reported on the eventual reunion – 'dear soul he has a perfect recollection of me he could not speak but kissed me & looked at me again & again, I could almost have said "Lord now let thou they servant depart in peace for mine eyes have seen thy salvation"'.[16]

From January 1822 until he entered Trinity College, Cambridge seven years later, Thackeray was a pupil at Charterhouse, Henry Carmichael-Smyth's old school. Charterhouse would take on a fictional life as Greyfriars, the institution which frames Colonel Newcome's life, and in whose care he dies as a resident pensioner. The experience of an English schooling had endearing manifestations through Thackeray's later life. He would not argue for fundamental changes in the public schools, nor even for reform in the manifestly unsatisfactory standards of the small preparatory schools which fed them. His sympathy for the hopes and anxieties of small boys emerged instead in modest practical gestures, as he introduced moments of unsolicited pleasure into their humdrum lives. In short, he liked to treat them by injecting a moment of colour into the dull routine of a 'Greyfriars' day. Unknown boys would be taken into shops to be bought jam tarts by the tall, amusing stranger who delighted in their simple enjoyment, and then passed on his way. He never forgot what it felt like to be a schoolboy – often unhappy, lonely, and not in control of one's life.

Thackeray's time at Charterhouse coincided with an eccentric teaching system introduced by its then headmaster, Dr John Russell, who contrived to expand student rather than teacher numbers by requiring selected boys in the higher forms to act as instructors for the lower ones. Perhaps there were boys with sufficient instinctive authority to impart something to their younger fellows, but these must have been rare. Discipline was maintained by flogging, Dr Russell's favoured implement being a bunch of birch, and the institutionalised fagging system of the English public school system, whereby a junior acted as a kind of unpaid servant to a senior boy, survived attempts to abolish it. Thackeray's introduction to a classical education came at the feet of the headmaster himself, whose teaching was remembered by a fellow pupil, George Venables, as 'vigorous, unsympathetic, and stern', while another, Martin Tupper, had only contempt for the regime of bullying. 'What should we think nowadays, of an irate schoolmaster smashing a child's head between two books in his shoulder-of-mutton hands till his nose bled?'[17] In Thackeray, we probably have a classic instance of someone able to learn far more outside the classroom than within it, and of forming his values accordingly. What he learned of human character and of the values of self-sufficiency would not be forgotten. But he left Charterhouse with only a shaky academic grounding, inadequately prepared for life as an undergraduate.

> W. Thackeray. Charterhouse
> 1825, 1826, 1827
> 1828.

Q. HORATII FLACCI

OPERA,

CUM SELECTIS SCHOLIIS,

ET

OBSERVATIONIBUS

BAXTERI, GESNERI,

ET

ZEUNII.

EDITIO NOVA CUM INDICE VERBORUM ET NOMINUM
COPIOSISSIMO:

IN USUM

SCHOLÆ CARTHUSIANÆ.
Charterhouse School!!!

Londini:

IMPENSIS G. ET W. B. WHITTAKER, J. NUNN, BALDWIN, CRADOCK ET JOY,
J. RICHARDSON, T. WILKIE, LACKINGTON, HUGHES, HARDING,
MAVOR ET LEPARD, ET R. HUNTER.

1822.

Some people think it a good school

Above: *Title page from Thackeray's school copy of Horace*

Opposite: *Doodle from Thackeray's school copy of Horace*

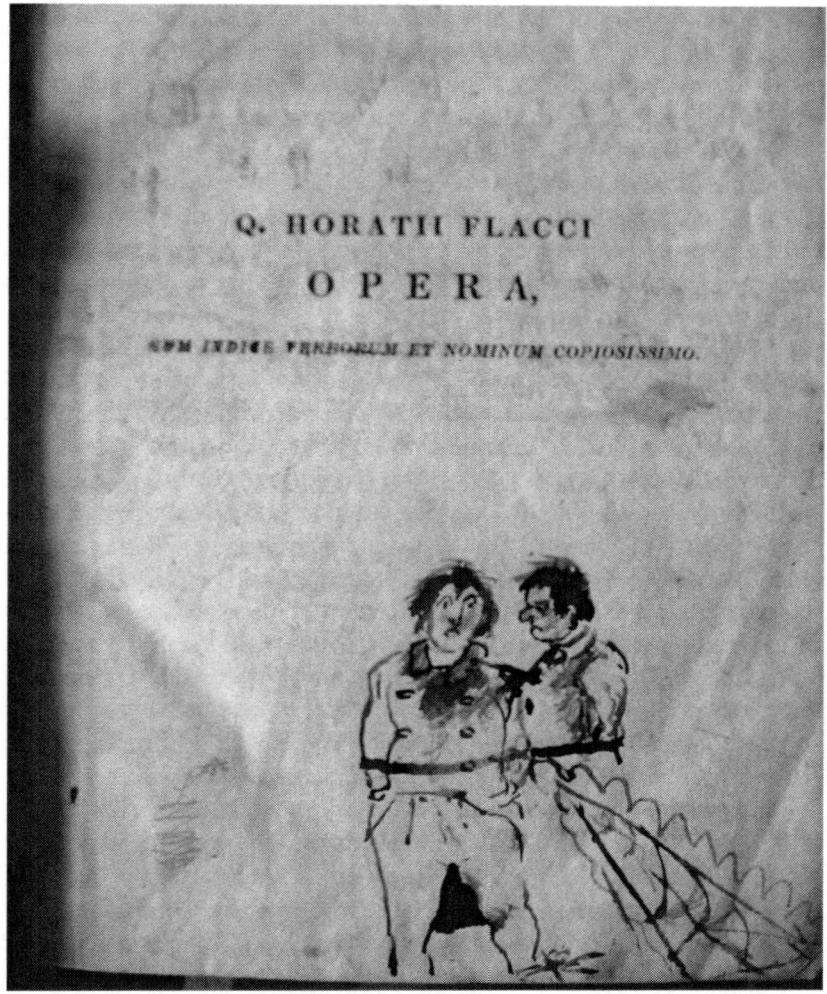

Once they had given up thoughts of returning to India, the Carmichael-Smyths settled first in Addiscombe, near Croydon, where Major Carmichael-Smyth was appointed the acting warden of the East India Company's military academy. The schoolboy Thackeray nagged his mother to communicate more regularly. 'I hope you will write to me soon at least oftener than you did last quarter & tell me all about Addiscombe.... Write again as quick as you can.'[18] She was a striking woman, tall – as was her son, who reached the height of six feet three by the time he left school – somewhat imperious, and with a strong religious conviction. Life in India had helped shape her attitudes, and now she began to move in English county society 'fascinating everyone who came her way'.[19] Her granddaughter and others remembered her as beautiful even in old age, and a dominant personality within her rather narrow world. She was not arrogant, but she could be autocratic and quick to judge. After Addiscombe, she and Henry moved to Ottery St Mary in Devon, where they planned to retire. This became home for the young Thackeray, and it was from here that he travelled by coach to Cambridge for the first time, Major Carmichael-Smyth accompanying him, a journey later reworked for *Pendennis* in which memories of undergraduate life in no way glamorise the reality of the life of the future writer.

Thackeray enrolled at Trinity College in February 1829, at once beginning an epistolary journal of this new life for his mother, just as his father a quarter of a century earlier had recorded the trivial incidents of his voyage to India. 'I am now about to begin my first journal, my dearest Mother, which will I hope be always sent, with the regularity with which it is now my full purpose to give to it.' Unsurprisingly, he seems to have known that that these good intentions would not last. Yet from the end of February until early June 1829, and perhaps for longer, he sent off every few days a candid account of his experiences. He tells of his readings in Greek and of struggles with mathematics for which he had been ill-prepared by Charterhouse – 'I have been working the Algebra today, but have lost all my chance even of mediocrity' – but such academic challenges were only to be expected. His mother must have felt more worried about the dinners, the wine parties, and the company that he was keeping. If she suppressed her anxieties during term time, they surfaced during the vacation. He spent the summer of 1829 in Paris, and his first letter home on 18 July must have alarmed her. 'We went last night to the Opera, and saw the Comte Ory, & a ballet the name of w^h. I forget – They have a certain dancing damsel yclept Taglioni who hath the most superb pair of pins, & maketh the most superb use of them that ever I saw dancer do before.... They are most inordinate card players here, & I am told play rather high.' And then on 6 August he declares that he has learnt a hard lesson at a fashionable gambling house on the Rue de Richelieu. 'The interest in the game Rouge et Noir is so powerful that I could not tear myself away until I lost my last piece – I dreamed of it all night – & thought of nothing else for several days, but thank God I did not <u>return</u>. The excitement has passed away now, but I hope I shall never be thrown in the way of the thing again, for I fear I could not resist.'

He probably thought that in adopting this tone of wide-eyed honesty he had disarmed his mother, which makes the ruffled dignity with which he met her subsequent reproof the more endearing. She

One: Scenes of All Sorts 17

knew him too well to think that in recognising his weaknesses he was somehow guarded against succumbing to them.

> I have this moment read your letter, my dear Mother, w^h. surprised me, and I confess hurt me, for I did not think I deserved those strong terms of reproof in which it was couched – I mentioned that I had been to Frascati's – but for what went I? to gain? No – It was a sight w^h. I perhaps might never have another opportunity of seeing, it was a curious chapter in the book of life, the perusal of w^h. has done me the greatest good – it has taught me not to trust so much in myself as before my pride or ignorance would have led me to do; it has shewn me that I could not, (as few could) resist the temptation of gambling, & it therefore has taught me – to keep away from it – The same motive which would have led me to a Theatre led me to Frascati's – I was obliged if I went to stake my ten francs at the table instead of paying at the door – If I had not done so <u>I should never have arrived at a piece of self knowledge, which I can conscientiously thank God for giving me</u>.... I have learnt the full extent of the evil. I have discovered my temperament & inclination with regard to it, and the necessity w^h. I did not then know of avoiding it – In what then am I blameable? I went with <u>no</u> bad desire, no desire for gain....
>
> Good bye till tonight my dearest Mother; & may God grant that you never again call me avaricious and mean when I am but curious, that you never again think because I before was ignorant that therefore I was good; or that because I am now aware of my own weakness I must be wicked.[20]

We know much less about his second year at Cambridge, as he kept no journal, or at least none has survived, and only a couple of letters to his mother are preserved. The scarcity of evidence is possibly significant, for in later years his daughter Anne destroyed letters and other papers touching on sensitive matters. Perhaps his mother, for similar reasons, did not keep everything that her son wrote to her. So we learn nothing at the time of the clandestine visit Thackeray paid to Paris during the Easter vacation in 1830 with Edward FitzGerald (the Cambridge contemporary to whom he felt closest), himself a future writer whose fame would rest on his translation of *The Rubáiyát of Omar Khayám*. The exotic allure of Paris was too great to resist, and some years later in a piece written for the *Britannia* Thackeray tells of an encounter with a woman of about thirty-five who claimed to have met him when she worked as a governess in England. 'In her private capacity she was a workwoman; she lived in the Rue Neuve St. Augustin, and I found her a few days afterwards eating garlic soup in a foul porter's lodge, from which she conducted me up a damp, mouldy staircase to her own apartment, on the seventh floor, with the air and politeness of a duchess.'[21] However unattractively Thackeray paints her, there is no doubt that he was intrigued.

All such Parisian temptations must have been hard to resist. Even before this Easter trip he had again been gambling at Cambridge despite the fulsome promises made just weeks earlier, falling easy prey to professionals who fleeced him of the enormous sum of £1,500 which he only finally settled when he came into his father's money in 1832. At the end of the academic year he was placed in the second class, with most of his friends ranked above him, and his academic ambitions ended with his decision not to return. He faced a difficult visit to Devon to offer explanations and to face recriminations or, perhaps worse, the silent disappointment of his mother. It is true that he had succeeded in having a few verses and brief articles published in the student newspaper *The Snob* and its successor, *The Gownsman*, hints of what was to follow. But Cambridge and its distractions lay behind him.

++++

When I said you were frivolous I meant no harm, all women are so I think from their education, and I want my wife to be better than all women.

To Isabella, 5 July 1836

It was not in William Thackeray's nature to sit around and mope. Resolved not to return to Cambridge, he persuaded his mother and Major Carmichael-Smyth to let him have some months on the continent, and began planning a visit to Dresden by gathering letters of introduction. It was agreed that after a period abroad he should return and commit himself to a profession, preferably the law. Travelling via Rotterdam and Frankfurt, he visited the University of Bonn and sampled student life before deciding to base himself in Weimar rather than Dresden. His mother's letters were delayed, so some weeks passed before he celebrated at having at last seen 'the old handwriting'.

He told her of meeting the greatest German of the age. 'I saw for the first time old Goethe today, he treated me very kindly & rather in

One: Scenes of All Sorts

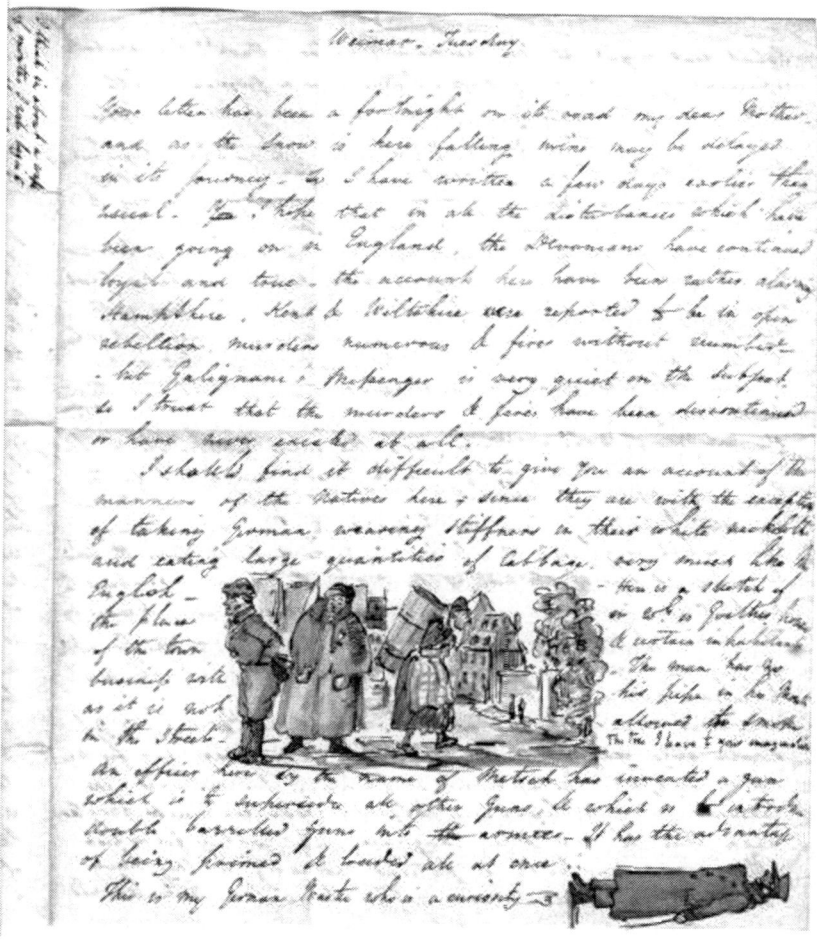

Pastel illustrations in a letter from Thackeray to his mother, Weimar 1830

a more distingué manner than he used the other Englishmen here... he sent me a summons this morning to come to him at 12, I sat with him for half an hour.' This was flattering attention, but he probably invested rather more energy in a flirtation whose history runs through a number of letters. Had it not been entirely innocent in nature, he is unlikely to have mentioned it to his ever alert mother, though she probably continued to worry anyway. 'The prettiest woman I ever saw in my life is here & I have within the last two days fallen in love with her; I trust I shall continue so for I find the sensation novel & pleasing – her name is – but I wont say what her name is – but if ever she becomes M^{rs}. Thackeray it will be well for her and myself.' This was

Melanie von Spiegel. By contrast, he found 'Madame de Goethe very kind but withal a great bore'.[22]

A month later his affections had been transferred. 'I am still violently in love but it is with another person; Tho' as there are only two young ladies at the Court of Weimar with whom one can fall in love, I don't know what I shall do at the end of another fortnight, about which time I expect again to be free.'[23] The object of his attention this time was Jenny von Pappenheim. She would recollect Thackeray as a particularly popular Englishman in Weimar, humorous, tall, and (as his father had been) skilful at entertaining the company with his lightning caricatures. But he lost the affections of both women once they recognised that he was not a serious player in the marriage market. Probably he had been put on his guard when he realised with what determination the game was played in Weimar. 'The old ladies here seem to be bent on marrying their daughters, two have told me that they did not wish much money for their Melanies or their Eugenies, but merely a competency – but I did not speak on the hint and as the respectable dowagers find they can make nothing of me they almost cut me.'[24]

By the end of the year his mother had heard more than enough, and from his reply we can assume that she sent a letter which attacked on several fronts. Her lingering irritation about his Cambridge years, and fresh anxieties at his current frivolities – she may have put it stronger – prevented her from keeping silent. His attitude spoke to her of a decided lack of seriousness. Then there was his immortal soul to worry about, for she was certain that he was neglecting his church attendance. Thackeray's self-justifying response voices his own disappointment in a wasted school and university experience. His mention of the new German theology that he has encountered, which would revolutionise biblical criticism in the years to come by challenging the literal interpretation of scripture to which Mrs Carmichael-Smyth unquestioningly adhered, skilfully deflected the attack by raising the spectre of a more powerful threat.

> Your letters always make me sorrowful, dearest Mother, for there seems some hidden cause of dissatisfaction, some distrust which you do not confess & cannot conceal & for which on looking into myself I can find no grounds or reason....
>
> You seem to take it so much to heart, that I gave up trying for Academical honors – perhaps Mother I was too young to form opinions but I did form them – & these told me that there was little use in studying what could after a certain

point be of no earthly use to me.... For ten years of my life I was at school, it was thought that this discipline of misery was necessary to improve & instruct me; with all the power I had I struggled against it – the system was persevered in – & the benefit of ten years schooling was a little Latin & a very little Greek.... You will think me ungrateful, because I set myself so resolutely against what I know to be your wish, I am very young but if I have had any experience at all it has been in the system of education which you wish me to adopt.... In my reading & my pursuits here I have had a freedom which I never enjoyed in England – & I hope you will feel the benefit it has done me.

....When I first came here I did not go to Church very regularly as my attendance there was productive but of small profit – as I begin to comprehend the language of course I shall attend more regularly – The doctrine here is not near so strict as in England – many of the dogmas by w^h. we hold are here disregarded as allegories or parables – or I fear by most people as fictions altogether. They call our Religion in England too 'objective' & not refined enough for their more mature understandings.[25]

He returned to England in March 1831, and late in May went to London where he took chambers and entered the Middle Temple to train for the promised legal career. He was attracted by its social trappings, for 'the Inns of Court provided a setting for an existence of gentlemanly idleness'.[26] Whether or not he knew before he started, it can have taken him very little time to realise that such a career was not for him, and although he found it convenient to keep his chambers on for the rest of his life – a strange decision – this was the extent of his commitment to the law.

The financial independence that was granted when he turned twenty-one in 1832 proved useful, if temporary, for subsequent failures in Indian investments effectively wiped out what remained of his inheritance by the end of 1833. But while the money lasted, he gained his first involvement with the print press, and unwisely (though only from a commercial viewpoint) bought a failing weekly paper called the National Standard, becoming its proprietor and editor. The paper closed by February 1834, but it was an introduction to London journalism, or at least to its rougher side. Even as he struggled to keep the National Standard afloat, Thackeray was considering another scheme which would lead him once again across the English channel to Paris. He wanted to be a painter.

Page from an album of Thackeray sketches.

His artistic ambition cannot have been a surprise to the Carmichael-Smyths, yet scarcely what his mother had been hoping for. There was plenty of evidence of a natural talent. From his earliest years, his letters regularly include a caricature or illustrative sketch, and those from Weimar are at times quite elaborate; the letters to Edward FitzGerald from autumn 1831 onwards are especially fine. The very first letter to his mother which has survived, written when he was six, contains a delicate drawing of a horse and rider, and his school books have similar evidence of idle but talented doodlings. Something of this skill at drawing and especially caricature was inherited by both of his daughters: their letters often contain a sketch or two, usually executed swiftly. In due course the facility passed to the grandson named after him, and although at one stage his mother hoped that Billy might make art his profession, nothing came of it. The highly successful John Everett Millais refused to recommend life as a jobbing painter, writing with relief after she had abandoned this idea that 'I am glad to hear you have given up the idea of making your boy an Artist, as it is going to be a bad business for some years to come. The moneymaking class who were the only patrons are becoming too wise to buy pictures, or have ceased to make money.'[27]

Sketches of people rather than topographical detail is what interested the Thackerays, father and daughters. It was not a gift he inherited from his mother, who may in any case have felt that this facility bordered on time-wasting, disappointing evidence of how father and son approached the serious business of life. A revealing comment by Thackeray's aunt Maria, written in a letter to his mother even before he had started at Charterhouse, is enough to suggest that the Becher women had regarded Richmond Thackeray as clever but lazy. Were they worried that it might all be coming out again in the son? 'Does not this great quickness and idleness except when roused, remind you of his poor father?'[28] On the other hand, when his mother saw her son for the first time after her arrival back in England in 1820, his resemblance to his father was both striking and comforting. 'He is the living image of his father, and God in heaven send that he may resemble him in all but his too short life! He is tall, stout, and sturdy. His eyes are become darker, but there is still the same dear expression. His drawing is wonderful.'[29]

Wonderful, but insubstantial perhaps. Yet in one respect Mrs Carmichael-Smyth could feel reassured about his new venture. When he left for Paris, it was to stay with her own mother, Mrs Butler, who had herself just moved to the capital. For the first few weeks the two lodged together at a boarding-house, and then transferred in October 1834 to the Rue de Provence, where Mrs Butler took rooms. Thackeray's new determination to acquire a formal artistic training took him daily to the Louvre to copy old masters, and to attend life classes. But Paris also offered the familiar distractions, now to be experienced within a bohemian milieu whose new opportunities both thrilled and shocked him. His fragmentary diary hints at erotic excitements. 'The conduct of the model, a pretty little woman, the men & the master of the establishment was about as disgusting as possible – The girl w^d. not pose but instead sung songs & cut capers; the men from sixty to sixteen seemed to be in habits of perfect familiarity with the model.' His grandmother was not told the details, but she seems to have voiced her concerns nonetheless, for at the end of this same diary entry Thackeray adds 'a few domestic storms & scolds'.[30] As for his painting, Edward FitzGerald was encouraging from a distance, but the technical challenges were considerable. With honest self-deprecation Thackeray shared his frustrations with another friend, admitting that 'I have got enough torn up pictures to roast an ox by – the sun riseth upon my efforts & goeth down on my failures, and I have become latterly so disgusted with myself, and art & every thing belonging to it, that for a month past I have been lying on sofas reading novels, and never touching a pencil.'[31]

He took the opportunity to renew his acquaintance with his father's younger sister, Charlotte and her husband John Ritchie, who had been especially kind to him when he had first arrived in England as a little boy. The Ritchies had made Paris their permanent home in 1830, like so many genteel English seeking out its cheaper living costs and relatively comfortable lifestyle. The Carmichael-Smyths would also make the move across the English channel in due course, in an attempt to stretch the value of Major Carmichael-Smyth's modest army pension. Thackeray's friendship with his younger cousin, William Ritchie, dates from this Parisian trip: Ritchie would eventually make his career in India. More than forty years later, long after both men were dead, their children tied the family knots even more tightly when second cousins Anne Thackeray and Richmond Ritchie married.

Thackeray also was a welcome visitor at the home of the *Morning Chronicle*'s Paris correspondent, Eyre Evans Crowe, and became acquainted with the Crowes' circle of English writers and painters. Two of Crowe's children return as important figures in Thackeray's later life, a son, also called Eyre Crowe, becoming his secretary and assistant during his first American trip, and Amy subsequently joining his household as a companion to his daughters. Amy Crowe would marry yet another Thackeray cousin, and, as if to complete the loop, their own elder daughter Margie Thackeray would marry another of William Ritchie's sons, Gerald.

Amongst the 1835 Parisian ex-patriot community was an Anglo-Irish family with strong roots in India. Quite how and where Thackeray met the Shawes is not clear. The father was dead, and his widow and children had recently been prompted to move to Paris for economic reasons. Like Thackeray, Isabella Gethin Shawe was born in India, in 1818, and she was just seventeen when they met. Why she in particular captivated him is difficult to fathom, but having willed himself to fall in love with someone, Isabella appeared as if on cue. She had a naïve charm and was musically talented, but she was also shy, not regarded as especially pretty, lacked firm opinions, and came with a formidable mother. Once he had fixed her as 'the gal of my art', Thackeray set about winning her no less determinedly than on all previous occasions when he had met with opposition and had got his way. It became his current project. He had declared to his mother back in the autumn of 1833 that he should marry, and even at that time told her of his need to find someone. 'I shall go back to Paris, I think, & marry somebody'; 'I want now to settle... to marry someone with money... going to Church regularly, rising early, & walking in the Park with M^{rs}. T. & the children'.[32] This is playfully put, but seriously meant. He needed simply to put a name and a face to the idea.

Isabella Shawe lacked money, but despite that significant detail the plan laid out two years earlier was now set in motion. If one pauses to

One: Scenes of All Sorts

wonder why in 1833 Thackeray sought out marriage, when his finances and career were very far from secure, then a need for emotional stability and an anchoring female influence must largely explain it. He wished to restore what he may have regarded as his entitlement, the supporting presence of a woman, a filling of the gap left by the mother from whom he had been removed as a child. Perhaps, too, the curious manner in which he chose to declare this ambition to his mother was a subliminal desire to punish her now for having sent him away.

By September of 1835 he was representing himself to William Ritchie as conventionally lovesick. 'I sleep not neither do I eat, only smoke a little & build castles in the clouds... God knows how it will end, I will, if I can, bolt before I have committed myself for better or worser, – but I don't think I shall have the power. My mamma has given me a five franc piece to amuse myself and stop away for a day, but like the foolish fascinated moth I flicker round the candle of my love.'[33]

But he had no intention of bolting. Instead he endeavoured to prove himself to Mrs Shawe, the only real obstacle to his plan of marrying her daughter. She would not have viewed his prospects with much confidence, and her own depleted income did not permit her to endow Isabella with anything. The Carmichael-Smyths had similar initial doubts, though they appear to have been persuaded by Thackeray's earnestness and ended by supporting his ambition. Perhaps he was just more used to winning their favour. At considerable personal financial risk, Major Carmichael-Smyth invested in and became chairman of the Metropolitan Newspaper Company, the vehicle by which he launched a radical journal called *The Constitutional and Public Ledger*, of which Thackeray was to be Paris correspondent. Funds were raised only slowly, and the first number of the paper was delayed beyond its planned launch date in May 1836.

The relationship with Isabella appears to have proceeded on his side only, with Thackeray cast as the importuning lover. He wrote to her in his most persuasive vein from London in April, recreating the make-believe world that he had spelled out three years earlier to his mother.

> My father says I could not do better than to marry, my mother says the same. I need not say that I agree with the opinion of my parents – so, dearest, make the little shifts ready, and the pretty night caps; and we will in a few few months, go & hear Bishop Luscombe read, and be married, and have children, & be happy ever after, as they are in the Story books – Does this news please you as it does

Isabella Thackeray, *pastel by Thackeray*

me? Are you ready and willing to give up your home, & your bedfellow, and your kind mother, to share the fate of a sulky grey headed old fellow with a small income, & a broken nose? – Dear little woman, think a great deal on this now, for it seems to me that up to the present time (& considering the small chance of our union you were wise) you have avoided any thoughts as to the change of your condition, & the change of sentiments & of duties, w^h. your marriage with me must entail.[34]

There are disturbing references to Isabella's health, indicating that even in comparative youth she was not strong. Whether the 'thinness' referred to was an early symptom of her later illness cannot now be known, but it does suggest that any medical treatment she may have been receiving was ineffective, for Thackeray presses her to try the alternative remedies in which his mother always placed her faith. 'I have been telling my Mother of your ills and your thinness, and she earnestly begs that you will go to one of the Homœopaths in Paris, and explain to him the whole state of your case. <u>Now I ask it as an especial favor that you should do this</u> – for the system if it be true will cure you, and if false can do you no possible harm, for the hundredth part of a grain of medicine is all w^h. they will give you to take.'

She took a week to reply, and although Isabella appeared to have reassured him, she seemed unable to understand that marriage would necessarily remove her from her mother's house and primary guardianship. It can be inferred that Isabella's letters devolve power and choices to Mrs Shawe.

> [W]hat in God's name have I been saying to hurt you (for I see you are hurt) and your Mother? – What a scoundrel I should be were I to endeavour to weaken such a tie as exists between you two – The separation to w^h. I alluded did not go farther than the bedroom – If I recollect rightly this was the chief object of my thoughts at the moment, and I opined that you would be unwilling to quit your bedfellow, and your present comfortable home for another with me. If you are my wife you must sleep in my bed and live in my house – voila tout – I have no latent plans – no desire to exclude you from those whom I sh^d. think very meanly of you, were you to neglect.[35]

Continued delay in the appearance of *The Constitutional* seems to have led Mrs Shawe to insist that marriage should be deferred, and early in July Thackeray agreed that there should be a cooling off period. He urged Isabella to continue to write, and even if these should be but a few lines, she should send them regularly; he even persuaded himself that absence would make her mother grow fonder of him – 'it will put the intimacy w^h. ought to exist between your Mother & me upon its proper footing; for I think that when we are not too intimate or familiar we shall be much better friends; and finally it will make my little Trot conquer two lazinesses that beset her, not writing letters, and lying abed'.³⁶ However, Mrs Shawe continued to exercise strong pressure on her daughter, resulting in what at first appeared to be a complete break. Then, in an episode curiously reminiscent of the early romance between the young Anne Beecher and Henry Carmichael-Smyth, Thackeray arranged for a sympathetic servant to smuggle a letter to Isabella. He presents himself as the victim whose consistently warm and honest love is met with coldness.

> My love for you is greater than I thought, for it has withstood this terrible three days trial. I have tried to leave you, & you will hardly credit me that I felt obliged to return – for I do not believe in spite of all this heartlessness on your part, that you ever can be other than my wife – You may recollect, that after our second quarrel, we made a kind of vow that, happen what would – you & I were bound together & married before God, & that I told you but a few nights since, that I had prayed to Him to give me aid in quelling any improper desires wʰ. might create your disgust or lessen me in yʳ. esteem.
>
> If you feel that after our three months' marriage, for I can call it no less, you are sick of me & my love, <u>tell me so with your own lips</u> – you have not spared me, God knows, through all this business & I see no reason why I should be called on to be polite, merely to spare you the bore of an interview.
>
> ... Should anything occur to your Mother wʰ. God forbid, where will you & your sister live? – with your Aunt Mary? – Or will you return to the man who loves you still, better than you deserve, Isabella – for if I have given needlessly vent to my feelings you don't know how often I have smothered them; if I have hurt you by my warmth, have you never wounded me by yʳ. coldness? ...
>
> However, take me or leave me – I never can love you as I have; although you fancy that my love for you was not '<u>pure</u>' enough – it was a love of wʰ. any woman in the world should have been proud, & wʰ. I never can give to any other – but still dearest, I love you; forgive me my trespasses as I here remit you yours, and you will restore happiness to your family, & to one whose misery you never can feel or know, please God.³⁷

One: Scenes of All Sorts

William and Isabella Out Walking, sketch by Thackeray

This insistence that Isabella ought to recognise him as deserving of her is extraordinary, but no less so is her immediate capitulation and facing up to her mother. The episode is fictionalised in Thackeray's late novel *Philip*, revealing how long-lasting was the harbouring of his resentment towards his mother-in-law, and there is an almost pathetic irony that in looking back over the years to his Parisian infatuation he described it to his friend and publisher George Smith as his 'absurdly imprudent marriage'.[38] They married on 20 August in the British Embassy, and Mrs Shawe was sufficiently reconciled to attend and sign as a witness.

Despite this troubled courtship, the first years of the marriage itself would be regarded by Thackeray as the happiest of his life. They had no money, and when they moved to their first set of rooms in the Rue Neuve St Augustin they spent Edward FitzGerald's wedding gift of cash on furniture. The idleness for which he had gently rebuked Isabella before they married now affected his own behaviour, but in confessing it to his mother he shifted the blame onto his naïve wife. 'I am ashamed and angry every morning of my life, but do what I will scold or laugh she won't get up, & I am only too glad of an excuse to lie in bed – fancy that out of the 24 hours we spend at least eleven in bed.'[39] He knew that this could only meet with his mother's disapproval, and indeed a few years later she skipped generations to extol the godly merits of early rising and wholesome work to Thackeray's two young daughters.

But at last *The Constitutional* had started to appear, and from mid-September Thackeray's commentary on the Parisian political scene was a regular item. Meanwhile he sought out other journalistic opportunities to boost his income. Larger writing ambitions also began to surface. In January 1837 he wrote to the publisher John Macrone proposing 'a book in 2 Wollums. with 20 drawings. entitled Rambles & Sketches in old and new Paris by WT. I have not of course written a word of it, that's why I offer it so cheap.'[40] He was asking £50 for the proposal, and wanted an immediate £20 on account. Nothing at the time came of the suggestion, but three years later *The Paris Sketch Book* appeared under Macrone's imprint.

We also hear Isabella's own voice for the first time, when she started to write to Mrs Carmichael-Smyth – 'dear Mother I may call you now' – urging Thackeray's parents to visit them. 'We are always looking forward to your coming to Paris so we often look at apartments with a sufficient number of bedrooms.' Hers is a gentle and kindly personality, living in the shadow of her husband perhaps but with its own humour and warmth. Within a few months of their marrying, she was also able to allude to her pregnancy – 'I suffer a little but for so pleasing a cause that I do not mind it.'[41] She seemed to have fully transferred her loyalty to Thackeray, whose relations with his new mother-in-law had not prospered – indeed he kept out of Mrs Shawe's way to avoid quarrels. 'Puss goes to her now and then, but I can't; I have no time and as little inclination – I don't know how it is that I have got to dislike her so.'[42] In these earliest days it is unlikely that the Thackerays would have been able to afford any domestic support, so that all the housekeeping responsibilities fell on Isabella. She would have had no training in household management, nor any personal experience of cleaning and cooking. (Thackeray once discreetly had to enquire of his mother how to make hash taste of something other than onions and water.) Even when their money ran to employing servants, they had to be managed effectively, and here too Isabella was wanting.

By the spring of 1837 the couple had given up Paris to stay with the Carmichael-Smyths in London, who had themselves moved up from Devon, to Albion Street, Hyde Park. There were self-evident financial reasons for doing so, but Thackeray also needed to be closer to the offices of *The Constitutional*, which was struggling. By March, Major Carmichael-Smyth was carrying most of the paper's costs. At the end of April, Thackeray became its managing director, whereupon he immediately wrote to shareholders in what turned out to be an unsuccessful appeal to fund the flagging publication. It closed at the beginning of July, leaving Carmichael-Smyth with heavy losses. He nevertheless earned his stepson's admiration for the honourable way in which he had borne his responsibilities.

The principal reason for the Thackerays joining the Carmichael-Smyths in London at this time may have had nothing to do with business at all, but in order that Isabella could be supported in the closing stages of her pregnancy, for on 9 June the Thackerays became parents for the first time. Looking back on it, Thackeray may well have reflected that staying in Paris for the birth would have been safer, for Isabella had a very difficult time. This was in part caused by the inadequacy of the homeopathic doctor whom Mrs Carmichael-Smyth had insisted should attend her daughter-in-law at Albion Street. Thackeray's daughter records how, shortly before he died, her father still recalled the very real dangers. 'Papa said, how when I was born he knew nothing about it & the homeopathic doctor nearly killed her, & he sent out & brought in another who only was in time to save her life.'[43] This same first daughter was named after paternal grandmother and mother, Anne Isabella – in fact she took both grandmothers' names as Isabella was also Mrs Shawe's given name. In a letter written to Annie in her mid-teens, Mrs Carmichael-Smyth wonders about the original spelling of her own name in a time when rules were more flexible. 'Your name is <u>Anne</u>, in the Paddington register. Mine is Ann I believe but I have always written it Anne.'[44]

Despite the trauma of her arrival, Annie seems to have been a perfectly healthy baby and soon became the focus of her parents' interest, especially after the arrival of her sister Jane, born a year later on 9 July 1838 and named after Isabella's unmarried sister as well as Thackeray's cousin, Jane Ritchie. Annie was old enough to be aware of 'dear little No 2', and was beginning to walk.

> Great fat deedle deedle, is extremely fond of her sister, but shows her affection in rather a rough manner, she would willingly poke out her little 2's eyes or pull her out of ones arms by her long robes, all out of pure love, she hushes her to sleep and exclaims oh! oh! in a very patronising manner. She held out her fat arms that the small babe might be put in but that was an experiment we were not willing to try, I am happy to say she promises fair to walk alone in a short time she can already go a short distance.[45]

The Carmichael-Smyths had left Albion Street and moved to Paris, so the Thackerays transferred to 13 Great Coram Street in Bloomsbury. They had taken no chances this time, for as Thackeray reported to Mrs Shawe three days after Jane's birth, 'The Doctor in attendance is no less a person than Sir Charles Herbert the very pink of accouchers',[46] and Isabella was also quick to reassure her that 'after the bad business we made of it last time I was determined to submit to black dose, castor oil pills, or any other abomination that was ordered'.

Thackeray had managed to secure regular writing for *Fraser's Magazine* to which he was contributing his first real success, the *Yellowplush Papers* (1837-40), with *Catherine* (his parody of Edward Bulwer's criminal romance genre) and *A Shabby Genteel Story* following in 1840. He maintained something of a peripatetic existence in these early years, travelling to Paris to stay with the Carmichael-Smyths, usually alone but at least once with Isabella. It was from Paris that, scarcely able to credit their current contentedness, he had written to her back in Great Coram Street in terms which would prove to have a cruel irony in view of the fragility of their situation and the sadness which would visit them. 'Here have we been nearly 2 years married & not a single unhappy day. Oh I do bless God for all this great happiness w^h. He has given us. It is so great that I almost tremble for the future, except that I humbly hope (for what man is certain about his own weakness and wickedness) our love is strong enough to stand any pressure from without, and as it is a gift greater than any fortune, is likewise one superior to poverty or sickness or any other worldly evil with w^h. Providence may visit us.'[47]

Exactly a year later came the first test, when Jane died after a chest infection. Thackeray was profoundly affected, and never forgot this daughter near whom he was to be buried in Kensal Green; Jane was one of the earliest occupants of the cemetery which had opened in 1832. He remembered her for her purity and innocence, 'as something charming that for a season we were allowed to enjoy.... We have sent to Heaven a little angel who came from us & loved us and God will understand her language & visit us mildly.'[48] Isabella was similarly stoical in writing to Mrs Carmichael-Smyth of her loss, showing a wisdom not usually associated with Thackeray's now-obscure wife. Even if some of the opinions were shaped by those of her husband, the freshness of expression is Isabella's own, and the way in which she tries to comfort her mother-in-law from the depths of her own loss is touching. It is likely that the start of her own mental decline is rooted in this first trauma, and was accelerated by the severe postnatal depression which followed Minny's birth in 1840. Meanwhile, we can only admire the measured insight, so painfully acquired.

> Her little heart seemed full of love for every body and such a gentle sweet tempered Lamb that it seems almost merciful she should not have had to struggle with this world. I sometimes grieve to think that she was so quickly taken, but how foolish, would I have had her pine and fade because it was sudden shock to me to have her suddenly removed. A child's death is dreadful but a child's suffering is ten thousand times worse. If we know our hearts right I do not think we question Gods justice but cannot one bow to the Divine will and yet mourn for the precious gift that was lent one so short a time and yet so long as to make one sensible for <u>all</u> its value... There is scarcely a minute I do not think of her so you cannot wonder if I write a great deal about her. But if it makes you grieve you must put a restraint on me.[49]

One cannot help but think that if only Isabella had continued to articulate her anxieties and feelings in this way, to sympathetic and understanding hearers, she might yet have diverted the full force of the gathering storm that was to put an end to the normal pattern of family and domestic life for all of the Thackerays.

Two

NOT YET ACTORS IN THE PLAY
(1839-1846)

There is a grand power of imagination about these little creatures....

Thackeray to his Mother
December 1839

Our understanding of Thackeray's world can now benefit from the addition to the available documentation of a fresh speaking voice, a witness for whom directly experienced events are filtered through memory in a process of personal narrative.

Anne Thackeray occupies a privileged position, for she is both part of the story and controls its retelling. In a recollection from her earliest childhood, her father is the benign but indistinct presence at his writing desk, not yet fully known to her. She claims to remember the moment before being carried into the room where he sits writing.

> Almost the first time I can remember my parents was at home in Great Coram Street on one occasion, when my mother took me upon her back, as she had a way of doing, and after hesitating for a moment at the door, carried me into a little ground-floor room, where some one sat bending over a desk. This some one lifted up his head and looked round at the people leaning over his chair. He seemed pleased, smiled at us, but remonstrated. Nowadays I know by experience that authors don't get on best, as a rule, when they are interrupted in their work – not even by their own particular families – but at that time it was all wondering, as I looked over my mother's shoulder.[1]

Whatever one's misgivings about the authenticity of this episode, the adult woman looking back seems to want us to value this as a transforming moment. Her willing it to be significant makes it so.

Thackeray's own accounts of domestic life catch its pleasures as well as its limitations. 'Missy's little voice I can hear carolling in the parlor. Isabella comes to pay me a visit every ½ minute or so, and I'm not as angry as I ought to be.'[2] He was always conscious of their hand-to-mouth existence which a writing success might alleviate. 'One good hit and I am made; all my works will then sell 50 per cent higher, and, please God, enable me to save for the little ones'. It is scarcely surprising that in such circumstances he found working at home difficult and wanted to escape, if only to spare Isabella his bad humour as deadlines approached. '[I] have been for a fortnight in the pains of labor: horrible they are: and dreadfully cross to my poor little wife in consequence. She had much better let me go away on these occasions but she won't.'[3] When Mrs Shawe came once to stay he maintained a low profile, his absence noted sadly by a wife who understood all too well certain aspects of his impulsive personality. 'I see nothing of William but this is all for the best I suppose. He went yesterday to Richmond. The painters get round him & tell him it is ten thousand pities he does not follow that vocation and W. says let us sell all & go to Rome. It must be all or nothing with him.'[4]

Isabella was a consistently reassuring presence for her daughter in these early days, though Annie is also able to recall the precise moment when she first understood Thackeray to be her father. 'The first time I remember Papa is standing at his knee & asking him to tell us the name of my doll and Papa said this is Miss Polly Perkins I think.'[5] If her father was more remote and indeed not always recognisable, Annie remembers that her mother would sit at the piano to sing and play dance tunes, her hair shining. From the nearby streets, the sounds of barrel organs penetrated into the Great Coram Street house, and the child was taken out to encounter that entrancing world. Her father is remembered as retrieving her and returning her to safety. 'Some one walking by came and lifted me up bodily on to his shoulder, and carried me away from the charming organ to my home, which was close by. As we went along, this stranger, as usual, became my father, whom I had not recognised at first.' In those days they called her Missy, or sometimes Nanny. Their Scottish nurse, Jessie Brodie, had joined them shortly before Jane was born, and remained loyally through the difficult times to come, even giving up the chance of marriage and choosing instead to stay in London. She was 'the best nurse in the world'.[6] In addition, the Thackerays had by now inherited a manservant, John Goldsworthy, who had previously been in service with the Carmichael-Smyths in Devonshire and moved with them up to London. 'I loved Old John. He used to teach me to sip porter out of a pint pot, and to take my part when I was naughty; I can hear him still calling for Missy's chop, and announcing the important fact that she was crying for her dinner. I had a fine time of it.'

Quite how the later reading of her father's letters framed Annie's adult memories of childhood is impossible to know, but she remained alert to the limitations of her method of recollection, with its natural tendency to fill in the gaps. 'And here the writer must confess that although she remembers these raptures and the go-cart and some picture-books and the drawing of a certain alphabet which was to teach her to read, she has reconstructed much of what happened from the scraps and letters of that time.'[7] She would find many references to her old-young self in those letters and other fragments of evidence. She was probably no more lively than any ordinarily intelligent child, but her father was intrigued by the intuitive world of imagination which she inhabited. He mused on its elusiveness, and the tendency of adults to suppress the freshness of the child's fantasy. 'There is a grand power of imagination about these little creatures, and a creative fancy and belief that is very curious to watch: it fades away in the light of common day: I am sure that the horrid matter-of-fact child-rearers Miss Edgeworth and the like, with their cursed twopenny-halfpenny realities do away with the child's most beautiful privilege. I am determined that Anny shall have a very extensive and instructive store of learning in Tom Thumbs, Jack-the-Giant-Killers &c.'[8]

As she looked back over these early memories, as a woman of sixty, Annie pondered the mystery of her own childish imagination in terms which her father would have recognised, recalling 'those dawning hours, when the whole world is illuminated and enchanting, when animals can speak – nay, when all nature speaks and inanimate things are alive, and when we are as gods, and unconscious of evil, and create existence for ourselves as we breathe'.

Even in these early years of his marriage Thackeray had health problems, especially with his digestion. It was something which for the remainder of his life Anne Carmichael-Smyth would try to monitor, urging on him some new homeopathic remedy and requesting his daughters to report on his progress. He took a grim fascination in the behaviour of his bowels, confident that he had his mother's sympathetic ear. 'I am writing under the influence of four grains of diabolical calomel. We were to have gone to Carlyle's tonight, but 4 good dinners last week were too much for my poor dear insides and I was compelled last night to dosify. What horrid poison to be sure – what a fine night of fever did it give me, and a sweet morrow of – never mind what. I am writing this in the – no I an't.'[9]

During the early part of 1840 Isabella was preparing for her next confinement, and Thackeray wanted his mother to come to stay for a few weeks. Probably to Isabella's relief, she kept away. He still found himself defending his young wife from his mother's accusations of slackness. 'You are I think rather hard upon Isabella: she gets up at eight o'clock now, & if she leaves the washment of the child to the nurse, at any rate the child is healthy and as clean as can be.'[10] Meanwhile, Annie was a distraction for both parents, with a precocious if shaky grasp of adult worries. 'Miss T remarks that the taytoes are very dear at a penny a bushel, and that she will only give five franks – I believe that on this matter the daughter knows very nearly as much as the mother, who has a noble want of the organ of number. The Child is the same, for though she knows all her letters, we can not get her to count two.'[11] It was a prophetic observation, for Annie would be regularly defeated in the practical business of managing her money, throughout her life making resolutions about spending less which were abandoned as easily as they were made. What was merely endearing in the two-year-old child drove Leslie Stephen, her future brother-in-law, almost to despair. But for Thackeray, there is discernible pride in the fact that she was unspoilt – 'she is a noble little girl that's the truth, and is not made too much of'.[12]

Thackeray was either slow to see that Isabella was growing more silent and withdrawn, or reluctant to attach significance to her behaviour. But he was troubled to realise just how much she depended upon him, comparing their situation with that of an acquaintance, Frank Bacon. 'His poor wife is just on the point of confinement. I don't like to think of her, or of where mine w^d. be, should God please to remove me. Pray heaven that I may live to leave something behind for her and the little ones.'

He removed himself temporarily from London to get some writing done, but returned in time for the arrival of his last child on 27 May. It appears to have been a trouble-free birth, doubtless helped by the absence of grandmothers. 'I think we have been all the better for quiet in the house: and find that the professional nurse does the business quite satisfactorily.'[13] The new daughter reminded him of Jane, and he looked to the ever-present Annie for company as Isabella and the baby gained strength. 'Missy is delightful she is very kind to me, and comes to see me in bed. The little baby is very like the dear one we lost – strangely like in voice.' Annie recalled this addition to the family in the memoir written forty years later for her niece, Laura. 'The first time I saw y^r. Mommee she was all wrapped in flannel & lying on our old nurses knee. My nurse said Come here Missy & look at y^r. little sister. And I said but I cant see her Brodie & Brodie said look at her kicking her little feet.'[14]

Only slowly does the evidence enable us to see the new child as someone in her own right, allowed to share the limelight with the precocious Annie. But at least she was no cause for anxiety. A month after the birth Isabella could assure her mother-in-law that she 'flourishes beautifully. I could wish it had been stouter, but all stout children are not strong'.[15] The baby's relative anonymity is not helped by the delay in giving her a name, and only shortly before her christening in late July was this settled as Harriet Marian. Isabella describes both the christening and Thackeray's good notices for the *Paris Sketch Book* in a letter which offers disquieting insights into her own mental condition and her sense of being abandoned by her young husband, who had taken himself off to Belgium.

> In the midst of all this the dear lamb has been christened 'Harriet Marian' so she can be called Polly and Harry and Harriet... I confess to you I feel myself excited my strength is not great and my head flies away with me as if it were a balloon. This is <u>mere</u> weakness and a walk will set me right again but in case there should be incoherence in my letter you will know what to attribute it to. William too I fear is a little agog for he thought he should like to see the Belgian pictures and so nothing would serve him but to put himself into a steam boat and set off for Antwerp. He says he will make a series of articles for Blackwood that it was necessary for his health and that he is sure that Titmarsh in Belgium will take as Titmarsh in Paris. [*'Michael Angelo Titmarsh' was the alias chosen by Thackeray for his reviews of pictures, written for 'Fraser's Magazine' two years earlier.*] I tried to persuade him not to go but it seems as if I was always to damp him, and that I am to go a round of old saws such as 'It is the tortoise and not the hare wins the race' mais enfin il ne m'écoute pas and I must e'en let him make his fortune his own way. I do mind my own business as much as possible but one cannot but be interested. He is to be back on the 15th he has plenty of grist as have we so it is not that makes one uneasy. I try to think my fears imaginary and exaggerated and that I am a coward by nature, but when people do not raise their expectations to too high a pitch they cannot be disappointed....
>
> I believe I am a goose for having written all this but you won't know what to think if you do not hear from me.[16]

Mrs Carmichael-Smyth must have been concerned to have received this, though we have no record of her response. Even as Isabella tried to set aside her own disappointment at her husband's absence, at the centre of her mounting distress is an unspoken fear that she is inhibiting him, that she is not really his match, that she is at fault for not liking being left alone. Isabella regularly sought advice from Thackeray's mother, who seemed to the young wife to be so much more practically-minded than herself. 'You know I have not got <u>your busy needle</u> now and mine is but a "slow coach."... Pray write me out "Froggy would a wooing go" and any other ballads.'[17] Trivial things, but Isabella was quick to measure herself against her mother-in-law and to find herself wanting.

On his return from Antwerp after a fortnight, Thackeray was so alarmed at Isabella's condition that he at once consulted their doctor. He quickly removed her to Margate to take the sea air.

> That young woman I am sorry to tell you I found in such an extraordinary state of languor and depression when I came home that old Powell counselled me to bring her immediately to the sea side, and here we are arrived this very night. She has got the better of her first complaint but this was succeeded by excessive lowness of spirits that came on in my absence... but this is our marriage day & thank God the fresh air & the sunshine & the little excitement of travel have done wonders for her, & she has gone to bed tired and happy. Don't allude to it at all, or only to say that you are charmed to hear she has got round.... There can be nothing the matter with her (but indigestion) for she has plenty of milk, and the infant is as fat & smiling as babe can be. It is always at her, & this pulls her down of course very much.[18]

Determined to enjoy the sea break, and remembering a happy time in his youth when the Carmichael-Smyths had brought him to Margate, he persuaded himself that Isabella simply needed the stimulus of change, for 'the air & bustle acted on her like a charm'. They stayed for about three weeks, during which any improvement in her mood was only minimal. Thackeray was patiently encouraging, but for the first time allowed that her condition might be more serious – 'of mornings especially her spirits are curiously low, she is so absent then that I don't like to trust her'.[19]

Probably he still did not quite realise that her 'languor' presaged something rather more severe. Modern clinicians might well have diagnosed puerperal psychosis, affecting about one in a thousand women after childbirth, with symptoms which may include depression, delusional behaviour, hallucinations and paranoia. Thackeray was right to fear leaving his wife alone, but not until twenty years later did Annie write of the time she was out with Isabella – it almost certainly relates to this Margate trip – and of 'walking on the sea shore with Mamma & she held me by the hand & once pulled me in a little way, & then her love struggled with her madness & so we came back to the little white house in w^h. we lived'.[20]

It was only now that Thackeray learned that an acquaintance of his mother's had visited Isabella several times during her pregnancy, undermining her already frail self-confidence by speaking of Mrs Carmichael-Smyth's doubts about her capability. It angered him. 'M^{rs}. P[arker] repeated to Isabella just before her confinement every word you said, about her faults not doing her duty & so on, & in the course of her depression the poor thing had worked up these charges so as to fancy herself a perfect demon of wickedness – God abandoned & the juice knows what: so that all the good of your reproof was that she became perfectly miserable, & did her duty less than ever. It was an unlucky time to lecture her that's all: when she is better talk away and amen. – This is of course a secret.' The reprimand was justified, but had come rather late in the day.

The family returned to London, but within days Thackeray acknowledged that the Margate trip had had no lasting effect. He came to a bold decision, and one which had dramatic consequences. Concerned at her daughter's silence, Mrs Shawe was now proposing to set off from Cork to visit her, and in order to pre-empt this Thackeray made arrangements to take the family to Ireland instead, convinced that seeing her mother and sister would do Isabella good. Although he had no wish to have the Shawes in London, he felt it was time to remind his mother-in-law of her duties to her daughter. 'Do what he will a man is but a bad nurse, and you & Jane must look to the little woman and get her back to spirits again.'[21] He had offered to the publishers Chapman and Hall an Irish travel book similar in scope to the *Paris Sketch Book*, for if Isabella and the children were placed with Mrs Shawe in Cork he might 'go wandering about as best I may'.[22] Securing an advance of £120, he undertook to complete the manuscript by 31 December, 'unless illness or any other domestic calamity sh^d intervene'.[23] The caution was well founded.

It is easy to blame Thackeray for failing to see that all was not well with Isabella before the crisis broke. Although the various manifestations of postnatal depression were not recognised by the

Victorians, the persistent strangeness in her behaviour ought to have triggered some concerns. Yet when he did act, it was courageously, as he began to face the full challenge of her illness and its consequences. Nowhere is this seen more starkly than in the grotesque farce of their Irish escapade. On 12 September he took Isabella, the two children and their nurse Brodie on a steamer bound from London to Cork, where they all arrived 'after a long horrible journey of three days and four nights that I can't think of now without shuddering'. At first he withholds from his mother the full horror of that journey, but says enough to reveal that Isabella was dangerously out of control. 'My dear wife's melancholy augmented to absolute insanity during the voyage, and I had to watch her for 3 nights (when she was positively making attempts to destroy herself,) and brought her here quite demented.'[24] Three weeks later he said more, fearing that his mother would otherwise hear it from one of Mrs Shawe's friends who had a sister in Paris. Things had rapidly deteriorated during the second day at sea.

> [T]he poor thing flung herself into the water (from the water-closet) & was twenty minutes floating in the sea, before the ship's boat even <u>saw</u> her. O my God what a dream it is! I hardly believe it now I write. She was found floating on her back, paddling with her hands, and had never sunk at all. This it was that told me her condition. I see now that she had been ill for weeks before, and yet I was obstinately blind to her state, and Powell & the surgeons must tell me that there was not the slightest reason to call a physician, that nothing was the matter with her, that change of air w^d. cure her & so on. O God what a mercy this was! I hardly remember the thing now – so sudden was it: it did not shock me at the time either. I don't know why: but it is better you should know it from me, than from any of M^{rs}. Spencer's gossips who might suddenly pour it out upon you at Paris.
>
> In the next night she made fresh attempts at destruction and the first week here was always attempting to quit the bed: You may fancy what rest I had. I had a riband round her waist, & to my waist, and this always woke me if she moved. But lately she has made no sort of similar attempt, and only yesterday spoke of it in terms of the greatest remorse and sorrow, nor will she I do believe fall again into the same frightful mania. But she has for the present the greatest dread of steamers, & I fear for some time to come putting her to the risk of a voyage.[25]

Mrs Shawe made it clear even before the Thackerays left London that she would not be able to accommodate them all, so Thackeray had taken lodgings next door. But having wrongly assumed that she would at least have room for Isabella so that she might be closely nursed, he railed against such unnatural behaviour. 'I don't like to tell you of the conduct of M^{rs}. Shawe: so unmotherly has it been. As far as bringing her daughter tea and dinner & sitting by her bedside she is well enough: but she has a spare room in her house and refused to receive her on account of her nerves (she has been very ill that's certain) & those of her darling Jane.'[26] It was galling to be accused of irresponsibility for having moved Isabella from London, and of having kept her away from her mother when she was well, only 'to be thrown on her in sickness'.

This behaviour only served to confirm his view that Isabella's mother was herself disturbed, 'a woman who is really & truly demented'. But he quickly discouraged his own mother from entering the fray. 'We have just had a scene – fancy that – in the midst of all this trouble she can't keep her monstrous tongue quiet. Don't you however come forward. It would only make matters worse.'[27] He was already minded that when Isabella could be moved, he would ask his mother to assist in her recovery, but then there began to be some signs of improvement. Isabella reproached herself for her behaviour, taking some pleasure again from the children, especially Annie who 'prayed God to bless her dear Mamma' – but only a couple of days later she lapsed into a listless depression.

Thackeray did his best to shelter the children from what was happening, carrying on as normally as he could for their sakes – 'he always laughed & made the best of his great deep sorrow'.[28] Amidst the turmoil, Annie seems only to have had pleasant recollections of the Irish adventure, recalling her time there with Minny. 'I can remember her as a little baby with a long green veil because her eyes used to be sore. We were in Ireland up on a hill – There were sloping fields leading to a great wide river & ships were floating, & in one of the fields some beautiful buttercups were growing.... One day the nurse let me tie the babys green veil on my hat & as I ran along it floated beautifully in the air.' But for Thackeray Ireland was a turning point, making him review his treatment of Isabella, with the result that he resolved to live a more simple domestic life by resisting the distractions and personal gratifications he had enjoyed as a bachelor. 'I must learn to love home more, and do my duty at the fire side as well as in my writing-room: and I do see how out of all this dreadful trial profit will come to us, if it shall please God to let us have the chance. Make me more humble, O

God, & less selfish: and give me strength to resist the small temptations of life that I may be fitted for the greater role.'[29] His good intentions anticipate a less stimulating personal life, which it would be hard for him to follow.

The Irish trip was a failure at every level. If he had hoped that a visit to her mother would raise Isabella's spirits, that evidently had not worked, and had served only to expose Mrs Shawe as a destructive liability. It had been impossible for him to make the necessary sorties for the Irish book to which he was now contractually committed, as his time was entirely given over to Isabella, with only Brodie to help – 'without her I don't know what would have become of us all'. Moreover, it was costly, and with nothing to show for it he had eaten into the £120 advance from Chapman and Hall. But not for a moment does one find Thackeray avoiding what he knew to be his duty. Immediately before setting out on the nightmarish steamer crossing to Cork, he had reflected on their current misfortunes and accepted his portion. 'O Titmarsh Titmarsh why did you marry? – why for better or for worse. Let us pray God to enable us to bear either.'[30]

He acted decisively in bringing the visit to an end. It was initiated by Mrs Shawe's irrational and 'odious' behaviour, and as he lay sleepless in bed, with Isabella worse again and with Annie crying, 'I said to myself why am I to stay longer here? – and this bright thought having occurred to me, I instantly felt myself happier, got up, walked to the Doctor who advised me to go by all means, and so came off at 2 o'clock by the Queen Steamer, giving M^{rs}. Shawe no hint of my departure until 1: when she was advising me to put Isabella into a mad-house.'[31] His little party reached Clifton, where he proposed to await the arrival of his mother from Paris, when together they would decide what should be done, perhaps placing Isabella into secure care in or near London – an asylum – and handing his children temporarily over to Mrs Carmichael-Smith. Since leaving Cork he had written a nine-page letter to Mrs Shawe, detailing the charges which he levelled against her; scarcely surprisingly, the letter has not survived, and their relationship did not improve. In the end, his mother did not come to Bristol, so the Thackerays moved on to London to close up the Coram Street house before starting for Paris, where support and comfort awaited them.

At the age of three, Annie understood little of her mother's condition at the time. The overnight journey to Paris was far more of a reality, and she always remembered her own role in it. Her father's nerves were close to breaking after the weeks of Isabella's sometimes dangerous unpredictability, and the stress of conveying her safely now across the Channel, so that Annie's own attention-seeking was not well received. She wrote two accounts of this journey, the first shortly after Thackeray's death. 'I remember him in the stage coach after Mamma went out of her mind. He was very grave & when I kicked & talked he told me I must be still or I should wake baby, & when I still went on he told me he must put out the light if I was not quiet, & then still I was not quiet & the light suddenly went out. Has the light gone out now for us?'[32] A more crafted public version composed thirty years later puts greater weight on her personal terror and her father's sternness, the memory of which clearly did stay with her.

> My father was in the corner of the diligence opposite to me and the nurse and the baby, and he struck a match, and lit up a little lantern, which he held up to amuse me. But I only cried the louder. Then he said gravely, 'If you go on crying you will wake the baby, and I shall put out the candle;' so I went on crying, and I woke the baby, who began to cry too; ... and my father blew out the lantern, and suddenly all was dark. I could not believe it, never before had I been so severely punished. 'Light it, light it,' I screamed. 'No,' said my father's voice in the dark, 'I told you I should put the light out if you cried.' ... I remember hearing him long afterwards speak of that dreadful night.... The next thing I remember is arriving quite cheerful at Paris, and my grandmother and my grandfather coming down the curling stairs to meet us in the early morning and opening their arms to us all.[33]

His daughters endured a long period of grief after his death, but even in their own worst moments Annie believed that his attempts to manage Isabella's illness required the greater courage. 'My poorest dearest – Was it more terrible than it is now for us – I think so for at least this is peace sometimes.'[34]

Paris was a turning-point in a number of ways, and for Thackeray something like a coming home. He decided to seek professional treatment for Isabella, which would include humouring his mother's keenness for alternative therapies. For Annie and Minny, Paris was all adventure. It would be their home for the next several years, living in the care of their grandparents once Thackeray had returned alone to London to work, for his expenses were mounting. His mother's readiness to take on this refugee family without a qualm threw the behaviour of Mrs Shawe into even starker contrast. It almost overwhelmed him to think of what he owed the Carmichael-Smyths and his mother's unmarried niece, his cousin Mary Graham, then living with them. He tried to express his feelings to Edward FitzGerald, with whom he was always unaffectedly frank. 'Since my calamity, I have learned to love all these people a great deal more – my mother especially. God bless her who has such a tender yearning big heart that I begin to cry when I think of her: and when I see her with the children, cleaving to them, am obliged to walk off for the sight is too much for me.'[35]

His first priority was to find a place for Isabella. Within weeks she became a residential patient at the clinic established near Paris at Ivry-sur-Seine by Jean Esquirol, a leading exponent of new techniques in treating the mentally ill. At first there were indications of progress in her case, but it was slow, Isabella experiencing the same morbid guilt which had manifested itself in Cork. 'She kissed me at first very warmly and with tears in her eyes, then she went away for me, as if she felt she was unworthy of having such a God of a husband. God help her.'

Annie remembered an incident soon after their arrival in Paris. Her great-grandmother, Mrs Butler, was also with them at this time, and four generations of the family joined the Parisian crowds to witness the return of Napoleon's remains from St Helena for re-burial on 15 December 1840. Father and daughter both recorded this event, Thackeray immediately for his *The Second Funeral of Napoleon*, in which his own family retinue feature anonymously (though as he said to FitzGerald of this essay 'you will read a pretty incident about [my mother] and the children apropos of the Napoleon procession'), and Annie years later recalling the childhood experience. 'As a baby holding my father's finger I had stared at the second funeral of Napoleon sweeping up the great roadway of the Champs Elysées. The ground was white with new-fallen snow, and I had never seen snow before; it seemed to me to be a part of the funeral; a mighty pall indeed, spread for the obsequies of so great a warrior.'[36]

The Carmichael-Smyths lived close to the Arc de Triomphe, in the Avenue Sainte Maria which led from the Faubourg du Roule. Their rented apartment was part of a house with a courtyard in which Annie would amuse herself alone or with Justine, the concierge's niece, for Minny was as yet still too young to play with her. On one side of the Avenue Sainte Maria was the convent where Justine went to school, and on its exterior wall was a faint fresco, 'representing a temple in a garden and clouds, and [a] bird with outstretched wings'. Annie would hear the convent bells and the sound of the nuns intoning the canonical hours, and one night she dreamt that she was in the convent garden and that from out of the frescoed temple stepped her father to take her home. It links with that other early recollection of his gathering her up in the London street where she had been dancing to the music of the barrel organ. Perhaps the memories have become mingled. There were many childish dreams, and when she woke 'from the dark corners of the room there used to come all sorts of strange things sailing up upon the darkness.... I have since heard that this seeing of pictures in the dark is not an uncommon faculty among children.'[37]

In January 1841 the Carmichael-Smyths and Mary Graham travelled to Italy to meet Major Carmichael-Smyth's brother, Charles, returning from India. Charles and the much younger Mary had corresponded and, at this distance, become engaged, determining to marry once he had reached Naples. In congratulating Mary, Thackeray reveals doubts about putting Isabella into institutional care, feeling that she would benefit more from the stimulus of travel, 'but there are 1 or 2 objections to move just now. In the first place she is really better and more sensible than she was, and has made a little advance. The Doctors don't see it but I do and am certain of it.'[38]

During the several months that the Carmichael-Smyths were away Mrs Butler oversaw the children in Paris, with Brodie as nurse, whilst Thackeray took lodgings closer to Isabella, enabling easier visiting. He could not have been more pleased with Mrs Butler's help, for she appeared to dote on Minny and played happily with her, although Annie thought that her great-grandmother probably considered Minny and herself 'inconveniently young'. Trips to see her father in his lodgings became something of an event. 'Very often he was dressing, and it was a privilege to see him shave, better still to watch him drawing pictures or tearing little processions of pigs with curly tails out of paper. Sometimes he was writing, and to my surprise and annoyance could not tear out little pigs.'[39] There is a something pathetic in his readiness to find improvements in Isabella, based more on hope than any sustained progress. '[T]he little woman is a little more active, reads out, speaks a little of a night, and yesterday when I was going away pressed me by words to stay – w^h. is always something. We had a long walk in the country. Her remarks were those of a child.'[40]

By early April, the doctors at the Ivry clinic had told him that they could do nothing more, so he decided to remove Isabella and take her home. But first, in a poignantly romantic gesture, he decided to ply her with champagne's medicinal properties.

> It did her a great deal of good & made her eyes sparkle, and actually for the first time these 6 months the poor little woman flung herself into my arms with all her heart and gave me a kiss.

At w^h. moment the waiter burst in.

This only served to mend matters for the lady went off in a peal of laughter the first these six months again; and since then I have had her at home not well, nor nearly well, but a hundred times better than she was this day week.[41]

He was becoming more sanguine about her being able to achieve some kind of peace of mind, and observed her sitting with Annie and falteringly telling her a story, unable to remember it all. 'We will have her back again please God – and it is an inexpressible happiness to me to have her away from that lonely place, and to see her even as she is.'[42] After a few weeks he secured home nursing support, which relieved him of some of the intense pressure. What saddened him most was her 'perfect indifference silence and sluggishness'. Writing on Minny's first birthday he was only able to report that 'She kissed the child when I told her of the circumstance, but does not care for it'.[43]

It was hard to decide where they should live. So far as his work was concerned, Thackeray could not view Paris as more than a temporary arrangement. He suggested to his stepfather that when the lease on Great Coram Street ran out they might all take a larger London house together. There should be a garden for the children, 'the Infantry', for he knew that his mother was pining for them and would 'never be happy till she has them under her wing'.[44] She meanwhile was coming up with alternative therapies for Isabella, having learnt of a sanatorium in Silesia where patients were given water treatments of various kinds, and the Parisian physician whom Thackeray consulted seemed to think that Isabella might benefit from it. By mid-August, he and Isabella had joined the Carmichael-Smyths in a sanatorium near Boppard on the Rhine, 'a kind of genteel hospital set up for the cure of almost all complaints by means of sweating & cold water'.[45] Isabella endured several weeks of the strict regime, while Major Carmichael-Smyth became an enthusiastic fellow participant in the rituals.

> The first days she would not stand the immense sluicing of the water-pipe, and I was obliged to go in with her. It would have made a fine picture – M^{rs}. Thack in the condition of our first parins, before they took to eating apples, and the great Titmarsh with nothing on but a petticoat leant him by his mother, and far too scanty to cover that immense posterior protuberance with w^h. nature has furnished him.... The Governor though by Heaven's blessing perfectly well,

nevertheless for the love of science gets up every morning at four, sweats for 4 hours, douches, forswears wine at dinner, douches again, and concludes the day's amusements by sitting for nearly an hour in a tub of icy-cold water... [Hydrosudopathy] has been the means of setting my dear little wife in her senses again.[46]

But as before, the improvement was short-lived. By February 1842 Thackeray finally accepted that he was unable to keep Isabella at home: as he had admitted to FitzGerald some months before '[I] am really with all the year's sufferings quite used up'. It had been a heroic struggle. He managed to secure a place in the clinic run by Dr Puzin in the Chaillot quarter of Paris, where Isabella was to remain for more than three years. He felt such animosity towards her mother, who had returned to Paris but refused any practical support, that he could only tell her of this latest arrangement through a third party. His contempt was becoming obsessive. 'I am sorry to trouble you with this kind of correspondence; but am compelled to <u>préciser</u> every one of my transactions with my wife's mother, in order that I may be able to show her relations when I go to Ireland in the Spring, what my real conduct with regard to her has been, – it has been somewhat misunderstood by M^{rs}. Shawe's family and I hope to be able to prove that <u>I</u> at least have not failed in my duty to the poor girl.'[47]

He had decided to return to Ireland to gather material for the long overdue *Irish Sketchbook*, but first he went to London and stayed with Charles and Mary Carmichael-Smyth in Great Coram Street. Annie and Minny remained in Paris with their grandparents, whilst their father maintained a furiously busy writing regime in order to fund his family commitments. Not until 1846 did his daughters rejoin him in London, but their mother would never again live within the family. She begins to disappear from view, to be assigned a role both by Thackeray's circle and his later commentators as the absent, demented wife, her looming absence portrayed as the silent tragedy of his life. Her story does not end here, but for now she moves quietly into the wings. She will live for a further half century, hardly triumphant but a survivor all the same, eventually forgotten by virtually everyone except her one remaining daughter. There would be a serenity to those final years, when she found peace in the home of the elderly carers with whom she lived in seaside tranquillity near Southend on the Essex coast, taking pleasure in the grandchildren whom her husband would not live to see, and who wept for her during her modest funeral.

++++

When first left in their grandparents' care, Minny was still not two, but at nearly five Annie was old enough to register the change even if its meaning escaped her. A mother who was institutionalised and an absent father may not seem the best of starts. But Annie's recollections never came close to suggesting that the girls felt in any way disadvantaged, perhaps because the years eventually spent in London with their father from 1846 until his death more than compensated for his absence during their Parisian exile. Thackeray's courage in trying to cope with Isabella's illness probably coloured Annie's view of this early period, and it saddened her to think back to his situation at this time. For her, the past could always come flooding back in a moment and whilst this was often a comforting reassurance, it could be melancholy too. 'Time flies, but the great wings come beating backwards again as one looks over the records of the days that were, and which indeed are also now, and not in the past only.'[48]

If their upbringing in Paris was unconventional, it provided stability and offered the diversions of a city which both sisters came to love and returned to many times. Their grandmother's role in these formative years was crucial. Most biographies portray her as a formidable old lady, wilful, overbearing and often wrong-headed, and on top of all this a tiresome Calvinist. A recent representation offers 'a self-opinionated old bigot', a target to be pitied for 'her faith in the powers of homeopathy was just as strong as any of her religious beliefs', with a husband safely sidelined as 'rather a fuddy-duddy'. The best that is allowed is that she 'meant to be kind but she was strict'.[49] She deserves better than this, and fortunately there is sufficient evidence from her later correspondence with her granddaughters to allow a more nuanced portrait.

When Anne Carmichael-Smyth took charge in 1842 she was just fifty. Perhaps she appeared older than she was, seeming closer in years to Major Carmichael-Smyth who at sixty-two played the grandfatherly role convincingly. 'Our Grandpapa who we used to call GP used to wear a short cloak he called a poncho & a straw hat & to buy Almanachs full of pictures w^h. he gave us to play with. He was a dear old man & we always thought it a treat to be with him.'[50] But Thackeray's mother was still an energetic, sociable and lively woman, and according to her granddaughter a leading figure in their small Anglo-French circle.

> My grandmother had a little society of her own at Paris, in the midst of which she seemed to reign from dignity and kindness of heart; her friends, it must be confessed, have not

> as yet become historic, but she herself was well worthy of a record. Grandmothers in books and memoirs are mostly alike, stately, old-fashioned, kindly, and critical. Mine was no exception to the general rule. She had been one of the most beautiful women of her time; she was very tall, with a queenly head and carriage; she always moved in a dignified way. She had an odd taste in dress, I remember, and used to walk out in a red merino cloak trimmed with ermine, which gave her the air of a retired empress wearing out her robes. She was a woman of strong feeling, somewhat imperious, with a passionate love for little children, and with extraordinary sympathy and enthusiasm for any one in trouble or in disgrace. How benevolently she used to look round the room at her many *protégés*, with her beautiful gray eyes! Her friends as a rule were shorter than she was and brisker, less serious and emotional. They adopted her views upon politics, religion, and homœopathy, or at all events did not venture to contradict them. But they certainly could not reach her heights, and her almost romantic passion of feeling.[51]

This suggests a strong and even eccentric personality, certainly, but also someone of style and sympathy. An unwavering religious conviction was balanced by a lively intelligence and an interest in political and social ideas. Of course, we are being given the partial view of a granddaughter reconstructing from former childish impressions the effect one adult had on others, but corroborating evidence in Thackeray's correspondence shows that Annie understood his mother's place in that Parisian world astutely. There were two distinguishing characteristics to this society of displaced British – impoverished gentility coupled with the smug provincialism of a 'twaddling mean society'.[52] It was populated by former Anglo-Indians who, like the Carmichael-Smyths, eked out a modest pension while maintaining the inward-looking social world familiar from their former life. Annie was struck by how they enjoyed living in France, and yet ignored the locals, an enduring characteristic of British expatriate communities. 'Oddly enough, though we talked French, and some of us even looked French, we knew no French people. From time to time at other houses I used to hear of real foreigners, but I don't remember seeing any at ours, except a *pasteur* who sometimes came, and a certain Vicomte de B.'[53]

This first stay would turn out to be their longest in Paris, but there would be further extended periods with their grandparents when

Thackeray undertook his two American tours. Annie's memories of French life are of people and incidents rather than of places, of 'the cheerful crowds and happy voices outside', the sensations from an enticing exterior world engaging with her interior imagination. The Thackeray girls became friendly with the children of their grandmother's circle of connections, especially Pauline and Laura Colmache and Alice and Henriette Corkran. It was the special moments which stayed with them, naturally, occasions whose significance ripened over time and came to have an almost magical meaning. This is a recurring theme for Annie, the idea of the past being transfigured into a kind of living present; 'the people walking in and out of the by-gone mansions of life were not, to our newly-opened eyes, the interesting personages many of them have since become; *then* they were men walking as trees before us, without names or histories, – *now* some of the very names mean for us the history of our time'.[54]

One Parisian memory suggests how these past experiences matured later for her. Three Scottish sisters, friends of her grandmother, were staying in Paris and Annie was sent to them with a note. Prompted by the letter, one of the sisters set out with a basketful of provisions to visit a musician in a side street off the Arc de Triomphe, and Annie accompanied her. The door was opened 'by a slight, delicate-looking man with long hair, bright eyes, and a thin, hooked nose'. There was an upright piano but no furniture in his room. The musician had not slept, but he had been composing, and he offered to play his new piece. The lady worried that it would tire him, but he sat at the piano and played, and tears rolled down her cheeks.

> I can't, alas, recall that music! I would give anything to remember it now; but the truth is, I was so interested in the people that I scarcely listened. When he stopped at last and looked round, the lady started up. 'You mustn't play any more,' she said; 'no more, no more, it's too beautiful' – and she praised him and thanked him in a tender, motherly, pitying sort of way, and then hurriedly said we must go; but as we took leave she added almost in a whisper with a humble apologising look – 'I have brought you some of that jelly, and my sister sent some of the wine you fancied the other day; pray, pray try to take a little'…. As we were coming downstairs she wiped her eyes again…. She looked hard at me as we drove away. 'Never forget that you have heard Chopin play,' she said with emotion, 'for soon no one will ever hear him play any more'.[55]

> I have nothing to send my dearest Anny but a little picture: – the picture is of some little girls I saw going to church, & one of them I thought was like Anny.
> Well, this is all I have to say. for there is no time, because the person is waiting who is going to take this. God bless the little girl to whom he is going to take it, & her little sister. Do you know their names and that their Papa loves them?

Earliest surviving letter from Thackeray to Annie (summer 1842)

Chopin would live until 1849, but this encounter can have occurred no later than 1846, when Annie would have been nine. The composer was in especially poor health during the early months of 1845, and 'the thought of death was never far from his mind'.[56]

At this time, she began receiving short letters from her father, carefully written out in print so that she would might read them for herself. Perhaps the first one which he wrote just for her dates from the summer of 1842, when he was collecting materials for the *Irish Sketchbook*.

> I have nothing to send my dearest Anny but a little picture:
> – the picture is of some little girls I saw going to church, & one of them I thought was like Anny.
>   Well, this is all I have to say: for there is no time, because the person is waiting who is going to take this. God bless the little girl to whom he is going to take it, & her little sister. Do you know their names and that their Papa loves them?[57]

He was in Ireland for several weeks, its sad associations from two years earlier constant reminders of his separation from the children. He was startled and surprisingly upset when a child in the arms of its nurse noticed him and called out 'Papa'. During these solitary years he visited Paris frequently, to see Isabella as well as the children. Having returned from such a trip in January 1843, he writes more expansively to the five-year-old Annie as if to a little adult, inviting her to recollect earlier, happy times and to look forward with optimism. His recounting of a sentimental little incident contrasts the situations of his daughters with children begging in the street.

> You will be well I hope in the spring when we will take a house by the seaside, and you can go into the fields and pick flowers, as you used to do at Margate: before Mamma was ill and when Baby was only a little child in arms. Please God, Mamma will be made well one day too....
> The other night as I was coming home I met in the street two little girls: and what do you think they were doing? –
> Although one was not bigger than you, and the other not so big as Baby, they were singing little songs in the street, in hopes that some one would give them money ... their mother was ill at home with three more children, and they had no bread to eat!
> So I thought of my two dear little girls and how comfortable they were and how their Granny gave them good meals and their Grandmamma a nice house to live in: and I brought the little girls to M^r. Hill the baker in Coram Street, and gave them a loaf and some money, and hope soon to give them some more. And this is all I have to say except God bless my dearest Nanny: and that I always say.[58]

Thackeray mentions his younger daughter relatively rarely as yet, but she was nonetheless a lively presence in her grandparents' apartment. His absence during the early years meant that the Carmichael-Smyths' influence on her upbringing was necessarily profound. Minny had scarcely known the mother who shortly after her birth retreated into illness, and was now removed from her, and as her father had moved back to London it was uncertain how and when they would rejoin him. Thackeray acknowledged that she had been disadvantaged. It was almost as if Minny – in fact, she had yet to acquire this affectionate family name – was implicated in the sadness of Isabella's decline. '[The letter] gave me great pleasure about poor little Marian whom I don't love as I ought. I am always thinking about Nanny but not of the little one God bless her; though for the first 3 months of her life I was immensely fond of her: but the mother makes half the children that's the truth: and I'm not afraid to make the confession to you.'[59]

Annie is able to offer suggestive glimpses of her sister growing up in Paris, though these memories were compiled more than thirty years later, after Minny's death. They have a particular kind of memorialising function in that they were written for Minny's daughter, for whose vulnerability Annie felt acutely. Whilst the account contains an authentic amount of detail, this picture of Minny's early childhood was recorded by a woman fighting to come to terms with the cruel death of a beloved sister.

> One night I dreamt somebody had cut the babys two little feet off & I scrambled out of bed & went to look at her & O I was so glad to see her warm & sound asleep. I had never loved her till then but then I loved her. We went into the country that year & we used to spend the day in a big forest under the trees & pick tiny little blue deep flowers that I made into wreaths & y^r. Mommee used to wear a tiny little pink frock. One day when we had just done some luncheon someone said look look at Baby, & baby was beginning to walk & holding on to the chairs. I was very naughty that day & I had refused to say grace, but my Grannie was so pleased with Baby for beginning to walk that I was forgiven. I used to be naughty every day like naughty Lucy. Once I picked some cherries off a tree once I kicked a gentleman's legs once I was shut up in a cupboard. I also ran away three times.[60]

Although Annie's aberrant behaviour during the summer of 1842 may have been a reaction to the absence of her parents, or perhaps was no more than attention-seeking prompted by the standard jealousy of a younger sibling, her grandmother was sufficiently anxious to alert the absent father, and from Dublin he wrote authorising the use of the whip, 'for where's a better cure for that sort of wilfulness and pride?'[61] There was to be no quick solution, for when he was in Paris the following year Thackeray again urged his mother to deal firmly with 'the little reprobate' – the children were with their grandparents at Montmorency – but was unwilling to administer the punishment himself. 'Pray do as GP advises: it is the shortest easiest and wholesomest of all corrections and will prevent I'm quite sure any scenes or conflicts for the future. Why hesitate? Every year the wilfulness will grow stronger, and your power to correct it less.'[62] Annie remembered the occasion well, unable as an adult to account for her behaviour as a child. 'One year we went to Montmorency where I was very unhappy & naughty & shut up in my room for a long time & I was whipped.'

These episodes did not spoil the general happiness of these Parisian years, especially when Minny was old enough to be someone with a real name, 'Baby' no longer. 'Grannie bought a nice little green cart for Minnie to go out in. Sometimes as a great treat I was allowed to get in too. We used to have big bits of bread given to us & a penny each & our nurse used to drag us to a little shop where they sold milk & we used to breakfast in the little shop & then go on to a green shady terrace & spend long mornings out of doors. Minnie drank her milk but never would eat much. She used to run away from the table & sometimes my Grannie used to give her her dinner under the table. She never liked Rhubarb or vegetables or puddings.'[63]

There was a new baby to distract them all in 1844, as the Carmichael-Smyths were also looking after Mary and Charles Carmichael's child whilst they were in India (they had dropped 'Smyth' from the surname about a year after they married). Charles junior – Cheri as he was always known – was a great novelty, and went with them all on the next summer holiday, when the Carmichael-Smyths rented a country house at Chaudfontaine, near Liège. 'In front of the house, with its many green shutters, was a courtyard, enclosed by green gates, where we used to breakfast, and outside the gates a long terraced road by the dried-up river, where I used to walk with my father, holding his hand. He would come for a day or two; sometimes he stayed at the villa, sometimes at a little inn in the village, a whitewashed place with trellises, where we would fetch him of a morning. He never remained very long with us; he came and went suddenly.'[64]

It was a strange childhood for an intelligent, observant girl like Annie, an early introduction to the notion that happiness was elusive. For it was whilst they were still in Belgium that Thackeray, having returned to England, was offered a free passage to the Middle East, an opportunity which he seized and which led to his *Notes of a Journey from Cornhill to Grand Cairo*. He would not return to the family at the Belgian villa, and it would be months before they saw him again. By the end of August he had reached Gibraltar. 'I enjoy myself very much all things considering (viz bugs musquitoes &c) and please God shall pass Xmas with you and my dear little girls. I wish Anny were here – she would see & understand quite as much as the best travellers. God bless her & all.'[65]

From Constantinople he wrote Isabella a letter full of lively description of the exotic new sights, illustrating it with several sketches and confining himself carefully to the language of the travelogue. He avoids personal issues other than gently reminding her of the water cure she had undergone back in 1841. There is nothing that would alert an innocent reader to the fact that he is writing to an invalid.

Watercolour of Annie, by Thackeray

Yesterday I was in the bazaars at Constantinople and was thinking of buying you by way of a present a little black slave girl – they are to be had for 10£ – but would you like a pair of papooshes better or a beautiful veil or Yackmack such as the Turkish ladies wear? You can only see their noses and eyes as they shuffle past in their yellow slippers, and I was warned off from a shop for looking at one too curiously.... Then I could describe to you a Turkish bath I took – how I was sweated and shampooed and kneaded by a great grinning Turk, as bad as you used to be at Chateau Boppart.[66]

He wrote some weeks later to his unmarried cousin Charlotte Ritchie about his wife's condition, Isabella having written in a manner that perhaps encouraged hopes of a restored normality. Charlotte and her family had supported Thackeray by continuing to visit her regularly at Chaillot. 'My wife's letter I think is far the best and most reasonable she has written yet: and it is almost equally gratifying to find that she continues to be happy and pleased with her home away from us all.'[67] He still had hopes of eventually reuniting his family, despite having accepted in 1842 that he was unable to cope with looking after Isabella himself. As he saw the young families of his friends growing up around him in London he yearned for the comfort of a home life. He had noted in his diary during his visit to the children at Chaudfontaine that 'I lose a great deal of the best kind of happiness by being deprived of their affectionate artless society.'[68]

Back in London in 1845 he arranged that his mother should bring the children to England for an early summer visit. They travelled to Southampton and went first to her Becher relations before moving on to London where Thackeray had rooms in St James's Street.

> Our Father was living in London in chambers opposite S^t. James Palace & he came to meet us at the station & immediately gave us each 2 wax dolls, & at breakfast he gave us bigger helps of jam than we have ever had in our lives & after breakfast he took us to feed the ducks in St James Park, & then he bought us picture books the Arabian Nights & Grimms Fairy Tales & then he took us to a diorama & to the Colosseum. I thought he would spend all the money he had in the world when I saw how much he had to pay for us. One day he took us in our flapping straw hats to see Aunt JOB who was quite a young lady with curls & who gave us a book.[69]

'Aunt JOB' was Jane Octavia Brookfield, wife of Thackeray's close Cambridge contemporary, the Reverend William Brookfield, and this mention suggests that it was not her first appearance on the scene. During the next few years Thackeray developed an intense friendship with Jane which, on his side at least, allowed some emotional release to compensate for his enforced return to what we must assume to be celibacy. Jane became for him an always unattainable female ideal, so that he attached to the 'My dear Lady' of his correspondence an almost courtly, chivalric significance. It is most unlikely that the relationship ever became sexual, but his passion was something of an open secret amongst their circle, and Jane herself does not seem – in the early years at least – to have done anything to discourage his attentions. Letters in which she addressed him as her 'dearest brother William' serve only to give a legitimising – or alternatively incestuous – dimension to this ultimately impenetrable relationship which reached its crisis during the cathartic composition of *Esmond*, completed in 1852. That novel about the unorthodox passion of an older, married woman for a younger man, and his for her daughter, is made less personal by being placed in the safety of the historically distant eighteenth century.

The visit to London coincided with Annie's eighth birthday on 9 June. The entire trip must have felt like an extended celebration, although the adults were slow to remember the date. Thackeray worried that Isabella might discover that the girls had come to London without her knowing, and felt guilty at keeping it from her. 'I was in a perplexity about the poor little woman and whether or not to tell her that the children had been here to see me.... This is Anny's birthday. I wonder whether her mother will remember it. Her father didn't: and poor Nanny wouldn't say a word but kept her secret, until my mother remembered it.'[70] He filled their visit with treats, taking them to the Zoological Gardens, Westminster Abbey, the Tower of London, the Chinese Exhibition and a final trip out to Richmond Park. 'And then comes tomorrow: and the dear little souls and the kind mother disappear in the distance – and I am left to my bachelor life again. If I did not know how much better a guardian they have in her than myself, they never should leave me.'

His hopes for Isabella's improvement proved illusory, for Annie tells of visits to Chaillot and then of the last occasion that the children were able to see her there. 'Our Mama was ill & she used to live with a Doctor in a big house with a great garden full of little paths & we used to go & spend the day with her & run after her down the long slopes of the garden. She was quite young with beautiful red-golden hair, one day when we came we found her sitting on the terrace with all her hair tumbling about her shoulders & somebody combing it out. Then the Doctor said it was better we should not go & see her anymore & we came away to England to live with our Papa.'[71]

Rather than abandoning Isabella in an establishment where she appeared to make no progress, Thackeray decided in October 1845 to bring her to London so that she could be nearer to him. His mother's friend, Mrs Gloyne, travelled to Paris to collect her, Thackeray meeting them in Boulogne and escorting them to London. He knew that it would not be possible to look after Isabella himself, placing her instead in the care of a Mrs Bakewell, 'an excellent worthy woman. The difference in the poor little woman's appearance is remarkable now that she has some one to look after her and keep her clean.... My visits please her exceedingly. God bless her so I go almost every other day.'[72]

During their last months in Paris, Annie started attending morning school with her friend Laura Colmache, and in the afternoon she would rejoin Minny whereupon they would play in the gardens of the Tuilleries. Their father spent Christmas in London with Isabella, from where he wrote to Annie at the close of the year.

> On Christmas day I dined with Mamma and she was very well and happy, only she grew very grave when we talked about you; and there were tears in her eyes the meaning of which I knew quite well. How glad I am that it is a black <u>puss</u> & not a black <u>nuss</u> you have got! I thought you did not know how to spell nurse & had spelt it en-you-double-ess. But I see the spelling gets better as the letters grow longer: they cannot be too long for me.... I would sooner have you gentle and humble-minded than ever so clever. Who was born on Christmas day? Somebody who was so great that all the world worships him; and so good that all the world loves him; and so gentle & humble that he never spoke an unkind word. But I hope Nanny is proud with no one. And there is a little sermon, and a great deal of love and affection from Papa. May God send my dearest children many happy new years.
>
> I wonder who will kiss Minny for me?[73]

Why this 'little sermon'? It appears that Annie's propensity for wilful naughtiness had not entirely disappeared, and that there were occasions when she could be resolutely 'difficult'. Not long before the girls joined him permanently in his new house in Kensington, he reported to Isabella's sister the despairing remarks that his mother had made in a recent letter. The grandmother was finding it increasingly hard to rein in the quick-witted granddaughter. 'Here is the last report just come from Paris about Anny. "I assure you Nanny wants a firmer hand than mine. She fights every inch of her way – if it's only to wash her face or put on her stockings she will not do it without an argument – She is so clever: so selfish: so generous: so tender-hearted yet so careless of giving pain." – I am afraid very much that she is going to be a man of genius: I would far sooner have had her an amiable

& affectionate woman – But little Minny will be that, please God, – and the Sisters love each other admirably.'[74] Minny would certainly fulfil his hopes, but her moral capacity – her decisiveness, loyalty and wisdom linked to a readiness quietly to crush her own ambitions for the sake of those she loved – these traits would not wholly emerge until after his death.

During the summer of 1846 he was actively looking for a house for them all, hoping that his parents would come from Paris with the girls, as he knew that his mother would be lost without them. But there was an apparently insurmountable difficulty in that Major Carmichael-Smyth's outstanding debts made him unwilling to come to England, as his creditors might apply to the law for redress. At the beginning of July, Thackeray had moved into the house in Young Street, Kensington, where he would complete *Vanity Fair* and go on to write *Pendennis* and *Esmond*. He wrote enthusiastically to his mother, urging them to join him without delay, hoping that even his stepfather might be persuaded.

> I know you won't be happy without him with that ingenious knack you have of making yourself uncomfortable: and I hope & pray in God that we shall all be able to live together and that I may not be deprived of my mother & my children. There are 2 capital bed-rooms & a little sitting room for you & GP – a famous bed room for G.M. [*Mrs Butler*] on the first floor – 2 rooms for the children on second very airy & comfortable; a couple of rooms big enough for Servants, & 2 little ones quite large enough for me – There's a good study for me down stairs & a dining room & drawing room, and a little court yard or garden and a little green house: and Kensington Gardens at the gate, and omnibuses every 2 minutes. What can mortal want more?...
>
> I have been opening the trunks to day. Full of the lumbering useless old books; and woful [*sic*] relics of old days – In one of them I find a power of old shirts of mine from India.[75]

There is serious intent here, a desire to make a home where they could all be happy. At first Mrs Carmichael-Smyth agreed to bring the children for a summer visit only, but that was put off. Thackeray continued to visit Isabella regularly, but there was only melancholy and decay surrounding him on the day that he took her to Camberwell Fair. 'I saw nothing funny or pleasant: only a great collection of ginger-bread booths and people swinging in merry-go-rounds. So we hired a cab & drove up beautiful Norwood Hill to Beulah Spa – There wasn't a soul in those charming gardens. Tents down, ponds seedy, roses moulting troubadours fled.'[76]

At last, in the autumn, his mother brought Annie and Minny from Paris, not for a holiday but for a trial period during which they would live with their father. Then she returned to Major Carmichael-Smyth, leaving behind the girls whose characters she had helped shape and to whom she was entirely devoted, the only mother that Minny had ever known. Annie would never forget their arrival at Young Street.

> We came one evening in the autumn. There were raging fires lighted & volumes of Punch were put out on the round drawingroom table & also beautiful red silk books that I was never tired of reading afterwards when I had had time to value it all. Upstairs was a dear little room with two little beds & some pictures. One was of a good boy doing a sum & another of a sleepy boy yawning on his way to bed, & then over the drawers hung Daniel O'Connel who used to make the most horrible faces at us. Your Mommee was six & she had dear little feet & such pretty blue eyes & long curls & she used to play by herself at all sorts of games – How bitterly she cried when our Grannie went away & left us.[77]

The girls settled in quickly and Thackeray determined that they should stay with him. By the beginning of December he writes to comfort his mother who was missing them sorely, but he is resolute. He did not want to lose them again, and perhaps sensed that he might not be able to cope if they did return.

> You know how it pains me to think of my dearest mother being unhappy; Anny read me your letter the other day: it brought back all sorts of early early times, and induced an irresistible burst of tears on my part, at w^h. the Child looked astonished. Her eyes were quite dry. They don't care: not even for you. They'll have to complain some day of the same indifference in your Grand-grandchildren. Now they are with me I am getting so fond of them that I can understand the pangs of the dear old mother who loses them: and who by instinct is 100 times fonder of them than ever a man could be. But it is best that they should be away from you: – at least that they should be away either from you or me. There can't be two first principles in a house. We should secretly be jealous of

one another: or I should resign the parental place altogether to you, and be a bachelor still. Whereas now God Almighty grant I may be a father to my children. Continual thoughts of them chase I don't know how many wickednesses out of my mind. Their society makes many of my old amusements seem trivial & shameful....

And how thankful this makes me to you & my dear old GP, who have kept the children for me and watched them so nobly & tenderly – Kind and affectionate hearts, dear & steadfast friends, for this I thank and bless you as the father of my children.[78]

Annie would give a second version of their arrival in Young Street some time after this first account, which is similar in all essentials, but as her recollection travels back over the years she adds one wistful reflection that seems to have occurred to her as if for the first time. 'Once more, after his first happy married years, my father had a home and a family – if a house, two young children, three servants, and a little black cat can be called a famly.'[79]

Three

OUR STREET
(1847-1852)

Suns long set begin to shine once more through the old Kensington study windows. My father's silvery-grey head is bending over his drawing-board as he sits at his work, serious, preoccupied, with the watercolour box open on the table beside him, and the tray full of well-remembered implements. To the writer her own childhood comes back and fills her world.

Annie's Preface
'Contributions to Punch'
Biographical Edition

With a sick wife and two young children to care for, Thackeray had come to realise that only in England could he hope to secure enough work to meet his expenses. Alone in London he established himself as an intensely busy freelance, active as a journalist and increasingly as a writer of fiction. A long connection with the comic-satirical periodical *Punch* began in 1842, his first regular contributions coming in 1844 with the travel pieces of the 'Fat Contributor', and by 1846 he was engaged on his latest series for that magazine, later republished as *The Book of Snobs*. When Annie and Minny rejoined him in the autumn he was at work on *Vanity Fair*, his first long novel, its opening number appearing at the start of 1847 under the imprint of Bradbury and Evans. The hoped-for rewards were slow in coming, and as late as March 1848 he would tell Edward FitzGerald that 'Vanity Fair does everything but pay'. But by then things had decidedly changed for him, and he walked on a bigger stage. He was moving within a perceptibly literary world, and his daughters were becoming old enough to appreciate the difference. *Punch* brought him into contact with its editors, Mark Lemon and Henry Mayhew, and with fellow contributors including Douglas Jerrold, Gilbert à Beckett and the illustrators Richard (Dicky) Doyle and John Leech, the latter of whom had been Thackeray's junior at Charterhouse. He saw something of FitzGerald again in these years, and also their mutual Cambridge friends, Alfred Tennyson and James Spedding.

Now that he had his children with him, Thackeray wanted to provide them with satisfactory home schooling and to continue what his mother had set in place in Paris. 13 Young Street had plenty of space up on the second floor for a schoolroom, and one of Mrs Carmichael-Smyth's Paris friends, an Irish woman, Bess Hamerton, was engaged to look after the girls, but she was more nanny than governess, and it was teaching that they now needed. Her unsuitability was painfully evident from Annie's guileless observations. 'Minie can read the printed letters very nicely and I think reads better by a goodeal though you must give her the merit of getting on by her self for Bess canot bear to teach.'[1] And Bess knew her limitations. 'I regret daily my incapability and repugnance to teaching, the former isn't to be cured, and the latter must be indured [*sic*].'[2] Thackeray saw that Annie did not respect Bess, neither her intellect nor her background. The fact that she was an intimate of Mrs Carmichael-Smyth made it awkward for him to have to point out – with some of the prejudices of the time – that Bess was 'not an English lady – that's the fact'. But he did not duck the issue. 'The child is the woman's superior in every respect: and subject to a vulgar worrying discipline w^h. makes her unhappy. She has once or twice shown a disposition to complain w^h. I have checked: but she has opened her heart to me today.... The commonplaces in that enormous brogue kill me: and she falls to worrying Nanny as soon as I go out. And so we part.'[3] That same day he wrote as honestly as he could to Bess.

> After all your care & kindness it seems very ungrateful to say to you 'Dont stay with us any more' but it w^d. be worse not to speak openly my mind now it is made up. You have not got the affection of the children. They are afraid of you: & though I know you have done your utmost & your best by them & by me – yet, right or wrong, I think the little girls won't give you their confidence, & that its best we sh^d. part....
>
> I have checked Anny twice or thrice when about to make complaints: I have just now had some talk with her and see from what she says & feels that were you to live ten years together, the ideas of both of you are so different, you could never be cordial.[4]

It had been a salutary realisation. As he observed to his mother, 'this is not the woman to rule such a delicate soul as my dearest Nanny's.

Three: Our Street 65

What a noble creature she is thank God. May I love her and be her friend more & more. As for Minny who can help loving her?'⁵

Annie remembered only her own behaviour at the time, which clearly made life miserable for all concerned. 'I think I must have been a very discontented child for it seems to me now that I was always in disgrace & that Bess used to call me a Viper. But with our Papa we were always happy.'⁶ The real problem was not Bess's rough edges so much as that Annie was jealously possessive. Now that she had found her father again, she feared that he would suddenly remove himself as on previous occasions. It was the same anxiety about being abandoned that had haunted Thackeray through his own early schooldays.

Minny could be mischievous in her own right, and Jane Brookfield once caught her 'throwing her shoe at the housemaid whom we did not like'.⁷ Both girls felt the threat of being displaced by the excellent manservant, Samuel James, 'afraid that Papa would like him better than us'. They all called him Jeames, after the footman Charles Jeames de la Pluche of the *Yellowplush Papers.* In later life, Annie became closer to this valued servant, able then to appreciate his kindness. James had noted his master's lack of all pretension and grandness, his perfect contentment with the cracked and unmatching cups and saucers brought out daily at breakfast. One morning a hamper arrived containing a set of fine breakfast china, the anonymous donor dedicating the gift 'To the famed M.A. Titmarsh of *Vanity Fair*'. It was only when Samuel James set out to Australia for a new situation that he at last broke his silence to reveal the truth. 'I sent you the breakfast things; you guessed a great many people, but you never guessed they came from me.'⁸

From Paris, Mrs Carmichael-Smyth wrote constantly to her granddaughters, kind, watchful and, in their way, wise letters, for despite his large heart she knew that her son could not be both father and mother to his children. She tackled Annie about her moments of unhappiness, believing that their cause was deep-rooted and that talking of her anxieties could alleviate the misery – 'every one is sad sometimes and then it is good to have a good cry ... & write to me what you think as well as what you do'.⁹ It was compensation, if some years too late, for not offering this kind of simple support to Isabella in her early married years. But not once is the girls' mother mentioned in these letters. It would have been a difficult subject, of course, although Isabella cannot have been far from her thoughts, partly prompted by Annie's troubling behaviour. The fear of hereditary transmission of mental abnormality made Thackeray and his mother watchful.

Annie's letters to her grandmother and a single note from Minny from these years constitute their earliest surviving writing. Compared with the few letters that Thackeray kept from his mother – she carefully preserved many of his, of course – the far larger number that survive to her granddaughters give a more rounded picture of the woman who influenced not just his attitudes but those of his children as well. They flesh out our understanding of the London life of the Thackerays during these years of his growing success, and reveal a woman of surprising wit and charm. The correspondence is above all valuable for its glimpses of mid-nineteenth-century Anglo-French life during a time of political and social change.

In his search for a suitable governess Thackeray described one in terms designed to reassure his mother – 'a Miss Drury – clergyman's daughter – all her relations gentlefolks – a miracle of sweet temper & gentleness and beloved by everybody – not pretty & 27'.[10] Mrs Carmichael-Smyth was persuaded, and looked forward to the new regime – 'it will be such a comfort to Papa, & every day you will be learning to be more useful to him, & that will be a comfort to you'.[11] To be told by Annie that Miss Drury was 'beautiful with large black eyes'[12] may not have been quite what Mrs Carmichael-Smyth wanted to hear, especially as Thackeray had offered a less flattering picture. If she felt anxious about the allure of diverting female companionship, it was only because her son had already alerted her to his failings. 'Unless I liked a Governess I couldn't live with her and if I did – O fie. The flesh is very weak, le coeur sent toujours le besoin d'aimer. What a mercy it is that I've kept clear hitherto.'[13] It becomes something of a running joke, on Thackeray's part at least. A month into Miss Drury's regime, he reiterated that 'I shan't fall in love with her'.[14]

Annie always remembered the Young Street house with affection, in the first years of her marriage returning to live just across the road from these scenes of her childhood. 'My father used to write in his study at the back of the house in Young Street.... Our garden was not tidy (though on one grand occasion a man came to mow the grass), but it was full of sweet things. There were verbenas – red, blue, and scented; and there were lovely stacks of flags, blades of green with purple heads between, and bunches of London Pride growing luxuriantly; and there were some blush roses at the end of the garden, which were not always quite eaten up by the caterpillars.'[15]

In 1847 Thackeray became entirely preoccupied with the monthly numbers of *Vanity Fair*, driven by the relentless deadlines for copy. In his case, this meant providing the illustrations as well. 'Towards the end of the month I get so nervous that I don't speak to anybody scarcely, and once actually got up in the middle of the night and came down & wrote in my night-shimee.'[16] For his daughters, being witnesses to the novel's composition was a great adventure, whilst their grandmother impatiently awaited each number, read them eagerly, and then passed the yellow-covered copies around her Parisian circle.

Dombey and Son had started to appear just a few months earlier, and the two serials ran contemporaneously. Comparisons were invidious, but irresistible. In mentioning the appearance of the March number of her father's novel, Annie actually seems to have become more involved with the story of Florence Dombey – 'the third number of Vanity fair is come out poor little Paul in Dombey is dead but the Father is so unhappy and unkind to poor Florence'.[17] Mrs Carmichael-Smyth too probably felt more comfortable with Dickens's moral certainties than with the ironies and realism of her son's writing. She occasionally included for her granddaughters one of her own stories designed for their instruction – plodding, religious in tone, and full of ennobling self-sacrifice. Despite calling one of them 'wonderful', Thackeray knew that they were unpublishable. She followed *Dombey and Son* from its start, borrowing the numbers from a neighbour, unusually affected by Dickens's treatment of his characters. But in picking up Annie's concern for Florence Dombey, she insists that there will be an appropriate outcome. 'Cruel old Dombey will be sure to be punished & good Florence will have the happiness of being his comforter in distress – & his stiff neck cloth will have the starch taken out – Miss Fitton lends it us & we send her V.F.: one to laugh at, the other to cry.'[18] She came across Catherine Dickens when the author and his wife were staying in Paris, just after *Vanity Fair* had started to appear. They compared notes about working-methods, hints of rivalry not far beneath the surface. 'I met M[rs]. Dickens who talked about Papa & you & I think we both tried which could say the handsomest things of Husband & son. Boz never goes out till after the 15th of the month nor sees any one at home.'[19]

Thackeray always remained a genuine admirer of Dickens's work and never set himself up in opposition. They had first met as early as 1836, since when a friendship had developed, although, as Gordon Ray puts it, 'Thackeray could not hide from himself the conviction that by his standards Dickens was not a gentleman'.[20] It was a relationship which entered rougher waters in later years. When the first number of *David Copperfield* appeared in 1849, Thackeray was enthusiastic. 'It has some of his very prettiest touches – those inimitable Dickens touches w[h]. make such a great man of him', but he also detected the influence of *Vanity Fair* in the writer's simpler style, his 'foregoing the use of fine words'.[21] To William Brookfield he was even more generous about the merits of *David Copperfield* – 'it beats the yellow chap of this month [*Pendennis*] hollow'.[22] Dickens organised a dinner as *Dombey and Son* came to an end, and insisted on Thackeray's presence – 'It couldn't be done without you' – but he was guarded about the other's novel. 'I am saving up the perusal of Vanity Fair until I shall have done Dombey.'[23]

Annie and Minny would serve either as models for Thackeray's illustrations, or as aids in their composition. 'One day we were the two naughty children rolling over & over on the ground, & there is a little picture of [Minny] sitting building cards upon a little three legged stool our Grannie had given us.'[24] They were conscious of the greater work going on around them as they tried to concentrate on their lessons upstairs. 'It used to be a joy to us as we swung our legs in the schoolroom ... to be called from these abstractions to take a share in the great living drama of *Punch* or "Vanity Fair" going on in the study below. We were to be trusted to stand upon chairs, to hold draperies and cast a shadow, to take the part of supers on our father's stage.'[25] It was a charmingly effective way of bringing the girls' likenesses before their young Parisian friends. 'What pretty pictures Papa has made, everybody knew them.'[26]

Mrs Carmichael-Smyth urged Thackeray to construct his characters within a less ambiguous moral framework, which of course misunderstands the principal strength of the novel. He sought to defend his social and moral vision.

> What I want is to make a set of people living without God in the world (only that is a cant phrase) greedy pompous mean perfectly self-satisfied for the most part and at ease about their superior virtue. Dobbin & poor Briggs are the only 2 people with real humility as yet. Amelia's is to come, when her scoundrel of a husband is well dead with a ball in his odious bowels; when she has had sufferings, a child, and a religion – But she has at present a quality above most people whizz: LOVE – by w^h. she shall be saved. Save me, save me too O my God and Father, cleanse my heart and teach me my duty.[27]

In view of the fictional character's weakly self-indulgent nature, it is curious that Thackeray should have borrowed George Osborne's name from a child in his mother's Parisian circle. As a result, her letters at times can be read as an almost surreal blend of her son's fiction with prosaic Parisian news as she sketches out the character's alternative history. 'George Osborne is such a funny little fellow, but I must say very troublesome; he is so fond of his books that he brings them to his Momme to read to her while she is dressing.'[28] One can only imagine the Osbornes' own puzzled interrogation of Mrs Carmichael-Smyth as the true nature of her son's characters emerged month by month.[29]

She was prepared to share her criticisms with her granddaughters, especially when Thackeray's portrayal of women as selfish creatures seemed to exclude the possibility of self-improvement. 'Mr Punch is very profound with new ideas about pattern wives – tell him from his Mamma that unlucky writers of the 19th century must submit to such penalties as politics talking wives unless they can find a paradise of Amelias.... I wish he would write a novel to shew what Mind Women might be who act from a better principle than self love. Poor old Man he has such a loving heart withal.'[30]

In the summer of 1847, Miss Drury left and the girls went to their grandparents until November. Not for the last time, Thackeray and his mother disagreed over the governess question, she insisting on a steadying female hand to look after the girls' interests, believing that they were being allowed to go about in increasingly shabby clothes. His daughters were sensitive to these atmospheres, aware of their father being treated as if he himself were still a child. After reacting badly, Thackeray quickly apologised once Major Carmichael-Smyth intervened.

> God forgive me if I have wronged you my dearest old Mother: the wrong has made two of us very miserable.... GP's letters were far from harsh they were admirable in kindness & gentleness....
>
> How to find a Governess is now the puzzle.... I repeatedly asked Miss D to get everything the children wanted – and didn't leave her any money for I thought GM would advance anything required – It wasn't much to expect from her... but I really didn't know the little ones wanted anything.

Shortly after this, Mrs Butler (GM) died in Paris, but before the news reached him, Thackeray wrote seeking his daughters' return, having secured the services of a Miss Alexander, 'a very nice plain kind-looking governess – about 28, with 6 or 7 brothers & sisters living at Richmond with their Pa & Ma'.[31] For a moment, he had toyed with an unusual offer made to him by William Brookfield, that they should join their households and share expenses. In view of his complex emotional dependency upon Brookfield's wife, this was an attractive suggestion, and therefore one he was wise to resist. With his mother, he is as frank as always. 'M^rs. B managing the children – loving her as I do – mong Dieu [*sic*] what a temptation it was! but you see the upshot. That would be dangerous, and so I keep off.'

By December the children were back in Kensington, and Mrs Carmichael-Smyth was encouraged by reports of 'plain' Miss Alexander, as she confided to the children. 'How glad I am your new little companion is so accomplished & cheerful & I daresay very amiable & that you are both very kind to her.'[32] There was the success of Thackeray's new Christmas book, *Our Street*, as well as the latest number of *Vanity Fair* to celebrate, but her son's financial entanglement in a failed railway company was a new worry, and she feared for his health. 'I am frightened at the notion of poor Papa getting into a horrid [law]suit – I see & hear of handsome things said of Our S^t. this n^r. of V.F. is very excellent – I wish he could get a holiday.'[33]

The Alexanders lived in Twickenham (not Richmond), at Chapel House, later Tennyson's home and the birthplace of his eldest son, whose christening Thackeray would attend. Annie and Minny might stay for a couple of nights at a time at Chapel House if Thackeray was out of town, and the scientific interests of Miss Alexander's father met with Mrs Carmichael-Smyth's strong approval. 'I have so often wished I knew anything of geology. It is the fashion to laugh & sneer at ladies who study these things, but I cant see the wit or good sense of it; all knowledge of nature is good, even if it only kept us from other things w^h. are not good, but it does more when it is pursued in the spirit of love. We may darn our stockings & make pies & puddings if need be, & still find time for such things.'[34]

In April 1848, a troubled and revolutionary year across Europe, fears of public disturbances when the Chartists arrived in London with their final petition led the government to swear in thousands of special constables, Thackeray amongst them. With a swagger suggesting that he took his duties about as seriously as he felt they warranted, Thackeray armed himself appropriately. From their Young Street window, Annie and Minny watched him enter the Greyhound inn, across the road, '& when he came out he was carrying a great purple staff with a lion & unicorn painted on it'. He nevertheless thought it wise to send the girls to the Alexanders for the night, where precautions were nervously taken, but all passed peacefully.

At the end of July, with *Vanity Fair* completed, the girls were again billeted in Twickenham while their father travelled to Brussels and Spa. His leaving triggered in Annie another bout of bad behaviour. 'I think I was out of temper & jealous & suspicious. Minnie was very happy & one day Henry Alexander said to me as we were all sitting in the garden What a pretty little girl your sister is: & I looked at her & I thought why what a pretty little girl she is.'[35] Thackeray failed to realise how his departure might upset them, which is curious in view of his own childhood insecurities – 'my daughters didn't seem much to care, though they have already discovered the emptiness of Captain Alexander and gave me to understand that they are tired of living with him'.[36]

Miss Alexander's reign in Young Street would not be a long one. She had scarcely crossed the threshold before Thackeray doubted her capacity to handle the precocious Annie. '[M]y dear old Nan goes on thinking for herself, and no small beer of herself – I am obliged to snub her continually, with delight at what she says all the time. They are noble children. Thank God. And the governess – a nuisance.'[37] By April the nuisance had become a 'bore' (and just a bit too plain, perhaps), despite always being 'good-humoured with all their factiousness and bent on doing her duty'.[38] It was as well that on becoming engaged she gave up the job. And yet, the safety of her dullness was exactly what reassured Thackeray's mother, concerned that the girls should have an overseer whose looks would go unremarked by their father. Before he left for Brussels, Thackeray had identified a possible German governess, but as things turned out there would be nobody new until a final appointment in 1850. Instead, the Carmichael-Smyths came to Kensington in October for an extended visit, whereupon his mother became 'my comfort my housekeeper and governess in chief'.[39]

In his unusual domestic circumstances, with his wife alive but lost to him, Thackeray tried to do his best for the daughters whose comforting presence reminded him of what might have been. As Annie later recalled, 'Ours was more or less a bachelor's establishment, and the arrangements of the house varied between a certain fastidiousness and the roughest simplicity. We had shabby table-cloths, alternating with some of my grandmother's fine linen.'[40] The sisters saw nothing unusual in it at the time, and were content with the household routines. 'One day my father said that he had been surprised to hear from his friend Sir Henry Davison how seriously our house struck people, compared to other houses: "But I think we are very happy as we are," said he – and so indeed we were.'[41] Just occasionally, on visits out, they were aware of being dressed dowdily, more attuned to their father's adult world and their grandparents' sober ways. The Dickens children became friends, particularly Kate Dickens, and they were invited to their parties. 'I remember watching the white satin shoes and long flowing white sashes of the little Dickens girls, who were just about our own age, but how much more graceful and beautifully dressed. Our sashes were bright plaids of red and blue, a tribute from one of our father's Scotch admirers (is it ungrateful to confess now after all these years that we could not bear them?)'[42] This magical other world contrasted with the realities of hand-me-down clothes. After their first New Year in Young Street, the nine-year-old Annie tells her grandmother that 'I have got a new white frock and Minnie has mine made up for her only think it was not a bit to big for her except the bodice wich was to long but the wast was just the size', and Mrs Carmichael-Smyth soaks up the detail and celebrates the frugality – 'and so my Minneks can wear Nanny's frock! What a deal of good English beef & mutton she must have eaten.'[43]

In one of the more searching observations from her later years, Annie finally admitted to the limitations of their life then, regretting that she and Minny had not thought to introduce a livelier regime for their father. It worried her that they might have been able to make him more content. 'There was certainly a want of initiation: in our house there was no one to suggest all sorts of delightful possibilities, which, as we grew up, might have been made more of; but looking back, I chiefly regret it in so far as I think he might have been happier if we had brought a little more action and sunshine into daily life, and taken a little more on our own responsibility, instead of making ourselves into his shadows.'[44] In fact, they provided him with more normal a family life than he might ever have thought possible, and their reward was to be treated as adults before their time.

++++

Unlike *Vanity Fair* with its range of protagonists and breadth of scale, Thackeray's next novel, *Pendennis*, the story of a young man who makes his way in the social and literary world, is crammed with autobiographical incident. Arthur Pendennis becomes Thackeray's fictional alter ego and will return in later works, replacing the previous mask of 'Michael Angelo Titmarsh' behind which the writer both concealed and revealed himself. The novel's composition ran alongside his intense feelings for Jane Brookfield, a friendship which on his side was illicit in intent – he desired her and when he did not see her wrote to her constantly – but though the relationship was never physically consummated, its potency was not lessened for him. When eventually

William Brookfield stopped Jane from asking Thackeray to the house, his reaction was that of a spurned lover.

From the outset, he justified his interest in Jane's happiness by what he insisted was Brookfield's neglect, but it helped that she was beautiful. 'I know the cause of a great part of her malady well enough – a husband whom she has loved with the most fanatical fondness and who – and who is my friend too – a good fellow upright generous kind to all the world except her.'[45] Brookfield was over-sensitive to the different social positions of his own and his wife's family. Jane was the youngest daughter of Charles Elton (later Baronet) of Clevedon Court, near Bristol, while he was the son of a Sheffield lawyer and the product of an oppressive, evangelical home. He loved his wife sincerely, but undemonstratively, and 'was something of a domestic tyrant and disapproved of uxoriousness on principle'.[46] Thackeray insisted on regarding it as a lonely marriage, since that forged a link between Jane and himself. The Brookfields were as yet childless. But very different reasons account for Thackeray's solitariness, and for the absence of sexual love. He saw that his daughters could replace much, but not all that was missing in his life. Already Annie seemed to him 'as wise as an old man. In 3 years she will be a charming companion to me: and fill up a part of a great vacuum w^h. exists inside me.'[47]

Writing to Jane from Spa, where he rested after completing *Vanity Fair*, he tried to plan the new work. 'But instead of Pen, ah Mon Dieu how one sits and thinks of all sorts of other things.'[48] By September he was back in Young Street, and contemplating a sad anniversary. 'Tomorrow it will be eight years since my poor dear little wife jumped into the great calm sunshiny sea off the Isle of Wight: and she has been dead or worse ever since.'[49] As Isabella's sister left for India, he remembered the charm and simple honesty of 'the dear artless creature' when they first met.

> What a whirl of life I've seen since then, but never her better I think: whose reason it pleased God to destroy before her body: and who cares for none of us now. Nest ce pas mourir tous les jours – dont you recollect her singing and her sweet sweet voice? She goes to Epsom tomorrow when you sail for India. Go, stay, die, prosper, she doesn't care. Amen. Her anxious little soul would have been alarmed at my prosperities such as they are. She was always afraid of people flattering me: and I get a deal of that sort of meat nowadays.[50]

When the Carmichael-Smyths arrived in Young Street in mid-October, Thackeray handed over management of his household to his

Autograph pages from Pendennis *(left leaf)*

Three: Our Street

Autograph pages from Pendennis *(right leaf)*

mother. The new novel was well under way, as he revealed to Jane Brookfield. 'Madam I did not think about you one bit all yesterday, being entirely occupied with my 2 new friends M^rs. Pendennis & her son M^r. Arthur Pendennis.'[51] And as Thackeray readily confided to the poet, Arthur Hugh Clough, the saintly Helen Pendennis was a portrait of Mrs Carmichael-Smyth.

He paid a short visit to the Brookfields in late October at Clevedon Court, Jane's ancestral home. William Brookfield having returned to London before his wife, Jane and Thackeray spent a further weekend there. An understanding was reached.

> Thackeray was alone one evening when Jane called him to her. She spoke of her constant ill health, or her loneliness, of her unhappiness.... After Thackeray had shown her how entirely he comprehended and sympathized with her, he went on to confide his own unhappiness to her. He told her of the details of his early history, he spoke of the fate that condemned him to remain perpetually a grass widower, he told her how little success meant to one who, like himself, had to return every evening to 'the old solitary nothingness.' The upshot of this interview was a tacit agreement that they would henceforth, like brother and sister, rely on each other for solace and support.[52]

Thackeray wrote lyrically of this visit. 'Ah, how happy I was then! I will always love it, that gracious house.'[53] This charged yet ultimately impotent relationship continued through the following year as *Pendennis* made progress.

The girls spent the summer of 1849 with their grandparents in Wales, ending up at Laugharne near Carmarthen, the seaside village where Dylan Thomas later lived and wrote. They got there by boat, but it was a perilous landing, and they nearly capsized amongst the rocks. During their absence Thackeray learnt of Jane's pregnancy, and a feeling of bitter jealousy kept him awake all night, 'but I grew to be much more wholesome in 24 hours, and to wish for this event more fiercely than anybody does except you I believe'.[54] In Brighton he coincided with Brookfield, visiting in his role as an Inspector of Schools, and Thackeray hurried to reassure his mother. 'Dont be alarmed M^rs. Inspectress isn't here.'[55] Alarm is almost certainly what Mrs Carmichael-Smyth did feel about the friendship with Jane, judging by the frequency with which he felt he needed to offer such reassurances.

Then, when his family were in Wales, Thackeray fell dangerously ill. Work on the novel halted, and he was for several weeks confined to his bed in Young Street. He had been taken ill at a dinner on 17 September given by Lady Rodd – his ankle gave way under him and he fell – and after a day or two his condition quickly deteriorated. He had symptoms of cholera, which was epidemic just then, 'bilious fever accompanied with inflammation of the liver & lungs & other parts'[56] and on the insistence of John Forster, Dickens's friend and physician Dr John Elliotson was called in and supervised his treatment. Thackeray's Kensington Square neighbour, the surgeon John Jones Merriman, also undertook daily medical visits, and Jane was a frequent visitor at the lonely house. There were serious fears that he might not recover.

Not until a month of his illness had passed did Thackeray allow Jane to alert his mother, by which time though still weak he was recovering quite well. The Carmichael-Smyth party immediately hired a carriage and set out from Wales, his mother made the more anxious by the church services and tolling bells signalling 'a day of prayer and solemn humiliation, which had been appointed for the cholera'.[57] They found him gaunt, and about to leave for Brighton to recuperate. 'He didnt know how anxious & unhappy we were.'[58]

And then it was his mother's turn to be incapacitated, by rheumatism. Thackeray was moved by the pathos of his stepfather's constant attention, a model of selfless love in the absence of an effective remedy. 'I dont know how he sleeps for a week past, but he lies on the edge of her bed on w^h. she is restless and moaning, and wont go to another room.'[59] Thackeray had taken up *Pendennis* again, and from this point regarded the medical profession rather differently from the ironic stance seen at the outset of the book, where Pendennis's father, an apothecary whose 'secret ambition ... had always been to be a gentleman', is the object of knowing mockery. Thackeray's recovery at the hands of skilled modern practitioners led him to dedicate the final book publication of the novel to John Elliotson, of whom an idealised portrait later appears in *Philip*. When his mother saw the dedication she approved of its wording – 'I am so glad he said "me & mine".'[60] There is an autumnal colouring to the book's later chapters, responsible perhaps for Annie's later view of the work and its reception. 'To myself and to many of my own generation it has always seemed as if there was a special music in "Pendennis," and the best wisdom of a strong heart beating under its yellow waistcoat.'[61]

The birth of Jane's daughter prompted the shortest of notes from Brookfield. 'It's a wench & came at 12.30 P.M. this day. Both seem well.'[62] That evening Thackeray sat down to write a touching letter to the newborn infant, one to be kept for her later years.

My dear Miss Brookfield

I send you my very best love and compliments upon your appearance in this world, where I hope you will long remain, so as to make your Mamma & Papa happy. Sometimes they will talk to you perhaps, about a gentleman who was a great friend of theirs once. He was a writer of books w^h. were popular in their day, but by the time you are able to read this they will be quite forgotten. Therefore the author himself did not much care about them: and he does not in the least wish you to read them. But what he would like you to remember is that he was very fond of your dear mother, and that he and your Papa were very good friends to one another, helping each other as occasion served in life.[63]

In time Magdalene Brookfield became his daughters' close friend, and eventually Annie's sister-in-law.

Within a week of the birth, and drawing upon his own experience of fatherhood, he found himself reassuring Jane that her reserved husband's affections for the baby would quickly develop. 'He will be immensely tender over the child when nobody's by, I'm sure of that: no father knows for a few months what it is: but they learn afterwards.'[64] But when he called to see Jane and her baby, he was not admitted to the house, and he was angered and hurt. She hurriedly sent an explanation, and announced the name chosen by her husband – 'everybody objects to it... W^m. chose it & I liked it too – Magdalene – so you must please to be on our side & approve it'. But Thackeray's ruffled feathers needed a little more smoothing. '[Y]ou should not have said that W.^{m} "shut the door" upon you – as if it had been a personal thing to you – I felt vexed that you should not have been the exception to his wish for privacy but this was perhaps unreasonable and you hardly know yet, how W.^{m} dislikes to betray any real feeling, whether painful or otherwise.... I believe in a few days time he w^d. have taken it quite as a matter of course that you sh^d. be here – tho' not to be admitted upstairs.'[65]

Did Thackeray register any warning signs? – quite probably not. When more than a year later Brookfield prevented Jane from seeing him, her unquestioning compliance hurt Thackeray's pride more than the abrupt collapse of their relationship. 'I have been played with by a woman, and flung over at a beck from the lord & master.'[66]

From the beginning of the friendship he had wanted Annie and Minny to see 'Aunt JOB' as someone special. In June 1849, he tried to pass some of the responsibility for Annie's birthday treat over to

Jane. 'Will you come out (being as I must consider you if you please, the children's aunt) at 2 or 3 o'clock or so and take innocent pleasures with them such as the Colosseum.... I dine out myself at 8 o'clock and should like them to share innocent pleasures with their relation.'[67] That repetition carries weight. A year on, he asked her to take the children for a month. 'I want them to love you, and wisey wussa. For what else do I care – let it be known from China to Peru, but them and my dear lady?'[68] Jane encouraged regular visits – 'there is Baby to comfort me while you are away, & I hope tomorrow Anny & Minny may come here to see me?'[69] Perhaps Annie assumed too great a familiarity at times with the woman whose affections her father craved, for he had to caution her about the niceties of letter-writing, and that scribbling caricatures in a letter to a lady like Mrs Brookfield was not quite the thing. 'I dont mean be affected and use fine words, but be careful grateful and ladylike.'[70] It was a salutary lesson.

The Thackerays came to know the Brookfields' friend Mrs Fanshawe, who in May 1850 invited Annie and Minny for a few weeks to Southampton where her husband was a curate – William Brookfield's former parish before his marriage. This was their first unaccompanied trip, Mrs Carmichael-Smyth having returned to Paris in May following the arrival of the excellent new governess, Miss Trulock. They became particularly friendly with the Fanshawes' daughter, Rosa, with whom they acted charades, a regular favourite pastime, involving on other occasions the children of the polymath Henry Cole, their Kensington neighbour and the future founder of the South Kensington Museum. Minny loved dressing up and play-acting, and as an adult going to 'the play' was her favourite indulgence whether in London, Paris, Boston or New York. Her earliest surviving letter describes a theatre visit – 'We have been to the play the last one was called the wood demon he was all drest in red and looked so pretty but Annie does not think so'[71] – and Annie more than once remarked on the instinctive, delicate quality of Minny's own performances, and her curious feeling of having been an actor in a former life. 'She acted better than any of us. She never seemed to do loud things or stamp or shout but she would say a little word or move a hand & somehow it meant more than all the rest of us together.'[72]

Both girls celebrated their birthdays that year in Southampton with the Fanshawes. Their grandmother used the anniversary to caution Annie about complacency, and, more weightily, the need to sustain a religious perspective. And her son's well-being was never far from her mind, for she knew just how valuable the nourishing presence of his daughters was to him.

> So my dearest Nanny is to 'arrive at the goal of her hopes' tomorrow! & <u>when</u> you have arrived my child, que faut il faire? a grave question at every stage of life's journey.... dear Nanny He is in the crowded city as well as in the great sea & the open plain & so, let us feel that redeeming love is the believers portion which nothing can wrest from us while we desire to hold fast by it. – You seem to have had a charming holiday, & now I hope you will soon be returning to cheer the dear old Pater.[73]

It was probably later in the summer that Mrs Carmichael-Smyth, now all too aware of her son's near-fatal illness the previous year, urged them to leave London and the Thames, fearing the water which they cooked with and of their breathing in 'that vile miasma'.[74] They should head for refreshing sea air, to 'Dr Brighton' as the Thackerays always called it. They did not take that trip; instead Thackeray spent some time alone on the continent in mid-September gathering topographical detail for his next Christmas book, *The Kickelburys on the Rhine*. He promised to take his daughters on a continental tour after returning from America – his first mention of thoughts of crossing the Atlantic – although the next year he would take them abroad in advance of this American trip.

The completion of *Pendennis* at the end of November was announced in an intimate disclosure to Jane. 'I was writing the last paragraphs of Pendennis in bed and the sun walked into the room, and supplied the last paragraph w^h. ends with an allusion about you, and w^h. I think means a benediction upon W^m. and your child and my dear lady.'[75] His mother had asked Annie and Minny to post her the latest numbers of the novel to Paris, as she had fallen behind in her reading since returning in May. In acknowledging their arrival she drew attention to Thackeray's illustrated initial letters for two chapters. 'I have had all the "Pens" in the papers but they make me very melancholy, the empty study chair, the swing with Mrs Brookfield & her frightened child: & <u>Papa's hand</u> so wonderfully like.'[76] In this latter illustration (for 'A Chapter of Match-Making') a man's steadying hand reaches out to a swing on which mother and child sit, the rest of his body discreetly out of picture. She was right to feel the melancholy behind this little drawing, emblematic of an entire relationship, but was unaware of its more suggestive iconographic allusion, linked most familiarly with the eighteenth-century French pastoral scenes of Fragonard, in which a girl on a swing can suggest a situation of sexual intimacy.

Thackeray's initial letter to chapter thirty-six of Pendennis

At the turn of 1851 Thackeray was making plans for the intended American lecture series on his favourite eighteenth-century English humourists, which he would first tour extensively in England and Scotland. It was conceived primarily as a money-making venture. He made early arrangements to leave Annie and Minny with his mother, although he would not set out until the end of the following year. They were all in Paris during January, his daughters staying with their grandparents whilst he put up separately in lodgings, intent on reading to gather material for the lectures. In the event, he also found plenty of diversions, including a chance to return to his former gambling haunts, playing into the early hours. Once again, he was touched by the simple humility of his mother and stepfather, whose poverty required them to settle for what he considered a numbing Anglo-Parisian existence, 'a dismal end to a career. A famous beauty and a soldier who has been in 20 battles and led a half dozen of storming parties to end in a garret – and its not the poverty I mean but the undignified dignity, the twopenny toadies, the twaddling mean society.'[77]

For her part, prompted by a reading of the verses which Thackeray wrote for the opening of the Great Exhibition in London on 1 May, Mrs Carmichael-Smyth was more expansive about her son's achievements than was usual. 'The post is this moment come & brought me Papas work – dearest Children there is no talking about such things as these – there is only to bow down before a Heavenly Father who has created the noble mind who has filled it with such good things & better better, oh how much better has given the heart that feels them – When people say "are you not proud of y^r son?" how I hate to hear that – proud – who dares to be proud? no no – it makes me more humble because more thankful.'[78]

The series of six lectures later published as *The English Humourists of the Eighteenth Century* were delivered first in London, in Willis's Rooms, St James's on successive Thursday afternoons starting on 22 May. His mother had been determined to attend this first one, but a business venture of Major Carmichael-Smyth's delayed her departure for London, much to her distress. 'I seem as if I had never known disappointment till now... & now I can only send my prayers where they always go & my blessings where they always fall upon my own old one that he speak good words from true thoughts.'[79] After a tentative start, Thackeray's delivery grew in confidence and he drew large audiences to what became successful society occasions. 'Duchesses and great ladies came in spite of the dog days... with bishops bigwigs and parliament men. Macaulay came to 5 lectures of the 6.'[80] The press coverage was generally very favourable.

After the London series, he took his daughters away for six weeks, and Annie would have us believe that they crossed Europe trailing scattered clothes and mislaid possessions in various major cities, returning with not much more than a chessboard. 'But it was all so lovely & so wonderful the things we didnt lose were the pictures & the places. I can see them now after all these long years & years when I look for them.'[81] It seems that her former outbursts of bad behaviour subsided once she had settled properly in Young Street, and now it was Minny's turn to cause concern. Her difficulties expressed themselves in jealousy of her sister. In the middle of the Rhine as they headed towards Wiesbaden Thackeray reported that 'Minny keeps all her claws for poor Nan. It's all smiles & good humour for me. The little hypocrite! the little vixen! the little woman! She has little Beckyfied ways and arts.'[82]

At Baden he was touched to witness Annie taking Minny on to her knee and telling her a story. Annie chose only to remember her sister as charming, like one of the many Madonna images they had seen, 'with her sweet eyes & peaceful wondering face – only she was funnier & cleverer than any of them, & made little jokes'.[83] Their grandmother's own memories of travel were stirred by the scenes they described to her later. It was from her as much as from their father that the girls developed the desire for new experiences which came from foreign travel, for she knew that what they had seen in Germany, Austria and Italy would stay with them. 'I long to hear such a deal about it – now that all the disagreements are passed you will think only of the charms – w^h. of all y^r resting places did you like best? Venice to me was anything but "gay".... If I can find my journal we will compare notes one of these days.'[84]

Thackeray's relationship with the Brookfields reached its crisis in September, following his return to England. In his absence, Brookfield had quarrelled with Jane and his health was close to collapse. A further confrontation led him to insist that Jane sever her friendship with Thackeray, finally and irrevocably. Thackeray reacted with fury, condemning Jane both for her flirtatiousness and for her capitulation. He and Brookfield met, and then each went his own way nursing grievances. By the end of the month, Thackeray's confused feelings expose a tangle of sympathies, with all concerned both right and wrong.

> O me – the only thing is Duty Duty Duty. Her husband is a good fellow and does love her: and I think of his constant fondness for me & kindness and how cruelly I've stabbed him and outraged him with my words – Well, I'd do it again

– though I wish that it could have been any other dagger than mine to strike the blow – The sword must have fallen someday or the other. I am glad that she did her duty and threw me over for him – and though in my moments of pique & rage I dont forgive her, I do at better times & say God bless her. But we must bear our fates. We shant and cant and musnt meet again as heretofore.[85]

It was impossible to conceal the depth of his hurt from the children, although they cannot have known the true cause of his unhappiness. A month later Lord and Lady Ashburton contrived a meeting between the parties, after which he could tell Annie that 'I'm very glad I came down to shake hands with poor Brookfield and poorer Mr^s. B. She looks & is worse than he I think',[86] and to his mother, who understood more, he reported that his new novel, *The History of Henry Esmond*, 'is getting on pretty well & gaily I mean – What I wrote a month ago is frightfully glum. And I shall write it better now that the fierceness of a certain pain is over.'[87] Nor did not spare her his moments of self-loathing. 'Very likely it's a woman I want more than any particular one: and some day may be investing a trull in the street with that priceless jewel my heart.'[88] The pain lasted for many more weeks, but he partly worked through it in *Esmond* whilst America would provide new outlets for his emotional fantasies. He longed to find sufficient contentment in the cheerful companionship of his daughters: 'what a brute a man is that he is always hankering after something unattainable!'

Regarded by Anthony Trollope as the finest English novel, *Esmond* was unusual in being the only one of Thackeray's written in three-volume form, and not published as a serial. It brought him into a close working friendship with the young entrepreneurial publisher George Murray Smith, who had known Thackeray since taking on *The Kickleburys on the Rhine*, his Christmas story for 1850. Their professional relations were not yet permanent, since Thackeray returned to Bradbury and Evans both for *The Newcomes* and *The Virginians*. As he toured the country with his lectures, he worked at *Esmond* in his hotel rooms, thankful that 'the printer's devil' was not standing at his shoulder. Annie confirms that the novel's composition was a less public process than before, no longer at the centre of the workings of the household. '"Esmond" did not seem to be a part of our lives, as "Pendennis" had been ... I cannot remember either the writing or the dictating, nor even hearing "Esmond" spoken of except very rarely.'[89]

Thackeray resolved to delay going to America whilst good money was still to be had by delivering his lectures at home, but knowing that he would soon be absent from his children for several months, he now began to take them with him on his social visiting. This included going to the Ashburtons in December, where Annie and Minny sampled the fashionable company into which their father was increasingly welcomed. Mrs Carmichael-Smyth remained healthily cynical about the values of good society, fiercely championing her son's independent achievements and fearful that he was allowing himself to be patronised in a desire to please. When the visit to the Ashburtons was still being contemplated, she made her views clear to her grandchildren. 'I think he was very right about y^r not going to Lady Ash-s while English Lords & Ladies have the vulgar idea that they do people a favor by <u>admitting</u> them to their society I would let them keep their favors – I shant forget old Miss Berry's speech about Papa "He has worked himself into our society & now we make quite a pet of him" – As an old and respectable Lady I admit her kindness but for "<u>our</u> society" – bah.'[90]

Defensively, Thackeray told his mother that those who accused the 'grandees' of snobbery were misjudging them. 'My dearest Nan is very popular and Minny too of course: & as they must have some friends, when they go into the world why not good ones? How much kindness haven't I had from people eager to serve me? It's we who make the haughtiness of the grandees – not they.'[91]

Mrs Carmichael-Smyth usually had to rely on her grandchildren for news of her son's health and well-being. 'I wish he w^d. send them, scraps though they be, its a comfort to have even his grumblings – but to hear he is "jolly," is a jolly making thing for me w^h. does not often happen'; 'its so wearying to the spirit not to get a line for so many weeks – send me any scraps of notes when he is away that have not home secrets.' There is a single revealing remark on *Esmond*. 'I hope the Novel is not so sad as you say.'[92] Thackeray had himself told her of Charlotte Brontë's reaction upon reading the first volume in manuscript, that she thought it 'admirable and odious – well I think it is very well done and melancholy too – but the melancholy part ends pretty well with Vol 1'.[93] Brontë's friendship with her publisher, George Smith, and through him her meeting with Thackeray are well known.

Miss Trulock was by some margin the most successful of the Thackeray governesses. She remained at Young Street until he went to America, and in these last months a part-time music teacher was also employed. Thackeray had known Mary Holmes from his parents' Devonshire days and now, as a Catholic convert in London, she sought his advice about prospective work as a governess. In turn, he found himself opening up to her about recent times, and reflecting upon the 'disappointed yearning' of his mother 'that she can't be all in all to me, mother sister wife everything but it mayn't be – There's hardly a subject on w^h. we don't differ.... When I was a boy at Larkbeare, I thought her an Angel & worshipped her. I see but a woman now, O so tender so loving so cruel.'⁹⁴

Unsettled by the political situation in France, Thackeray tried without success to persuade the Carmichael-Smyths to transfer to London whilst he was away. 'France must end in battle...And I wish to Heaven you were here, and out of it.'⁹⁵ His stepfather had solid republican instincts – 'he is very weary & disheartened about his dear republic. Everybody asks what is to come next?'⁹⁶ – his mother remaining intrigued by the frailties and vanities of human behaviour. 'It's the nature of true genius to be humble, but I heard something the other day to the contrary w^h. so vexed me – a lady told me that she heard Hans Andersen read some of his own tales to the king of Denmark, & was beyond measure disgusted at the vanity he displayed – so petty, so seeking for or rather greedy of applause.'⁹⁷ She became friendly with Robert and Elizabeth Barrett Browning who were in Paris at this time, the young Pen Browning bringing her own son's childhood back to her. 'Mrs Browning has such a dear little boy at 3 years old, he does as Papa used & draws figures & houses & has learned his letters without any teaching.'⁹⁸

The evidence of Thackeray's letters would be sufficient to suggest that his mother's was a forceful though not unsympathetic personality. Indeed her own correspondence allows a more complex and subtle figure to emerge, an original thinker with ideas unusual for her time and social position. One cannot imagine, for example, that many of those from the 'twaddling mean society' of the Anglo-Parisian community dismissed so quickly by Thackeray would articulate the kind of ideas that she shared so readily with the elder of her granddaughters, aged just fourteen.

> One thing is clear that women must attend to their families, w^h. of course takes much of their time, but how much is spent unprofitably – there is a noble study for the embellishment of the new worlds that are rising, & that is architecture. What is to prevent women from studying it & making it a profession? – a clever active loving hearted woman will always find useful employment however, but must toil for it, in youth & in age – One thing I am quite sure of, that active employment is one of the most effective parts of happiness, & a time will come when people wont waste their hours in hot crowded rooms, where nobody cares for anybody & only

remarks their presence by the fashion of their dress, or the manner of their exit or entrée.[99]

In some ways Minny would embrace this independent spirit even more readily than Annie, showing a distinct interest in interior design and domestic architecture. In 1868 she became excited by the boldness and innovation of the new houses that she saw being built in New York, and wished that she too could become a house builder. That this was not mere whimsy is suggested by something said after her early death in 1875. A Dublin newspaper, passing on the current London gossip to its own readers, assigned to Minny a talent inherited from her father, 'his great genius for design and caricature.... The double talent of the father was thus transmitted in equal portions to the daughters. While to the eldest was bequeathed the literary gift, the younger inherited his bright and sparkling artistic fancy.'[100]

In the months before he left for America, Thackeray grew closer to Minny, realising that she had had to vie for his attention and affection. 'I try to take down Minny's pertness and desire to shine, by telling her that the best of all qualities in the world is not wit but good-nature. God bless her. She is a charming little dear.'[101] Annie sketches Minny's emerging personality during the Young Street years, an intuitive child alert to atmosphere and to the needs of others. She loved animals, maintaining 'a menagerie of snails and flies in the sunny window-sill',[102] and was skilled in nursing those around her. 'Her little hands always seemed to send pain away – once when her little kitten was ill she stroked it quite well.'[103] She opted for Dickens's fictional characters rather than her father's as a source for names for her stray cats; 'she had Nicholas Nickleby, a huge gray tabby, and Martin Chuzzlewit, and a poor little half-starved Barnaby Rudge'.[104] Her palpable energy came out in her natural talent for acting, but also in movement too. 'She used to dance about on the little green lawn & her long thick curls used to shine so, that I used to look out of window at them[;] sometimes she would turn round & round as quick as she could go & then her hair would seem like a burning bush.'[105]

The manuscript of *Esmond* was finished at the end of May. The Thackerays set out for the continent, met the Carmichael-Smyths and travelled with them to holiday in Germany. It was Thackeray's intention to revisit several of the places they had enjoyed the previous summer, after which he planned to leave his daughters in Paris and prepare for America. But after not much more than a week he returned alone, taking a good seven weeks to reach London, via Nuremberg, Munich, Salzburg, Vienna, Berlin, Hanover and Brussels. The impulsive decision avoided the rituals of formal leave-taking which he hated, although Annie explains it differently. 'He had to correct the proofs of *Esmond* before he left, and to give some more lectures in the provinces, and to wind up things at home.'[106] All that may have been true, but it does not adequately explain why he then took so long to get back.

To Kate Perry and her sister he probably gets close to the truth – 'being with 'em was like traversing the cart and fitting the halter, an endless leave taking: so suddenly I jumped off at Frankfurt and left them to their good old Granny: who will never own that she was delighted to have them without their Papa, and will now command her little kingdom entirely in her own way.'[107] His conclusion is not at all fair to his mother, who according to Annie was 'very miserable and nervous' at the prospect of his departure to America. In fact she utterly opposed his going, believing that his children needed him and that he would be directionless without them. She urged him to return to fetch his daughters as soon as he could, much as it would sadden her to be separated from them. Above all, she was unconvinced of his need to make money in America, and composed an impassioned but measured letter for his forty-first birthday, by which time they had reached Paris although he was still journeying back to England.

> Forty & one years my dearest dearest & the thankful old Mother still writes her blessing & presently we shall be asking it in the house of GOD, not more His perhaps than this w^h. holds so much love.... I feel all y^r low spirits at every letter that comes f^m you. Why in the name of goodness sh^d you continue this separation f^m. the children – Why go to America? surely you are not so used up for England that you cant go on with y^r work among y^r own people – I hate the thought of y^r going – & <u>dont for a moment fancy</u> that the pleasure of having the young ones with me can compensate for the idea that you are unhappy in the separation f^m. them & running risks to add a few hundreds to y^r fortune – finish y^r tour <u>well</u>, finish y^r home lectures & instead of going to America come & fetch the children in Sept.^{ber} – why not? My great grief at being separated f^m them was as pure a maternal feeling as exists, because I know no one could supply my place to them, not my own gratification in their pleasant prattle – the necessity on their part no longer exists, materially – therefore do not let the idea of any disappointment to me, influence you....

> We could have thoroughly enjoyed all the glorious things you put before us in our trip but there was always the idea that we were putting our hands into the money bag, & that you had separated because 'the party was too large' – Last year you could not work with the maids, this year you cant work without them, what is to be done – please GOD you keep well through the heat.[108]

He would not be persuaded. By September he had resumed the lecture circuit, ending in Liverpool from where he would sail. To Annie he wrote encouraging instructions as to what she should do in his absence. 'Learn dancing or whatever it may be with all your heart and soul: and play me some good music when I see you again.' Nor had he forgotten the significance of the month for them all. '14 Sepr. is 12 years since your mothers illness was declared.'[109]

The time for his departure was drawing close. The series of lectures in Liverpool was not well attended – 'not above 200 and the Philharmonic Hall at Liverpool the most beautiful room I've seen is made for 2500.... It is like a dinner for 20, and 3 people to eat it.'[110] Waiting to begin the long journey with Eyre Crowe, who accompanied him as his companion and secretary, Thackeray fired off last letters to family and friends, sending to some of them copies of the just-published *Esmond*. He had been moved when, back in April, he had received from Edward FitzGerald a quite unexpected promise of a legacy of £1,000 that would eventually come to Annie and Minny. FitzGerald had asked for no fuss about this, nor did he want others to know of the future gift. It had been prompted by his going through Thackeray's letters since 1831, and burning most of them, mainly because 'I thought that if I were to die before setting my house in order those letters might fall into unwise hands, and perhaps (now that you are become famous) get published according to the vile fashion of the day.' He was anxious to express the loyalty of his affection more tangibly. 'I shall hope however to keep my eye upon your girls in case you should die before me which is not very likely. Annie is verily a chip of the old Block.'[111] Thackeray now asked FitzGerald to look after his daughters' interests should this turn out to be a final parting.

> My dearest old friend
> I mustn't go away without shaking your hand and saying Farewell and God bless you – If anything happens to me you by these presents must get ready the Book of Ballads w^h. you like and w^h. I had not time to prepare before embarking on this voyage. And I should like my daughters to remember

that you are the best and oldest friend their Father ever had; and that you would act as such: as my literary executor and so forth – My books would yield something as copyright – and should anything occur I have commissioned friends in good place to get a pension for my little wife – I should have insured my life but for my complaint (a stricture) w^h. I am told increases the payment so much that it is not worth the premium. Does not this read gloomily? – Well, who knows what Fate is in store; and I feel not at all downcast but very grave and solemn just on the brink of a great voyage –

I shall send you a copy of Esmond tomorrow or so w^h. you shall yawn over when you are inclined.[112]

His mind was easy. His last message before departure went to Annie and Minny in Paris. 'I dont think I have the heart to write a long letter – it would be like a long parting and that you know I cant abear – Its beautiful calm weather I'm to have a cabin to myself in consequence of my illustrious character and so poor Eyre will go puke in private.' The following morning he added a hurried postscript, a final departing wave to his distant family. 'The little steamer just coming to take us to the big one. God Almighty bless & keep my dearest children & mother.'[113]

Four

A LITTLE RAIN OF DOLLARS
(1852-1855)

God bless my darlings and teach us the Truth. Every one of us in every fact, book, circumstance of life sees a different meaning & moral and so it must be about religion. But we can all love each other and say Our Father.

Thackeray to Annie
October 1852

It comes as no surprise to discover that the kind and gentle Henry Carmichael-Smyth was the model for Colonel Newcome. When in June 1852 Thackeray suddenly left Annie and Minny with their grandparents and returned alone to London, it had fallen to his stepfather to restore a measure of tranquillity. The old man diverted the girls and calmed his wife, already anxious at the prospect of her son's American trip. 'Our dear old grandfather did his best to cheer us all, and after we had parted from my father he made out all sorts of pleasant little plans, and ordered various special *compotes* and tartlets at the hotels suited to our youthful appetites.' The eccentric Newcome charm occasionally embarrassed his young charges, such as when he signed the hotel guest book as 'Schmid Major, en retraite, avec Madame sa épouse et ses deux Mademoiselles', the hotel staff then transferring these details to the dinner-table to identify their places. 'My grandmother, sad as she was, began to laugh, and we all entreated our dear old Major to make some changes in the inscription, but he stuck to it, and would not alter a single letter.'[1]

As they continued on their itinerary through Switzerland, Mrs Carmichael-Smyth found consolation at Geneva in the Calvinist community. She took Annie to a sparsely-attended service near their hotel, and they were introduced to the elderly man who had built the chapel. César Malan sought to discover from Annie her religious feelings and her aspirations for the future. She stumbled over her answers, then burst into tears. Afterwards, it was her grandfather who comforted her, assuring her that matters of doctrine and interpretation were for those whose life had been given to close reading of scripture, 'and we had therefore better leave all such speculations entirely to them'.[2] It sounds like the kind of reserved diplomacy in which he had learned to become well-practised.

Much has been made of Mrs Carmichael-Smyth's insistence that her granddaughters should be appropriately instructed in matters of faith, such that a confrontation between mother and son was almost certainly unavoidable. Annie and Minny spent the later summer at their grandparents' summer retreat in Mennecy, where during daily bible readings Mrs Carmichael-Smyth insisted on the literal truth of scripture. She would not shrink from her duty of instruction, but accepted Thackeray's right to place his daughters in the care of someone who would more closely follow his own wishes, much as that would grieve her. She composed a letter which Annie beseeched her not to send, and which indeed was held back for four months.

> And now to come to the painful difference that alas! & alas is come between us.... It seems to me that the difference between us is just this, you put them to sea without a compass & pointing to a star, tell them they are to keep it before them & that they will arrive at it.... Poor Nanny's is a stiff heart of unbelief, & it came upon me like a thunderbolt when I heard her declare that she 'did not care for the old Testament & considered the New only historical' – it was tremendous to hear such words, & my only consolation is that she can give no reason for her unbelief –
>
> I dont think you would place them with any one who would encourage infidelity, but I am perplexed as to whether I sh^d. retain my charge & submit to the pain or whether they should be placed in y^r. absence under any other care that you may select.[3]

The Mennecy house leased by the Carmichael-Smyths had been formerly a hunting-lodge owned by Henry IV, and in more recent years converted into a farm. Mrs Carmichael-Smyth introduced some modest comforts, including a piano which had been hired in Corbeil. This was the focus of summer evening gatherings, to which the local Mennecy worthies were invited, figures who would later people Annie's portrayals of French provincial life in *The Village on the Cliff* (1866-7). Along the terrace at the end of the garden grew pumpkins and vines which became heavy with fruit in the late summer.

Back in Paris for the winter months, Annie and Minny were sent to scripture classes under the guidance of the charismatic French pastor, Adolphe Monod. For Annie, at least, this was intended by her grandmother as a necessary preparation for confirmation. Thackeray tried to counterbalance his mother's influence by giving his children licence to think for themselves, confident that Annie's sharp intelligence and Minny's instinctive scepticism would be enough to withstand what he considered the excesses of what they would encounter. He advised diplomacy, but also encouraged private questioning. 'I should read all the books that Granny wishes, if I were you: and you must come to your own deductions about them as every honest man and woman must and does.' He instinctively rebelled against dogmatic assertion, making a barely veiled reference to his mother's fervent hope that his daughters would be won for her cause. 'What person possessing the secret of Divine Truth by w^h. she or he is assured of Heaven and w^h. idea she or he worships as if it was God, but must pass nights of tears and days of grief and lamentation if persons naturally dear cannot be got to see this necessary truth?' He believed in a historical Jesus, and in a Bible that was the record of ordinarily flawed men. 'To my mind Scripture only means a writing and Bible means a Book. It contains Divine Truths: and the history of a Divine Character: but imperfect [and] not containing a thousandth part of Him – and it would be an untruth before God were I to hide my feelings from my dearest children.'[4] By sending this manifesto to his daughters – which his mother would read – her influence was fatally weakened from the outset, as he must have foreseen.

Thackeray learned of the scripture classes from Minny, who wrote to him around the time that he disembarked at Boston on 12 November. 'We shall go tomorrow to M^r. Monods and he is to preach a sermon every week to us and other young ladies and we are to write down what he says. I daresay I will make a very nice hash of it though Grannie and every one says he preaches very good sermons.'[5] But Annie does not suggest that attendance was an unwelcome task for her. 'To-day we have been to M. Monod's Cours, and presented our "analyses" tied with red ribbon.... There are about twenty girls and twenty mothers all round the room.'[6] She told her Kensington friend Laetitia Cole about the classes which, together with her piano practice and other lessons kept her very busy. 'Grannie takes us to a Cour, that is a confirmation cour, but as Minnie is so young she only listens as for me I have 5 or 6 pages to write twice a week a great deal to read besides.'[7] In her next letter to America she discloses her concern about having to accept contradictions in scripture as matters of faith. 'I am afraid Grannie is still miserable about me, but it bothers me when the clergymen say that everybody ought to think alike and follow the one true way, forgetting that it is they who want people to think alike, that is, as they do.... I am sure when Christ talks about "My words" He means His own, not the Bible, as Grannie says.'[8]

But her later recollection of these classes would be decidedly ambivalent. She shared her father's liberal scepticism, and yet Monod's saintly character impressed her profoundly. She believed in him, but not in all that he had to say. Something bordering on mild sexual hysteria was present in the room during his sessions, attended by adoring young girls and their parents.

> To me [Auguste Monod] seemed the St. Paul of my own time; and those classes which cost so many tears, and which gave rise to so much agitated discussion, are still among the most touching and heart-reaching experiences of my life. I can see the girls' faces now, as they listened to their beloved *pasteur*. Our hearts were in our lessons, as his was in his teaching, undoubtedly; we were all in earnest and ready to follow; only, though I longed to be convinced, I could only admire and love the lesson and the teacher as well.[9]

She wanted to believe, but her loyalty to her father ran very deep. Monod is remembered more informally in her memoir of Minny, and Thackeray's influence over his daughters' thinking is made explicit.

> [Monod] thought a great many things wrong w^h our own Papa thought right & a great many things right that our Papa thought untrue: but he was a good man & did his duty & when he preached to us, it was not what he said but his whole heart & life that seemed to reach us. The girls used to sob & shake & I am sure we did only we wanted to tell him that we thought there was no harm in being happy & laughing & in being interested in plays & stories, & that our Papa said this world was as much God's world as that other world for which M^r. Monod wanted us to live alone.[10]

When he learnt that Annie and Minny were attending Monod's classes, Thackeray probably considered carefully before deciding to tell his mother of his distaste. Although wanting to be gentle, he was nevertheless firm.

> I must write you a line, and kiss my dearest old Mother, though we differ ever so much about the Old Testament.

> What a deal of heart-burning & unkindness what division between friends has that book cased! ... I wouldn't have the children whilst with you go to other than your church: but seeing you uncomfortable about Anny & poor Nan unhappy that you are so (a word from each is enough to show me what is going on) I can't help myself, but must speak my mind. I wouldn't have the girls Lovatites or belonging to that sect of Xtians because I dont think their doctrine is a true one.... I wrote Private on that letter to Anny w^h. hurt you – I meant you not to read it: not that I want to keep secrets from you but simply not to talk about a subject on w^h. I must speak and we can't agree.[11]

Mrs Carmichael-Smyth now sent the letter that she had held back for four months along with her reply to her son, justifying the consistent honesty of her own position. She takes him to task for telling Annie to read whatever books she gave her, only to contradict such open-mindedness by objecting to his daughters' attendance at the scripture sessions.

> With regard to Mr Monod's Scriptural lessons, you deal somewhat hardly – If there had been time to ask y^r consent previous to the commencement of the course I should have done so magré the carte blanche you gave to Annie in that letter to w^h. you allude, 'to read whatever books I put into her hands to hear what I had to say' & so forth – & now you come down upon me with a sledge hammer blow saying 'you knew I sh^d. not like it that my children sh^d be sitting under a French Calv: & of course I am unhappy'. But there was no time, & the teaching is so entirely apart from sectarian or dogmatical features, that I do not think any Christian of whatever denomination could object to it.... I have one thing to say by w^h. you may free y^{r}self from any apprehension of y^r. children thinking, or believing otherwise than as you do; they have but one Creed & that is 'Papa' – & so may you be directed for their & your immortal welfare, my task is done; but that you may see that I did not undertake it with any desire to thwart your authority, I send you the letter I wrote before you sailed, & only did not send it at Annies urgent request – So my dearest old Man may GOD give you the health & strength for the combat, there is no need I think for disquietude about worldly affairs.[12]

In this battle of wills between mother and son, grandmother and father, he had triumphed, but she emerges with undamaged integrity. His response was conciliatory, for he knew that he had hurt her, and he probably agreed that the girls should continue with Monod's classes despite his lingering disquiet. The quarrel subsided but rumbled on as – for his part at least – they agreed to differ.

After his return from America, and on Annie's sixteenth birthday, his mother raised the delicate topic of her confirmation, but she did not mince her words, wanting to know what was to be done about it. Preparing a young person properly was a duty not to be ignored, and in the grandmother's view so loving and yet so freethinking a girl as Annie was in danger of placing herself in peril.

> My dearest old Man I fancy you are thinking of what happened this day 16 years ago, & how a beautiful child was born which called you Father & how she is now a fine honest creature to be thankful for, & still more to pray for – such ardent feelings, such an overflowing heart of love, with such insouciance; notions of female independence which never can be realised, of self knowledge which is no knowledge at all, for she does not know herself poor child (who does?) & an idea of her own wisdom, w^h. is not uncommon either at 16... She is now come to the age when every Christian child ratifies the vows made for them & reviews the testimony which our Lord commanded 'in remembrance that He died for us' – what will you do about it?... You know I would have been but too thankful to have helped you on the way, but we dont travel by the same road, & the dilemma is a serious one – to neglect the ordinance is surely wrong, & what Minister of the Church of Christ would administer it to her, if she avowed the fatal opinion 'The Bible is not the Word of GOD, I dont believe in the Old Testament & the New I think is only historical'? – There is in this wise no revealed religion to this poor child.[13]

For Annie and Minny, the adults' religious war probably did not dominate their lives in the way that this impassioned correspondence might suggest. But it was a cause of great anguish for Mrs Carmichael-Smyth, who regarded it as her personal failing, whilst Annie drew on this exposure to French Protestantism ten years later as fruitful material for her first novel, *The Story of Elizabeth*.

Four: A Little Rain of Dollars

++++

When Thackeray left for America to make money, he gave no signs of being curious about encountering the new world. He quickly ruled out the idea of an American travel book, conscious of the adverse local reception of Dickens' *American Notes*, and knowing that to compose one on the basis of only a few months' travelling was unwise. 'It seems impudent to write a book; and mere sketches now are somehow below my rank in the world – I mean a grave old gentleman, father of young ladies, mustn't be comic and grinning too much.'[14]

At first, he resisted diversions from his main intention – 'the goose lays much too good eggs for that – and theres no time for writing or seeing'.[15] He was astonished at how easily the cash rolled in, principally from his lecturing but also from publishing deals. He had hopes of pulling in something in the region of £4,000, although by the end of the trip this was probably something closer to £2,500. On top of this, he managed to secure some publishing deals. His naïve delight at his financial prospects is endearing at first, but his persistent discussion of his earnings in letter after letter becomes tedious. He assumed that his correspondents shared his enthusiasm. 'I know that you will be glad to hear of my good luck present & prospective and that there is a chance at last for my little women.... It is a little rain of dollars pray Heaven to send plenty of the rain.'[16] By the end of the year he already seems to have been committed to a second visit with a new set of lectures, as a final solution to all money worries.

It was inevitable that for someone without preconceptions, he would be intrigued by what he saw. In New York, where he settled himself into the Clarendon Hotel, it was the 'rush of life' which appealed, the constant building and rebuilding and the sense of opportunities being seized. 'The houses are always being torn down and built up again.... Nobody is quiet here.' He could not help being impressed by the persuasive sense of democratic idealism. 'Everybody seems his neighbour's equal. They begin without a dollar and make fortunes in 5 years.' He was moved by the generosity and affection of his hosts and 'everywhere a love for the old country quite curious nay touching to remark'.[17] Above all, as he wrote to Minny from Philadelphia, he was struck by the vastness of scale and the youthfulness of the country, in comparison with tired old Europe. Fifteen years later she would travel over much of the ground he had covered, carrying his enthusiasm in her memory, although her own response to what she encountered was to be rather different.

> Empires more immense than any the old world has known are waiting their time here. In 10 years we shall cross to Europe in a week and for 5£; in 50 the population will treble that of Britain – Everybody prospers. There are scarce any poor. For hundreds of years more there is room and food and work for whoever comes. In travelling in Europe our confounded English pride only fortifies itself, and we feel that we are better than 'those foreigners' but it's worth while coming here that we may think small beer of ourselves afterwards. Greater nations than ours ever have been, are born in America and Australia – and Truth will be spoken and Freedom will be practised, and God will be worshipped among them, as they never have been with the antiquarian trammels that bind us in the Old World. I look at this, and speculate on this bright Future, as an Astronomer of a Star; and admire and worship the beautiful goodness of God.[18]

The one issue about which Thackeray was ambivalent was that of black emancipation. There is evident racial anxiety in his endeavour to square the circle, apparently justifying slavery whilst refusing to accept that human creatures can be bought and sold. He doubted whether he would have time to go to so far south as New Orleans, 'though I want to see slaves & slave-countries with my own eyes. I dont believe Blacky is my man & my brother, though God forbid I should own him or flog him, or part him from his wife & children.'[19] He alludes here to the popular Wedgwood company design of a chained African slave with the caption 'Am I Not a Man and a Brother?', a familiar image for the abolitionists. But Mrs Carmichael-Smyth, by contrast, took a radical abolitionist position, influenced by her reading of Harriet Beecher Stowe and her own solidly evangelical beliefs.

From the nation's capital, Washington, Thackeray clarifies his position a few weeks later. He cannot support slavery, but nor does he believe in racial equality. In terms which at the time were not untypical even for people, like him, of a liberal Christian stance – the Thackerays would happily name their pet dogs after the black servants in *The Virginians* – he offers physiognomic differences as evidence of racial inferiority.

> They are not my men & brethren, these strange people with retreating foreheads, with great obtruding lips & jaws: with capacities for thought, pleasure, endurance quite different to mine. They are not suffering as you are impassioning yourself for their wrongs as you read M^{rs}. Stowe they are grinning &

Four: A Little Rain of Dollars

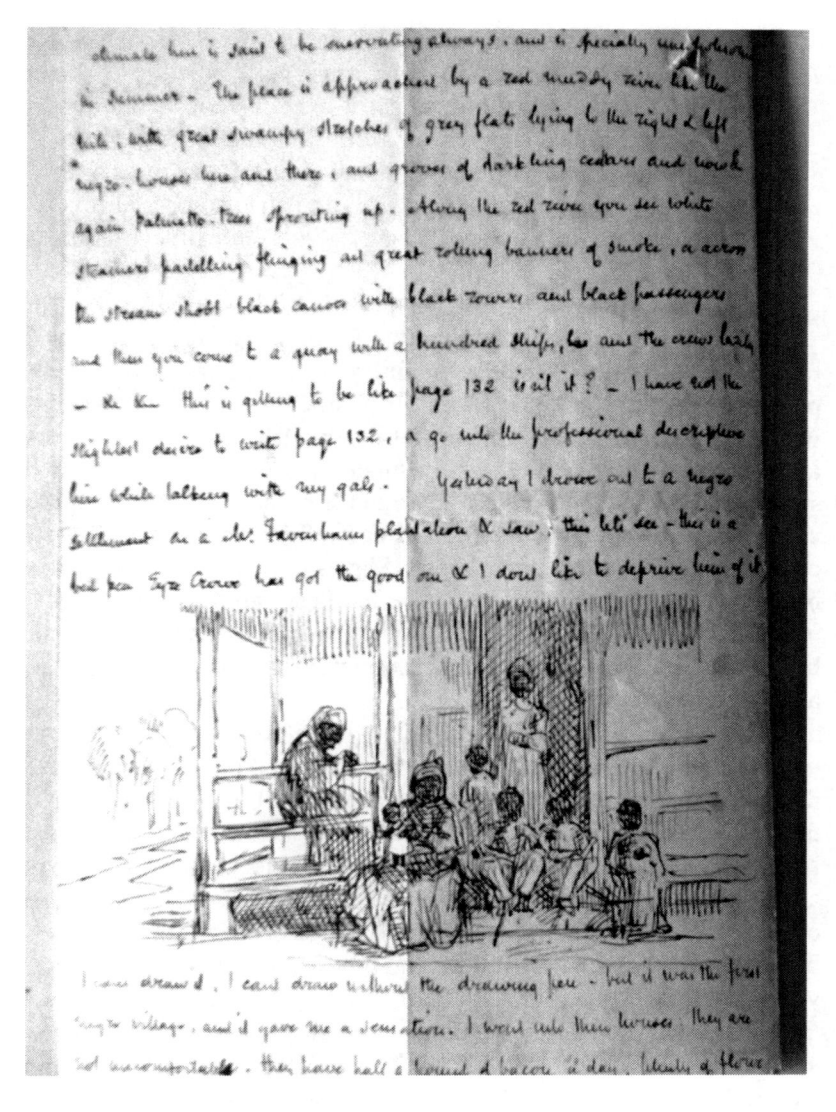

Thackeray's letter to Annie and Minny, with sketch of slaves, written from Savannah 1853

joking in the sun; roaring with laughter as they stand about the streets in squads; very civil, kind & gentle, even winning in their manner when you accost them at gentlemen's houses, where they do all the service. But they don't seem to me to be the same as white men, any more than asses are the same animals as horses; I don't mean this disrespectfully, but simply that there is such a difference of colour, habits, conformation of brains, that we must acknowledge it, & can't by any rhetorical phrase get it over; Sambo is not my man & my brother; the very aspect of his face is grotesque & inferior. I can't help seeing & owning this; at the same time of course denying any white man's right to hold this fellow-creature in bondage & make goods & chattels of him & his issue.[20]

He clinches his case for leaving things alone by suggesting that the problem would resolve itself in the future with the introduction of low-paid, hard-working immigrant labour from China, whereupon slavery would be seen to be inefficient and costly. Travelling further south, to Richmond, Charleston and Savannah, he encountered more of the slave population. The children charmed him, and also their apparent contentment. 'They have the best of food, of doctors when they are ill, of comfortable provision in old age. Slaves they are and that's wrong: but admitting that sad fact, they are the best cared for poor that the world knows of.'[21] He leaves the topic to which he saw no resolution by concluding that immediate emancipation would 'be ruin to them and their masters too'.[22]

He was on more familiar though not necessarily safer ground when searching out female consolation in New York. America's great distance from home allowed him to place on his hastily rebuilt altar the new object of his fantasy, this time the daughter of George Baxter, a New York businessman. Sally Baxter was nineteen. Her father owned a warehouse in Wall Street, and the family lived in the Brown House on Second Avenue, between 20th and 21st Streets. Thackeray quickly became friendly with Mrs Baxter and the two daughters, Sally and her younger sister, Lucy. For him, Sally was an embodiment of Beatrix Esmond. It was an innocent passion, a passing infatuation, but there is something disconcerting in his adopted caricature of elderly admirer succumbing to a young girl's coquettish charms. Perhaps Sally Baxter was merely flattered that the famous foreign novelist should enjoy her company. Or maybe she chose to play the part assigned to her, knowing him to be a temporary fixture. As he prepared to leave New York for Boston, Thackeray is remarkably frank with his mother. 'I have been actually in love for 3 days with a pretty wild girl of 19 (and was never more delighted in my life than by discovering that I could have this malady over again) and am sure that my own peace of mind is immensely increased by leaving Europe. When I began to write Esmond how miserable I was! I can contemplate that grief now and put it into a book: and the end of my flirtation with Miss Sally Baxter here is that I have got a new character for a novel – though to be sure she is astoundingly like Beatrix.'[23]

Mrs Carmichael-Smyth probably kept her silence about Sally, but Minny was not inclined to be charitable. 'I hope your young ladies in the brocades are quite well, & particularly Miss Sally what an ugly name she has got fancy a Novel with Sally for the title.'[24] Thackeray wrote to Mrs Baxter a few days after his departure from New York, apologising for having taken the liberty of kissing her daughters when taking his leave of them. 'I ask your pardon but I didn't mean any harm and I hope M^r. Baxter shall kiss my daughters though they are not so pretty as his – But they are as good as any man's.'[25] He even mentioned Sally to Jane Brookfield, claiming, not quite truthfully, that a momentary infatuation with 'Beatrix' was already behind him. 'I have basked in her bright eyes, but Ah, me! I don't care for her, and shall hear of her marrying a New York buck with a feeling of perfect pleasure.'[26] Just a week before, he had written to ask George Smith to prepare 'a quantity of very pretty note-paper envelopes &c., blue edged, & the deuce knows what', with Sally's initials as a monogram – 'They are for a very pretty young lady, who is not the only one of that sort at New-York.'[27]

Gordon Ray may be right in believing that Thackeray 'cultivated this last love in the hope that it might sever permanently the cords that bound him to Mrs. Brookfield'.[28] The pain had diminished, but it would never entirely recede. 'I would not have not had her love for any thing in the world. It's apart from desire, or jealousy of any one else, that I think of her and shall always. There is nothing I know or have ever read or thought of so lovely as her nature is; the dark spirit is on her poor husband still I fear.'[29]

His daughters wrote regularly from Paris and in their turn awaited his letters eagerly. And the fierce pride that he had in Annie and Minny was reinforced each time he had news from them. He told Lucy that Annie had written about a wedding party where there had been dancing, 'and my dearest homely fat Nanny is quite contented with her little share of partners, and the admiration her little sister gets. Well, Anny has one faithful swain and admirer, who loves her quite as much as a girl need desire: and that gentleman is now writing to Miss Lucy Baxter.'[30] He had a tendency to write like this about his daughters, and particularly about Annie, in unguarded terms which might seem less than supportive. Flattery, however, was not his way, and there was nothing false in his affection for any of his family. He saw the pure gold in Annie earlier than anybody else, a capacity for loving that enriched the lives of those whom she touched. He saw also a future for her as a writer. 'When my weary old quill is worn to the stump, please God she'll be able to use that honest pen of her's.'[31] To Mrs Procter he predicted that 'she shall be the writer in the family soon, and I shall subside into a professorship of Deportment'.[32]

There are two moments of passing sadness at this time, reminders of what might have been. He thinks it best that the girls should not write to Isabella in his absence, as letters would probably upset her. His hopes fade that she might one day return to them, and might be to them almost as a sister. 'Her intelligence has slept during the times theirs was developing. I doubt whether she ought to come back; and whether, Fate having put that awful 12 years barrier and death between us, it would be happy for her to be reinstated into our world.'[33] Twelve years. It was longer still since Jane had gone from him, but nor had she been forgotten. 'I wonder whether those sweet little cherubs develop in an after world and grow, and note us who love them?'[34]

He made his decision to leave for home suddenly, in characteristic fashion 'one-half an hour before my berths were taken this morning',[35] and on board the *Europa* wrote George Baxter a farewell note – 'partings are the dreariest events of life and were always best done quickly'.[36] After arrival in England he went first to Young Street for about ten days before crossing to France and to the welcome of his family. One of his first letters from London was to Mrs Baxter, and he mused on the strangeness of chance which throws fellow ship passengers together for a few days where they form an intimacy, only to shake hands at parting with no likelihood of meeting again. But America, and New York in particular, had made its lasting effect on him. 'I've not forgotten <u>you</u> yet – No, please God, – I look at the Sunset very very kindly, and do you know I haven't had the heart to move my watch from New York time?'[37]

Thackeray's mother and daughters patiently waited in Paris for his reappearance, but then were almost too excited to open the door to him. Sitting together in the early evening on the red sofa in their grandparents' little study, Annie and Minny heard the door bell. 'My heart beat so I couldn't move & then the bell rang again, and then we <u>rushed</u> to open it.'[38] Mrs Baxter knew what the effect of his arrival would have on his family, and longed to hear that they were reunited. 'Make a place for us, in the hearts of those you love – for I feel we shall know them face to face some day.'[39] Thackeray was delighted to find his daughters grown, well and content, but the tedium of his mother's circle made him melancholy. 'Anny is grown a complete woman – not pretty a bit – but with a healthy fair complexion....

Minny is no beauty neither but quite pretty enough for me: and I would not change them for girls 10 times as handsome.... I have not been into the world at all: and have been here a week and it seems an age. From a twaddling society what can you expect but twaddling? It's hard that there should be something narrowing about narrow circumstances.'[40]

It was time to remove the girls from that stupefying atmosphere, but the perennial problem of finding the right governess had to be faced and he returned to London to start the hunt. It was particularly hard for his mother, whose long months of devotion were soon to be over. Yet she had consistently argued that his must be the principal responsibility for his daughters, and, even if sometimes he chose to believe differently, she had no wish to supplant him. A fortnight after his arrival in Paris, she wrote a mother's letter of thanks for the Baxters' friendship, predicting her son's eventual return to America with Annie and Minny.

> I shall know that they have a maternal friend among the many who will welcome them – & you & y^r charming daughters will love these children as you love their Father – We are at this moment awaiting the appearance of a governess to be their companion & instructress if it is decided that they return to Kensington – I would fain keep them under my wing, if it were possible, but they make their Father's home w^h. is of the first importance, & I yield my place to the stranger.[41]

On Annie's sixteenth birthday, when he was being urged to present her for confirmation, Thackeray acknowledged the indispensability of his children – 'as it is an ascertained fact that I can't live without female friends I shall have a pair at home, in my own women, who'll understand my ways, laugh at my jokes, console me when I'm dismal &c, as is the wont and duty of women in life'.[42] It was certainly the role he constructed for his women.

He was in Paris again at the end of the month, in the meantime having engaged a new manservant, Charles Pearman, formerly a footman in a London club. He wanted to take Annie and Minny to Switzerland where he might start his new novel, and then to spend the winter in Rome. But the frailty of his stepfather made him think that Italy might have to wait, and that he should spend the time in Paris doing his duty 'filially as well as paternally'.[43] The warmth of his affection would soon emerge in his characterisation of Colonel Newcome, as Mrs Baxter was quick to spot. Despite never having met Carmichael-Smyth, she had clearly heard much about him, for once she had read the second number of *The Newcomes* she observed that 'The Indian Colonel must be drawn from the kind old Stepfather – I think.'[44]

The Thackerays left Paris on 6 July, travelling to Nancy, Mannheim and Baden Baden where they stopped for about ten days. During the time that he was working on his novel, he knew that he was not good company. 'When we are moving it is well enough: but when I am absorbed in my work, and thinking of it out of work-hours I am a bad companion.' He admitted to a technical limitation in having to draw on 'those well-remembered regions' of his childhood as a way of starting his books. 'One of Dickens's immense superiorities over me is the great fecundity of his imagination. He has written 10 books and lo I am worn out after two.'[45] It did not help that images of Jane Brookfield still haunted him. It was always she whom he placed in the vacant railway carriage seat opposite or imagined alongside him when there was a fine view to be shared.

His own preoccupations led him to be indulgent with Annie and Minny, particularly with their timekeeping. Annie would return late from a walk before breakfast, Minny covering for her, sure that she had glimpsed her sister, 'hinting that I had best wait till she came…. Enter Miss Thackeray with a face shining like a full moon.'[46] At Vevey he wrote to Sally Baxter, making himself a subject for self-mockery, contrasting her youth with his grandfatherly desires. 'Theres a time for all things: for brilliant young Sarah Baxters; bright eyes and coquetry and triumphs and passions and filial duties – for old folks like me; art and ambition and money-getting and parental cares.'[47] There was a crowd of Americans at the Vevey hotel, the women pretty, the men 'so awfully vulgar'. He was tickled by what one of them had written in the visitors' book, where in response to the standard query 'Whither going' the Reverend J. Smith had declared, 'over the whole lot'.

On 6 August they were in Berne, where he worked on the third number of *The Newcomes*. Annie remembers a walk in a field, their father silent and preoccupied, lost in his thoughts. 'We waited till he came back to us, saying he now saw his way quite clearly, and he was cheerful and in good spirits as we returned to the inn.'[48] Annie was increasingly acting as her father's amanuensis, a familiar if intermittent role during the rest of his life, for her good-nature, patience and humour – 'a certain grave mirth w^h. is delightful to watch' – was the perfect balm to her father as he struggled with composition. Did Minny feel any lingering jealousies? There were none of the difficulties which had emerged on their earlier foreign trip, yet set alongside Annie 'Minny is not so good but she is a good little puss',[49] which is strangely equivocal.

Page of The Newcomes *in Annie's hand, with Thackeray's annotations.*

They arrived back in London at the end of August, having been delayed at Frankfurt where Thackeray suffered a 'smart fever' for three days, with symptoms 'uncommonly like the affair 3 or 4 years ago: but ending more happily and quickly than that'.[50] It was sufficient warning for him to consider once again his daughters' future. For one who thought so unsentimentally about his own death, it is strange that he should have left his affairs unsettled. Instead, he enlisted the support of friends to oversee the welfare of his children. Remarkably, in view of all the recent history between them, he now wrote to Brookfield, sending a box of cigars and recalling the days when they would smoke and drink together.

> When I was ill the other day I made a sort of will in w^h. I begged you & FitzGerald to act as a sort of guardians to the children, and that you'd have them every year to stay with you and your dear wife. God bless you both now after 2 years asunder, when there are no more rages on my part, I pray you to forget savage words, as I do (for I don't remember what I said or wrote only that a great deal of it was furious & unjust) – Forget all this if you can and remember the friend of old days.[51]

He could scarcely entrust Brookfield with anything more precious.

He seemed seized by a restlessness, taking Annie and Minny back from London to Paris to their grandparents, returning alone once more for a few weeks to London and then rejoining them. He had decided after all that they should spend the winter months in Rome, though he would have preferred to slip away on his own and be spared the ceremonies of departure. 'I wish the girls would let me go by myself for a month, & they w^d. but they wouldn't forgive me afterwards.'[52] He had finalised the arrangements to move house, as the lease on Young Street was about to expire. This time he decided to buy not rent, taking a house in Onslow Square, Brompton, to which they would move after their return in the spring.

Thackeray's poor health continued during their extended Italian journey, a time which affected his daughters profoundly. 'It almost seems to me now that all the rest of my life dates in some measure from those old Roman days, which were all the more vivid because my sister and I were still spectators and not yet actors in the play.'[53] Even so, Annie concedes that it was a trip 'which was trying in many ways',[54] alluding not just to her father's illness, which flared up again in Rome, but also to the scarlet fever that laid both sisters low at Naples and required a period of quarantine. Accompanied by Thackeray's servant, Charles Pearman, they started from Paris at the end of November in bitterly cold weather, travelling by steamer down the Rhone and then by train from Avignon to Marseilles, from where they took the overnight boat to Genoa. Thackeray's bout of 'illfluelza' receded as they travelled, but Annie was conscious of the journey being more of an adventure for them than it was for him. They all wrote separately to Mrs Carmichael-Smyth from Marseilles, Minny noting that the town was full of Turks, three of whom had travelled from Avignon with them, 'but they dident smell very nice'.[55]

Upon reaching Genoa, there was a day to spend onshore, so they took the train to Pisa where they admired the cathedral and its famous bell-tower, 'aslant in the sunlight for a background'. Returning to the quayside in Genoa, and with time pressing, they engaged a dubious group of sailors to row them back to the ship. A few yards from the quayside the boatmen played out a familiar scam, refusing to go further unless they were paid more.

> Then the steamer sent up two more rockets, which rose through the twilight, bidding us hurry; and then suddenly my father rose up in the stern of the boat where he was sitting, and standing tall and erect, and in an anger such as I had never seen him in before or after in all my life, he shouted out in loud and indignant English, 'D—n you, go on!' a simple malediction which carried more force than all the Italian polysyllables and expostulations of our companions. To our surprise and great relief, the men seemed frightened, and took to their oars again and began to row, grumbling and muttering.[56]

Their last stop before Rome was Civita Vecchia, from where they travelled by road in a decrepit post-chaise. Thackeray had heard rumours of brigands, and the dangers were real enough, but the journey is portrayed by Annie as a wonderful romance, where an antique pastoral world gives way to Christian imagery as the great basilica of St Peter's is first sighted looming in the twilight across the Campagna. One of the traces of the carriage broke, and in a moment shadowy figures appeared from nowhere.

> We were surrounded by people as if by magic – satyrs, shepherds, strange bearded creatures with conical hats, and with pitchforks in their hands. The sun was just setting, and dazzling into our faces all the time.... [A]fter a good deal of conversation with the postilions, the satyrs and fauns went their way with their pitchforks, leaving us, to our inexpressible relief, to continue our journey. Then came the dusk at last, and the road seemed longer and longer. I think I had fallen asleep in my corner, when my father put his hand on my shoulder. 'Look!' he said; and I looked, and, lo! there rose the dusky dome of St. Peter's, gray upon the dark-blue sky.[57]

The local charms passed Thackeray by. 'Every miserable official at every post house, customs, what not holds out his swindling hand and begs.'[58] But the English society in Rome appealed to him. Robert Browning recommended lodgings in the Via Della Croce, above a pastry-cook's. They would be there for two months, patronising the cake shop below and making arrangements for their dinners to be delivered from a nearby trattoria. There was some confusion the first time, for they managed to overlook the iron box left in the hall, but when eventually they opened it, 'smoking still upon the hot plates, was spread a meal like something in a fairy tale – roast birds and dressed meat, a loaf of brown bread and *compotes* of fruit, and a salad and a bottle of wine'.[59]

For the first fortnight Thackeray wrote nothing, giving himself over as chaperon to his daughters. 'Not one word of writing have I done as yet', he told the Baxters, 'and to be sure have been ill for the last 4 days; with an attack of – well of leeches blisters calomel. I have been ill once a month for the last 5 months. I who never was ill in <u>our</u> country'[60] (he meant America). Annie was enraptured by Rome, but Minny's levelheadedness made her less susceptible to first impressions. People would comment later on her practicality, so different from Annie's spontaneity and vagueness; but Minny was far from being just solidly reliable, for she was sharply observant and witty. It was Minny who, during Tennyson's visit to Young Street, looked up in the middle of reading Dickens to enquire 'Papa, why do you not write books like *Nicholas Nickleby*?'[61] Thackeray asked himself the same question repeatedly.

During those two months the Thackerays became intimate with quite a lively circle, so that the girls went visiting and not always in the company of their father. Kind friends doubtless were aware of his need to work. They were often with the recently-married Adelaide Sartoris – the celebrated operatic singer and sister of the actress Fanny Kemble – and also met people like Walter Scott's son-in-law and biographer, John Lockhart, Mary Brotherton (an old family friend), and the diplomat Alexander MacBean who kept them supplied with novels by Bulwer Lytton and Disraeli. Thackeray paid for them to have Italian lessons. On the last day of the old year, he reflected on their first month. They had still to set foot in the Vatican, nor had they been to any galleries, but they had got to know Rome and its colourful street life by walking – 'it is always bright new and nobly picturesque – much more to my taste than churches smelling of stale perfumes, and statued all over with lies. There's a capital English parson.... But O deary deary me, the Newcomes wont get on; and their author is in a dismal way.'[62]

Many years later Annie asserted that Mrs Browning and Mrs Sartoris were the people they liked best in Rome, an impression confirmed at the time by Thackeray, who added Emelyn Story to the list of those who went out of their way to be kind to his daughters. William Wetmore Story had been visiting Europe regularly since 1847, and settled permanently in Rome in 1856. Thackeray's new sympathy for America made Story's Bostonian roots attractive, and he offered the family his unconditional friendship at a time of personal tragedy, after the death of their young son. 'We often urged him to forget us, and not to be drawn into the depths of our sorrow, but rather to disport himself in the cordial sunshine of appreciation, among his own people, to which he had so good a right. But he would not hear of this, and came again and again, with a kindness and sympathy never to be forgotten.... Under what people called his cynical exterior and manner, his was the kindest and truest heart that ever beat, large in its sympathies and gracious in its giving.'[63]

As the Storys tried to recover from their grief, their daughter Edith fell ill and was confined to bed. Sitting with the little girl in her sickroom, Thackeray began a tale which would become *The Rose and the Ring*, and Edith 'was always so happily to remember that, chapter by chapter, the immortal work had, in the old Roman days, between daylight and dusk, as the great author sat on the edge of her bed, been tried on her'.[64] The story actually had its origins in a set of illustrative cards of fantastic characters which he made for his daughters' Twelfth Night party. Each card picked from a lottery resulted in the reward of a cream-cake from the downstairs pastry-shop. Musing over the abandoned pictures where they lay scattered after the party, Thackeray arranged them into a pattern, and the idea for the tale was born.

The Thackeray girls had probably first met the Brownings in Paris when staying with their grandparents, their Roman reunion allowing a friendship to develop. It may well have been from this time that a curious story originates, the sole source for which is a page of typed notes with manuscript annotations by Annie's daughter, Hester. One cannot even determine the author, but it would have been someone known to the Brownings. Ariana Curtis is a possible candidate, especially as she also knew Annie and Hester well in later years.

> Anny Thackeray had the power of clairvoyance, which bothered her and which she heartily mistrusted. In Rome Mrs Browning discovered that she was a sensitive medium for automatic writing. Lady Ritchie's description of her séances with Mrs Browning remain vividly with me. Mrs Browning

on her sofa, a smouldering log fire – (whatever the season of the year Mrs Browning always had a fire) – Anny sitting close to the sofa at a little table, both of them intent and absorbed, and the pencil in Anny's hand, guided by an invisible spirit writing and writing. Time ceases to exist with the interest of it all, and then the sudden return of Mr Browning from his walk brings everything to an abrupt end. Morning after morning Anny went to sit, and then to her horror she began to find that the communicating spirit had such a hold over her that even when away from Mrs Browning, her pen would write not her own words, but the words of the spirit.[65]

There seems no reason to doubt the authenticity of this story, though Annie never mentions participating either in séances or automatic writing, activities very popular then. Still, the mid 1850s was just the time when Annie would have been most susceptible to such adult influence, and her father had been a far from sceptical observer at séances in New York. Though he dismissed much of it as 'dreary & foolish superstition', the evidence of his own eyes was persuasive – 'I wouldn't have believed in a table turning 3 weeks ago – and that I have seen and swear to.'[66]

They left Rome for Naples on 8 February, Thackeray all too conscious of the inhibiting effects of work and illness. But the city had worked its magic. Nothing was finer than the sunset over St Peter's – 'Gods what a flaming splendor it is!'[67] It pleased him to think that his daughters would have lasting memories to tell to their own children. The living history and timeless landscapes supplied a perspective to his passing quarrels, and he seemed able to accept that his religious differences with his mother were mere matters of detail. 'In a very few years and the doubts shall be over and we shall see darkly no more.'[68]

During their first weeks in Naples Thackeray finished two numbers of *The Newcomes*, and also began revising *The Rose and the Ring* as his next Christmas book. Then Annie without warning fell ill with a sore throat and headache which got steadily worse until a doctor diagnosed scarlet fever. It was her first real illness. Reviving the role previously played out for Edith Story, Thackeray now read to her portions of *The Rose and the Ring* as he rewrote them, noting in his diary how Minny was 'a dear little nurse'. But within the week Minny had also succumbed, as was almost inevitable with this contagious childhood disease. The doctor was able to recommend an Irish nurse, and in due course Annie recovered sufficiently to encourage her sister 'who is wofully frightened, and would fancy herself much worse than she is but for Anny's example'.[69]

It had been a shock to Thackeray, used to coping with his own illnesses but suddenly presented with a parent's fears. He would constantly check on the girls, quietly entering their room at night. 'So the Father of all of us sends illness death care grief out of w^h. come love steadfastness consolation.' It was just the kind of thing which his mother might have written. But it also made him conscious that the company of two young daughters necessarily constrained him. He had to put Neapolitan society beyond his reach, which was frustrating for it seemed to be 'curious and pleasant' – familiar alarm bells here for his mother. 'But with daughters who are of no age, it was impossible.' During their convalescence, in effect a quarantine period, he fell ill again with his familiar internal problems, probably aggravated by what the Victorians called 'Roman fever'. For ten days all three of them lay quietly in their rooms, with limited service as the hotel waiters feared infection, but with views of Capri and the dazzlingly blue Mediterranean for comfort. Their slow recovery meant there was no time to visit Florence, and on 30 March they began the return journey through France.

They stayed for a couple of weeks in Paris before Thackeray returned alone to 'O such a dreary old house at Kensington'.[70] It was dreary because it was empty, but Young Street and its Kensington Square community had been a real home to Thackeray and his daughters for eight years. They would shortly leave it for the newly-purchased Onslow Square house, an imposing property where they continued to be happy but which they never held in quite the same affection. Annie tried her best when she called it 'a pleasant, bowery sort of home, with green curtains and carpets, looking out upon the elm-trees of Onslow Square. We lived for seven years at No. 36, and it was there he wrote the "Lectures on the Georges," and the end of "The Newcomes," and the "Virginians," part of "Philip," and many of the "Roundabout Papers".'[71] This was also the house from where he edited the *Cornhill* magazine and which therefore saw virtually all the significant work of his last years. During the first weeks of May he bought furnishings for Onslow Square and prepared it for his daughters' arrival. He contemplated their future with his characteristic blend of affection and selfishness, which would be startling were it not so appealingly honest. 'I had a line from my dear little women 3 days ago and yesterday bought them 2 nice new beds and hope to make a pooty room for them at 36 Onslow Sq. What Comforts they are to me! – My dearest old Fat is the best girl I see anywhere: and I am brutally happy that she is not handsome enough to fall in love with: so that I hope she'll stay by me for many a year yet.'[72] Indeed, both daughters were to stay for all of the few years he had left.

His relationship with Mary and Charles Carmichael now reached something of a crisis, having been strained in recent years. The problem lay with Mary, who appears to have been jealous of Thackeray, accusing him of showing no affection towards her, even 'charging my poor girls with misrepresentations'. He had no quarrel with Charles, and had a great affection for their little boy, Chéri, whom he had been prepared to sponsor through college, but Mary's erratic behaviour made any continued association impossible. 'Genteel estrangement' was his preferred solution, and he urged his mother not to be drawn into the inevitable repercussions. Mary Carmichael served to confirm his distrust of a certain kind of female, the archetype for which was his mother-in-law, Mrs Shawe. 'I hope you won't "take on" over much; or be affected by what she says any more than by what any other insane woman says – she is as certainly crazy as my wife is.'[73]

Thackeray finally transferred to Onslow Square on 18 May, and set off the next day to bring Annie and Minny back from France. After his death Annie recalled that first night at the new house, and thought still further back to the writing of *Pendennis* when he had been so ill in Young Street.

> I said to Papa ... I am so glad you did not die when you were so ill. We should never have known you then or learnt to care for you & Papa said – a little hurt & yet touched too – I have thought so myself but I do not think it right ever to talk sentimentally about ones feelings. Papa said next morning that as he was in bed the night before & as he was looking about & thinking how comfortable it looked, he could not help wondering, what the end of it all would be, & whether this was the room in which he would die one day.[74]

By early June a large house in Boulogne had been located for the summer, just as he had started writing more freely with all the business of moving completed. The Carmichael-Smyths set out from Paris, stopping off on their way to Boulogne at St-Valery-sur-Somme, from where Annie and Minny were sent their grandmother's usual anxieties and tips for good housekeeping, fussy but well-intentioned. 'If the house has not been occupied during the damp weather it will be necessary that it should be opened & the Mattresses aired &c before we sleep there – Papa said that [the servants] Eliza & Charles were to follow you, but surely it would be better to take them with you, or send them by "long sea" with the baggage, to arrive about the same time.'⁷⁵ By the end of the month they were all together at Boulogne, at the Château de Bréquerecque. The town was full of soldiers, whose billet the girls overlooked from their garden, from where they could see them singing and dancing. Catherine Dickens was also in Boulogne that year. Thackeray tended to come and go, spending a week in Paris and much of the time in London during the quiet weeks of late summer with everyone away. The illness that had flared up in Rome continued to nag, and Boulogne seemed not to agree with him either. He found the garden there damp and unwholesome. Nevertheless, he made good progress on *The Newcomes*, was relieved to discover that his fears for his American investments in railway bonds were unfounded, and continued to tidy up *The Rose and the Ring* ready for Christmas publication.

Annie and Minny were back with their father in Onslow Square by September, and his lingering illness led Mrs Carmichael-Smyth to suggest, not without some caution, the kind of alternative treatments that his stepfather was undertaking. It appears to have been Major Carmichael-Smyth's own idea that Thackeray should try magnetism. 'I am thankful to say dear GP is receiving benefit f^m. the magnetic chain, the operator was obliged to apply his strongest chain before it touched him at all & today he moves much better.... Its a great proof to me that he requires electricity – he says he wishes Papa w^d try galvinism to strengthen his internals – those strong doses of steel will play the d—l with his head – Tunbridge Wells water & air w^d do him a world of good.'⁷⁶

But Thackeray's new great triumph was in finding an ideal companion to his daughters, for now aged seventeen and fourteen they were scarcely in need of a governess any more. After the withdrawal of a Miss Evans because of illness in her family, a better option presented itself in the form of Amy Crowe, the daughter of his old friend and sister to Eyre Crowe, who had been Thackeray's secretary-companion in America. Amy had cared for her mother during her final illness, 'quite angelic in goodness and fidelity',⁷⁷ and now needed a fresh purpose in life. Thackeray was delighted to be able to ask her to join his household as the girls' companion and his housekeeper.

> [M]y girls jumped for joy at the notion that you would come to them and indeed, my dear, if you will, I shall thank God to have you with them. <u>Your coming will be of the very greatest comfort & service to all of us</u>. There is no family in all the country that wants such a person as much as we do. You will not be a charge to me but do me the greatest kindness; save me money; take infinite care off my shoulders – you <u>must</u>

Annie in a studio photograph taken about 1854

come that is the word. You & the girls will have your floor to yourselves up stairs, and I shall feel what I have never felt for years that there's somebody with them whom we all like, who can look to me and them, who will be with them when I am away, and ease me of a part of the responsibility I feel about them.[78]

Four: A Little Rain of Dollars   115

Minny in a studio photograph taken about 1854

It did seem like an ideal solution, and Amy would move in and live with them without interruption until her marriage to Edward Thackeray late in 1862. But immediately before her arrival Mrs Carmichael-Smyth had concerns; she did not question Amy's suitability, but was worried that her son's persuasive personality and strong opinions might overpower the girl's own meek religious convictions and weaken her simple faith.

> At this moment she reads the Bible & she believes it through GOD's grace to be His word; while she believes that, she must be comforted. But if by a certain chopping of logic, a Man whom she sincerely loves & knows to have the kindest of hearts & most powerful of intellects tells her or argues before her that it is not His word, but that certain fallible creatures like herself, have set forth the most stupendous assertions, declaring them to be truths which GOD Himself has pronounced; while in reality they are only entitled to the same credit with any other historian, w^d. it be matter of surprise, if that simple faith were shaken, & she let go a sheet anchor to tear upon a broken reed?... If you & y^r dearest Father can believe that you are 'joint heirs with Christ to the Kingdom of Heaven,' upon man's word alone, I say that my faith is as a grain of mustard seed as compared to yours.... And now let us have done with this – I must believe that we are approximate in spirit if not in the letter – I have not answered Amy's letter yet but I shall rejoice to hear that she is with you for all y^r sakes.[79]

It was not a lasting anxiety, for a few weeks later she was celebrating Amy Crowe's successful integration as 'scolder and rower' into the Onslow Square establishment. She continued to promote magnetism, but only in carefully controlled circumstances. Her husband's experience did not sound like an unqualified success. 'GPs heel, I hope will be all right when the burns the chain has made have healed. Meanwhile I dont advise anyone to try it, when it must touch the skin.'[80]

Mrs Carmichael-Smyth's latest activity amongst the expatriate community was the organising of support for the Crimean war-wounded and their dependents. She was frustrated to find herself rather a lone voice in Paris when she heard what was being done for the war effort in London. She encouraged Annie and Minny to do their bit in the provision of comforts for the soldiers at the front.

> I'm very much obliged to Min for wishing to send me a 'post mortem' account of my oldest love. I prefer a viventure if you please, & I hope he will be wise in his diet & exercise, & take boiled rice, not so very dry, for its hard of digestion, but boiled very tender, no potatoes, sometimes onions – Nanny dear why dont you take the hip bath, rubbing well after it & taking a walk brisk in the Square – it has set in very cold here. We are trying to get up an amateur concert for our poor

widows & orphans but people are so slow, so insensible. How touching it is to hear of the efforts of all classes in England schoolboys subscribing a week's pock^t money, a little girl writing a poem w^h. has sold for 20£, prisoners f^m. their cells, poor pensioners, & we in this city we can do nothing.... What can I do? poor helpless, my head wont let me work, but your young fingers work – work I beseech you, for the wives & children if you cant for the flannel waistcoats.... If every woman in England who has the means w^d. makes one flan: waistcoat even, not a soldier w^d be without.[81]

Illness was once again inhibiting Thackeray, and he decided to send the girls to Paris for Christmas to give himself a better chance of beating his deadlines. He wanted *The Newcomes* finished so that he could write a new lecture series for America, still anxious to set aside a secure legacy for his daughters and absent wife. Not much is heard of Isabella during these years, though in early November his brother-in-law had reported that she 'is much better, and does not look 26'.[82] Thackeray's own visits may have ceased altogether. He would tell a friend a few months later that Isabella appeared not to miss any of them, 'and the care of her serves to maintain a very worthy old couple who treat her with the utmost kindness and watchfulness – so that her illness serves for some good'.[83] Yet despite the tragedy of his marriage, and his difficult relationship with the impossible Mrs Shawe, Thackeray remained dutiful to Isabella's family, even to the extent of writing privately to the English minister at the Hague about another of her brothers, Henry Shawe, who since leaving the Indian army had been ruined by drink. 'I would gladly pay his board for a few weeks or months, & defray the charge of a small plain outfit, such as w^d. be suitable to one in his condition – a few shirts, woollens, clothes &c.'[84]

During her granddaughters' Parisian Christmas and in the weeks to come, Mrs Carmichael-Smyth's concern about the Crimea heightened their consciousness of its horrors, for they saw wounded soldiers fortunate enough to have been sent back to France and England. 'We met such a fine young Crimean at Paris one day, with one leg doubled up, I have not seen so many here, w^h. I am not sorry for, it makes me perfectly unhappy when I see those poor crippled heros.'[85] The months leading up to their father's second American trip were spent in combating illness and clearing the decks, and he hoped for the space to 'try Vichy or some other Jordan for a cure'.[86] Major Carmichael-Smyth's own poor health took them yet again to Paris and it was there at the beginning of July that Thackeray completed *The Newcomes* 'with a very sad heart'.⁸⁷

As Annie approached her eighteenth birthday, she wrote to Mrs Fanshawe in Southampton, seeking advice about her future and hinting at a certain restlessness, a growing dissatisfaction perhaps with the likely direction of her future life, the first indication of ambition and of desires that could not easily be discussed at home.

> I cant make out what it is just now but I am continually longing for something but I don't know what.... There is one thing wʰ. seems delightful. When we are old & go to parties with papa, & make breakfast & write for him – I should like a profession so much – not to spend my life crochetting [*sic*] mending my clothes & reading novels – wʰ. seems the employment of English ladies unless they teach dirty little children to read wʰ. is well enough in its way – but no work to the mind – & I don't want to write poetry & flummery – so I am in a fix what to do when I leave off lessons. Please write by my birthday & give good advice for I have no one much to talk to & I like my jaw very much indeed. Papa says in a few years we shall only have 200£ a year to live upon & as my favourite Miss Martineau says it is far nobler to earn than to save. I think I should like to earn very much & become celebrated like the aforesaid Harriet who is one of the only sensible women living beside thee & me & 2 or 3 more I know.⁸⁸

Perhaps Mrs Fanshawe responded in the way that Annie hoped. Perhaps she told her that of course she must be a writer. Evidently it was not yet a discussion to be had with her father. His thoughts were taken up with America, but because of his stepfather's frailty he had to resolve after all to leave Annie and Minny in Paris and not take them as his companions. Mrs Baxter remained keen for him to bring them to New York, but 'we have debated, the girls & I, and agreed with very heavy hearts that it is best they stay behind & take care of Granny & Colonel Newcome'.⁸⁹

His own passage was booked for 13 October, and the time remaining was devoted to preparing his iconoclastic set of lectures on British monarchs, *The Four Georges*; they were still being completed as he crossed the Atlantic. There is a sense of déjà vu about these last weeks, of the notes of farewell to friends, and then the last letter from Liverpool written on his mother's birthday, having arranged for his daughters to travel to Paris to their grandparents. 'I should like them to learn French with a master, not a mistress, or German with D^r. Kalisch who lives Rue des petites Écuries.'[90] Two years had made all the difference to Annie and Minny, for he was leaving behind self-aware young women accustomed to being their father's companions, watchful for his welfare. They felt the parting more painfully on this occasion, as Annie later recalled. 'That was a heartache worse than the first time, for he had never been well since that Roman fever & I was old eno' to be anxious now.'[91]

Five

TOWARDS THE UNKNOWN OCEAN
(1855-1862)

[W]here's the pleasure of staying when the feast is over and the flowers withered and the guests gone –

Thackeray to Anne Procter
26 November 1856

During his second American trip, Thackeray travelled further than before, spending less time in New York (where the Clarendon Hotel was again his base), and getting as far south as New Orleans. After four months, he announced that 'your Pa is prospering and at Midsummer will actually be worth 10000£ – At present it is only a little more than 8.... I think little Dorrit capital as far as I have read – (Do you perceive the connexion of ideas? I was thinking to myself how much is Dickens worth? I suppose).'[1] He endured the relentless travelling and endless cycles of lectures, for 'the making of dollars is the object of this tour – I want these for the sake of the young ones at home and against the rainy day w^h. cant be far distant – My health is a good deal hit – since I made a journey to Rome 2 years ago I never have been well from one ailment or another.'[2]

The novelty of first impressions was lacking this time, but there were more personal disappointments too. He was pulled up short when he learnt of Sally Baxter's engagement, passing off as a joke what had come as startling news. 'Sally is not improved. She has been awfully flattered since I went away and O Minny! What do you think shes going to be – to be – mum mum – married! – w^h. I don't envy the young man – who they say is a fine fellow.'[3] Sally comes off worst in a comparison with Jane Brookfield 'who is always noble and pure and generous and unselfish – am rather ashamed that I sh^d. have let this wild American girl be fond of me'.[4] To present himself as the recipient of former unlooked-for affections is at best a partial reading of the facts. He was invited to the wedding, but was able to offer his absence in Boston and a feverish chill as convenient reasons for not travelling to New York. The strength of the Baxters' friendship had considerable calls upon his loyalty, such that 'I feel as if I was doing wrong though I am doing right',[5] but doubtless the occasion would have been impossible for him.

He was able to tell Annie afterwards that the wedding had gone off 'very smartly', and disingenuously would spin a story about Sally being the one inclined towards fantasy and coquettishness, trusting that his own daughter will marry for real love – and only to a man with the wherewithal to keep her. This curious sequence of ideas was prompted by his attention being drawn to a possible attachment between the eighteen-year-old Annie and a clergyman called Creyke. Thackeray was sufficiently startled by his mother's unsubstantiated news to make his views brutally clear to the daughter who could deny him nothing.

> My girls I suppose must undergo the common lot; but I hope they wont Sallify – Indulge in <u>amours de tête</u> I mean. Indeed I dont like to think of their entering into that business at all unless upon good reasonable steady grounds – with a Tomkins who is likely to make them happy and has enough to keep them – and who above all falls in love with them first.... No my dearest old Fat you mustnt hanker after a penniless young clergyman with one lung. It is as much as I can do to scrape together enough to keep my 3 daughters (your mother being one): and you must no more think about a penniless husband, than I can think about striking work – these luxuries do not belong to our station. Besides has he ever thought about you? Girls are romantic, visionary, love beautiful whiskers & so forth – but every time a girl permits herself to <u>think</u> an advance of this sort she hurts herself – loses somewhat of her dignity, rubs off a little of her maiden-bloom. Keep yours on your cheeks till 50 if necessary.... I dont say banish him from your mind – perhaps it is a fatal pashn ravaging your young bussom – perhaps only a fancy w^h. has left already a head that has taken in a deal of novels – but settle it in your mind that it would be just as right for you to marry Charles Pearman (what do I say? Charles is healthy & can make his 40£ a year) as poor Creyke.[6]

No more is heard of this match until after his return to London, when it is dismissed as nonsense, an imagining of his mother's. Annie laughed it off, but for Thackeray a lingering doubt remained. 'No, if there had been anything in it, I am sure my girl w^d. have told me.'[7] Having felt the heat of his reactions, 'dearest old Fat' may have chosen to guard some of her secrets closely, even having to ask Mrs Fanshawe for advice about her possible future career, for 'I have no one much to talk to'. In some matters, her father was the one least able to offer an objective opinion. Having to confront the possibility of Annie's marrying and the question of her future independence made him concede that she might succeed as a writer, though not in terms which can have given her much confidence. 'Perhaps Nan will be able to write and earn for herself – it's not unlikely – yes it's unlikely, but not impossible.'[8] To his mother, he is far more generous in his assessment. 'Her drawing is very good in spite of what the Master may say – much better than mine at her age, and so is her writing too.'[9]

Revisiting America did not change Thackeray's views on slavery, but his interest in the people intensified. He set out his final position on black emancipation to Mrs Procter, predicting a time 'when the sufferings of the negroes will be awful – when they begin to fall in value and cost more than they are worth – then will be the pinch for the poor wretches, whom the selfish white race will wish to be rid of'.[10] He made time to sit and sketch individual slaves, particularly the children whom he found irresistible. 'I wish I had a sketch book and a hundred of them drawn.'[11] In New Orleans it was disconcerting to be mistaken for a slave owner. 'A man came up to me in the street & asked me if I could sign him any one who wanted to buy a field hand? It was because I looked like a Kentucky farmer my friends tell me, that this obliging offer was made to me.'[12] But he never risks taking the slave issue too seriously, reverting without difficulty to a mix of humour and routine prejudice. 'If one of these imps w^d. remain little I think I would buy him and put him into buttons as a page for the young ladies – but presently he will become big, lazy, lying, not sweet smelling doing the 4th. of a white mans work and costing more to keep.'

Because on this occasion he saw less of New York society and spent more time in provincial towns, he was struck everywhere by the lack of refinements. The southern landscapes he found dreary enough, but the coarse manners of his travelling companions were positively upsetting. He still had not accustomed himself to the spitting, to fingers substituting for handkerchiefs, and to gross dining habits – 'by Heavens at the ladies' table yesterday every single woman had her knife down her throat'.[13] He had been in generally good health on the last occasion; this time his recent medical history made him altogether more cautious and wiser, an ageing writer in a young country which was moving on at an ever-quickening pace. He was unable to shift his feverish chill, whilst an old urinary complaint was discomforting because of the way it constrained him in public. He admitted to his daughters having had a 'shivering fit' during dinner – 'thats 4 fits I have had since I have been in New York' – and to William Wetmore Story he was more explicit. 'And now I'll tell you of something else besides chill & fever w^h. I carry about: an irritation of the bladder w^h. causes me great inconvenience, & is sometimes very awkward in lady's society.'[14] On the return voyage in May he was ill on the boat, and told Mrs Baxter of his intention to 'lay myself up either in London or Paris, and see if this crazy old hull of mine can be patched up & made sea-worthy again. The best thing I can do for the next 3 months is to devote myself to being ill.'[15]

In the second half of August he took his daughters for a short trip; they started at Calais, moved through Belgium to Spa, Dusseldorf, and thence to Aix la Chapelle 'w^h. disagreed with me as it always does'.[16] Amy Crowe received letters from Spa, Annie reporting on their itinerary – Ghent was 'an uncommonly jolly old town with a moat & gables & convents & all the people wear crinoline'[17] – whilst the practical Minny conserved her travelogue – 'it'll be something to talk about in the long winter evenings' – feeling that Amy would be more interested to learn of the risks they took at night. 'Yesterday we got wet twice then we went to the play & it was so cold that we had an air tight charcole stove live in our bed room like what people kill themselves with & I expected that we would both be dead in the morning.'[18] They turned back to Paris on getting news of the death of one of Major Carmichael-Smyth's sisters-in-law, assuming that the Carmichael-Smyths, themselves travelling in Germany, would be returning home and in need of support. But they found themselves alone in Paris, so whilst his daughters stayed with his cousin, Charlotte Ritchie, Thackeray put up in the Hôtel Bristol in the Place Vendôme.

Paris was also their destination later in October when it was Mrs Carmichael-Smyth's turn to be taken ill, and Thackeray's daughters took charge of their grandparents. Anne Carmichael-Smyth's 'nervous' complaint remained undiagnosed, despite a procession of homoeopathic and conventional doctors, and Thackeray began to resent the demands that it was placing on Annie and Minny. 'In all these botherations the girls are behaving like trumps.'[19] Compelled to make adjustments to his touring schedule for *The Four Georges* he assigned, not entirely fairly, an almost wilful selfishness to his parents' behaviour. 'Why, nearly 3 months have been wasted in this dodging about and sentimentality.'[20] He refused to accept that his mother's condition was serious, although her recovery took several weeks. Despite the evidence of his own past domestic history, Thackeray could still be reluctant to acknowledge illnesses other than those with definite physical symptoms.

Observing her grandmother at firsthand, Annie was more astute in recognising what was evidently a depressive condition. Writing to Amy from le Havre on the Channel coast, to where she and Minny insisted on taking their grandparents 'in the face of all the friends', she monitored the patient carefully.

> She bore the journey famously slept it through & had a better night than she had had for 6 weeks she said & is really a great deal better. But you know after a nervous fever one need not be surprised at nervous attacks occasionally particularly when one has had them before the illness & that is what Granny will insist upon doing & theres no talking her out of it. She had a bad one last night the 1.st for ten days, Eliza came & called me up, & there she was groaning & moaning & starting poor dear, & so wretched it became quite melancholico-comic at last.... Its dreadful to think of going off and leaving them all by themselves those two dear old people & so we shall stay till Xmas at all events.[21]

This sympathetic diagnosis contrasts starkly with Thackeray's insistence that his daughters should spend Christmas with him. 'I wish she could be convinced that her illness is not much. I thought nothing of it when I saw her the first day.'[22] He confided in the indispensable Amy Crowe, his 'dear little Dorrit', that his mother might urge her to go to Paris in place of Annie and Minny. 'So if you are written to say you think you ought to ask my consent (as you ought Miss) and write and ask it and then I will refuse it.'[23] He thought that it was the years of caring for his stepfather that had debilitated his mother, and that her lively spirit had been worn down by the increasingly sedentary old man. There was probably something in this. He agreed with Annie that his parents should move to London to stay with them, but knew that his stepfather would be as reluctant as ever to leave Paris.

And yet, perhaps Thackeray was anxious about broader, long-term problems, for in the midst of the fussing over his mother he feared for the possibility of inherited nervous weakness. 'I lay awake hours & hours last night trying to see a way out of this doubt and trouble & gloom. And my poor wife's youngest daughter mustn't be subject to too much of it. I always tremble about my little Minny.'[24] By the turn of the year his mother was slowly improving, was taking an infusion of hops to assist her digestion and eating 'like a Trojan'. It had been a long time since she had written to her granddaughters, and she felt as if she was emerging into the light again, 'like wakening out of a long sleep'.[25]

During the time that his mother was at le Havre and still far from recovery, Thackeray delivered repeated cycles of *The Four Georges* in Scotland, virtually his uninterrupted occupation between November 1856 and the end of May 1857. Preoccupied with work and family worries, he yet found time to write thoughtfully to his old friend Anne Benson Procter, whose mother had died. His fine letter serenely evokes hopes for another, unknown world, in language which is measured and free from sentimentality.

> Thinking of it is thinking of God Inscrutable Immeasurable endless, beginningless, Supreme, awfully Solitary. Little children step off this earth into the Infinite and we tear our hearts out over their sweet cold hands and smiling faces that drop indifferent when you cease holding them and smile as the lid is closing over them – I dont fancy we deplore the old who have had enough of living & striving and have buried so many others, and must be weary of living – it seems time for them to go – for where's the pleasure of staying when the feast is over and the flowers withered and the guests gone – Isn't it better to blow the light out than sit on among the broken meats, and collapsed jellies, and vapid heeltaps? I go – to what I don't know – but to God's next world w^h. is His and He made it – one paces up & down the shore yet awhile – and looks towards the Unknown Ocean, and thinks of the traveller whose boat sailed yesterday. Those we love can but walk down to the pier with us – the voyage we must make alone – except for the young or very happy I can't say I am sorry for any one who dies – & now havent I got a score of letters to write about business? I came in just now from Glasgow, am off again tomorrow plunge about all next month reading these old papers, and behold one day shall be silent – let us scrape together a little money for tomorrow we die.[26]

He was aged forty-five in 1856, hardly an old man even for the standards of the time. Yet there is a definite weariness about Thackeray's later years, primarily owing to his continuous ill-health of course, and now coupled with a tiredness of ambition. Although a final testing commitment lay ahead in the form of the editorship of the *Cornhill*

– a job for which he would have been temperamentally unsuited even when in the best of health – after his return from America there is increasingly the feeling of an account being settled. His energies were expended on activities which dragged him down – the long lecture-tour for *The Four Georges*, bringing in good money but little personal satisfaction; the coming quarrel with Edmund Yates and the 'Garrick affair', whose essential triviality he might have dismissed in earlier years but which was now to become a distracting obsession; and the familiar struggle to complete his novel before the *Cornhill* swallowed all of his time.

But there is no self-pity, no suggestion that he had earned a right to be spared his full share of ordinary suffering. Instead, he sought a diversion from the routine drudgery of the writer's round. This is perhaps the best explanation for his allowing himself to be persuaded to try for an Oxford parliamentary seat in July 1857; that, and the notion that it was the sort of thing to which a man of his background might legitimately aspire. There had been earlier proposals that he should stand, which he had not accepted, but as he wrote to his mother from Bath, 'the beautiful city where Miss Ann Becher first danced with Captain GP', he was now tempted to show his hand. 'Just when the novel-writing faculty is pretty well used up here is independence a place in Parliament and who knows what afterwards?... I shant be happy in politics and they'll interfere with my digestion – but with the game there, it seems faint-hearted not to play it.'[27] If he had strongly-held political views, he had not previously made them evident. At Oxford he stood against the Whig nominee, but was not a success on the hustings, and like Colonel Newcome was out of his depth in the electioneering machine. Addressing a crowd of noisy voters was not the same as delivering a lecture. His defeat was certainly not a humiliation (he lost by sixty-five votes to an experienced candidate), but it put a close to his political ambitions. It had also been a costly vanity, resulting in personal expenditure of nearly £900.

No sooner had he delivered his final series of lectures than he started *The Virginians*, for which Bradbury and Evans promised the enormous sum of £6,000. '[I] am straightway going to a book w^h. in consequence of the popularity of these lectures is paid to me twice as much as any former production.'[28] The size of the payments made him worry whether he could produce value for money. 'I dont think the Virginians is good yet though it has taken me an immense deal of trouble but I know it will be good at the end. I tremble for the poor publishers who give me 300£ a number – I dont think they can afford it and shall have the melancholy duty of disgorging.'[29] In this novel he would combine his fondness for eighteenth-century themes with a new admiration for the New World, for it deals with family divisions caused by the American revolution. At the same time, by a web of subtle genealogical links he manages to make connections with other novels, to *Esmond* and to a strand of the pre-history of *Pendennis* – the novel whose eponymous hero also becomes the narrator of two of its successors, *The Newcomes* and Thackeray's final completed novel, *Philip*.

For Christmas 1857 he went with his daughters and Amy Crowe to stay at Walton-on-Thames with 'a Merchant Prince', the American banker Russell Sturgis and his family. Thackeray delighted in the lavish entertainment, as much for himself as for his daughters. The wide-eyed wonder of Sturgis's children charmed him, and Julian Sturgis remembered the writer being 'moved to tears at the rapture of my youngest brother at the sight of his first Christmas-tree'.[30] Thackeray was in much need of this break, for his parents were now staying at Onslow Square, which inevitably put a strain on his writing routine.

Other people's visiting was now his source for news of his wife's condition. It became another of the list of duties that Amy Crowe took on as his housekeeper. 'Good accounts from poor Isabella. Her fever is over. Amy brought back the very best report of her and of the care taken of her.'[31] Preoccupied with his writing, Thackeray was resigned to enjoying social life vicariously, for Annie and Minny 'do all the fun and observation of the family now. Their talk is capital: it is delightful to hear the prattle, as they come home from their parties.'[32] *The Virginians* ground on through 1858, its historical detail requiring visits to the British Museum where he took meticulous notes. 'I am myself so constantly unwell now that I begin to think my turn to be called cannot be delayed very long. These Virginians take me as much time as if I was writing a History.'[33] It was a particular pleasure to receive news of the reception of the book in America, and to be told that locals admired his convincing pictures of Virginian life. He had great respect for Washington Irving, and to learn of his unsolicited good opinion was very satisfying. The eminent American writer commented that 'I know what he is capable of doing, a man of great mind, far superior to Dickens. Dickens's prejudices are too limited to make such a book as Thackeray is capable of making of the "Virginians"'.[34] For Thackeray, who was all too ready to give to Dickens the first place as the finer writer, this must have been encouraging, boosting his confidence just as relations between the two men were about to get awkward. In May Thackeray became innocently entangled in the rumours about Ellen Ternan, concerning which he tried to correct an error. 'Last week going into the Garrick I heard that D is separated from his wife on account of an intrigue with his sister in law. No says I no such thing – its with an actress – and the other story has not got to Dickens's ears but this has – and he fancies that I am going about abusing him! We shall never be allowed to be friends that's clear.'[35] The incident helps explain why Dickens was so ready to take Edmund Yates's part in the Garrick affair.

Both Dickens and Thackeray belonged to the Garrick Club, many of whose members were drawn from the literary world. The Garrick controversy began when the young journalist Edmund Yates, a fellow member, published in *Town Talk* in June 1858 a trivial and mean-spirited piece critical of Thackeray's character and sincerity, describing his conversation as 'affectedly good natured and benevolent'. Yates asserted not just that *Esmond* was 'still-born' and that the English reception of the *Four Georges* lectures had been 'dead failures', but went on to claim for good measure that 'his success is on the wane ... [and] there is a want of heart in all he writes'.[36] Thackeray's fury led him formally to complain about the behaviour of this fellow Club member, and instead of letting the dust settle he succeeded in having Yates expelled. Dickens somewhat disingenuously acted as Yates's adviser, but also tried to mediate with Thackeray, thereby prolonging something which would have been best ignored. Thackeray was upset at what he regarded as ungentlemanly behaviour, a reaction probably disproportionate since Yates was an insignificant figure. More personally costly was the break with Dickens, which was only repaired shortly before Thackeray's death. Nevertheless, Thackeray's belief that his fellow novelist was the superior writer never wavered.

He found some relief by escaping to Germany and Switzerland for much of July and August, but was increasingly troubled by his old intestinal problem, as well as the distressingly painful stricture of the urethra. The fact that Annie and Minny seemed such permanent fixtures was a great comfort, but he acknowledged that his motives were less than worthy. 'Nobody in the least is coming to marry them – and nobody I am sure is wanted, by their selfish parent – Annys happiness makes almost me happy.... When I am lying upstairs in bed you know dreadfully ill with those spasms, and yet secretly quite contented and easy, I say to myself "Good God what a good girl that is! Amen".'[37]

In September Mrs Carmichael-Smyth was knocked down and suffered a hip fracture on her way to visit her sick son at the Hôtel Bristol in Paris. He put an almost tragic gloss on the episode, which seemed to be bringing to a sad close the heroic role he had assigned to her. 'So in decrepitude and ill health, and straitened circumstances ends one who began beautiful & brilliant with a world of admirers round about her.'[38] His mother improved, if rather slowly, and his initial melancholy passed. But increasingly he found himself sympathising with friends after the death of a parent, causing him each time to reflect on his own approaching exit, a prospect he faced with very little regret. He regularly employed the familiar metaphor of departure on a journey, always reluctant to prolong leave-taking and favouring the quick and silent removal, without tears or the opportunity for second thoughts. He wrote to Dr John Brown, whose father had died, that 'he was ready I suppose, and had his passport made out for his journey. Next comes our little turn to pack up and depart. To stay is well enough: but shall we be very sorry to go? What more is there in life that we haven't tried? What that we have tried is so very much worth repetition or endurance?'[39]

His attacks would retreat for a time. At the end of January 1859 Annie was able to confirm that her father was 'fresh and eager for work' and had already started the March number of *The Virginians*. 'Except for a one-day attack on Xmas day he has not been ill for nearly six weeks.'[40] But this was merely an unusually prolonged respite, for by mid-February he was writing to his mother from his bed. He had put himself under the care of his friend Dr Henry Thompson, and owned a copy of his recent specialist work, *Pathology and Treatment of the Stricture of the Urethra*. Thompson had already tried some treatment on Thackeray, but with only short-term success. 'I am in for a second bout of Thompson – an accident rendered the first inefficacious, & left almost all the ground to be gone over again.'[41] These interventions at best eased his problems. He seriously considered surgical treatment for which Thompson's success rate was good – the 'little touch of the knife w^h. is hardly felt' – but his concerns about the inevitable interruption to work meant that the decision about surgery was delayed until eventually time ran out on him. It amused him that his daughters hoped that prayer might intercede on his behalf. 'I asked [Minny] why the natural laws were to be interrupted in my particular case?... I have a right to say O Father give me submission to bear cheerfully (if possible) & patiently my sufferings but I cant request any special change in my behalf from the ordinary processes, or see any special Divine <u>animus</u> superintending my illnesses or wellnesses.'

Annie's observations about the on-going quarrel with Yates and difficulties with Dickens throw light on the distress it caused her father, and she found herself drawn into the widely-held fascination with the Ellen Ternan story.

Sketch by Thackeray

About the Garrick: its only ½ as exciting as it used to be. Papas getting disgusted. Everybody's been bullying him about his susceptibility. M^r. Dickens finding he w^d. have to be put up in the witness box wrote off to Papa to say that could not the lamentable affair be arranged.... I am getting confused & indignant Papa says the story is that Charley [Dickens] met his Father & Miss Whatsname Whatever the actress out walking on Hampstead Heath. But I dont believe a word of the scandal – After all the stories told of us we can afford to disbelieve it of other people.[42]

This rumbled on until March 1859, with Yates contemplating legal action against the Garrick but then publishing a final pamphlet instead. Thackeray wisely maintained his silence, perhaps because of his daughters' insistence. 'We are begging our Jupiter to keep in his thunder & not even read it & as he has taken to paying great attention to what we say lately perhaps he wont.'[43] At last he put behind him an episode from which no party emerged untarnished.

By the time that Yates was firing off his pamphlet, Thackeray had signed a contract with George Smith, agreeing to write for a new magazine to be launched in January 1860. The terms were exceptionally favourable, for Smith was keen to secure Thackeray, probably at any price. The story is well-known – Smith tells it himself – of how he visited Thackeray with the written offer that he hoped would secure him for the as yet unnamed magazine, how he wondered 'whether you will consider it, or will at once consign it to your wastepaper-basket', and how Thackeray, recognising of course the generosity of the terms 'with a droll smile [said] "I am not going to put such a document as *this* into my wastepaper-basket"'.[44] The original contract survives, in Smith's own hand, amongst the Thackeray family papers.[45]

> Smith Elder & Co have it in contemplation to commence the publication of a monthly Magazine on January 1st. 1860. They are desirous of inducing M^r. Thackeray to contribute to their periodical and they make the following proposal to M^r. Thackeray.
>
> 1/. That he shall write either one or two novels of the ordinary size for publication in the Magazine – one twelfth portion of each novel (estimated to be about equal to one number of a serial) to appear in each number of the Magazine.
>
> 2/. That M^r. Thackeray shall assign to Smith Elder & Co. the right to publish the novels in their Magazine and in a separate form afterwards, and to all sums to be received for the work from American and Continental Publishers
>
> 3/. That Smith Elder & Co shall pay M^r. Thackeray £350 each month
>
> 4/. That the profits of all editions of the novels published at a lower price than the first edition shall be equally divided between M^r. Thackeray and Smith Elder & Co.
>
> 65 Cornhill
> February 19th. 1859

The change from serving as a well-paid contributor to taking on in addition the editorship occurred sometime during the summer. Having tried and failed to secure as editor Thomas Hughes, the author of *Tom Brown's School Days*, and Thackeray's friend Alexander Scott, Principal of Owens College in Manchester, Smith considered other names but none seemed quite right. The answer came to him during his morning ride on Wimbledon Common.

> [T]hat good genius which has so often helped me whispered in my ear, 'Why should not Mr. Thackeray edit the magazine, you yourself doing what is necessary to supplement any

want of business qualifications on his part? You know that he has a fine literary judgment, a great reputation with men of letters as well as with the public, and any writer would be proud to contribute to a periodical under his editorship.'

After breakfast I drove straight to Thackeray's house in Onslow Square, talked to him of my difficulty, and induced him to accept the editorship, for which he was to receive a salary of 1,000l. a year.[46]

As the birth of this new venture approached, time and illness caught up with the Carmichael-Smyths who finally decided to leave Paris, as Thackeray records. 'Since her accident in September last, she shows that she is 67 years old, and walks very very slowly on her stick. Her husband is 80 and pretty well, and as good and gentle as old Colonel Newcome in his last days. We want to persuade them to a house at Brighton where we can be within reach, and she can get sermons of any required strength & length.'[47] The Carmichael-Smyths had been staying at Hythe near Folkestone all through September, but by the beginning of October they were still undecided what to do, and Thackeray gently pushed them towards a decision. Rather than moving to Brighton as he had hoped, they took a house near Onslow Square, at 52 Brompton Crescent. It would be their last move.

++++

With the final number of *The Virginians* completed on 7 September and his best fiction now behind him, Thackeray started to prepare for the inaugural number of the *Cornhill* and the start of his final adventure. He greatly admired the design of the magazine's paper wrappers, and liked the idea of launching the new vessel in its fresh yellow livery, as 'the good ship dips over the bar, and bounds away into the blue water'. Conscious that his partner lacked business skills, Smith controlled this side of the enterprise himself – indeed, the whole venture was at his financial risk – but neither of them foresaw that Thackeray's aversion to the drudgeries and disciplines of editorship would eventually drive him away. Yet in the months before the first issue of January 1860, both men were tireless in working for its success and in the securing of future contributors. The phenomenal reception of the early numbers, measured in high sales and the enthusiastic response of its readership, is captured by Henry James in his recall at the end of his life 'of the arrival, from the first number, of the orange-covered earlier Cornhill – the thrill of each composing item of that first number especially recoverable in its intensity. Is anything like that thrill possible today – for a submerged and blinded and deafened generation, a generation so smothered in quantity and number that discrimination, under the gasp, has neither air to breathe nor room to turn round?'[48]

The rediscovery of Smith's *Cornhill* letters to Thackeray permits a fresh view of their working relationship and of the early history of the magazine. Annie alluded to this correspondence in her preface to *Philip* for the Biographical Edition, although she made no use of it there. Matters of publishing policy were not really the kind of thing which interested her. She kept the letters, but bundled them together and put them aside. 'Messrs. Smith & Elder worked hard and converted their editor's suggestions into facts and realities, with an energy and a liberality very remarkable. I have a pile of old letters from them about *The Cornhill Magazine*, which are an example in themselves – punctual, orderly, sparing no trouble. There are more than one on the same day, entering in to every detail.'[49]

Having initiated discussions with a prospective author, Thackeray would leave Smith to clinch the deal. 'I will write to Trollope saying how we want to have him – you on your side please write offering the cash.'[50] Securing *Framley Parsonage* as a serial to open the January number proved to be crucial in sustaining the exceptional sales of the early months. An attempt to persuade the historian Thomas Carlyle to contribute something was unsuccessful – 'Is there any hope? Can you help an old friend? Have you never an unedited chapterkin, or a subject on w^h. you wish to speak to the public?'[51] Alfred Tennyson sent 'Tithonus' for the second number, though he expressed concern that Thackeray should have taken on the editorial role at all, the poet believing that such an arrangement must inevitably compromise a serious writer's freedom.

On balance, Tennyson was probably right. The routine nature of the work which now engaged Thackeray's energies was draining, not least when dealing with aspiring contributors. In addition, the two men had decided that their joint agreement should be required for each contribution accepted, an arrangement which began to creak even before the inaugural number appeared. There would be instances of Thackeray implying that what Smith had called his 'fine literary judgement' ought to prevail. It seems that he would tend to accept pieces and expect his partner's rubber stamp. 'My goodness! I daren't write to him & say it wont do – I wrote only yesterday to say I had sent to have it put into type.... I think you are too squeamish about the articles. Churchill, Bell, Edwards are all readable – the geniuses are very very rare.'[52] Smith took time to be persuaded of the merits of verses by the young Thomas Hood – 'I expect to find that I have been strangely mistaken as to their quality' – but the poems would appear during the opening few numbers. Thackeray was not beyond a little gentle bullying and threats. 'You are not converted about Hood's verses but I am sure they are true metal'; 'You must not refuse them or you will make a fool of me.'[53]

One must not take at face value Smith's subsequent claim that 'I used to drive round to his house in Onslow Square nearly every morning, and we discussed manuscripts and subjects together'.[54] That may have been how it worked at first, but his letters only occasionally mention prospective visits, in a context suggesting that they were scarcely daily, and Smith was evidently sensitive to the possibility that he was intruding. 'I will come for your decision tomorrow morning and if you say yes, will not interrupt you for five minutes'; 'I had intended to come to Onslow Square this morning but I thought that I had better not interrupt you.'[55] It is more likely that most of the detailed business was dealt with by correspondence, a messenger conveying the frequent exchanges between the *Cornhill* office and Brompton. Much later Annie recalled Smith visiting, 'driving in early, morning after morning, on his way to business, carrying a certain black bag full of papers and correspondence, and generally arriving about breakfast time'.[56] But her impressions of the period were filtered through Smith's account of the enterprise, and she remained typically hazy over detail. 'I am told that my Father demurred at first to the suggestion of editing the Cornhill.... I have an impression, also, besides the play, of very hard work and continuous work at that time; of a stream of notes and messengers from Messrs Smith and Elder; of consultations, calculations.'

Within a few months, the *modus operandi* for the working partnership was apparent. If Thackeray supplied undeniable literary gravitas and expertise, most of the hands-on work in assembling each number lay with the publisher. As Smith tried to beat each issue into shape, he did so with a barely-concealed anxiety that perhaps was not fully shared by Thackeray, whose own habits of working right up to a publishing deadline may have inured him to the concerns of the practical businessman. It was probably frustrating for Smith always to be the one to have to seek answers and suggest solutions, and doubtless he would have welcomed a shared sense of urgency. His letter sent as the deadline loomed for the June 1860 issue captures the tone.

> We are getting rather into a corner with the present number – I enclose a list of the contents as it may be made up – but you will observe that 'Muscular Hero Worship' and 'Sir Self

and Womankind' are included. The latter you did not think up to the mark, but what are we to do. As regards 'Muscular Hero Worship' I have taken out a good deal but even now I don't think it ought to go into the same number with your Roundabout Paper....

Can you give me the words for your Illustration of 'Lovel'?[57]

Much more to the novelist's taste were Smith's monthly dinners for contributors at his Gloucester Square home, for which in a number of instances he sent the invitations through Thackeray. The artists Frederic Leighton and Sir Edwin Landseer were secured in this way, as was Herman Merivale. In drawing up one guest list, Smith also remembered to ask Thackeray to puff the phenomenal sales of the magazine in the forthcoming number, thus tackling rivals who were talking them down.

I have asked Fields the American Publisher – who will I hope be interested in the CHM by and bye. I like him better than the Harpers. We are now 20 or with Mr Merivale 21 – and if he comes we ought to have another to make the table even.

We published the number this morning, and the demand has been as brisk as ever. I hear that people won't believe in our circulation – and talk of it as 30000. Could there be a little modest swagger on this point in the Preface.[58]

Smith's use of the term 'preface' for Thackeray's regular series of 'Roundabout Papers' captures one of their functions, as editorial introductions to individual numbers of the magazine. Sometimes they include internal references to neighbouring articles, and although they can read oddly when detached from that context this did not prevent Thackeray from agreeing to their republication as an independent volume. The first of the Roundabouts, 'On a Lazy Idle Boy', famously ends with the metaphor of a ship's voyage, emblematic of the optimistic adventure of the freshly-launched *Cornhill*, but the piece also defines (in more domestic terms) the magazine's rationale as a home for serious non-fiction ('plain wholesome tea and bread-and-butter') and not just for the latest serials ('tarts and ices'). Too much indulgence, it was suggested, dulled the taste for things of substance, and Thackeray imagines Dickens, Dumas and others enjoying fiction by other writers, but merely as a diversion. 'I make no doubt that the eminent parties above named all partake of novels in moderation

– eat jellies – but mainly nourish themselves upon wholesome roast and boiled.' Though he refused to take his craft over-seriously, his own fiction, with its broad canvas, episodic, complex plots with their persistent undercurrent of contemporary and historical allusions and expansive range of characters, demanded much of his readership.

Smith's wish to celebrate the outstanding sales of the first six issues resulted in a Roundabout Paper, 'On Some Late Great Victories', in which Thackeray began by writing about successful military skirmishes solely as a pretext for highlighting triumphs of a more prosaic nature in the literary market-place. 'The victories which I wish especially to commemorate in this the last article of our first volume, are the six great, complete, prodigious, and undeniable victories, achieved by the corps which the editor of the Cornhill Magazine has the honour to command.... "I say more than a hundred thousand purchasers – and I believe *as much as a million readers*!"' This effectively reproduced the point which Smith had made during the printing of the second number – '75000 of No 2 have been disposed of, and we are printing 100000! I hope this notable fact will excite attention and increase the demand. If only ten people read each copy (a moderate average) there are a million of readers.'[59]

At such times, Smith knew that he was receiving full value from his editor. And, of course, Thackeray's personal writing commitments for the *Cornhill* were extensive. *Lovel the Widower* appeared from January-June 1860, followed at once by *The Four Georges*, their first publication since being delivered as lectures. *Philip* started in January 1861, a novel which returned to his autobiographical vein by recalling early attempts at artistic training in Paris and which would, as he confided to Smith, 'tell pretty much the career of W.M.T. in the first years of his ruin and absurdly imprudent marriage'.[60] It ran monthly until August 1862. In addition to all of this, there were the regular series of Roundabouts and other occasional pieces.

Early in November 1860 Smith pressed for advertising copy for Thackeray's new work, so that he might provide an insert in the December number – 'Can you let me have the title and drawing for the advertisement slip of the new serial?'[61] It seems that on previously raising the matter Thackeray had not been best pleased with these further demands, though he quickly apologised. 'I am very sorry about the contretemps of yesterday. I never thought about the advertisement of the new story, any more than that S E & Co would announce it.'[62] The blurb was duly delivered, but so tight against the publishing deadline that not all of the December copies could include it. 'We shall not be able to insert it in all the copies of the Magazine, and had I kept it back

Page of the Roundabout Paper *'On Ribbons' in Minny's hand, with Thackeray's annotations*

until tomorrow 30000 or 40000 must have gone without it. Swain has not done justice to your Drawing but he had very little time, and I hope you will let it pass.'[63]

Over the next few days, a revealing exchange shows Thackeray undecided on his final title for his serial, and Smith making encouraging suggestions.

Thackeray to Smith [29 November][64]
Swain has got the 3 Initials and design for the large cut. A man in conversation used the words 'Fit for nothing' yesterday. Hang him, why did he not speak a week sooner

Smith to Thackeray 29 November
Why not call it 'Fit for Nothing or the Adventures of Philip' &c? It's not too late.... You know that Philip is the name of C Dickens' hero.[65]

Thackeray to Smith [?29 November]
As the posters are out, let Philip stand – and see if we cant make a good fight against tother Philip.

Smith to Thackeray 3 December
It occurred to me yesterday that we should lose the best part of the title of the story if we put no more than 'Philip' at the top of the first chapter. The title will appear no where else but in the advertisements until the story is completed. I have had the first page altered for you to see, but I don't know that it doesn't look best as it stood. Please say how it shall stand.

Thackeray to Smith [December]
How do you like

The adventures of
PHILIP
on his way through the world
Showing who robbed him, who helped him, and who passed him by.

The book will be called Philip, and it is as good a name as any other.

Thackeray was frequently ill when writing the early chapters of *Philip*, delaying its progress, so that by the end of April Smith had to report that the habitual late arrival of the numbers was causing problems with their American partner, Harpers. 'I hope we shall have "Philip" in good time. Low refused to take the sheets of the present number for Harper in consequence of our not presenting them early enough and we only induced him to take them by promising to keep back for a week the copies we send to America for sale. He has frequently complained and I doubt if he will renew the arrangements at the end of the year.'[66] Thackeray responded breezily. 'Make your mind easy. I expect we shall go into 25 pages – 23 are at the printers and the 2 last I have <u>had</u> copied, and will leave at the Printing office to send with the proofs to Low.'[67] His copyist on this occasion was Minny.

By July he could be more positive again – 'Here's Philip Thank God in good time'[68] – but this month also saw something of a crisis in the relations between the two men, with Thackeray again wanting to accept pieces which Smith subsequently vetoed. An article about the actor/playwright Charles Fechter by Mrs Pollock, together with an 'amusing little Irish fable' by Charles McKay, appealed sufficiently to Thackeray for him to want to take them – perhaps unwisely he had already given an undertaking to Mrs Pollock to that effect – but Smith was unconvinced. Thackeray knew that neither piece was worth fighting over, but his pride was pricked. An unsent draft of the letter written on 9 July shows that his departure as editor could only be a matter of time, offering stark evidence that Thackeray knew the best days of the *Cornhill* adventure were behind him. In the parts which he did not send Smith, he addressed the declining sales of the magazine, which had fallen away since its early and unprecedented success. Circulation had dropped by 1,000 since the completion of *Framley Parsonage* in April, and Trollope's next serial was not due to begin until August. Thackeray felt that his own salary should return to that originally paid when he first took on the editorship, which Smith had subsequently doubled: 'after Michaelmas say, instead of 166.6.8 let it be 83.3.4. – I don't say sooner, because I am as poor as may be, with those building engagements'. At the end of September, he was still being paid the higher salary, though by then even the ever-generous Smith thought that an adjustment might be warranted. 'I hope I may not have to come to you next month with a long face, and a proposal about the amount'.[69] But the more revealing aspect is Thackeray's recognition that their differences over editorial decisions was probably irreconcilable, and he did not want to lose Smith's friendship. '[Y]ou know there does not live a man for whom I entertain a greater personal regard and confidence. But about authors, artists, articles, we have such a difference of opinion that I own the future is very glum' (here he first wrote 'dark and cloudy').[70]

By December, a final disagreement over a piece by Herman Merivale sealed Thackeray's future with the *Cornhill*. He passed the manuscript to Smith and adopted a tone of special pleading, rather than arguing for the article on its merits. 'You must, please, let me accept the article from this good old friend and well-known Scholar. Let me have a word that I may write him a yes.'⁷¹ Smith's reply does not survive, but unlike his editor he had bothered to read Merivale's piece before deciding against it. The tone of Thackeray's answer is measured, but sad and reflective, the response of one whose frail health was to be expended on such trivial battles no longer.

> You have the pull over me in the argument, that you have read the paper, and I have not.
> BUT it is written by an eminent scholar and practised writer, whose works are received with welcome by the old reviews; and I should have accepted it, as you have accepted others, upon the character of the author.
> We agreed that both of us should have a veto upon articles, and in this case I can't complain if you exercise your's. [sic] We shall lose Merivale. I am sorry.⁷²

If there were any more disputes, we have no record of them. Thackeray took the next few weeks to reflect on his position, but surely did not doubt the eventual outcome. A final exchange of correspondence followed two meetings, on 3 and 5 March. In sadly accepting his editor's resignation, Smith conveys the strong impression that he had been misrepresented in Thackeray's opinion of him. Yet the affection remained on both sides.

> I have received your Notes of the 4th and 6th. Instant, and I am grateful to you for the kind manner in which you have conveyed to me the important and unexpected communication they contain.
> I forbear from entering into any discussion on the subject; but, perhaps I may be allowed to express my opinion that you have not been well advised. If, in your construction of my conduct towards you in respect of the 'Cornhill Magazine' you have done me any injustice, or if you are acting under a misconception of my feelings or motives, I dare say you will some day discover that you have been mistaken – and I shall then be set right in your opinion.
> In the mean time I must, of course, accept your decision as to withdrawing from the Editorship of the Magazine – though I deeply regret it – especially as you seem to think (I hope groundlessly) that it is necessary for me to acquiesce in your determination in order to preserve your friendship.⁷³

They agreed that the resignation announcement should not occur until 25 March, the date recorded on Thackeray's letter to *Cornhill* contributors, inserted as a slip into the April 1862 number. In this final public statement as editor, he returns once more to the image of the sea-bound voyage, but as seen and understood now by a weary and wiser captain. 'Those who have travelled on shipboard know what a careworn, oppressed, uncomfortable man the captain is. Meals disturbed, quiet impossible, rest interrupted – such is the lot of captains. This one resigns his commission.... I believe my own special readers will agree that my books will not suffer when their Author is released from the daily tasks of reading, accepting, refusing, losing and finding the works of other people. To say No has often cost me a morning's peace and a day's work.'[74] Particularly, it is fair to add, when his own inclination was to say 'Yes'.

Six

HERE IS NIGHT AND REST
(1860-1863)

Good night, friends, old and young! The night will fall: the stories must end: and the best friends must part.

Final lines of *Philip*

Virtually all of Thackeray's surviving correspondence during the more than two years that he edited the *Cornhill* relates to the routine business of the magazine. Letters to friends are fewer and shorter than before, and in one he depicted the dulling cycle of a routine in which he felt himself trapped. 'I have a Magazine once a month, a fever attack once a month, the charge of old folks and young folks whom I have to take to the country or arrange for at home – a great deal of business & bad health, and very little order.'[1] Nor did the volume of personal correspondence pick up once he was freed from the *Cornhill*, and few letters can be dated to these last months of his life.

There are, however, other authorities for the closing scenes of one of the great figures of the mid-Victorian period. Long before this, Annie and Minny had begun to emerge as informative and witty correspondents, even if relatively few of their letters written before their father's death survive. Although she had been keeping a diary each year, the journal which Annie later compiled from them only starts from 1860. Her diaries for the earlier years were either lost or destroyed even before the journal was constructed in the late 1890s, and the condition of the survivors was probably fragile. As she noted on the journal's opening page, '1860 an old book gnawed & torn by Gumbo our puppy. He used to eat every conceivable thing.' Once she had selected from and edited those diaries which had survived, they were burnt.

Annie's journal is valuable and frustrating in equal measure, an amalgamation of materials which represent her old and young selves.

Whilst many entries were probably copied into the journal verbatim, elsewhere there is editing, refinement, and omission. What was once clear can become clouded. The journal is therefore an essential supplement to other materials, but it has its own story to tell, and it chooses not to tell everything.

After completion of *The Virginians* in September 1859, father and daughters went travelling, during which the first number of the *Cornhill* was being planned. Annie thrilled at the squalor of much of what they saw as they passed through France. Their Bordeaux hotel was filthy, 'some swell apartments reeking with dinner, & no wonder', and they visited wine vaults in the old quarter, 'quite awful enough goodness knows with rampant fungi & creeping & slimy & oozy horrors'. At the quay they were attracted by the flat-bottomed barges, one of them piled high with onions and just one old woman crouching in it, so Annie proudly passed on one of her father's puns, with its contemporary literary reference. 'Papa called her The Lady of Shalott.'[2] In retelling the story years later she confessed to not knowing Tennyson's poem at the time, and that her father had to explain the joke.

From Genoa, Thackeray brought Mrs Baxter up to date on news of the last year or two. 'I have had at least 20 attacks of confounded spasms, w^h. are death-like whilst they last − (I mean I hardly know what happens what with pain, laudanum, & so forth) and then 2 or 3 days of recovery, and then the printer's devil at the door again, and the unavoidable chapter to be done − The unhappy book is all the worse for the ill health of the author.'[3] When they reached Switzerland Annie was taken ill with dysentery, 'not dangerous the Doctor says, but tedious',[4] and Minny proved her customary worth as a nurse.

The startling initial success of the *Cornhill* contributed to Thackeray's wish for a move to grander living quarters, fit for an editor, and he fixed on a property at Kensington Palace Green, just a few hundred yards from their old Young Street home, but altogether more fashionable. He told Smith that it was where he hoped one day to write his history of the reign of Queen Anne. That work would never even be started, but the house itself was completely rebuilt in Queen Anne style, paid for by his *Cornhill* earnings, and it was two years before they could take possession.

Annie and Minny were now moving within the literary and social circle to which as Thackeray's daughters they were given access. Most days would involve visiting, followed by an evening event or dinner, sometimes invited as their father's companions but increasingly in their own right too. At Onslow Square, they were Thackeray's hostesses. His new financial success purchased comforts for them all, with gestures towards a new kind of status, including a carriage and pair. They had also become involved in 'good works', giving tea-parties for local poor children with 'a good deal of district visiting & workhouse'.[5] It was what many Victorian women of their class did.

Annie exaggerated Thackeray's personal satisfaction in his *Cornhill* work, but the editorship carried a certain cachet. And for her, a new world was about to open up. Surrounded by manuscripts arriving from hopeful contributors made her conscious of a magazine's constant need for publishable material, and it was surely inevitable that she should develop the ambition first expressed five years earlier to Mrs Fanshawe. A great flow of writing projects in her teenage years had been abandoned at her father's insistence that first she should read more. Even as a child she had composed little plays and other pieces for the amusement of her friends and family. As early as 1847, her grandmother noted this 'fancy for writing plays', and recently her father had seen in her the facility which might earn her some kind of living. Annie's early letters show a liveliness of imagination and fluency of style, but in discouraging her from rushing into print, Thackeray wanted to protect her from being judged harshly as his daughter. Above all, he wanted her to develop the confidence which would benefit from good examples. Asked forty years later when she had first started writing, Annie told George Smith that 'I had written several novels & a tragedy but at the age of 15 my papa forbade me to waste my time [on] any more scrabbling & directed me to read <u>other</u> peoples books. I never wrote any more, except one short fairytale, till one day he said he had got a very nice subject for me and that he thought I might now begin to write again & that was Little Scholars w^h. he christened for me & of w^h. he corrected the stops & the spelling & w^h. you published to my (still) pride & rapture.'[6]

'Little Scholars' took up the topic of charity schools and appeared in May 1860, to be followed by many more pieces for the *Cornhill*. Her father knew that it ought to be published, but he doubted his objectivity and placed Annie's fate in Smith's hands. His first instinct had been to encourage her to send it to *Blackwood's Magazine*, but then thought better of losing out to a rival. 'And in the meanwhile comes a little Contribution called "Poor Scholars" w^h. I send you, and w^h. moistened my paternal spectacles. It is the article I talked of sending to Blackwood; but why should CornHill lose such a sweet paper, because it was my dear girl who wrote it? Papas, however, are bad judges – you decide whether we shall have it or not. And if we take it, shall we take it for this month, & keep over Higgins for June?'[7] That last practical question anticipates Smith's approval, and his endorsement of the proposed publishing schedule. Smith replied at once.

> I have only been able to look at the Manuscript you sent me this morning. I cannot read it, here, amidst continual interruptions, but I have seen enough of it to say, please let us have it for No 5 and allow Mr Higgins' article to stand over until June....
>
> I don't like to commit myself to an opinion about the 'Little Scholars' until I have read the M.S., but I think it will be found charmingly fresh and genuine, and I have fallen against some passages which will moisten other than paternal eyes. Please give my humble duty to our distinguished Contributor.[8]

Paternal pride led Thackeray to encourage friends to hunt out the piece. 'Read the Cornhill Magazine for May the article little Scholars is by my dear old fat Anny.'[9] Predictably malicious comments appeared by Edmund Yates in *The New York Times* to the effect that the *Cornhill* was in decline, that George Smith knew nothing about literature, and that 'Little Scholars' 'bears traces of being touched up by the parental hand'. These remarks were picked up and partly reported in the *Saturday Review*, and Thackeray's anger resulted in the measured irony of his Roundabout 'On Screens in Dining Rooms', which scorned 'Mr. Nameless' and censured 'Mr. Saturday Reviewer' in a manner which made him confident that 'our friend won't sin again'.[10]

Acquaintances continued to send their best wishes for the magazine's success, Thomas Carlyle doing so in the kind of nautical terms that Thackeray himself enjoyed. 'Fair wind and full sea to you in this hitherto so successful voyage; for which the omens certainly are on all sides good.'[11] He took his daughters to Tunbridge Wells for some of the summer of 1860, from where Minny described the shaming behaviour of their puppy, named after one of the black servants in *The Virginians*. '[Y]esterday we met a little boy walking between two nurses who must have been a little Marquis at least for he had such a lovely blue velvet frock on. Gumbo no sooner sees him than he dashes forward with his dirty paws & jumps on the little blue velvet back and tries to bite his feathers and his curls.'[12] The sisters succeeded in persuading their grandparents to come to Tunbridge, a prospect which alarmed their father. 'Yes, but where am I to sit, and how am I to work with those old folks in a house w^h. is already too full?'[13] In the middle of September they snatched a week or so in Holland, looking at galleries. In Amsterdam Annie concluded that Rembrandt had no equal, receiving the parental endorsement: 'Papa said so too'.

Plans by the Baxters to come to England in the autumn did not materialise. On Christmas Day Thackeray wrote to New York, sad to hear of the secession of South Carolina after the election of Lincoln as President, for the married Sally Baxter was living in the first state to break from the Union. 'Is it this horrid Separation that has prevented your all coming to Europe.... My dear relations are furious at my arrogance extravagance & presumption in building a handsome house, and one of them who never made a joke in his life said yesterday to me "You ought to call it Vanity Fair".'[14]

Forty years after they were written, Annie pasted her New Year's resolutions for 1861 into her journal with a comment which reflected the reality. 'Good resolutions (1901 still making them!)'

> Work 3 hours a day
> Keep house &ct 1 & a half
>
> | 8 to 9 | 10 to 12 | 12 to 1.30 | 2.30 to 5.30 |
> |---|---|---|---|
> | bkfast &ct. | go out | read | drive &ct |
> | 5.30 . 6.30 | 6.30 . 7 | | |
> | read | dress | | |
>
> and write of an evening:
> spend £5 a month.
> Have spent 10 a month as yet.

January opened sadly with the illness and death of Thackeray's old friend, Jane Elliot. She and her sister, Kate Perry, had acted as his intimate confidantes all through the Jane Brookfield affair. The closest experience that Annie had yet had of death touched her deeply.

> We went to Mrs Elliots one eve^g & she was very kind & said I have been ill, very ill indeed. Then she asked us to go again on a certain day. On the 9 of Jan we heard that she was dead.... I remember running up to Papas room he was in his shirt sleeves dressing & I hugged him round the waist & cried. That day I went to Chesham Place & saw her in her coffin. I had never seen anyone dead before. She looked very noble very kind. I seemed to love her as I had never loved her before.
>
> 15 [January]. Papa called us quite cheerfully to go to Mrs Elliots funeral & he & Minnie & I stood together.

But the matter-of-factness with which her father viewed death struck home, for within days Annie was writing to her grandmother's Parisian friend, Mrs Corkran, explaining why she had been feeling low. 'But now as is the usual way I believe we have forgotten all about it & put

Death aside until it gives us another reminder and Im sure this is what was intended & that Life was given to live with & not only to help us to brood over Death.'[15] Minny shared their father's capacity to focus upon the business of living, although his own death proved to be the exception, representing a loss which both daughters found impossible to accept.

Jane Elliot had been closely involved in charity school work – probably the inspiration for Annie's 'Little Scholars' – and Thackeray was keen to ensure that they should help in the work that she had left. He pressed the point on Kate Perry. 'What can we do for the schools? That is what she would like best. The girls will gladly go and work there; and their Father will give anything you want.'[16] It was not mere talk, for at the end of the month Annie records going 'to Mrs Elliots schools, saw Miss Perry there'.

There were now two Thackerays writing at Onslow Square. The first number of *Philip* appeared in January; 'Little Scholars' had been followed by 'How I Quitted Naples', and now Annie was tidying up another *Cornhill* piece, 'Toilers and Spinsters', touching on the work of the Society for Promoting the Employment of Women. On 8 February she and Amy Crowe collected Mrs Carmichael-Smyth and in the carriage and pair drove to Pall Mall where George Smith had opened a second Smith, Elder office in January. He accepted the contribution, and it appeared in March. The essay is enlightened and informed, but at the same time a prisoner of its social assumptions, with its clear distinction between 'ladies' and 'women'. Having seen women at work in a printing-press and as legal copyists she concludes that where poverty is the alternative, 'ladies' should not shun the dignity of women's work.

> In these two places I have seen in what way ladies have tried to help, not ladies, but women of a higher class than needlewomen and shopwomen and servants. Ladies – those unlucky individuals whose feelings have been trained up to that sensitive pitch which seems the result of education and cultivation, and which makes the performance of the common offices of life a pain and a penalty to them – might perhaps at a pinch find a livelihood in either of these offices, or add enough to their store to enable them at least to live up to their cultivated feelings.... Scarcely any work that is honest and productive can be degrading.

Such class-ridden assertions are scarcely to be wondered at. Her own social and sexual naïveté was not helped by the occasional crass, if presumably well-intentioned interventions of her father, all too conscious that 'no one has come to marry either of my dear girls'.[17] There was a ghastly moment at a fashionable ball in Dover Street, when Thackeray approached the only man wearing a black tie. 'Papa said to him I will give you 2/6 if you will dance with my daughter. I liked dancing but not the tie or the 2/6.'[18] But no-one was more naturally tender-hearted and comforting at moments of personal crisis. Annie was once taken ill when visiting friends at Little Holland House, and had to stay overnight. 'When Papa came to see me at Mrs Irvines I said I was so <u>frightened</u> when I thought I was dying. He said I once thought I was dying & I wasnt frightened please God when the <u>real</u> thing comes one is not frightened & this was because you were <u>not</u> dying.'

Even now, Annie and Minny were surprisingly unworldly and guileless, showing a gaucheness which may have reflected their motherless, bookish circumstances. They were susceptible to natural beauty and responsive to people and ideas, but clothes and fashion passed them by. Sitting up one evening in Onslow Square waiting for her sister's return from a ball, Annie leant from the window to witness the sunrise, captivated by the moment. It came as a surprise the next day to be told by a friend what really mattered. 'Lolla Sterling reproached me & said you didn't get her up nicely eno' – We never thought about her dress either of us.' The relationship which this suggests, that somehow the twenty-one-year-old Minny was still under Annie's care, is revealing. Yet in Annie's first ever letter to Mrs Baxter, written just at this time, she sets out Minny's quiet strength and resourcefulness. 'Im nearly 24 & Minny nearly 21 and absurdly young for her age for she still likes playing with children and kittens & hates reading & is very shy tho' she does not show it & very clever tho' she does not do any thing in particular and always helps me out of scrapes w^h. I am always getting into.'[19] Minny developed a refined taste in clothes and confident ideas about design, whereas for Annie getting such things right would always be a matter of chance.

As news of the opening skirmish in the Civil War came in with the attack on Fort Sumter in Charleston Harbour, Annie provides Mrs Baxter with a wonderfully concise checklist of the Onslow Square household and the faint aura of chaos which filled it.

> Do you know what our household consists of 1. a little dog with a curly tail. 2. 3. Jack & Jill two puppies that squeak a good deal 4 a little cat passionately attached to Papa, & she purrs & jumps on his knee & wont be turned off. 5 a certain kind gentleman whose picture I send you – tho' to

me it is not him a bit. 6 Miss Anny 7 Miss Minny... Then there is Amy Crowe who has lived with us these 7 years & who is one of the best and gentlest & kindest of women and then there is a faithful but tearful & affected cook, a pretty little maid called Fanny who is literary & quotes the Cornhill Magazine; and a gawky housemaid; and also a faithful reckless youth who breaks the china & tumbles down stairs & is called the Butler... The news of the Fort-battle came in after I began my letter and now I am almost ashamed to send such twaddle when you must be think[ing] & talking of wars & politics and presidents – and anything but puppies and kittens.

During July news of the death of 'our dear Mrs Browning' reached them from Italy. Elizabeth Barrett Browning's last poem had appeared in June in the *Cornhill*, and she had written to Thackeray sending her customary affectionate greetings to his daughters. 'Where are you all, Annie, Minnie – why don't you come and see us in Rome? My husband bids me give you his kind regards, and I shall send Pen's love with mine to your dear girls.'[20] Thackeray took his daughters to Folkestone, a frequent resting-place when he was in search of sea air and calm. This time it was Annie who was ailing. The girls said their goodbyes to their grandparents, for the Carmichael-Smyths were heading north to Scotland on a trip of their own. It was the last time that they would see their grandfather – 'he was over 80 but very young'.

Thackeray had reached that point in *Philip* which was most closely autobiographical, the years of his 'ruin and absurdly imprudent marriage', recalled with unnerving honesty from the distance of a quarter of a century. After a month in Folkestone he travelled to France, beset by 'sickness and spasms accompanied with diarrhoea',[21] and Amy Crowe and his daughters left for north Wales and a little adventure of their own, Sir Anthony de Rothschild joking with them that the 'Misses Thackeray [were] going to Wales to get Welsh husbands'. They stayed with Amy Crowe's married sister at Bronywendon and visited Caernarvon and Llandudno. On 10 September, Annie and Amy were returning from a mountain trip, and on seeing a telegraph boy approaching feared bad news, for they had heard nothing of Thackeray for several days. 'We were frightened about him. The news of our dear dear GPs death seemed almost a relief at the moment. We 3 girls set off at night bravely under stars & then by Chester & by Carlisle & thro the Cumberland passes late at night we got to Ayr.' Their relief at discovering that Thackeray had already arrived from France and was asleep was such that they rushed to wake him. It had been a quick and peaceful end for their grandfather, who had been ill only for a matter of hours and 'quite well and cheerful the night before he was sent for'.[22] He was buried the day after their arrival in Ayr, '& the sun shone & we came away & Grannie came with us & lived in Onslow Sq. She looked so tall & beautiful in her black & he too looked so big & so noble taking care of her.'[23] It was 'the first break that came in our home'.

Mrs Carmichael-Smyth soon became restless for Paris again, making several visits, some quite extended, during her last years. Her son had predicted her future precisely. 'There's a little clique of old ladies there who are very fond of her and with whom she is a much more important personage than she is in this great city. If anything happens to the Major she will go to Paris and give us the slip and grumble when she is there and presently come back.'[24] He wondered whether she was due East India Company pension benefits accruing from her short first marriage to his father, Richmond Thackeray, and he enlisted George Smith's help – the firm of Smith, Elder having significant Indian interests. The records of the Bengal Civil Fund had gone missing, but Smith asserted that 'if M^{rs}. Smyth received any pension from the Fund during her first widowhood, there is not the slightest doubt but that she will now be entitled to the same pension – and I would strongly advise her to make an application for it'.[25] But there were no recollections of any earlier pension. There had been confusion before Richmond's death in 1815, and Thackeray told of his father's anger when a relation failed to subscribe to the Fund, 'but on the other hand he thought he had left his widow and son provided for, so we can't, you see, make a claim as of right'.[26]

After his stepfather's death, Thackeray again considered having the surgical procedure which might sort out 'my old thorn in the flesh',[27] but prevaricated once he heard of recent failures for the operation. He decided that he needed to finish *Philip* first, and his constant balancing of the medical risks against the likely benefits meant that a right moment for the treatment never came. Even a successful operation could not have prevented his death from stroke, except that it would have removed the stricture as a source of stress and given him greater comfort and social ease in his last years. But having virtually resolved by the end of 1861 to give up the *Cornhill*, and with the completion of the Palace Green house drawing closer, he was able to contemplate a less harassed future.

The prospect of the move was exciting for all of them. It was Minny who suggested putting on a play for their friends in the large vacant rooms of Palace Green, a salute to the house in advance of the move itself. Thackeray's never-staged 1855 comedy *The Wolves and the Lamb* could be seen at last; he had recently recast it as a short novel, *Lovel the Widower*, for the opening few numbers of the *Cornhill*. It was the kind of imaginative idea that came readily to his younger daughter. Realising that that she was the best-organised of all of them, Thackeray had appointed her his 'housekeeper', responsible for instructing the servants and managing the household budget. This subtly rewarded her strengths whilst freeing Annie to inhabit the imaginative world which increasingly attracted her. It would be Minny who proposed that they should have 'a great poor childrens feast on N.Y. Day in the new house. Why not?'[28] Nothing came of this, but plans for the play-making went ahead, Thackeray seeking a special favour of the kind which George Smith was always happy to expedite. 'Will you have the Wolves & the Lamb printed for us? The girls are wild to act it.'[29] Smith entered into the spirit of the enterprise at once. 'I shall be delighted to print the Play for the Ladies – and when we come to the rose colored Play bills we will prove our taste. I will submit a specimen page of the Play to the Stage Managers very soon.'[30] This happy transaction occurred just as Thackeray and Smith approached the crisis of their *Cornhill* relationship, an indication that the foundations of the friendship itself were never seriously threatened.

At the turn of the year, 36 Onslow Square played host to young Willie Ritchie, eldest son of Thackeray's cousin William (who was based in Calcutta as legal member of the Governor-General's council). The Ritchie children lived with their aunts Charlotte and Jane in India and became steadily closer to the Thackerays after William Ritchie's death on 22 March, the news of which did not reach London until mid-April. Ten-year-old Willie was a pupil at a small English preparatory school, Whitnash Rectory near Leamington in Warwickshire. For Thackeray, the circumstances recalled his own childhood, sent from Calcutta to be schooled in England and dependent on the kindnesses of previously unknown relatives, and during the Christmas holiday Willie joined his Thackeray cousins to be pampered. A rare portion of Minny's diary survives for the first few days of January, giving a flavour of the entertainments which the cousins enjoyed together. 'Henny Cole & Emily Cope called to ask me to go next day to the Messiah after lunch went with Willie to the South Kensington Museum. Willie rather liked the raw produce but had no notion of pictures. Papa wanted to take him to the Pantomime but Willie w^d not go as Anny wanted to go too & c^d. not at that time.' They fitted in the pantomime at the Haymarket two days later – 'very good Little Miss Muffat & the big spider & little boy blue'. In between expeditions and walks with Willie, Minny found time to copy out the latest number of *Philip* for posting to the American publishers. Both daughters now shared these copying and occasional amanuensis roles; pages survive in Minny's hand of a 'Roundabout Paper' written to Thackeray's dictation with his own annotations.[31] (See illustration on p.137.)

Minny's well-organised rehearsal schedule culminated in two performances of *The Wolves and the Lamb* given by the W (Empty) [*WMT*] House Theatricals on 24 and 25 February, exactly a month before their move to the house itself. Annie sat and watched the evening rehearsal, entranced as friends were translated into creatures of fantasy.

> The theatre was put up in the dining room at Palace Green & the play came to life in the most wonderful & enchanting way. It was all alight coloured moving interesting, the people were all themselves & yet other selves. Minny as a peasant girl in a big mob cap was the sweetest & merriest thing that ever was seen. Herman [Merivale] as Capt Touchit thrilling & delightful – hansome little Sir C Young as Milliken with a profile a grand air Bella Bayne as Mrs Prior was simply perfect. Mrs Caulfield was only herself but Minnie as Mrs Milliken aged portentous – I shrieked with excitement over her mittens & her prunella shoes.... Papa was amused & delighted – Everyone was in fun & good humour clapping laughing admiring. Amy looked after the properties. We have a little china cup in the drawingroom w^h was put out for a stage property & I can hear my daddy telling us to take it away. Its about the best bit of china I have got he said. It w^d be a pity to break it.

A few days before the performances Minny wrote to invite the Smiths, wanting to enlist their loyal and loud support. 'Will you ask Mr Smith to be sure to applaud even if every thing should go wrong.'[32] The triumph of the evenings was chronicled proudly by Annie, no performer herself and happy to enjoy Minny's success. 'I remember standing by Papa when all was over & saying goodbye to the guests. Many of them I didnt know & had been asked by the actors. I remember such an odd feeling came over me. I suppose this is the summit I shall never feel so jubilant so grand so wildly important & happy again – It was a sort of feeling like fate knocking at the door.'

Independent witnesses testify to Minny's talent for acting. The sister-in-law of Jane (Jeanie) Nassau Senior (the married sister of Thomas Hughes) remembers that her portrayal was 'admirably droll', for she 'was a first-rate actress'.[33] Blanche Ritchie, Willie's sister, was

Six: Here is Night and Rest   153

Sketch by Thackeray

still living in Paris when the *Wolves and the Lamb* was performed, but would soon come to London after the death of her father. On a number of occasions during the months which followed she saw evidence of Minny's talent, and the memories remained with her fifty years later.

> The youngest daughter of the house, Minny Thackeray, afterwards Mrs. Leslie Stephen, with a complexion of milk and roses, and sunny nineteen-year-old hair, had impersonated Lovel's deposed mother-in-law with a front, and irresistible wit.... Mrs. Leslie Stephen had a beautiful and flexible voice, most apt at reproducing comedy but low-toned in a crowd, and especially making itself felt amongst many voices, as John Addington Symonds once pointed out to me. She had the gift of creating calm.[34]

Minny's creativity was not confined to acting. She was a Thackeray too, and in February her father commented on a story that she was composing. 'I think Harriet had best be left alone altogether, or certainly wait until it is completed. The author is very doubtful about it. So is her Papa.'[35] 'The Fox and the Cat, An Irish Fable' was duly completed, and at some stage set up in print and proof-corrected by her father, but it was not until 1911 and Annie's Centenary Edition of her father's works that her sister's long-forgotten work was finally published.[36] None of the several surviving fragments and ideas for other stories was ever completed.

Just over a week after the theatrical house-warmings Thackeray resigned as *Cornhill* editor, even as Annie was working on her first piece of sustained fiction, *The Story of Elizabeth*, which ran for five consecutive numbers of the magazine from September. 'It was when we were leaving Onslow Sq. that I began Elizabeth & scrawled away in the window to the sound of the Church bells that used to fill the green drawingroom.... [Minny] said write about our life at Paris Annie ... & so I wrote my first novel as hard as I could write on all sorts of untidy scraps of paper & then I stuffed it away & did not think any more of it, in the great events of the play & the move.'[37]

The long-awaited transfer to Palace Green occurred on 24 March. Meanwhile, Sally Baxter – Sally Hampton since her marriage – was dying of consumption in Charleston and writing her last letter to Thackeray, the sounds of the Fort Sumter band carrying her back to ballroom days, and to memories of her kind English admirer. The Civil War separated her from her family in New York, and her own loyalties were divided. It was easier for her to send word to England than to communicate with her parents in the north.

> I am far different from the gay girl you perhaps remember, years and years ago. I have been at death's door for many months now with one hemorrage [*sic*] after another wasting my little remaining strength. My poor Father and Mother, my only sister, do not even know that I live, or if they do, only that, – for a year we have had little intercourse, – for six months, none. I hear from them now and again to say they live and are well. If you get this, write and tell them of me, or send the letter. If you care to write to me, and you will care, I am sure, when you think how doubly dear the letter will be to me now, send it enclosed to the house of Fraser, Trenhold and Co., Liverpool, directed inside to me, Charleston. It will run the blockade, and come to me safely and secretly, or go to the bottom of the fathomless ocean, that tells no tales.[38]

Sally's letter probably reached England soon after the news of William Ritchie's death in India. Thackeray travelled to Paris to be with Charlotte and Jane and the Ritchie children, who, as he commented

Six: Here is Night and Rest

drily, seemed remarkably untroubled in their loss. 'The children [are] like children. All gone to the grandes eaux at Versailles.'[39] For them, India seemed a long way away; for him, America was less so. Back in his new Kensington surroundings, he would write to New York offering sympathy and more tangible support, for memories of earlier times seemed very poignant now.

> I know what your feelings are; loyal Northerns though you may be, with the daughter and grandchildren in the South who look at us out of our photograph book so innocent & pretty.... Now tell me my dear kind good Baxter and wife – there may be troubles at home – no dividends – the deuce to pay. I know a fellow who is not rich, for he has spent all his money in building this fine house: all but a very little – but who knows? Draw on me for 500£ at 3 months after date: and I am your man. You wont be angry? You may be worth millions; and laugh at my impudence: – I dont know but I dont mean no harm. Only I remember and shall all my life the kindness and hospitality of the dear old brown house.[40]

Everything seemed to be changing. Copying a hair style seen modelled on a statue in the 1862 London Exhibition, Minny altered her appearance to something more adult. 'She turned it up in pretty loose wavy loops instead of the little tight plats she had always worn & her cheeks became pink and I felt very proud of her.'[41] Perhaps this was the occasion when she and Annie took the two eldest Ritchie girls, Gussie and Blanche to the Exhibition, and Blanche bought ices for them all. The widowed Mrs Ritchie arrived home from India in June and came to stay, and Annie grew very fond of her future mother-in-law. Her grandmother wrote from Paris to Annie for her twenty-fourth birthday, reflecting quietly on a year of sadness. 'Well well they are happy years that gave us our dearest Nan & we grow old in welcoming them – & thinking of bygones that make the eyes dim & the heart lonely, while they draw us nearer to the Home where there is no more sorrow or separation.'[42]

Thackeray put the final touches to *Philip* at the start of July, the pressures of work lifting from his shoulders in the peace of the new house. 'Sitting in this beautiful room, surrounded by ease and comfort and finishing the story, I stop writing for a minute or two, with rather a full heart.'[43] He seemed ready to stand aside for Annie whose serial would shortly start to appear. 'I think the novel-writing vein is used up though, and you may be sure some kind critics will say as much for

Letter from Minny Thackeray to Annie Thackeray, with sketch, 1862

me before long. Anny's style is admirable, and Smith and Elder are in raptures about it. But she is very modest and I am mistrustful too. I am sure I shant love her a bit better for being successful. They are both of them beginning to bewail their Virginity in the mountains.'[44]

Another cousin, Edward Thackeray, had become a frequent visitor during 1862. It rapidly became evident that he was interested in Amy

Crowe, a friendship which the household encouraged even though the thought of losing her was painful. Mrs Carmichael-Smyth wondered whether the visits would ever lead to anything – 'why does Edward come so often, he'll be getting <u>lackadaisycle</u> [*sic*] & that wont do by no means'.[45] Edward duly proposed and was at first refused, at which point Annie and Minny talked to Amy about her true feelings. On 25 July they encouraged Edward to ask again, and three days later 'everything was happily settled. He had cared for Amy for a year.' What was hardest to contemplate was that his position in the Indian army meant that they would leave England, the latest in the clan of Thackerays and Ritchies to undertake the difficult passage. But gaining Amy for the family placed a permanent seal upon the exceptional friendship that she had offered them for years. The wedding was fixed for 6 December at St Mary Abbott's in Kensington, and naturally Amy would be married from Palace Green.

At the beginning of November Annie suffered one of the neuralgia attacks which plagued her from this time onwards, and her father insisted that she should accompany Julia Margaret Cameron to her Freshwater home in the Isle of Wight to revive. Mrs Cameron, shortly to discover the genius for photography which made her famous, would become even closer to the Thackeray sisters in the years after their father's death, drawing them into her intimate Freshwater circle which included the Tennysons, the painter George Frederic Watts and her sister, Sara Prinsep (who with her husband Thoby Prinsep were the long-term patrons of Watts). Her niece, Julia Jackson, became one of Annie's most intimate friends, a role which acquired a special poignancy when, after Minny's death, Julia became Leslie Stephen's second wife.

Annie had already witnessed Mrs Cameron's startling talent for embarrassing her friends, having gone with her in London to hear William Brookfield preach. 'Mrs Cameron led the way into the gallery & took up her place in the front exactly facing the pulpit. When the service was over & Mr Brookfield appeared climbing the pulpit stairs his head was so near us that we could almost have touched him. M^{rs}. Cameron chose this moment to lean forward & kiss her hand repeatedly. Poor M^r. Brookfield sank suddenly down upon his knees & buried his face in the pulpit cushion'. Once she reached Freshwater, Annie wrote to her friend Jeanie Senior. 'Its great fun here & I came, not to be made well so much as for a lark. M^{rs}. Cameron is so kind – The cottage is like a little scene at the play – Here is M^{rs}. Cameron in a blue little jacket writing letters at the table there is M^r. Watts in an arm chair talking about you – He says you are his old friend & that he knows no

such intellect (I was not desired to send this part of the message)....
Ive had my head turned by taking a walk and talking a talk with M^r. Tennyson – He is very good to know – I really think one is better for having seen him – at least one w^d. like to be.'[46]

Minny kept her sister supplied with the Kensington gossip. It seemed that everyone was getting engaged around them, and Annie was told to keep secret the news that their friend Ella Merivale would probably marry Peere Williams-Freeman. 'Papa came down to have some chicken just as Edward had eaten the two wings. I felt as if I could have eaten E, but Papa said he liked legs so I forgive him. I am afraid you must think this rather commonplace after your Tennysonian walks.'[47] Annie was back for the rather delightful supper party at Palace Green before Amy's marriage, organised according to a novel do-it-yourself theme. Each member of the small circle of hand-picked guests was assigned a different dish to prepare. Thackeray and the great Hungarian violinist Joseph Joachim were paired off to make a salad, a task which they undertook with great attention to detail. It is unlikely that any of those present had ever before stepped into a kitchen in the course of their adult lives, certainly not with the intention of attempting anything useful once they were within its doors. But at least the salad should have been edible.

The Thackerays missed Amy dreadfully after her marriage, and Christmas Eve was melancholy. Even the fires went out. On Christmas Day Thackeray wrote to the Baxters, having learnt of the expected death of Sally, and shared in their grief by recalling the loss of Jane so many years before. He would always remember Sally as he had known her in New York. 'What a bright creature! What a laugh, a life, a happiness! And it is all gone: and you dear people sit bewailing your darling.... This morning I was lying awake in the grey looking out at the elms, and thinking of your dear Sarah. God be with us. I dont feel much care about dying. As we love our children, wont our Father love us?'[48] Their Christmas sadness dissipated towards the new year, and they took a walk with Edward and Amy and went to the pantomime. The newly-weds did not leave for India until later in January, which was when Annie became aware of her father's distress at losing the woman who had become like a third daughter to him. 'Just been to see Amy & Edward off. I remember her back getting into the cab in the mist. God speed to them. Knocked at Papas door he wouldn't let me in.'

Later in the year, she wrote one of the reflective self-assessments which became something of a speciality, years afterwards copying it into her journal. It is a surprise to discover that at twenty-six she felt she might have reached 'a difficult age', but a recognition that her comfortable life lacked risk, that there was a danger of trading happiness for dreaming, indicates a yearning for something beyond her current experience. This was not a romantic or emotional frustration so much as a fear of opportunities being lost for ever.

> Here is a page written in 1863. It is morbid but sensible ... a little more courage honour uprightness and decision – Perhaps mine is a difficult age – its possible I feel older than there is any need for at 26. At all events if I dont take myself smartly in hand my future existence will be embittered by my feebleness and irresolution. It is difficult to remember things of every sort without unnecessary agonies. It is a great thing to lead a diligent and conscientious life & I do so hate being either the one or the other. Another great thing [is] to feel quietly settled down & to take things worst or best as they may happen to come. I am sometimes wretched about the house & the unnecessary expences for which Papa has to toil & weary. I am sometimes miserable about my Min because I think she is not so happy as she might be. Happiness is I do believe a very negative blessing after all. Happiness takes away a thousand other means of enjoyment, of understanding of speculating of dreaming.

She endeavoured to convey these private thoughts to her aunt, Jane Shawe. It is a troubled letter, dwelling on the passage of time and inevitable mortality, and the breakdown that would follow her father's death a very few months later is scarcely to be wondered at in one already close to nervous collapse.

> I get more & more puzzled & dazzled every year I live. I cant understand anything, or <u>you</u>, or myself, or going to church or keeping away, or how I dare to be happy or how I dare to be unhappy. I am afraid of the future I dont want to live the past over again, I dont want to last for ever I dont want to ever to stop [*sic*] I don't like doing right & I don't like doing <u>wrong</u>, & yet existing is delightful. I wonder, shall we ever understand? – I daresay not – I cant imagine that our intelligence should ever grasp the infinite – I cant imagine why I have suddenly begun to write all this to you – Except that I began to think as I wrote how unequal fates seemed to be & then I told myself how they were equalised in reality & how the great Leveller comes at last & sweeps down the tall poppies & the weeds and

the daisies with his scythe, and I suppose in some mysterious way that makes it all right & even....

Kensington has been the making of us all. Onslow Square was too depressing & relaxing there is no doubt of it. Theres been a series of weddings – all my friends married long ago. All Minnies are marrying now, a pretty Mary Irvine our cousin, Ella Merivale & Isabella Buller all within a month. I shd like M^r. Somebody to turn up one day. Dear me! how nice that would be.[49]

This inner discontent appears to have arisen around her birthday, when her awareness of the years passing was naturally at its most acute. In the 'clasp book', the separate short journal written just after her father's death in which intense feelings of guilt and loss are laid bare, she recalls the three of them dining at the Star and Garter on Richmond Hill. 'It seems no use to reproach myself about Papa. It does not make me love him more. I will try please God to do as he likes & to love him always. I pray God to make us always love him so that at the end we may meet once more & be his children still. I remember he said on my last birthday You are reproaching yourself about every thing today.... But O what a happy day it was all the same.'[50]

During this final year Thackeray worked on *Denis Duval*, his unfinished last novel which, as he promised to George Smith, would contain 'no moral reflections and plenty of adventures'.[51] As with the previous works located in the eighteenth century, it involved much preparatory historical research, including happy days spent at the British Museum. But there was time for a number of short trips with Annie and Minny; at Easter to Fryston Hall in Yorkshire, where they visited Richard Monckton Milnes – soon to be Lord Houghton – and then to Hampsthwaite, ancestral home of the Thackerays; to Hampshire where the girls stayed with Mrs Sartoris at Warnford whilst he travelled to Ryde to check out topographical details for *Denis Duval*; and finally to Paris for their last foreign trip together. Before they left for France in August, Mrs Carmichael-Smyth journeyed north with Charlotte, Gussie and Blanche Ritchie, stopping at Carlisle and Edinburgh. Then the Ritchies continued on to Fife to visit their cousins, Sir John and Lady Low, but Mrs Carmichael-Smyth had already given them the slip. 'I didnt go with Char & the 2 Ritchies, urgent tho' they were, Char even took upon herself to write to Lady Low that I was coming w^h: I was sorry for, & truth to say didn't wish to be there with such a party, but dear good Char, she would have it & I had nothing for it but to come away while they were sight seeing.'[52] This decidedly eccentric disappearing trick was a variant of her son's technique of removing himself without warning from the scene, though that tended to be to avoid the difficulties of farewells.

The Thackerays journeyed via Brussels, Dinant and Rheims, and in Paris revisited the old scenes once more, staying in the Hôtel des Deux Mondes where they were allocated the best rooms. They managed to lose and find their luggage, and Annie additionally lost (and found) first her money and then her umbrella. At the Louvre she appreciated the contrast between 'all the delicious balmy glitter without, all the calm wonders within', and decided that a Veronese was the finest picture seen that day.

It was Minny's turn to be out of sorts in September, and 'she began to droop somehow'. Annie and her grandmother persuaded Thackeray to send Minny off to Scotland for a complete change, first to their friends the Prescotts and then to the Lows at Cupar, the destination which Mrs Carmichael-Smyth had herself avoided. During her three weeks away, Minny wrote constantly to Annie, as was their invariable custom when either was away from home. She reveals a rather touching insecurity in needing to be reassured that her father was missing her, now that Annie had him to herself. '<u>Ask Papa to send me a message</u> does Papa miss me at all of course you do.' 'M[rs] B[lackwood] says that she adores Papa as much as ever, & if Papa sends her a more affectionate message than he sends me I will neither deliver it nor ever come home again.'[53] But she should not have doubted him, for when her father's friend, Dr John Brown, urged her to extend her trip by staying with his family in Edinburgh, Thackeray asked Brown to allow 'my little Min' to come straight back to London, framing a tactful letter to release her. 'She seems to be enjoying herself greatly: but when she has done with the Lows, I think she ought to come back to her Papa & sister. We three get on so comfortably together, that the house is not the house, when one is away. I know how kind you and your children would be to her. But Anny wants her companion, and a month will give her as much change of air as please God will be good for her.'[54]

Minny revelled in the local colour and the various hangers-on and elderly 'aunts' at Cupar, one of whom 'bothered me today by asking me if my Papa was a handsome man. I said I did not know & she thought it very stupid of me so I described him as well as I could & then she looked at me finally & said, but would he be a handsome man if it wasnt for his nose.'[55] The Thackeray brand of dry humour is often in evidence, including her description of a dour service at St Andrews, where she had to endure two sermons in succession from the same preacher – 'there was a little boy behind me who made me uncomfortable by expectorating throughout the whole service, however poor child one could hardly grudge him that little amusement with those 2 long sermons to sit out'.[56]

Thackeray's final excursion with both of his daughters was probably on the first Sunday in December, when evening service at the Temple church was followed by tea with Herman Charles Merivale, who had acted in *The Wolves and the Lamb* performances. Annie and Minny collected Lady Colvile in their carriage, and then drove through Hyde Park to the Athenaeum to pick up their father. He observed that they were twenty minutes late – not that he was used to their being on time – 'but he did not mind, and it was O so pleasant'. As the church was full they could not all sit together, and afterwards Thackeray waited outside as his daughters came up to him, 'standing quite still with his back turned to us', quietly singing over the evening hymn himself, 'so simple and unaffected & so entirely to the purpose'. They walked in the late afternoon sunshine in the Temple garden, and then went to Merivale's room where tea was set out. 'And Papa laughed because we were so pleased and happy and looked at the pictures on the walls.'[57] Throughout her life, Annie had a rare capacity to take an intense, concentrated pleasure from small prosaic events like this, which then became endowed with a lasting meaning. This account, written just months after Thackeray's death, looked back to that afternoon visit, and Annie was determined to regard the memory as emblematic of hope. 'It is ungrateful to be so sick with grief – Perhaps when we come out of this Temple we shall find him gone on a little way before us and waiting to lead us out into the open air.' The episode remained with her and ten years later she drew on it for a scene in *Old Kensington*.

Their grandmother was with them for Christmas that year. Thackeray had not been well for some weeks, with periodic attacks of 'spasms' and the old stricture troubles. A week before his death he wrote from his bed to Smith, where he had spent four days 'with an instrument of torture inserted in my urethra',[58] and with Henry Thompson in regular attendance. Yet again he contemplated having the operation, 'the grand coup', but as usual he resolved to undertake it only after completing his work in hand, in this case *Denis Duval*. That same night he managed to leave his bed to accompany Annie on the short walk across Kensington High Street and down Young Street, where they dined at the house of his old medical friend and former neighbour in Kensington Square, John Jones Merriman. The doctor recalled that

Six: Here is Night and Rest 163

Young Street and Thackeray's house, second on the left-hand side, photographed by John Jones Merriman, 1868

As he entered I saw he was not well, and with his usual kindness he said: 'I would only have turned out to come to you as an old friend.'... My friend stayed late, his daughter going on to some other party, and I strolled up Young Street with him; we halted by 'No. 13', when he alluded to older times and happy days there; he told me 'Vanity Fair' was his greatest work, and the 'Cane-bottomed Chair' his favorite ballad; and we parted at the top of 'Our Street,' never to meet again alive in this world.[59]

A well-respected surgeon and something of a local historian, Merriman appears also to have been a keen amateur photographer, following the example of his uncle, James Merriman. A group of his photographs survive from the 1860s, among them two similar 1868 views of Young Street, taken from the upper floor – perhaps a balcony – of one of the first houses on the east side of Kensington Square. The Greyhound Inn with its distinctive overhanging sign is clearly visible in the foreground, and we look up Young Street to the High Street at the top end. These are possibly the earliest surviving photographs of Young Street and of Thackeray's former house, taken just five years after the author's death.[60] None of the buildings now remain, with the sole exception of 13 Young Street itself. The current Greyhound Inn has been completely rebuilt. But these rather faded images offer a haunting glimpse of the route of that last walk. As they turned the corner from Kensington Square and approached the familiar bow-fronted façade of No 13, Thackeray paused to make his remarks to Merriman about *Vanity Fair*, and then they moved on up the street.

The evening following their dinner with the Merrimans was spent quietly at home, and they thought back over their trips that year, including the week at Paris, Thackeray picking up Annie's new diary for 1864 and noting that the year began on a Friday. 'And I said little thinking – Papa I assure you Friday is our lucky day. Indeed it will be a happy year.'[61] After lunch on Sunday, 'we sat by the fire, we three & talked to one another. We talked about Mamma and about M[rs]. Brookfield & Papa said that after all there was no one like her. So tender so womanly except perhaps you girls said Papa.' He recalled how at the time of Annie's birth the presence of a homeopathic doctor had nearly proved disastrous, and that the regular practitioner had been called only just in time. Anne and Minny left their father and took a walk with Dickens's daughter Kate and her husband, Charles Collins, and later Thackeray took Collins up to his room to show him something. 'M[r]. Collins has since told us that he noticed that Papa was quite tired & out of breath when he got upstairs.' There was a minor misunderstanding in the evening, for Annie had agreed to go out for dinner although Thackeray was entertaining the Collinses, Herman Merivale and Charles Cayley. 'Papa said to me "You are not going are you?" And I said – I suppose I must as they sent for me. I thought you

Six: Here is Night and Rest   165

meant me to go. Papa said "no I had nothing to do with it" – I was so sad, so silly, so foolish, that I felt as if I could not bear to be at home.'

The next morning she went into his room early, 'and I remember that he was so gentle that I could not help a sort of <u>pang</u>.... He lunched with us & we talked about the dinner-party the day before.... And as we were going out Papa came walking out of the study saying, I came to see if the carriage was there. Minny & I crossed the road & Papa looked after us & stopped behind. It was the only time almost this ever happened & I thought so then to myself.' Thackeray went later to the Athenaeum and Dickens would recall their last meeting there and how Thackeray had admitted that his recent bout of illness 'quite took the power of work out of him'.[62] Later he called on Charles and Kate Collins, irritated by something Edmund Yates had written, this time about The New Shakespeare Committee. That he raised it first with them upset Annie on her return. 'I pray God to be forgiven for my wicked anger and absurd jealousy', but she discussed it with him before breakfast on Tuesday morning, by which time he had resolved to leave Yates alone. 'I heard his step overhead as I was sitting writing in my little room. I waited for the first time in my life I think to finish before going to him. When I did at last he was gone out in the carriage they told me.'

Annie records that on the Wednesday

> Fanny said M^r. Thackeray is not well Miss, & I went into his room in a sort-of rage of sorryness. And Papa who lay very still with large-large eyes took my hand in his & said – It can't be helped darling. Then he added I did not take enough medicine last night. I have taken some more I shall be better presently. Thank God all my wickedness went away & I stood by his bed forgetting to go & only thinking of him. Then he put up the paper to his mouth & signed me to leave him.

During the afternoon, Annie heard him coughing, but the doctor called and reassured them that he would recover the next day. She took a walk, and later the servant said that her father was already much better. 'And then I thought all was well'. Her later journal simply records for 23 December, 'Papa ill again with spasms. That night was the last.'

In the early morning of Thursday Annie had a vivid dream. 'I was with Papa climbing a very high hill. We went higher & higher so that I had never seen anything like it before. And Papa was pointing out something to me w^h I could not see & presently left me & I seemed to come down alone. He said write to Mr Longman. I said I have written.' She woke, and had only just dressed when she was alarmed by the

Sketch of Thackeray, by Frederick Walker

sound of crying. 'I went out of my room to the landing & Charles the servant met me. He is dead Miss he said. He is dead. Then Grannie came from her room.'[63]

During the hours which followed, the rituals of death took over. Merriman was summoned at once as the nearest physician, and judged that death must have occurred in the early hours, between two and three. He recorded the cause as 'Disordered digestion 10 days. Excessive vomiting 24 hours. Cerebral effusion', commenting later that 'effusion had taken place into his powerful and great brain.'[64] Thackeray died in his bed during this cerebral haemorrhage, and secondary accounts indicate that it was not a peaceful end. 'From Thackeray's position, "lying back, with his arms over his head," "as if he had tried to take one more breath," it was assumed that he must have died "in great pain".'[65] Kate Collins arrived quickly and spent the day with the Thackeray women. Charles Collins went first to see Dickens to tell him the news before returning to join his wife. They saw the body, and Charles wrote to his brother Wilkie that 'I shall never forget the day which we passed at the house... or the horror of seeing him lying there so dreadfully changed'.[66] Kate and Charles changed their Christmas plans and eventually managed to persuade Annie, Minny and their grandmother to come to stay with them until the funeral.

It was only a week since Merriman had strolled back with Thackeray from his dinner in Kensington Square, the two friends remembering the happy Young Street days of Vanity Fair and Pendennis. At the top end they parted, but one can imagine Merriman standing quietly to watch as his old friend crossed over the High Street and turned right, passing from sight towards Palace Green, walking on alone towards that 'better country where there is no night'.[67] In the event, for those closest to him Thackeray's death involved as much guilt as grief. It is painful to read Annie's desolate and honest account of the last week of her father's life, written soon after his death when she even questioned her own reason. '[I]n these last days I think I must have been almost out of my mind at times. I can remember thoughts so impatient so unloyal so irritable & wicked. An absurd jealousy & suspicion had seized hold of me. The last day my Father lived I went to church & prayed so fervently for myself to be delivered from it, that I did not think to pray for him.' Elsewhere she is scarcely coherent, collapsing into a single narrative events which probably happened at different times or in a different sequence, but a raw truth cuts through, providing a plangent view of what his going meant to the immediate family.

Seven

ALL THIS ENDLESS YEAR
(1863-1865)

When I write to you I almost feel as if all the years had gone back & he was with you – only a few days journey off.
Annie to Mrs Baxter in New York
24 October 1864

In the quiet of the Palace Green house during the days before the funeral, Annie felt the constant presence of her father. As she lay exhausted, two days after his death, she thought that he stood by her bed and spoke to her. 'Are you sick my child?' His exceptional height required a coffin 'so long it was like him & I felt as if my head was on his breast'. Charles Collins felt the sadness profoundly, and feared for 'how the poor girls will get through the funeral'.[1] Their grandmother did not attend, but supported by Henry Cole, Annie and Minny were present at Kensal Green cemetery on 30 December, and 'it seemed as if he was with us the whole time'.[2] A plot was chosen close to that of Jane Thackeray, the daughter remembered tenderly during each of the twenty-four years since her death. There were large numbers at the mortuary chapel at midday, estimated as at least two thousand people, and although they included Dickens, Browning, Trollope, John Everett Millais and George Lewes, as well as former *Punch* colleagues and close friends like George Smith and the Collinses, the papers noted the crowds of ordinary people, a gathering of his unknown readers. Millais saw some colourfully-dressed women near the grave whose 'scarlet and blue feathers shone out prominently', and they had to be moved away to make space for the official party of family and friends. The inference that these were prostitutes is probably correct, Millais concluding that they were there 'from curiosity, I suppose'.[3] Assumptions that they were personally known to Thackeray are no more than that, but if true would indicate a genuine affection from working women for a former client.

Friends were generous in their support of the Thackeray women in the days to come. Henry and Marian Cole, Kate and Charles Collins, the Merivales, Fitzjames Stephen, George and Elizabeth Smith and Jane Brookfield provided immediate, practical advice. The disposal of Palace Green and finding somewhere cheaper to live had to be an early priority. Annie and Minny left for the Isle of Wight where during the first fortnight of January they stayed in one of Julia Margaret Cameron's Freshwater cottages, their grandmother probably retreating to the refuge of her Parisian friends. The sisters felt calm in the company of Tennyson, their father's friend since Cambridge days. 'It seemed to us that perhaps there more than anywhere else we might find some gleam of the light of our home, with the friend who had known him and belonged to his life and whom he trusted.'[4] Hardinge Hay Cameron, Mrs Cameron's son, tried to distract Minny by encouraging her to paint. Annie imagined funerals 'passing along the downs', but the desolate seascapes were somehow consoling. Once they had returned to London, they stayed with Kate and Charles Collins again. The prized carriage and pair, a poignant representation of a no longer affordable former life, was bought by Mrs Ritchie for £165. They began securing their father's papers and removing the Palace Green things which they wanted to keep as the grim business of househunting began, but all they seemed to see were 'horrid little houses everywhere'.

At the end of January the sisters travelled to stay in the country house near Wimborne in Dorset taken by Augusta Ritchie and her children since their return from India, and Mrs Carmichael-Smyth joined them there. The Ritchie and Thackeray cousins would become regular correspondents, and Emily, the third Ritchie daughter, always known as Pinkie, provided Annie with the most important friendship of her adult life. At Wimborne, a sad time was not made easier by a 'terrible religious discussion' with Mrs Carmichael-Smyth, the liberal views of her granddaughters being beyond her comprehension, but not something she could let pass unremarked. 'It used to make us miserable [and] to make her so unhappy. Minnie used to be made down right ill & I used to get half distracted.'[5]

And still Annie was dreaming of her father, 'such vivid dreams that I woke up feeling as if I had been actually with him. He used to tell me not to exaggerate my feeling.' She and Minny moved on to Adelaide Sartoris's country house at Warnford in Hampshire, where they experienced feelings of almost desperate loneliness. The large house was curiously claustrophobic, and as Annie gazed out to the hills beyond and watched the circling rooks, she seemed 'stifled &

Sketch by Thackeray

closed on every side & I feel as if some day they will come rolling down & close in & overwhelm the house'.

Thackeray had been troubled about his daughters' prospects were they to live with their grandmother, fearing that her oppressive love would smother them. Annie had once walked into the dining-room and found him gazing into the fire. 'And he said I have been thinking that in fact it will be a very dismal life for you when I am gone. I have a great mind to put it into my will that you are not to live with Grannie.' But although he had started to rethink his intentions, deciding that he no longer need to leave a legacy to Amy Crowe once marriage had given her financial security, a revised will was never signed. When asked why he needed to make one at all, it seems that in the disposal of his assets he wanted the costs of Isabella's future needs to be properly covered, but 'I cannot afford to give her a third'. An investment portfolio drawn from his estate would instead ensure her ongoing care.

Yet it seems unlikely that the sisters could ever seriously have considered living apart from their grandmother. They knew their duty too well for that, but nor were they prepared to move permanently to

Paris, her own preferred solution. Annie endeavoured to present their prospects cheerfully to a friend – 'all our affairs are beginning to go more smoothly. Minny doesnt care a bit but I do because I do so long long for a sort of a home. We are going to live with Granny & you must come & see us some times my dear wont you?'[6]

During their absence from London, Henry Cole's wife watched over Palace Green – in fact they never returned to live there – and she raised concerns about Mrs Carmichael-Smyth's future. Annie's response was quick and, for her, resolute. It was a matter of doing the right thing, whilst not compromising on principles.

> <u>Of course</u> we mean to try & do our duty by Grannie.... You know that I am not dishonest or apt to say things of myself that are not true, & now that Papa is gone I feel very strongly that my <u>first</u> duty in life is to try & make my sister as happy as it will ever be possible to be, & my <u>second</u> to comfort & take care of my poor dear old Grannie. I cannot help the first being the pleasantest – it was pleasantest always to be with Papa & yet it was the most right. It makes me very unhappy to think you & M^{rs}. Brookfield & Grannie evidently think me wrong – we are only too glad to live with Grannie if she will like it, but from her letters I cannot understand what she w^{d}. like except going to live abroad.[7]

They left the sale of house and contents in the hands of others, their urgent need being to realise some of the capital swallowed up by their father's expenditure on rebuilding Palace Green. His papers were a different matter, and Annie was determined that they should not be dispersed. Although she had found many documents she now remembered others, including 'a little old thick green book in Papas bedroom with Private written by him upon the back.... Would you dear M^{rs}. Cole put it safe away & lock it up – I am so afraid of valuers or servants &ct looking into it.' On 11 March the sisters crossed the Solent and returned to Freshwater, in the same week that Palace Green was sold to the Huths, who paid £10,000 for it. Henry Huth was a banker and bibliophile, and his wife Augusta – 'kind Mrs Huth' as Leslie Stephen called her – was earnestly interested in fashionable ideas. Stephen was cautious of her intellectual enthusiasms, but she was to be instrumental in encouraging his romance with Minny when the Thackeray sisters joined the Huths in Switzerland in 1866.

At Freshwater, the sisters' attempts at self-catering and at leading the simple life was diversion of a kind. Arriving in the early morning, they bought bread and jam and ate breakfast sitting in the window of their cottage. Their plan was to return to London in a fortnight and heal the rift with their grandmother, but they stayed for just a week before taking lodgings at Brompton Square, and then from mid-April they were offered the short-term loan of Heath Cottage in Putney by Julia Margaret Cameron. Their grandmother's behaviour continued to be volatile. In trying to talk reasonably about their differences, Annie managed to make things worse. 'I asked Grannie why she had been so angry with us. M cried out do be quiet. Grannie left the table & said she w^d. never get over it. Went out together all the same & dined together. Minny not well. Don't attempt explanations – dont write them.'

Annie's anxieties about the vulnerability of Thackeray's private papers had been well founded. There was something of a crisis when it was discovered that a piece of furniture which had been sold contained a collection of his letters hidden in a drawer. George Smith and Frederick Greenwood were able quickly to retrieve these, but it was another reason for self-recrimination. 'I blamed myself very much for having let the things be sold without going thro them & looking in the drawers.'

But at least their househunting was making progress. Guided by Henry Cole, they settled on a house in Onslow Gardens, Brompton, a new development leading off Onslow Square which when they viewed it 'looked sunshiny & pleasant enough'. It would not be ready until the autumn and would cost £2,250, but meanwhile the Putney cottage suited them. From there Annie told Mrs Baxter of their recent history, and hinted at the possibility of a future without the father who had given meaning to all of their past life.

> I have not written before because I can only write about Papa & sometimes I <u>cant</u> – When I am worried & troubled about other things then it seems a sort of desecration. I thought of you often & often when I was in his study burning & putting away papers in a sort of dream – There were one of two letters to you begun there was a packet of Sally's letters – I burnt them too and kissed them before I put them into the fire…. Forgive me for speaking of your daughter as I speak. To me the dead are dearer than the living and more alive at times. I think Papa knows perhaps I am writing to you now. Our home where you were once to have come is sold – We have only kept enough furniture for a small house where we are going to live with my Grandmother we believe – Friends are kindness itself there is money enough because Papa was

Seven: All This Endless Year

> always working for us, and our pain is far far less than it has been – It seems to us that sorrow at first is not sorrow but a terrible physical suffering.... We are in a little cottage on Putney Heath all the gorse is coming out & the green trees; & the birds are singing, & it is much better than London lodgings.... Minny & the little dog are standing at the garden gate. Here come some children with flowers who tell us it is Mayday....
>
> We are going to live in some new houses near Onslow Square.... My sister & I have bought the house & my grandmother is to rent it of us & we are to live with her. We try not to look forward much & to get thro each day as it comes. Granny is very kind, but very ill & feeble and every thing seems uncertain and dim. But we have had so much sunshine in our lives such a measure of love that we must not complain now if the light is hidden for a while.[8]

There would still be tensions in relations with their grandmother, but coming to a decision about a house and insisting that she must live with them prompted a grateful response from Paris. 'Ah dearest Nan if you knew what a cordial y^r letter is to my old stupid head you w^d thank GOD that you had been shewn the way to make me happy – no no – I dont want the name of its being my house. I want only that we should live as we ought to live, loving & loved & therefore happy.'[9]

The future of Thackeray's copyrights remained to be resolved. George Smith was placed in a delicate position here, for his astute business instincts wanted to secure them for his firm. But as a sincere friend, he was concerned that the writer's daughters should obtain the best possible settlement, and was prepared to pay more for the copyrights than they were probably worth in the short-term, for Thackeray's sales were in decline. Smith had known how the future financial welfare of his family had preoccupied the author in his last years, the motivation behind two American trips and the exhausting lecture-circuits there and at home. And he knew too of Thackeray's tendency to spend beyond his income. Smith wasted no time in negotiating directly with those acting for the sisters, principally Herman Merivale and Henry Cole, for his genuine desire to protect their interests was firmly grounded.

In February, their father's friend Russell Sturgis told the sisters of an American publisher's offer of £100 with possible royalties for the right to produce a collected Thackeray edition in the States. Asked for an opinion, Smith recommended refusal, but his firm's potential interests made it a matter of some delicacy.

> I have the less hesitation in giving you this advice because putting aside all other considerations I am sure that it must not be worth your while to undergo the labour that would be imposed on you if you assented to their wishes for 'the sum of £100 to be paid at early dates during the publication of the Books'.... You need not hesitate to refer any such question as the present one to me, and if it will save you trouble I will write to such people for you. The only questions on which I cannot advise you are those in regard to which our interests would be opposed, or might appear to be opposed – such for instance was the question in regard to your copyright. I could not advise you to sell what I should have endeavoured to buy. All your friends appear however to have agreed on that subject.[10]

He did not press the women about the copyrights, but a month later there had been some progress, for with the sale of Palace Green settled, the time now seemed right to move towards an agreement.

> Nothing could be more satisfactory to my mind than to know that in any negotiations for the sale of the copyrights of your Fathers Books your own and your Sister's interests will be jealously guarded. I am in no fear that you will suppose that I wish to purchase the copyrights on any but such terms as are most favourable to you – and if I seemed to ask for any preference it only came to this – that, if my firm's proposals were as good as any others we should have the gratification of publishing your Fathers Books.[11]

As negotiations went forward, Smith broached what was arguably an even more delicate matter with Annie. In March, the *Cornhill* had begun to publish the eight completed chapters of *Denis Duval*, which Thackeray had left as corrected proofs. They provided sufficient material for four numbers of the magazine, but it would leave the June issue short and inevitably the story stopped abruptly in midstream. Smith knew of Thackeray's unusually elaborate preparations for the novel, and that notes had been left, perhaps indicating how the narrative might have been developed. He was also conscious that the sisters would need to consent to the publication of any kind of explanatory commentary, for already they felt fiercely protective towards the Thackeray legacy and their emotions were raw during these first months of loss. But Smith knew that they were likely to be in possession of uniquely privileged insights about their father's intentions for the novel, and that these needed to be preserved, whilst on a more personal level he was wise

Seven: All This Endless Year

enough to believe that for Annie the preparation of a concluding essay for *Denis Duval* could prove to be cathartic.

He chose his moment with care. Less than a month before the last of the *Denis Duval* material appeared he broached the subject, knowing that Annie would have been incapable of considering it any sooner, and that even now he was risking a rebuff.

> Trusting entirely to your consideration of the necessities of the case, I venture to trouble you with a little difficulty which is by no means a matter of business merely.
>
> M^r. Thackeray's story 'Denis Duval' breaks off in the next number of 'The Cornhill Magazine'. This last portion makes only 14 pages: it ends abruptly. To leave the story <u>there</u>, as it were, without a word of it's [sic] design, or a word of any sort, is a kind of thing which I cannot contemplate with any complacency. I don't know whether I am <u>quite</u> right in the selection of the words, but there seems to me something more than disrespectful, something almost indecent, in ending M^r. Thackeray's last work in that abrupt way, in a Magazine for which he did so much. And yet what can I do? I will tell you what I should like to do, or to see done, and leave myself then entirely in your hands, satisfied beforehand that the instinct of his daughter and his friends, must be superior to the judgement of his publisher and friends. I should like to see a line drawn after the abrupt portion of 'Denis Duval' and then a few words to this effect – put in my rough unliterary way 'Here ends the last work of W M Thackeray all that we can do now is to gather up what we have learned of his projects for the story and to give them to the public which respected his work' and then to set forth what bits of notes Mr Thackeray may have made for the Story – I myself have a letter in which much of this appears: other notes may exist (memorandum Book) and it occurs to me that he may have talked with you about his plans. Let us piece all this together – not in a formal or diffuse way, but closely and briefly; and end <u>so</u>. Perfectly ready to bow to your view of the matter, I must say I feel very strongly that this would be a course the most respectful to your Father's memory, and most satisfactory to the tens of thousands who will certainly be anxious to learn as much as they can about the work.
>
> Is it too much to ask you to perform this little task; or may I ask it? If you could bring yourself to write the few

lines necessary to put together whatever may be known or discoverable about your Father's plans for 'Denis Duval' that would be the very best thing from every point of view; and I need not assure you that the fact of your doing it might be kept strictly secret, if you pleased. But if not, then perhaps you will kindly furnish me with any particulars, on paper or in your memory, which may help us to close the story with some account of what it might have been. Of course, whatever were done would be submitted to you in proof; and nothing should appear that did not perfectly satisfy your judgement and affection.

And here I end this troublesome long letter. It <u>is</u> troublesome; but I have much confidence that you will agree with me that <u>something</u> should be done in the way I have suggested, and of course nothing could be done without reference to you.[12]

He had put his case skilfully and sensitively. Annie was tempted, stipulating as her one proviso that her own involvement should remain anonymous, effectively endorsing the solution which Smith had already put in her mind. He sent her the letter in his possession and offered to get any relevant material in the British Museum checked, for Annie already had the related notebook in which her father had made his research notes. In compliance with Smith's request, she began to sketch out the novel's possible future progress, and in only a few days sent him a draft, as he was pressing to go to print. 'I have strung some of the notes together – & put in some of the things Papa told me – in his words as nearly as I could…. At first we thought we could <u>never</u> find the heart to go on with this little task & could only cry over it – but now that it is done I am very very glad – & even if it is not what you quite want. I am sure nobody else could have understood the little half words he has written, to whom he had not talked about it.'[13]

In the June *Cornhill* the final completed chapter of *Denis Duval* was followed by a 'Note by the Editor' – actually the piece written entirely by Annie. It opens in her distinctive yet understated voice, gracefully developing the suggested opening that Smith had included in his original letter to her. 'The readers of the *Cornhill Magazine* have now read the last line written by William Makepeace Thackeray. The story breaks off as his life ended – full of vigour, and blooming with new promise like the apple-trees in this month of May.' Annie had worked feverishly in the two weeks since writing that letter to Mrs Baxter, when the appearance of children at their Putney garden gate with flowers had broken her reverie and reminded her that it was Mayday. Contented to feel that she had done her duty by her father, she was left close to exhaustion.

During their weeks at Heath Cottage the Thackeray sisters made several visits to their father's old friends Bryan and Anne Procter, whose house was something of a refuge for 'boys, girls & sick & sorry people'. The day before her birthday Annie sat in the Procters' garden, surrounded by the sounds and sights of early summer, and reflected on the twelve months' past. 'Pray God bless us alive & dead who love each other. I know not what else to pray for.' Always more grounded, Minny reminded her that 'while we are bodies it is no use pretending we are spirits'.[14]

For the summer months, she and Minny planned a continental trip, joining their grandmother and Charlotte Ritchie in Paris before travelling together to the Pyrenees. Minny's health was a concern, for she was so 'thin & so wan at times that I can't bear it',[15] but their medical friend Dr de Mussy reassured her. '[T]hank God it was only my own foolishness & want of trust, shall I call it, & yesterday when he came she was quite well & herself again but he <u>was</u> so kind & prescribed for sick hearts as well as sick bodies by this kindness.'[16] Mrs Carmichael-Smyth believed Minny to be experiencing the same listlessness that had affected her during the previous autumn, when she had gone to Scotland to recover. Her homespun diagnosis may well have been close to the truth.

> You know how Papa used to say when anyone was out of sorts, 'it was the liver,' & then dear soul he thought a blue pill w^d. put all to rights, but there was a mistake. If it is an aggravation of last years attack, it has its origin in the same source, added to by the state of mind no doubt – & I hope you explained to the D^r. that this attack was of the same nature as last years, otherwise he will fall into the error of believing it to proceed solely f^m. the present state of the spirits after sorrow.... [D]ont you remember how we both saw the necessity of change of air, & Scotland did her all the good in the world, as I'm sure the move will again D.V.[17]

Although their grandmother had proposed the Pyrenean trip, once she knew of Minny's frailty she urged them not to overreach themselves – 'do be quite sure in y^r own minds about the Py^r: its quite immaterial to me'. She was also cost-conscious, for the inevitable expenses attached to moving house would follow their return, although she casually threw in as a well-judged afterthought the notion that it might profit

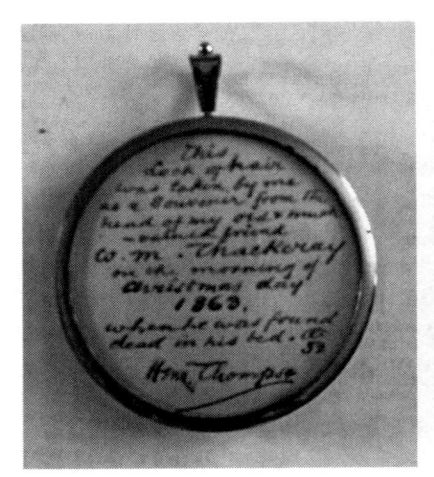

Left: *Locket of Thackeray's hair taken after death. Inscription reads: 'This lock of hair was taken by me as a Souvenir from the head of my old & much-valued friend W.M. Thackeray on the morning of Christmas day 1863, when he was found dead in his bed, aet 52. Henry Thompson' [Thackeray died in the early morning of Christmas Eve].* **Right:** *Reverse of locket, showing Thackeray's white hair.*

Annie's writing. 'Still if you incline to it with the prospect of new ideas for a story, & the minds & body's health, you couldnt have a better opportunity.'[18] They left for Paris in late June, having first arranged for a ring containing a lock of their father's hair to be sent to George Smith. He was immensely touched, and wrote to Bagneres de Bigorre in the Pyrenees. 'I think you and your Sister are the only people in the world who can understand how much I value it.' Together, they comprised quite a group of English women at Bigorre; Annie and Minny, their grandmother, Charlotte Ritchie, their cousin Selina Shakespear and at least one other in their party. Most wore conventional black during the period of mourning, and the locals 'took us for a community of nuns & Grannie was the Abbess'. Smith told them that the dean of Westminster Abbey had agreed that there should be a memorial bust of their father in Poets' Corner, 'not that there could have been any doubt on the subject'.[19] In a typically thoughtful gesture, he offered to send copies of the *Times* as well as a weekly paper, which they gladly took up. News of the bust was a tonic, and something of Annie's dry humour starts to reappear in her grateful response to his offer of newspapers. 'It gives quite a distinction here to have a paper, people lend it about in a patronising way w^h. we long to imitate. Even the Hotel keeper shews a marked difference. One lady has arranged for a 2^د. days Times to be forwarded to her – She is the Queen of the Place.'[20]

The business of the copyrights was also proceeding smoothly in their absence. George Smith continued to deal with the sisters openly and honestly, eventually buying the copyrights for a generous £5,000 and permitting them to keep whatever of their father's letters and other unpublished papers and drawings they currently owned, although the rights over any future publication would rest with the firm. Annie knew that they had been treated favourably and that her father would himself have been surprised at the value which Smith had placed upon his work. 'We have had much more for Papa's copyrights than he expected.'[21] Smith's was an almost avuncular role, and when later he became godfather to Annie's daughter his generosity embraced the next generation, for he presented Hester with £1,000 on her twelfth birthday in 1890. But his astute business judgment also meant that his firm secured a deal sufficiently watertight to ensure the rights of future publication of any kind of Thackeray materials. In order to recoup the significant initial investment it had been necessary to secure all unpublished items in whatever form they might exist. The document assigning the copyright stretched to nearly three thousand words, drawn up by lawyers as determined to close all loopholes as they were resolute in their avoidance of the full stop.

> Whereas William Makepeace Thackeray late of Palace Green aforesaid Esquire deceased departed this life on the twenty fourth day of December one thousand eight hundred and sixty three intestate and on the fifth day of March one thousand eight hundred and sixty four Letters of Administration of his personal estate and effects were granted to the said Anne Isabella Thackeray and Harriet Marian Thackeray the Daughters and only next of kin of the said William Makepeace Thackeray in the principal Registry of Her Majesty's Court of Probate And Whereas the said William Makepeace Thackeray at divers times during his lifetime wrote composed and edited and compiled and may have translated various works of Fiction books lectures letters essays reviews poems contributions to Newspapers and periodical publications articles in periodicals critiques diaries and other Literary Compositions and also designed drew painted sketched etched and engraved various drawings pictures paintings and caricatures either for the illustration of his works books and other Literary compositions or otherwise....[22]

There is a great deal more in the same vein. After July in the Pyrenees, the touring party began slowly to move north again, passing through Tours and le Mans as they headed towards the Normandy coast. At Arromanches the lodgings proved to be uncomfortable, but they were cheered to overhear strangers talking about *Vanity Fair*. Walking along the sands with Minny, Annie felt as if she was carrying an invisible heavy weight, but then Minny jumped over a rock, she followed, and 'the load seemed lighter'.[23] The next day they were at Caen, where they had hoped the English consul would endorse some papers so that they might withdraw more ready money, but he was away and they wandered rather aimlessly around the streets. Whilst their grandmother sat resting, to their delight the elder Herman Merivale appeared as if from nowhere, a guardian angel instantly able to provide them with funds. The Merivales had rented a house in Caen, and this unplanned encounter led him to arrange for the completed copyright agreement to be sent from England, resulting in the signatures of the Thackeray sisters being witnessed on 20 August by Merivale himself and the proprietor of their Caen hotel.

A quarrel with their grandmother, from which Annie suffered 'an agony of self-reproach', was followed the next evening by a worse one when she 'suddenly burst upon us. It was horrible torture.' Minny thought that Mrs Carmichael-Smyth was 'half mad', and the atmosphere was dispelled only when Annie 'went off into hystericks... w^h. was the best thing I could do'. As there was no pressing need for them to return home, they stayed on in Normandy for most of September, with Arromanches as their base. Annie's vivid dreams about her father continued, as did her preoccupations with feelings of morbid guilt. 'I said to him – if I could only live my life again.'[24] Shortly before Annie and Minny prepared to return to England and she to Paris, their grandmother talked to them for hours about the past, recalling her first husband, Richmond Thackeray. Probably it was the first time since her re-marriage that the former Anne Becher had thought and spoken so intensely about Thackeray's father, nearly fifty years dead, and of her early days in India.

They parted at Lisieux, and on 26 September Annie and Minny crossed from le Havre to Southampton, making their way to the Ritchies at Wimborne before coming to Onslow Gardens where their grandmother would join them in November. They wrote immediately upon their arrival in England, and she responded by sending them a house-warming message, hoping that calm might at last return to their lives, that the peace of a new home would represent 'a happy termination to y^r. wanderings'. She had things to settle in Paris and a wedding to attend, and even now there was something ominous about the way in which she saw their future together. 'I will write about business hereafter, the tooth must be drawn before we enter upon our new functions & I pray that we may be guided by right judgement putting aside egoisme & looking to the fulfilment of duty.'[25] It sounded as if she would insist on some ground-rules. But Onslow Gardens did indeed act like a balm upon the young women, for their arrival there felt not so much like entering a new house as a homecoming. 'It was all bright & alight with flowers. We thought we should have found it dark & dreary but we almost cried with joy instead of sorrow to be at home & with Papa again.'[26]

A month after they had moved in, Annie could contemplate a future in which some of the old normalities might be restored. 'Now that the house is in order & we have done with carpenters &ct we must look about I suppose & find something to do & to be interested in – It is very difficult – I try & write a little but I have nothing to say – It is like speaking when one is not thinking of what one says – I suppose we must take to some schools or sick people & do the best we can. Economising is an employment after all & fortunately we have chosen rather too dear a house.'[27] Minny was much recovered, at times reminding Annie strikingly of their father, not in her look only but in her speech and affectionate ways; 'sometimes she says things so like him that it is a wonder. She can remember things he said & liked & his words, & she has all his tenderness.' The news of the sudden death of the illustrator John Leech, a friend from Thackeray's *Punch* days, and before that a fellow Charterhouse pupil, was both a shock and a sadness. It was at times such as this that the sisters missed their father's sure handling of difficult moments, with his mixture of encouragement and gentle sympathy. 'We want him so much now to go & comfort Mrs Leech. He could be so tender & so cheerful too.'[28]

According to plan, Thackeray's mother joined her granddaughters in mid-November. It was her farewell to France, undertaken not without considerable reluctance and with no great expectations as to what awaited her. 'Me voici dearest Children & truly one must "love much" to leave these bright skies for fogland & all its dreariness.'[29] It was not the best time to travel, and as she spent a few final days in Boulogne, waiting for good weather for the crossing to Folkestone, her granddaughters needed to remind themselves that this vein of bleak pessimism was not her natural voice, and doubtless they hoped that, like their own sadness, it would ease as the pain of their collective loss receded. But whereas for them there was the prospect of carving out a future sustained by the memory of a father whose inspiring love could shape their lives to come, for her there was only loss, with husband, child and home all gone. Yet her last weeks in Onslow Gardens have an almost elegiac quality to them, or at least that is how Annie portrays them. They welcomed her return, already sufficiently happy in the new house to believe that they could live contentedly with her again. 'Grannie came back suddenly & to our great pleasure in November. She liked the house & settled down.' Annie and Minny had gone to Brighton to stay with the George Smiths, and when they returned on 13 November they found their grandmother freshly arrived from France, sitting peacefully by the fire. Gone were the arguments and the fractiousness, and once again she offered the pure, unqualified love of earlier years during what turned out to be her final weeks. Just two days before her death she made a dramatic declaration which helps explain much about their quarrels on spiritual matters during the previous months. She was calm at last after experiencing a sustained period of religious uncertainty. As they took a walk together, 'she said she had changed her mind about many things – specially abt. Religious things & that she could now sympathise far more than she had once done with what our Father had to think & say.'[30] It was a remarkable admission, this late change from dogmatic assurance to the possibility of doubt, and paradoxically it allowed her a serenity and peace of mind that she had not known before.

The anniversary of Thackeray's death was just days away, and they decided to spend it quietly together. It was their grandmother who on 18 December sensitively raised the matter, wanting to know how they wished to observe the time. 'We said we should like to stay quietly with her & not to go away. She had been so sweet, so very very kind of late.' That evening they reminisced, as they had at the end of their summer visit to the Pyrenees, of days long past. 'She said she was not very well but she was so sweet so tender that it seemed like old days. She told us all the dear old stories once more – Her youth her happy time at Bath India & the Grandfathers.'[31] She remembered the romance of how Richmond Thackeray had wooed her, of his arrival on a white horse, of his proposal and her acceptance. They had something to eat at about nine, and Annie assigns to this last supper a sacramental significance, for 'Grannie God bless her broke bread & gave it to us'. Only taking a little soup for herself, she ensured that her granddaughters ate well and looked at Minny 'with tender eyes of love'. An hour later, the women turned to their final reading for the day, Annie choosing Keble's *The Christian Year* while her grandmother silently studied from the psalms for a while before announcing that it was time for her to go to her rest. 'Then she gave me a great long tender kiss & then another & went away and as she went I thank God that I remember saying thank God in my heart.' It was a final parting, of the kind that the women had been denied in the case of their father and so it had the quality of a benediction now. The sisters sat together by the fire, and they heard a little noise and then were called by Fanny, the maid. Their grandmother had quietly died as she had been preparing for bed.

Ten days later, Annie sat down to write to Mrs Synge. She and Minny were in Brighton where they had gone with their father's cousin, Jane Ritchie, who had come from Paris as soon as she heard of Mrs Carmichael-Smyth's death. This latest sadness represented a form of termination, for whereas all of the last twelve months had involved an unbroken process of coming to terms with their father's death, the sale of Palace Green, the move to Onslow Gardens and anxiety about their grandmother's future, they were now required to start afresh rather than simply to struggle on. They had found it too much of an ordeal to attend the Kensal Green funeral, where Thackeray's mother was buried with her son on Christmas Eve, the anniversary of his death.

> We had been dreading Christmas for weeks past, but we did not think what a second Christmas it was to be. And yet strangely to ourselves even – though the last semblance of home & protecting love is gone – this new sorrow seems to have eased the weary pain w^h. has ached & ached all this endless year. I think now, even if one of us 2 were to die the other would almost feel as if she had only gone home. For home does seem there more than here at times. Grannie was buried on Christmas Eve – but all our strength & courage failed us & we could not go again, it was this day year that we left our Father there. We came here a few days ago with my cousin Jane Ritchie – I think for the present we shall live on in Onslow Gardens – the future must settle itself – I have no heart to make plans or schemes.[32]

In early June 1865, Annie would add a final portion to the short journal compiled during the initial desolation after her father's death, 'where my poor sick heart tried to write its pain'. She wrote in the room where her grandmother had died six months before, and now experienced great peace and a sensation of the dark months at last being dispelled by light. This sense of calm had begun to arrive on the night before their grandmother's funeral, when the sisters sat quietly in the house with Jane Ritchie. It was the anniversary of the terrible night during which Thackeray had died. Annie was struck by the transfiguring smile on Minny's face when she fell asleep. 'The room seemed to grow light, a strange brightness & perfect peace & happiness came over me.... I think the brightness of their love must have fallen upon us.' Minny had persuaded her that their deep sorrow was evidence of the transforming power of love, offered as a gift from those who had gone before. Until then, Annie had been assaulted by feelings of guilt about Thackeray's death, that they had not sufficiently proved their love to him and that the suddenness of his going was a punishment. 'I used to think that it would be a sign that our failings towards our Father were forgiven if my dearest Grannie were to go at peace with us at hand.' They had been given that sign, but now she accepted that it had not been required. 'Yesterday Minny said to me Anny how can you dare to complain? – our small troubles we can forget & our greatest sorrows are our greatest blessings – Her words have been ringing in my ears ever since.'[33]

Once she had completed this addition to her journal, a few days after Minny's twenty-fifth birthday and shortly before she would herself be twenty-eight, Annie closed the book and fastened its brass clasp with no thoughts of opening it again. Minny was right. They had been out of the world long enough, and it was time for Thackeray's daughters to confront the next phase of their lives.

Eight

A WOMAN'S CARES AND JOYS
(1865-1867)

I have the same feeling in happiness as in sorrow, which is that it is impossible that love should end here – or we should never be allowed to love so dearly.

Minny to Julia Jackson
25 December 1866

When he first met Thackeray's daughters in March 1865, over lunch in his mother's Bayswater house in Porchester Square where he and his sister Caroline still lived, Leslie Stephen revealed that his favourite novel was *Vanity Fair*. This was not designed to humour them, but was the truth. He was thirty-two, and just beginning to develop a career as a critic and essayist. He had not known Thackeray, but his elder brother Fitzjames (Fitzy) had been on friendly terms since early *Cornhill* days, recruited to provide articles on political and legal matters. A lawyer by profession, Fitzjames had been amongst those who advised the sisters after their father's death.

A fortnight later, Caroline Stephen was sharing the Thackerays' lodgings at Freshwater,[1] next door to Benjamin Jowett's Balliol reading group, and Annie was amused by the usual sprinkling of artistic types clustering attentively around Julia Margaret Cameron and Tennyson. 'Everybody here is either a genius or a poet or a painter or peculiar in some way poor Miss Stephen says is there nobody commonplace.'[2] She enjoyed Caroline's company, and they took moonlit strolls together. During this same Freshwater visit Fitzjames sent Annie a volume of his republished essays 'which you appear to have the peculiarly good taste to admire…. One essay on Lord Macaulay was praised I remember by your father. I wrote it one morning between 1.30 am & 6.30 am between hard days work in Court.'[3] He wrote having enjoyed one of her *Pall Mall Gazette* contributions, venturing to suggest ways in which she might benefit from a regime of serious reading in history.

> The style & taste are excellent, & you have inherited your father's keen & quick eye for all kinds of delicate shades & touches. May I say to you what I used sometimes to say to and write about him? What you want is knowledge. If you were in the habit of reading more & harder books it would give that graceful style & quick power of observation something to go upon.... If I had my time to myself I would read histories & biographies & think about them. If I could not trust myself to do so steadily I would read the best collections of historical & other essays that I could find. There are several in the present day which are as good as good can be – Lord Macaulay's, my father's, Mr Mill's (though you w^d. perhaps find them a little hard they are admirably good) M^r. Senior's in some cases, M^r. Merivale's &c &c. As to the histories their name is legion, but they are not so very very many after all. Grote's History of Greece Arnold's History of Rome, C. Merivale's history of the early Roman Empire, Milman's History of Christianity & of later Christianity make up altogether $12+3+7+9 = 31$ 8^{ve} volumes which would last you perhaps for two years & a half if you read a volume a month, which would not take you two hours a day or anything like it. 15 pages a day are 450 8vo pages in 30 days, & if you read these books so as to know them well or even pretty well they would open a new world to you.

Annie would have taken no offence at the unsolicited advice, which was well-intentioned, nor at the preachy, faintly patronising tone, but this regime of earnest dullness, reflecting Fitzy's inexhaustible capacity for work, would not be followed.

Leslie Stephen's conscious registering of Minny's personality dates from that first lunchtime meeting. In a later private family memoir written for the children of his second marriage, he described a time when he had not previously given serious thought to the idea that he might himself marry. 'I was shy, diffident, and fully impressed with the conviction acquired at Cambridge that I was an old don – a superannuated bachelor standing apart from all thought of domestic happiness.'[4] This encounter occurred a few months after he left Cambridge to forge a literary career in London, and Minny's entry into his field of vision startled him into seeing an opportunity being offered and of his need to come to a decision about himself. 'And so I had and took the chance of falling in love with my darling Minny.' It is curious that he should put it like this, as somehow being all a matter of will or deliberate choice, though Leslie was certainly susceptible to appearances. At first it was Minny's look which charmed him. 'The most striking features, I think, were the beautiful eyes – the form inherited, I think, from her father and beautiful in form rather than in colour. They were a blue-gray. I do not think that she could be called beautiful; but the face was interesting and attractive to me (I fancy not to me alone! but I speak for myself) from the first.'[5] Are we to understand that Leslie had to fight off rivals? According to Annie, as soon as Leslie and Minny were married both Alan Cole (Henry Cole's son), and Herman Charles Merivale (Minny's acting partner in the Palace Green play) seemed disappointed that her sister was no longer single. Yet neither had shown his hand sooner.

To learn anything of Minny's behaviour and feelings in the months before her engagement, we have to rely on the observations of others. Leslie's later account was recalling events from a considerable distance, but it is also complicated by performing the function of representing his second wife, Julia, to her children as saint and angel, as 'all that is holy and all that is endearing in human affection'.[6] As there could be no room for a rival candidate, the Minny of Leslie's narrative is depicted as making much of the early running in their romance, drawing him in by provoking within him an affection sufficient to overcome his natural reticence. After that inaugural lunch at Lady Stephen's on 23 March, the sisters next came across Leslie with Henry Sidgwick at the end of May, Annie merely noting that 'Leslie fled from us'. Was it shyness, or anxiety because he was unpractised in dealing with unfamiliar emotions? Yet three days later several of the Stephens – Fitzy and his wife Mary, together with two of his children and Leslie himself – invited the Thackeray sisters to join them on a river trip from Henley to Maidenhead, 'a heavenly day in a boat', according to Annie. Everything remained formal between them still, as Fitzy recalled for Annie when thinking back to those happy days: 'it was all M^r. Stephen & Miss Thackeray & there was the usual difficulty in distinguishing between M^r. S & M^r. L.S. & Miss Th. & Miss H.M. Th. I recollect I had blistered one of my hands slightly, & as I handed you out of the boat at Maidenhead you noticed it & made such pretty speeches about being afraid you had hurt me.'[7]

George Smith's regular Friday dinner at Hampstead the next week was perhaps the occasion recollected by Leslie, when they sat together and Mrs Gaskell 'foresaw that Minny Thackeray would become my wife. It is probable enough that our mutual feelings were sufficiently transparent to a looker-on.'[8] The next day he called on Annie and Minny, rare enough for a man unaccustomed to social visiting. But he places the rapprochement a whole year later, at Annie's birthday picnic in the Surrey countryside in June 1866, when the guests included the painters, Frederic Leighton and Val Prinsep (son of Thoby and Sara Prinsep), that he 'began to perceive that Minny was somehow drawing nearer to me. I must have perceived it, indeed, before this; but this particular occasion was a kind of revelation to me: it marked a distinct step in advance. She showed a gentle pleasure when the accidents of the day brought us together.'[9]

Annie confirms that this occasion was a turning-point, though her perception is subtly different in registering that it was Leslie whose behaviour was now different. Maybe she already knew Minny's heart. 'Picnic very great success. Mrs Sartoris, Leighton Val [Prinsep] Julia Jackson Leslie Herman [Merivale] &ct &ct. Made up my mind that Leslie was serious & that he really cared for Minnie. Lunch at the Inn tea under the great trees – carts to the station – Mrs Sartoris singing.'[10] It was more than a year since they had met, so there was little of the whirlwind in their romance. What Leslie only makes clear later is that this was also the occasion when he was first introduced to Julia Jackson, already a friend of the Thackeray sisters. Jeanie Senior asked Leslie for his view of Julia. 'I forget the words of my reply, but the substance was, she is the most beautiful girl I ever saw.... I do not remember that I spoke to her. I saw and remembered her, as I might have seen and remembered the Sistine Madonna or any other representation of superlative beauty.'[11] There is a significant contrast in his representation and characterisation of the two women he would marry – his memories of Minny's 'gentle pleasure' in his presence, and of Julia transfixing him as something wholly unattainable. Both narratives are self-serving. He surrenders to (and thus gains) Minny, and despite her being 'the complete reconciliation and fulfilment of all conditions of feminine beauty',[12] Julia will eventually fall to an all-conquering Leslie.

If Minny really was the keener party initially, there were reasons for her to have appreciated qualities in this diffident man who had perhaps assumed that marriage was not for him. A serious manner was no disadvantage, certainly, especially when coupled with a vein of dry, sardonic humour that would have appealed to the Thackeray trait for (self) mockery. Leslie was developing a career in journalism and essay writing, not unlike her father's early years, though he was very different in being a less obviously clubbable man who disdained the fashionable social world upon whose attentions the novelist had come to depend. Nor was the religious scepticism which compelled Leslie to resign his Cambridge tutorship necessarily a disqualification, for an agnostic belief in human virtues was not that far removed from the liberal Christian position of the Thackerays, which had distressed their grandmother so much. By this time he had grown the full beard which in his photographic portraits, ironically enough, gives him the look of a slightly wild Old Testament prophet. When they met, she was already twenty-five and he seven years older. Time was moving on, brought home for Minny as younger friends and members of her family circle settled into marriage. So a serious, sceptical and quietly witty man may have had distinct attractions to a Thackeray daughter. And then there was that fondness for *Vanity Fair*.

By the summer picnic in 1866 an event had occurred which would profoundly affect the daily lives of both sisters. Since Amy Crowe's marriage to Edward Thackeray four years earlier, they had kept in touch with her in India, learning of the birth of a daughter, Margaret (Margie). In 1864, Amy had been urging them to visit – 'you w^d. make lots of money writing India pleasantly for the P.M.G. No one has ever done it as you w^d.... I wish oh so many things but the chief & principal – that you were growing happier – & Minny fat.'[13] They did not go, for it would have been soon after they had moved to Onslow Gardens, when they were preparing to receive their grandmother. Neither of them was ever to visit India, that starting- and meeting-place for Thackerays and Ritchies, a country whose exoticism and remoteness were evoked so frequently in their father's fiction. And then in August 1865 arrived 'the dreadful news from India', that Amy had caught a fever and died soon after the birth of her second daughter, named after Annie who noted of this latest sadness that 'it seemed as if I had known it long ago'.[14]

Edward Thackeray made immediate plans to return with his two infant daughters, and even before his arrival in Europe Annie and Minny had begun to consider taking on the rearing of Amy's children in the role of step-aunts. They crossed to Paris and stayed with Charlotte and Jane Ritchie, met Edward and a week later returned to Onslow Gardens with the two little girls. Jane Ritchie was already showing signs of her final illness, her death six weeks later serving to add to their sadness and reflection as the anniversaries of the deaths of Thackeray and their grandmother approached. Minny used one of her father's letters to affirm his constant theme that one should not pity the departed, but care for and support the survivors. The presence of children offered hope, and Minny found an intense pleasure in looking after Margie and Anny, who reminded the sisters of Amy during this inevitably sad season. '[T]here

Sketch by Thackeray

is one thing at Christmas time that makes it seem even cheerful to us & that is when we think of the thousands of happy little children who are enjoying their holidays & merrymaking – and who have never known sorrow or parting – children are indeed a blessing, as we begin to find from our babies, altho indeed they shall never come between us.'[15]

At this stage no final decision had been made about the little girls, and Minny knew that it could not assumed that they would permanently be with them, though she hoped that they might. 'Edward has made up his mind to stay at Chatham for a year – & I think it is best he should, for he could not bear the thought of going back at once, poor fellow – I never look forward to keeping the dear babies long – but while we have them they are indeed a happiness to us.' Gradually it was settled that the children should remain at Onslow Gardens whilst Edward planned his future, and this gradually took on the status of a semi-permanent solution, at least until his re-marriage some years later. He made financial provision for his daughters (though over the years had to be encouraged to supply extras for them), and Onslow Gardens acquired a new vitality as a procession of nurses and nannies

Eight: A Woman's Cares and Joys

came and went. At the start of her 1866 journal Annie summarised the themes for the year. 'Writing the Village on the Cliff. Established with Margie & Annie & nurses. Seeing people.' When the time came, Leslie could have been in no doubt that marriage to Minny would bring with it a household with two little girls as an established fixture. Much to his credit, he did not demur.

In July the Thackerays arranged for Margie and Anny to go to Wimborne to stay with the Ritchies, and themselves accepted Mrs Huth's invitation to join her family group in Switzerland. Leslie, a celebrated climber who had become President of the Alpine Club in 1865, agreed to meet them there. 'I fancy that Mrs. Huth and other persons concerned had some inkling of what was likely to result from such a meeting.'[16] The Thackerays went first to Paris to see Charlotte Ritchie, with whom they visited Jane's tomb in Montmartre. 'I can see her kneeling & kissing the gravestone.'[17] They travelled overnight to Geneva to meet the Huths, and the next day were at Chamonix, Annie working on *The Village on the Cliff* all the while. This novel which drew, as *The Story of Elizabeth* had done, on Annie's memories of French provincial life experienced in the years growing up under her grandmother's care, had started its serialisation in the *Cornhill* in July, and continued until February 1867.

The progress of this party of English travellers was recorded by Annie during the next few days.

> 21. July. Started for the Tete Noir on mules on & on & on Martigny & Visp desolation horrors
>
> 24. Goblin world. Mules passes chalets cheerful villagers voices bustle – little Inn up in the mountains
>
> 25 July passes torrents & sunshine – Mr Stephen coming over the pass to meet us. He had been waiting about & heard two travellers f^m. St Nicholas saying that we were on the way. What a caravan we were! – Mrs Huth Dely Gennie Dicky me Minny the maid the guides each leading a mule.
>
> 26. Walked to a glacier lunched under a tree. Riffelhorn – O such a day at night moonlight & mountains & snowy eerie world
>
> 27. 8000 feet over the sea Garner Grat overdone
>
> 28 Perched on a Rock over a glacier
>
> 29 Leslie S left us. I feel low & anxious & cant think what to think. Sleepy, want to work. Is he serious; is he only flirting with my Min. Last night he said Brownings lines were ringing in his head 'Just for a handful of silver he left them'.

> I remember how we all sat out at night in the little Inn garden & how I awoke & heard the guides & Ls early start & how <u>scared</u> I felt for my M.
> At St Nicholas we found a farewell note sticking in the glass f^m. LS. saying he should come & see us in London. Everything seemed different.

Leslie remembered the same few days, anxious at the prospect of surrendering his bachelor existence but admitting the reality of his love for Minny. Once again he chose to portray himself as the one who was hunted out, though by now he was an increasingly willing victim.

> I went to Zermatt – the trysting-place – alone. The Huths went first to Chamonix; and my Minny used afterwards to tell how she had dragged the whole party thence to Zermatt and how Anny had said to her, 'You must really not ask every young Alpine traveller, where is Mr. Leslie Stephen?' I meanwhile heard one day of their approach and walked down the valley to meet them. One of my sacred places ever afterwards was a point where the road winds round a little bluff near Täsch. Thence I descried the party approaching on mules – there was then no railway or even carriage-road – and I walked back with them to Zermatt. I passed there two or three days of the happiest and took my Minny (not then mine) upon the Görner Glacier and up to the Riffel. How well I remember sitting on a little grassy platform under the Riffel-Horn with Anny, Minny and Miss Huth! I began to know that my fate was fixed. Yet, rather perversely, I chose to keep an engagement which I had made with [James] Bryce (already known by his *Roman Empire*) and went with him to Vienna (where I first met George Meredith) and Transylvania. I returned in the autumn to London and still for a time waited and hesitated; not that I was not in love, but that I was still troubled by some of my old doubts and diffidence.[18]

Annie's role through all of this is curious. Above all she sought happiness for Minny, solemnly declaring this to be 'my first duty in life', but marriage would inevitably mean a change in status for them both. She was scrutinising Leslie carefully, and in some ways finding him wanting, or at least ambiguous in his intentions. She should readily be forgiven any passing feelings of jealousy, for Annie may already have concluded that at her age marriage was something that happened to other, younger, better-looking people. Leslie himself said of Annie that she 'could never be called good-looking – unless the word means looking good and Minny was very like her, but very superior in appearance if judged by the ordinary rules. Anny's face was always ill-drawn or clumsy, though singularly amiable and intelligent: Minny was like her *minus* the clumsiness.'[19] Yet the sisters were inseparable. Emotionally interdependent, they were an integral unit. It was perhaps always self-evident to Leslie that marriage would not separate his wife from her sister, and that Annie came as a further integral component of the household.

In the end, it was Annie who precipitated Leslie into action, believing him to have had quite enough time to luxuriate in his uncertainties. On 3 December Caroline Stephen invited the sisters to Porchester Square, but Annie stood firm. 'I refused & said that we had been more than enough & that I felt if Leslie wanted to see Minnie he must come to us.' Leslie is disingenuously coy about this message relayed back to him. 'I heard at last some sort of rumour that Minny or Anny felt some annoyance at my conduct. One day, therefore, I lunched by myself at the Oxford and Cambridge Club; thought over the whole affair in a philosophical spirit; and went to 16 Onslow Gardens, where I found Minny alone and made her a little speech which I had carefully thought out, setting forth all my feelings and the reason for the offer with which I concluded. Her simple "Yes" dispersed all memory of the "reasons". There was one quite sufficient reason!'[20] His hint of having taken time to mull things over does not match Annie's claim that she had propelled him into a decision, for the day after Caroline delivered her message, he was on the Onslow Gardens doorstep, and as he and Minny talked, Annie was upstairs struggling with the end of her novel.

> 4 of December the great Reform Procession. Leslie Stephen came & asked Minnie to marry him. And Minnie said yes. Heigh! Ho! how happy I am. God bless them & help me & bless my darling.
>
> I was finishing the Village [on the Cliff] when she came up to tell me. Two days after Tennyson came & I asked him to help me with the last paragraph. I was over wrought & I could see the characters of my story walking in the air – very much smaller than life like a bright colour magic lantern. I have heard of this odd impression from others since then.[21]

Soon after this engagement, Blanche Ritchie married the Eton College schoolmaster and writer, Frank Warre Cornish (he later become Vice-Provost of Eton), at Wimborne. Influenza prevented

Annie from going, so Minny and Leslie went to Dorset without her, taking Margie as a bridesmaid. Minny summarised events after the wedding breakfast, the married couple having departed in the Thackerays' former carriage. It was her first public appearance with Leslie since their engagement, and clearly he had made a significant concession in attending a gathering of largely unknown Ritchies, though the presence of Robert Browning and Kegan Paul gave him congenial people to talk to. Minny knew that he was trying hard, but true to fashion Leslie 'seemed much inclined to swear', and was distracted by the loss of his portmanteau on the train journey to Dorset, which only reappeared after a couple of days.

> The wedding is just over and Blanchie has gone off in the poor old carriage with Felici on the box, but the guests are still rambling about in the hall & Leslie is going for a little walk with Mr Paul & Mr Browning and then coming back for me – I should have enjoyed it myself more if Leslie had liked it better but I am afraid he has felt it rather fearful except for me – & I can quite fancy myself not much enjoying such a wedding in his family if I did not know them – his spirits however like most peoples always rise with his meals, w^h. are fortunately very good here just now ... Mrs Paul rushed up and kissed me – and they all say that we are much in love with each other. I dont know what Leslie would do here if it wasnt for me except that of course he wouldnt be here at all – shall do my best never to take him to any respectable place again – but bohemia he will like I know.[22]

Annie felt the approaching change even more acutely than Minny, for whom it could only help soften the loss of their father. A letter to Lady Houghton captures her uncertainty, generous as always yet newly vulnerable, longing for Thackeray now that Minny was removing herself a little from the shared memories of the past and stepping confidently into the next phase of her life.

> She is so very very happy thank God & is going to marry Mr Stephen who is very happy too. I think if I were not so fond of him I should rather envy him. He is FitzJames Stephens younger brother & I think he lost his heart almost the very first time he ever saw her & she has always liked him better than anybody else & now I cannot tell you how happy they are – I never saw 2 people enjoy one anothers society more than my two & if only I had Papa to talk to about it I should

> want nothing else. But I am quite sure he would have liked him & I know that you & dear Lord Houghton will like to hear of her happiness.[23]

Their friend, Charlotte Williams-Wynn, asked just the right question. She remembered seeing Minny years before when she was sick with scarlet fever in Italy, but it was for Annie she felt now. Knowing just how much the sisters lived for each other, what would the future arrangements be? 'A certain, little, wistful sick face in a bed at Naples comes before me now so vividly than I can hardly believe <u>that</u> child should now be about to take on herself a woman's cares & joys! Tell me dear; what do <u>you</u> do? It must, I think be a "<u>marriage a trois</u>".'[24]

Annie continued to be weakened by 'flu over Christmas, so she and Minny spent it with the generously welcoming Lady Stephen and Caroline whilst Leslie was in Cambridge, shortly to terminate the academic life which resignation of his fellowship had meant. His principal purpose for staying there now was to secure the re-election of his friend, Henry Fawcett, to a fellowship at Trinity Hall. He and Minny wrote daily during their eight-day separation, and she soon overcame the slight awkwardness that writing to a lover involved. The season was a poignant one. 'I feel rather shy about writing to you, I hope I shall not often have much need of writing to you dear Leslie.... Tomorrow will bring me a letter and tell me all about it – and I wish it was tomorrow although it is Christmas day & I do not much like Christmas days – but I shall be very thankful on this one & happier than I ever expected to be.'[25] Leslie concluded his own letter on Christmas Day by acknowledging her role in rescuing him from his old life. 'Here alone, I feel that morbid sentiment wh. old Fawcett talks about creeping in upon me & I hope, but scarcely expect, that I shall be able to keep it at arm's length till Monday next. Whether I do or dont, I shall not cease to cling to thoughts of you as the happiest thing I have left.'[26]

On Christmas Day, the doctor decided that Annie could return to Onslow Gardens, and that night she and Minny quarreled, trivially enough, but sufficient to draw her attention to the inevitability of change with its repercussions. 'My Min & I spent the eve^g together squabbled called each other names what should I do without her to squabble with.'[27] That day, Minny had written to Julia Jackson about the death of Holman Hunt's wife, the sisters once again presented with memories of their own loss. 'To us this season of the year is one which naturally makes us think & feel with those who have had to go through the terrible parting – and I am sure that being as happy as I am does not make one less sorry for those who are unhappy – Indeed I have the same feeling in happiness as in sorrow, which is that it is impossible that love should end here – or we should never be allowed to love so dearly.'[28] To Leslie, she could not help remarking on the pettiness of the world which he described so minutely.

> Your letters do not give me a happier impression of Cambridge life than I had evolved out of myself. It seems to me very dreary, & rather small, & I cannot help feeling angry that you should have passed so many of your best years there, & very thankful that you are quit of the whole business not that it can have done you any harm, for I don't believe that anything on this earth would do you harm – but it would be enough to demoralise most people & very likely does – I have a great many opinions about Cambridge that I do not feel quite equal to giving you just yet – particularly as they would be too radical to please you, & of course a Don must be more or less of a conservative.[29]

Alone in Cambridge Leslie was surrounded by evidence of the life he was leaving behind. He set out the reasons why he favoured a June marriage, knowing that even in the first excitement of her own happiness, Minny was feeling her sister's anguish in having to adjust to the change. On his part, Leslie was entirely sanguine about Annie's situation, wanting to protect her from the jibes which might come for continuing to live with her married sister. He insisted that there was no reason why she should not be able to maintain her independence within the new arrangement. 'If we agree to June, there is no particular hurry about houses. But dont you think it would be worth while to enquire into that house of Leech's, whereof we spoke? I say so for this reason amongst others; it seemed by your account to be a large one & consequently one in wh. there would be plenty of room for <u>all</u> of us. The more I think, the more I am convinced that Anny should in no way separate from us &, if we were committed to a suitable house, the matter would be settled for good & she could be teased about it in no way.'[30]

Having heard a rumour that John Leech's widow might wish to move from her Kensington house, Minny thought that it might suit the three of them. Encouraged by Leslie, she visited Mrs Leech, but the house was not available. 'I saw an oldfashioned house to let in Kensington Square that we can go & look at when you come home, it will be a very nice occupation for us to look over houses – I have rather a fancy for a house with a studio, or some big room to make a nice healthy smoking room.' But for Minny, it was unimportant where they lived, for all that

Eight: A Woman's Cares and Joys

mattered was that the three should keep together – 'wherever I am as long as you are there & Anny, I shall be sure to like it'. She concludes in a blur of anticipated domestic happiness, already alert to his short temper at disturbed routines and personal inconveniences. A tiepin had been mislaid when they had gone to Dorset for Blanche and Frank's wedding, and unlike the lost portmanteau had yet to turn up. 'They have promised to look about everywhere for it – please dont be angry with me. I assure you I am very sorry that you should lose anything you like the only thing I can think of to comfort you, is to have our bureau bear set as a pin for you.'[31]

A few days before Leslie returned on New Year's Eve came the triumph of Henry Fawcett's fellowship election, something of a coup for Leslie who had worked hard to procure sufficient votes. Minny was politely pleased with the news, and genuinely surprised to find how much she had missed him. 'It is very absurd that you & I should want each other so much after having done without for all these years – I suppose it is human nature – but it must be very inconvenient sometimes, when people are not of one mind or so fortunate altogether as we are – I was delighted to hear the good news about Mr Fawcett – & believe that it was entirely your doing.'[32] In his reply, Leslie offered a striking admission to the redemptive qualities of Minny's love, an expectation of happiness that would be fully vindicated during the nine years they would have together.

> I feel what you say, as to the strangeness that we who have done without each other all these years should now miss each other so much. It *is* strange in one sense; & it will do me good to feel, more than I felt before, how indispensable you have become to me, & how much I am & always shall be in need of your kindness. But I can understand it as far as I am concerned. You say in one of your letters that Cambridge cannot have done me harm. I hope, & believe, that it has not dried me up into a hopeless mummy, walking about 'to save funeral expenses', & with a soul that ought to rattle like a pea in a pod.... I am quite conscious of the defects wh. such a life has produced in my character, though you have kindly overlooked them, or not yet found them out. But, my dearest Minny, I hope also that I am not too far gone to be revived by the love of such a woman as you. What I can do to deserve your affection, I shall do not only out of love for you, but in the hopes of improving myself & restoring my faculties that have been cramped by disuse.[33]

He was back in London the day she received this, and that night, the last of the old year, Annie sat upstairs and left the lovers happy in their own company. It was another moment when she felt intensely close to her father. Even in her wistfulness she only felt contentment for Minny, and a childlike hopefulness for the future. 'Still ailing. Minnie & Leslie down stairs. I read over some old letters in bed & cried & said my prayers. Pray God make us good & cheerful & simple & faithful. Pray God bless Papa wherever he is & M & make all crooked paths straight. & Thank God for his great new mercy to us & for my dearests happiness.'[34]

There are scarcely any journal entries for 1867, the year of the marriage. This may simply reflect that Annie either lost or did not keep a diary for that year, so that nothing was available by the time she compiled the journal thirty years later. The few entries pull together a few almost random details, although the presence of dates does imply that some original record survived. But it seems strange that there should be no moment of reflection on the year's signal event, as there invariably is on other red-letter occasions through the journal. Instead, the months leading up to the wedding are captured in the briefest of remarks.

> 28 Jan. Came home f^m. Brighton better. Pipes burst. Seeing a great deal of Millais, Collins, &ct
> 16. Feb Village on the Cliff came home in a book.[35] Leslie & Minny engaged couple. Amberleys coming a good deal.
> We spent some weeks at Wimbledon in the Spring.
> 4th of May to Southend to see Mama.

Nor are there many clues in the sparse surviving correspondence from these months to indicate what Annie was thinking. As word of the engagement spread, friends were sensitive to the change in life which this would bring to both sisters. One acquaintance picked up on the rumours that Annie would still be living with Leslie and Minny, news which reassured her. 'I hope it is true that you will not be separated, so that there will not be that pang, which even the happiest marriage of a sister cannot quite compensate.'[36] The painter G.F. Watts, by now a close Freshwater friend, offered Minny congratulations and a rather special wedding gift. 'You will believe how very glad I am & how much I wish you every possible happiness without my attempting to tell you. What shall I give you for your wedding present, a portrait of Mr Stephens [sic], or of your sister Annie?'[37] Minny chose Annie.

Leslie proved to be a sympathetic and sensitive prospective brother-in-law, reassuring Annie about her secure place in his affections. He

Eight: A Woman's Cares and Joys

enlisted her support against the tyrannical rule he playfully assigned to Minny, who insisted that he accompany her to parties, and who did her best to take his wardrobe in hand. As Annie stayed to put the final touches to *The Village on the Cliff* in Brighton, where they had both gone after Christmas, Minny returned to Lady Stephen's house from where Leslie wrote playfully and in search of sympathy. But there was a serious purpose, as his closing plea and undertaking to Annie reveals.

> I was cruelly subjected to Mrs Huth's party last night, being trotted out in spite of pathetic remonstrances, wh. did not soften Minny's heart. On the contrary, she affected to believe that I secretly wished for it & I was made to stand upon my legs looking very glum & sulky for an hour & a half & being sulked at by Coles, Hoares & persons of that description ... Mamma says that she likes to see me brought to order, but I hope that you will sympathise with me because you have suffered under the same tyranny.
>
> ... I shall be very glad when you come back, even though you take my tormentor out of this house & all that dreary long way across the park. – It is pleasant to have if not an auxiliary at least a fellow sufferer under Minny.
>
> You see I cant write about anything else as yet, at least when writing to you. Don't be jealous in consequence & forgive me as soon as possible (I know you haven't yet) for carrying off your sister. I will try to make it up.[38]

That pointed phrase used in the journal – 'Leslie & Minny engaged couple' – encapsulates what these months meant to her. Just as she had watched Minny surrendering herself to the magic of the Palace Green theatricals, emblematic of a dramatic world apparently unavailable to Annie herself, so now her sister's already altered state anticipated the rituals of an approaching married life unavailable to spinsterhood. Being engaged transformed Minny and Leslie into a couple with a defined future, with the privileges and duties attached to that undeniably powerful status. The same journal entry recalls the other significant event of early 1867, the novel's publication. The title page carries the place and date of its formal completion, 'Brighton, January 27th, 1867', and also a dedication, to 'Harriet Thackeray'. It is understandable that Annie should have wanted to associate her sister with this book redolent of shared French summers spent with their grandparents, as well as the very last one on the Normandy coast in the months before their grandmother died, but curious that she should record Minny in this formal way just as her name was about to change for ever. Nobody ever called her Harriet anyway, and in six months 'Thackeray' would surrender to 'Stephen'. It is almost as if in thus fixing the dedicatee, Annie was ensuring for Minny's name a permanence which would in all other ways soon be lost, with the inference that the significance of birth and family transcended the accident of marriage.

News of the approaching marriage spread beyond London, relayed in the society columns of one or two regional papers, but not without some reporting errors. *The Newcastle Courant* declared on 15 February that Leslie was to marry Annie, 'the daughter of the great novelist, and herself one of the most rising of our writers of fiction'. It was perhaps an understandable error, though one capable of upsetting all of those concerned. Leslie would have been irritated less by being assigned to the wrong sister than by the way he was described as 'a tolerably well-known writer'.

He would willingly have been spared some of the engagement rituals. Though he tried to laugh off having to make visits as Minny's fiancé, in his opinion it really was so much wasted time. Ten days before the marriage, he wrote one of his six-monthly letters to his Boston friend, Oliver Wendell Holmes Jr, summing up his transformed status. Behind the wit, there is anxiety at the loss of freedom entailed in such a commitment. Certain Alpine exploits would be curtailed by his new responsibilities.

> A man, when engaged, is to other men little better than a brute beast & I have been more so (if that is grammar). Miss Thackeray's sister has been rather unwell. I am happy to say she has quite got over it & consequently we have been living about in suburban lodgings after a scrambling rigmarole sort of way, with my lodgings, for the sake of propriety (damn it) a quarter of a mile off, & my books left at home & my Miss flying all over the place... being formally introduced to all sorts of friends & relatives who generally inform me they knew Mr Thackeray when he was a boy at school & seem to think that I ought to have done so, & having to tear off to dinner-parties at the other end of London & generally getting into a state of confusion, perplexity & muddle wh., thank God, once more, – I am not usually so pious – is rapidly coming to an end. In fact being engaged is very pleasant, though it is rather a waste of time, but I hope marriage will be better still & I am quite certain that after months of London fog (not but that what London has the finest climate in the

Watercolour by Thackeray

world mind you) I shall be devilish glad to see once more the Jungfrau Mönch & Eiger. Shall I be allowed to risk my (now) precious limbs in ascending any of these mountains? I dont know, but I must say I shall grudge the deprivation, even though it will be jolly loafing about the valleys.[39]

They had given up thoughts of finding a new house, and instead 16 Onslow Gardens became home for them all for several years. Leslie simply moved in, and assumed the status of head of household. At first, Annie appeared to think it important that she should live separately at least for some of the time. She took a cottage in Henley-on-Thames whilst the Stephens were on honeymoon, and they joined her there on their return. She spent much of the rest of that first year in Henley, travelling up to London regularly from Oxfordshire, but by December she had returned to Onslow Gardens. Although she kept the cottage into 1868, she had resolved to give it up. It was 'lonely and expensive'. As Annie moved back to London permanently, Leslie felt that they were joining her rather than the other way round. 'She was certainly the most conspicuous figure in the house.'[40]

The wedding was early in the day, at 8 a.m. in the adjacent church in Onslow Square, to make the minimum of fuss and to allow a quick escape to France 'to avoid all folly of breakfasts', as Leslie put it. For Minny, there was an obvious sadness in not having her father to give her away, but having known the daughters ever since their Young Street days twenty years before, Henry Cole offered to perform this duty. Because he was coming from Paris, there was some doubt as to whether he would actually appear in time, and Herman Merivale stood by as a deputy. Cole's biographers capture the quiet drama of his appearance. 'But when the words "Who giveth?" were spoken, a figure, until then unobserved, emerged from the shadow of a pillar and solemnly said: "I do." It was Henry Cole perfectly dressed for the occasion: how he had crossed the Channel was never known.'[41] In fact, Cole had been back in London for a day or so, so he was just ordinarily late.

Later that day, having crossed to Boulogne, Minny was already concerned to know how Annie was coping in her absence. 'My own darling how I do hope that you are not moping for me. I am already thinking a great deal of coming back to Henley.'[42] Leslie suffered from hay fever all the way from Folkestone, and she had been constantly seasick. As for Annie, she would spend the next day or two in a mood of somewhat unreal excitement. She wrote the day following the wedding, after travelling to Eton to stay with Edward Thackeray's brother and his wife, St John and Louisa Thackeray. On the train down she had been amused to be taken for the Miss Thackeray who had just got married. Before leaving Onslow Gardens she had packed up the valuables, but otherwise left the house in a state of confusion. Imagining the newly-weds as free-spirited birds flying away from her was depressing, but she dismissed that thought with recollections of the previous day in a breathless and chaotic letter symptomatic of her state of mind.

> Darling I forgot to tell you yesterday that I am quite amazed & ashamed of being so happy. I thought I shouldnt have eaten left off crying cared about anything – It all went off after luncheon & I met the girls at the Station and we came down with Mr Gurney in the train with a rose in his buttonhole, who seemed puzzled & I think thought I had been married that morning.... Darling we found y^r thimble w^h. I have got in my purse as a little sign of you. I look at your picture but it isnt you & I'll send you mine as soon as I get it back – I will try & write to you again before I go but this little conversation is distracting. Katie & I packed up all your plate into Cornhill

box no 1 yesterday & all y^r trinkets into the loveletterbox all the flowers were flowering & all the chairs in a confusion and all the house horrible when I came away – I was so glad to get off & to come here to this queer little colony. Two kind little birds came flying across the park right over my head & I thought they were you & Leslie, and I can't tell you how happy it made me for yesterday morning when I looked out the first thing I saw were two birds flying away over the house tops & that made me miserable.... Gussie's love to you & Leslie & she saw M^r. Cole exhausted with his mornings labour fast asleep in a hansom. Three people have asked me if you & Alan [Cole] were ever in love, because they say they shall never forget the expression on his face. Goodbye goodbye my dear dearest. Give Leslie my love & tell him I like him much better than anybody else I ever knew for my brother. I enclose my card. Do buy some Liebig if you can. I did mean to put some up.

George Eliot is here and everybody is much excited. Goodbye once more.[43]

The next day she provided more reactions to the wedding. The smallness of scale had disappointed some and confused others. Jane Brookfield's postman commented that there had only been two carriages, thinking that 'Miss Thackeray might have had a grander wedding'. Annie was herself planning to leave for Paris. 'I shall like to be where you have been & to gather up the fragments of the beloved piqué dress.' But she was also troubled by what she had seen in the *Times*. 'O my dear there has a cruel blow indeed been inflicted – Caroline & I made out a little thing for the paper, & Fitzjames of his own accord put another in all wrong with every thing we had meant to leave out & he didnt put S^t. John in & so when I came down this morning poor S^t. John flung the paper away with a face of agony & groaned out "They havent put me in at all".' At Eton, she had been alternately amused and touched by the attention paid by George Eliot to Anny and Margie, and by George Lewes asking after Minny's and her own composure during the ceremony.

My mind is still confused – I nearly arranged to go to Antwerp to stay with the Huths but I didnt fancy sleeping at Brussels all alone & so I shall go with M^r. Cole tomorrow & try & cheer up Alan. Perhaps he may transfer his affections to me. Herman says that Leslie is a very fine fellow & very nice indeed to you but that he feels as if he had had one hand cut off.

> George Eliot was in the Eton playing fields yesterday when Blanche & the children were sitting on a little low wall together. Blanche said two hideous but majestic forms came up walking [*she includes a sketch*] like that very quick and all doubled up – & some one said this is little Margaret Thackeray & George Eliot ran after her cried out George George! what a darling little girl kissed both her hands & then rushed after the baby & said they were the dearest little children that she had often heard of them & then Mr Lewes came up & said and was Miss Thackeray much agitated during her marriage & when Blanche said no he said & Annie how did she bear it, at w^h. Mr Cornish opened his eyes & gave a start of surprise.[44]

She and Gussie Ritchie visited the Henley cottage, and were disappointed to find it shut up and the garden overgrown, but Annie looked forward to Minny's reappearance when they could all be comfortable there. Meanwhile, she prepared to return to London the next day, and to see Lady Stephen and Caroline. Lady Stephen had attended another wedding the day following her son's, an altogether grander affair as she reported to the honeymooners, with perhaps a small hint of disappointment that their own nuptials had not been more showy. 'We had such a different wedding from yours yesterday!... 8 bridesmaids covered with tulle & blue ribbons & flowers – ladies gorgeously apparelled & a magnificent breakfast tables going the whole length of the two large rooms covered with every delicacy.' She knew that Minny was anxious about Annie, and thoughtfully reassured her – 'now this morning she has come herself looking so bright & so happy'.[45]

Annie was calming down. In the company of Leslie's mother and sister she was with sympathetic spirits, and together they thought fondly of their absent travellers. 'Dear Lady Stephen & Caroline are so good to me. I quite feel a sort of coming home feel when I come here much more than at home when you arn't there. They look very well & we are all thinking of the same two things & praying God bless them.'[46]

Nine

A GREAT ENORMOUS HALF GROWN PLACE
(1867-1868)

It seems as if Leslie & I had lived together all our lives like you & I, & had never been separated & never will, as please God you & I never will.

Minny to Annie
23 June 1867

Minny slipped so easily into marriage that it seemed almost like a continuation of her former life. On her wedding trip she wrote every day to Annie, letters crowded with detail – an itinerary of the day's activities, comments about the people at the table d'hôte and everyone encountered that day worthy of mention, what somebody said, the layout of a hotel room, the view through a window, a description of the street outside. She now added to this established repertoire her observations on married life, having discovered that husbands supplied ample comic material, particularly one like Leslie whose dress sense was rudimentary. 'Leslie is always ready to help me to pack but his notions of folding are rather vague'; 'he is always perfectly happy & thinks he is very cautious if he has what he calls a change of one wringing wet suit to another'.

There were familiar topographical landmarks to report – at Berne they put up in the Hôtel Fauçon, where Thackeray had stayed with his daughters fifteen years before, for despite new hotels having sprung up since then, 'I thought I should like this best'.[1] Although the idea led to nothing, they began to talk of building a chalet at Murren so that they might return regularly. In the usual style of British middle-class travellers, the couple saw fellow foreign visitors as a source of great irritation. At Interlaken Minny was distracted and perhaps embarrassed by the boorishness of a newly-married German couple. Leslie took against Germans in particular, 'what he calls damndutchmen', but also their fellow English, 'beings of the contemptibilist shopkeeper order'. He feared for the future of Alpine walking. 'Alas! If Cocknies come even now what will it be in a few years?'[2]

As the days passed, Minny felt more comfortable in her new role.

> Darling I should like you to be married once just for a week to see how pleasant it is & then I sh^d like your husband to disappear.... It seems as if Leslie & I had lived together all our lives like you & I, & had never been separated & never will, as please God you & I never will – darling when you are on one side of me & Leslie on the other, it seems to me that I shall have no earthly anxiety & as perfect happiness as ever anyone had in this world – but when you are away from me, I cannot help being just a little anxious & afraid that you are not quite happy – but I know that it will make you happy to think of me & my Lez. I cannot talk of what he is, any more than I could of you darling – or my own Papa – but I feel as if we should all be happy in heaven together some day, & indeed life is more like heaven than life to me just now. This is a private Spoony letter for you alone my own darling, but you see the rainy weather doesnt affect our happiness much.[3]

Perhaps she believed that marriage was not now going to happen for Annie, that age and opportunity had conspired against her. Yet Minny's own changed status gave her sister the freedom to develop her career as the unchallenged Thackeray daughter. As Froude wrote to Annie, 'I shall be much surprised if you do not carry on into the next generation the fame of the name which you bear'.[4]

Meanwhile, Annie was in Paris, staying first with Henry Cole and his family – Cole was overseeing the British section of the Universal Exhibition – and then with Pinkie and her aunt, Charlotte Ritchie. She sent letters to await Minny's arrival at Zermatt. 'M^r. Cole says he met an unknown individual yesterday who exclaimed so Leslie Stephen has married Miss Thackeray, an excellent good fellow: he then went on to tell Mr Cole that some of the guides were very unhappy about it & said this w^d. be an end of him. For I suppose a guide naturally thinks that theres nothing else going on anywhere but climbing up & down mountains.'[5] She went on a picnic to Versailles on 6 July with the Cole sisters, during which it poured. In the soaking rain, Annie for a moment forgot herself and started hunting for Minny. 'I got into an absurd fuss at the Picnic thinking you were wet through somewhere out in the rain, not seeing you come up with any of the people. It was only for a minute & I have <u>never</u> minded being away from you so little though I shant be sorry when the 3 last pens are written out darling & I see y^r dear old round face again & Leslies long one.' The intense dreams had returned, perhaps brought on by meeting a Mrs Perkins in Paris, 'a pretty lady with a pretty sister Papa used to tell us about. I dont remember much, but I know he was a little in love with the sister.... I dreamt of you all night long & a sea shore & Papa & Baby somehow jumped out of my arms & rushed into the sea it was a melancholy happy sort of dream.'[6] It strangely echoes the story of her mother, who years before in a moment of mental lapse had led Annie into the sea at Margate before recovering herself and pulling her back to safety.

The haphazard organisation of the wedding continued to have ramifications, and Annie had found herself settling unpaid fees for the church and its officials like the parish clerk and pew-opener. 'Mr Gibbs said that comes of not having a best man: but I think if you were going to be married to Leslie again you wouldnt do it differently & the Coles still talk about the bridesmaids.'

By 8 July Minny and Leslie were on their way via St Luc to Zermatt, scene of their romantic encounter the year before. They did ample justice to the enormous, cholesterol-charged meals put before them, and Leslie documented one of them, confident of Annie's interest.

> We have been up the Bella Tola & come down again & had dinner, of wh. this is our bill of fare. (I have partaken fully of every dish – Min of some)
>
> Soup. Bread. Water. souché
> Bouillie beef with grease in a separate dish
> Mashed potatoes
> Ham. & cold french beans
> Batter pudding (baked) with cherries (encored under the impression that it was the last)
> Liver, mashed potatoes & grease (in the same dish)
> Veal, potatoes, & salad & grease
> Custards (eaten very freely under the impression that it was the last)
> Boiled batter pudding with cherries (eaten still more freely under the impression, happily nearly true, that it was the last)
> Figs, nuts & a particularly stodgy pastry.

After this you cant expect a flowing description of scenery, but this has been a very successful day. Dear Min is asleep – whether from the effects of mountain air or of cherry-pie. She always takes naps on her mule after lunch, so I guess it is cherry pie. Excuse this rather disgusting P.S. We are very well & very happy & enjoying every day very much – in spite of cherries & batter.[7]

As they pursued their gruelling journey on foot and mule through idyllic scenery towards Zermatt, Minny was surprised to realise that '3 weeks of married life have passed over our heads'. They were travelling through scenes of some of Leslie's earlier Alpine triumphs, and they stopped overnight in the village from which he had ascended the Rothhorn, choosing not the inn where he had stayed before, 'one of those black pigsty looking places', but a new one which turned out to be infested with fleas. They reached St Niklaus on 12 July, their last stop before Zermatt, and although the guide had had to cut steps in order for Minny's mule to find a footing in the snow, from here the journey would be simpler. This was fortunate, for the weather showed signs of breaking again.

It was a great treat in Zermatt to be handed a clutch of Annie's characteristically undated letters from Paris. 'Leslie tried to arrange them for me by the postmarks but it was impossible, so I read them all higgledy piggeldy.' She scanned them for clues to Annie's state of mind, fearing melancholy, or worse – 'your letters gave me rather a dismal feel about the middle of them, for I saw that you had been out of sorts & tired while staying at the Coles, but I cheered up when Mrs Brookfield came. I do so hope she did, somehow I always felt that you w^d be unwell at the Coles, & told Charlotte so.'[8] By this time, Annie had returned to England, and was writing to thank George Smith for sending a copy of the third edition of *The Village on the Cliff*. 'I have had such a pleasant little trip & such happy letters from my bride & bridegroom who are scrambling about, Minny on, & Leslie walking beside the mule wh. has to have steps cut out for it as if it was a member of the A.C. [Alpine Club].'[9]

Already Minny was thinking ahead to their return, and took charge of the domestic planning, both in terms of the servants and the furnishings. Annie had been buying some things in Paris, mainly bits of porcelain, but Minny was conscious that both the Henley cottage (where they would initially be staying) and indeed Onslow Gardens needed taking in hand. 'I am beginning to think a great deal ab^t. Henley furniture – your Paris things sound very nice indeed – Only it seems to

Sketch by Thackeray

me that most of our furniture will be a little ornamental china.... You must not (<u>this is a strictly private letter</u>) buy any 4 post beds for me & Leslie – for it would be very uncomfortable for us, as he sleeps with nothing at all on except a sheet, & I like heaps of clothes. I think you had best take every thing you can from Onslow Gardens & Leslie & I can fill up the gaps in OG.'

Their original plan had always included taking in the Dolomites and Venice, where Minny intended buying glass, but they were enjoying themselves so much in Zermatt that they decided to abandon that part of the return leg and instead head directly towards Milan and St Moritz, before stopping at Zürich en route to Paris. Zermatt also brought back memories of the previous year for Leslie, who in a note added to one of Minny's letters included Annie in his recollections of that previous trip. 'It is a beautiful moonlight night just like last year & I can see the Matterhorn out of the window also just like it was last year.... The Huths are not here & Miss Thackeray is not here; nor indeed can Miss Minny T. be said to be here properly speaking: but there is a very pleasant person present who strongly reminds me of her & I think of the other Miss T. very often & very affectionately.'[10] The day before departing Zermatt they took a little picnic with them and found some edelweiss, which Minny divided up and enclosed in letters to Annie and to Blanche Warre Cornish. As she said to Blanche, it 'only grows very high up & all the guides & climbers wear a bit in their hats – & I know that it is a most lucky little flower'.[11]

The Stephens had no expectation that they would be adding to the size of the Onslow Gardens household. 'Lez & I both think that we had better make ourselves comfortable as we dont think we shall have any children & when we do we can make different arrangements.'[12] In a note written after she had gone to bed and which presumably she would not read, Leslie added to Minny's next letter a few lines for Annie. 'I am (private & confidential) very glad that we have skirted Venice &c in this hot weather',[13] which may indicate his thoughts that the possible health risks of the city should be avoided so as to maximise the chances of a successful pregnancy. His wife's own expectation of childlessness was a theme to which she returned ten days later, when the sight of some English children made her more wistful about the notion of having one of her own. 'I was much pleased by the attentions of 2 nice Yorkshire schoolboys one of them was very fat & freckled with red hair & I took a great fancy to him because I thought that if ever I had a son he w^d be like this boy – however I dont think theres the slightest chance of my having one.'[14]

Minny had long put behind her the tiny appetite of her infant years, taking the same kind of pleasure in trying different gastronomic novelties as had her father. There was a memorable prune omelette with rum before they reached St Niklaus, and shortly before they crossed the frontier into Italy 'we had the most delicious dinner that you ever tasted with stewed peaches & chamois & gerkins & other delicacies'. For her, Switzerland was undeniably grand and its landscape heroic, but Italy additionally offered a vibrancy and vitality drawn from the lives of its peasantry and the beauty of its children. There was an authenticity about the people, who appealed to her far more than they ever could to Leslie – 'my feelings rose into my heart & Leslie tried to quench them. We hadnt been in the country two minutes before long files of peasants came trooping down the road looking like brown virgins & Elizabeths with red handkerchiefs on & such dear little soft eyed children like squirrels.'[15] Leslie thought Milan shabby and dirty, whereas for her it was the smartest of Italian towns. As she remarked to Leslie's sister, she could not imagine what he would make of Rome. His disapproval of the surroundings seems to have led him to strike something of a pose, much to Minny's amusement – 'he is now swaggering up & down the street with the Milanese dandies in his marriage coat & white waistcoat on the strength of w^h. I was called milady yesterday. Leslie has taken the poor dandies here in horror. They are a trifle oily, but he looks at them as if he wouldnt touch them with the tongs.'[16]

Minny continued to make plans, with ideas for regular guests at Onslow Gardens. 'We mean to have people to dinner every other Sunday & no dinner on the alternate ones so as to give the servants a holliday.'[17] She had worked out that on their return they would stay just one night with Lady Stephen and Caroline 'because I shall be so very anxious to go to Henley & see Anny', and now that their noses were turned towards England she was eager to get back. Nevertheless the wedding trip had been a signal success. 'It is the greatest nonsense to say that new married couples are shy & miserable – I should advise all of them to go to Switzerland.'[18] Despite all her doubts, she was returning as yet unaware of the fact that she was pregnant. After two days in Paris, spent hurrying to dressmakers and attending the Paris Universal Exhibition, they crossed to Dover on 2 August and arrived by train at Victoria.

The way in which Minny writes about Henley suggests that the cottage was intended to be a country residence for them all, with Onslow Gardens as their London house. Had Annie simply wanted her own base, why did she not take somewhere else in London, so that she could continue to have easy access to her large network of friends? Minny was insistent that her sister should not feel in any way set apart from Leslie and herself, and may have been less happy about two houses in the first place. But although Annie spent much of the rest of the summer and autumn at Henley, it was hard to see it as a real home. She lacked the objects and people round her to make it seem like one, so was especially grateful to George Smith for supplying a Thackeray portrait which she hung in the cottage. 'It is not quite him, & yet it brings him to me so plainly that it has given a home feeling to this little place w^h. it never had before. I look at it when I come home & it makes my thought of him very real – to me.'[19]

As Minny's plans for buying Venetian glassware had to be abandoned, Frederic Leighton offered to buy things on their behalf as he passed through Venice on his return from Lindos, near Rhodes. It was no idle promise, for he wrote from Lindos for the details which Annie, inevitably, had forgotten to give him before he left London. He insisted that it would be no burden for him – 'I will choose the prettiest things in the world for you and they shall be very cheap' – and then went on to describe the startling beauty of his travels with all the wonder of a Renaissance cosmographer.

> For myself I have seen many wonderful places and such queer folk since we met and am enjoying myself very much. I have seen countries where the geese are pelicans and the cows buffaloes, where the frogs are tortoises and the caterpillars lizards – I have seen the sea bluer than sapphires and covered with white gulls as thick as daisies in May – I have seen Mosques wrought exquisitely in white marble and inlaid with tiles blue and green like the deep sea – I have seen men bristling with daggers and pistols like a pincushion with pins and women with slippers over their boots…. I will tell you all about my journey when I get home if you care to hear it – and may, I hope, be able to show you some sketches that will give you an idea of some of the most striking parts.[20]

Writing from Henley, Leslie let Oliver Wendell Holmes know of his return, regretful to have missed 'bounding from peak to peak across the fathomless abysses of the glaciers', but believing himself saved from Cambridge donnishness. The newly-established household took daily boating trips on the Thames, but it was too soporific an environment to satisfy him for long. 'My sister-in-law has taken a cottage here; a little ivy covered romantic cottage & suitable for a popular authoress & consequently a trifle damp…. It is a small scenery, but exquisitely finished & pleasant to live in. It stinks of country-gentlemen & retired ½ pay officers.'[21] It was not long before he was yearning for London.

> 16 Onslow Gardens is a paradise to me, & I like the streets and gutters round there better than all the lanes & commons of Surrey. I would rather be a doorkeeper in the South Kensington Museum than dwell in the palaces of the country squires. In fact, I am getting decidedly bored & find myself thinking very often of my dear little study & its books & my rocking-chair & comforts – I dont think you know what comfort means & you rather prefer living in a confused litter & writing on odds and ends of paper in disorderly rooms with nothing to sit on. I cant bear it and shall not really settle to my work till I get back again.[22]

But the fresh air and tranquillity provided a welcome haven during the early weeks of Minny's pregnancy. When Leslie next wrote to Holmes, at the end of December and now back in London, he announced that in the previous weeks she had spent much of her time 'very unwell' confined to the sofa. 'She is getting better, however, & her illness is not of a nature to give me much anxiety, except as it offers prospect that in a certain number of months I shall be a father.'[23] In fact, both he and Annie were very concerned. If on days when the sisters were apart Minny was not herself well enough to write, Leslie provided Annie with the latest bulletin. In February, she was visiting the Rothschilds at Mentmore Towers in Bedfordshire when the telegram came to call her back to Onslow Gardens and an unhappy outcome. 'Horrid journey up. thank God she was safe but the poor little boy had come too soon & did not live.'[24] She enlisted other members of the family as distractions for Minny, including Gussie Ritchie. 'I long for you to come & charm away poor Mins troubles again. She has been as bad as ever, but thank God this morg she seems more bonny.'[25]

Of Minny's feelings there is no record of this time. Her letters have been lost, or silently pruned. That she was physically weak is certain, but in her journal Annie's simply records that 'early in April we went to Freshwater & Minnie got well'. In June Leslie told Holmes of the loss, and of his intention to bring Minny to America in the autumn. 'The baby was born prematurely. It was a trial for us both, but I am happy to say, that she is now perfectly well & strong. We are therefore more at liberty than we might have been.'[26] Leslie may well have seen an American trip as a healing distraction for Minny, but it was an adventure he had envisaged even before their marriage. More than a year earlier he had told Holmes of Minny's keenness to cross the Atlantic, despite being 'somewhat secesh in her principles'.[27] Siding with the former secessionist southern states had been the standard English position during the Civil War, but it was not Leslie's view. He looked forward to re-visiting the United States, 'more especially that pure & reformed part of them wh. surrounds Boston'.

Their passage was booked for 8 August from Liverpool, on board the *China*, a Cunard steamship, and travelling with them was Herman Charles Merivale, set to promote his play-writing ventures in Boston and New York. They left London by train, Annie seeing them off before returning to Oatlands Park, the Walton-on-Thames country hotel where William Wetmore Story's family and a group of fellow New England Brahmins spent the summer. Annie, Minny and Leslie had all been some days with the Storys and their guests while final preparations for the American trip were made, and from where Annie wrote ahead to Mrs Baxter in New York, dreading the moment when Minny would leave her.

> Your letter came yesterday when Minny was in London buying her little provisions for America, & I could not help opening it & beginning to cry over your dear kind familiar handwriting – It was a happy little cry making me feel that my dear was indeed going, but going to find one place at least where she would be at home & at peace with friends of our dearest Fathers choosing.... I feel as if a little bit of my life & ease of heart was going & yet I think I am right to stay behind – She is so true & clear & she looks with such simple bright eyes that I dont even feel as if I could keep my conscience straight without her for very long – Leslie too is a dear good old fellow & he adores Minny in his silent <u>dobbin</u> like way.... Outside theres the garden & the birds all singing in the sunshine. It seems like a little bit of USA here, the Storys are delightfully companionable, M^r. [Thomas Gold] Appleton as kind as kind can be, & there is a nice M^r. Dexter who can talk to us about all of you & that is always a bond.[28]

At the end of July, Annie had made one of her innumerable resolutions to rein in her expenses and 'to live less for fun', which was immediately set aside as this stay at Oatlands was 'fun from beginning to end once Minnie had gone away to America'.[29] Yet compared with the Alpine wedding trip, the pain of separation was more intense and poignant this time, for not only was the distance so much greater and the risks of the journey more acute, there was additionally all the unspoken knowledge that Minny was following the route undertaken by their father on his two American trips. The time before the departure seemed so reminiscent of those previous adventures, the waiting in Liverpool for transfer to the ship, the final letters home before the silence that inevitably followed as communications with the land were lost during the passage itself. Minny wrote on the Friday night from their Liverpool hotel, 'a bugeous looking place', imagining Annie's comfortable bed at Oatlands. In fact, her sister was already experiencing the trauma of separation. '7. August My dear went to America. All battered to the Station at night to say goodbye once again. The train started as I got there. What a dreary night. I woke up with a fall & went to the window. Cats yowling moon high over fleecy clouds.' For Annie, parting always seemed to be associated with disturbing images of nightmare and loss, welling up from her unconscious and linked to fears that stretched back to earliest childhood, of memories of her father's sudden departures from them without a word of farewell, leading to that final cruel removal when he embarked on the great journey into silence.

++++

Minny's American experience would be mixed, very much a journey of two halves. She learned to enjoy New York thoroughly, and took a shine to Baltimore, but she hated Washington and remained decidedly ambivalent about the overt intellectual self-confidence of Boston and Cambridge. Her sometimes contradictory opinions reflect the poor health she suffered during the first weeks of their trip. Once she had recovered, she rapidly revised her initial estimates of the country and the people, and hoped to return with Annie. It appears to have been Annie's own decision not to accompany them this time, probably because she was unwilling to leave Margie and Anny for so long. Perhaps, too, she balked at the idea of being a constant travelling companion to the married couple for three months. Yet only a year before she had been writing enthusiastically to James Fields in Boston about the prospect of tracing her father's old routes, though sadly not in his company. 'It is a thing w^h. has been talked of for years past in our house but the realisation will not be what we used to picture to ourselves in our long after dinner talks with Papa.'[30]

The passage from Liverpool to New York took ten days, and by the evening on 18 August the travellers were settled into a comfortable suite in the Clarendon Hotel on Fourth Avenue, favoured by European visitors, and where Thackeray had stayed on both of his trips. Minny posted off to Annie her on-board record of the crossing as soon as they arrived. Their experience was typical of passengers who could afford the relative comfort of a cabin, with access to the saloons on the upper decks, a paradise compared with the squalid conditions of those crowded into steerage. In the depths of the boat, whole families travelled with their life possessions as they emigrated to the New World. She makes no mention of this category of passenger, and indeed would never have seen them once they were stowed below, but every New York crossing would have had its share. They were the reason the boat docked at Queenstown in county Cork (the port is now called Cobh), stopping long enough to take on the Irish labourers needed to construct America's burgeoning road and rail infrastructure.

At first Minny was pleased with their cabin, but then spent as little time below as possible, only sleeping there. 'The only nasty part is the downstairs arrangements w^h. are beastly stuffy but the air on deck is more delicious than any thing you can imagine, it is something like mountain air only much softer.'[31] The poor sanitation made it impossible for her to stay below deck for long, whilst in the public saloons the mingled smells of food and sickness could be unsavoury. 'I am going to write you a letter in the ladies cabin w^h. until this morning I was afraid to enter but having at last done so found it far less smelly than the Saloon where people are constantly eating – & there is an open window w^h. is a blessing – for the beastly German Jews never let us open them in the Saloon. Fortunately they are not allowed to be sick in the public rooms or on deck except quite at the end of the ship which makes it much nicer than it would otherwise be.'[32] Before leaving England, William Wetmore Story's friend, Thomas Gold Appleton, had insisted that she should take on board with her a comfortable chair, which proved invaluable for sitting out in the fresh air. Appleton had also provided a note of introduction to the amiable captain, and although Leslie and Minny wanted no special favours or privileges, 'he said that I was always to ask him for anything I wanted & to send to him if he wasnt there, & he always shows his teeth at me – w^h. is his way of smiling'.

By the third day out in the Atlantic, they had settled into the routines of shipboard life. The weather was not at all rough, apart from the 'nasty foggy mizzle & rain – w^h. damps one thro & thro'. One needs to look no further for the source of the bronchial symptoms which struck soon after their arrival in New York, and then made her life miserable for the first six weeks of their tour. As she sat on deck, or in the saloon with Leslie or Herman in attendance, this Thackeray daughter recorded the little dramas and comic absurdities of their fellow passengers. 'Its rather nice being a lady on board – for there is a battle w^h. goes on here just like the one at Oatlands about the windows – & Herman with a voice of thunder says to the enemy – Sir a <u>Lady</u> desires to have this window open. Sir if the window is not opened the <u>Lady</u> will leave the room.' They ate constantly, as large meals appeared at regular intervals. 'Leslie says he has grown enormously fat & I dont wonder.' But sitting out for so much of the time was taking its toll on them. They were quickly weather beaten, and this was enough for Minny to caution Annie, always prone to cold and flu, about making the crossing in order to join them later.

> Leslies appearance is most disreputable so is mine – My gown has shrunk & almost tumbled to bits & we are both

> red & blowsy. I ought to have had a waterproof short dress to come over in they are the only ones that keep tidy – for I have often sat in the drizzle almost without moving from 8 in the morning till 10 at night – & there is no kind of shelter & it is impossible to keep up an umbrella. Think of all this if you have the least notion of coming over – but I almost advise you not darling – for at the best the passage is a beastly thing & we shall soon be back.

The night before they disembarked there was dancing on board – 'they found a fiddler in the 2nd cabin who could play Yankee doodle in several measures'. They passed Staten Island, 'just like the Isle of Wight', then waited an age before being allowed on shore, whereupon they were all herded into a leaking shed from where the luggage had to be retrieved before clearing the customs check.

> Then Herman got a carriage at 7 dollars to take us to the hotel – but it is only in New York that carriages are so dear – then all the carriages drove into a great wooden tunnel – & the tunnel went across to New York – for tunnels are steam boats here – The boats here are the only things that have struck me & Herman particularly – they are more mad & unearthly than anything you can imagine. Some of them like houses 5 or 6 stories high with balconies, some of them like towers some of them like I dont know what, all sorts of bulging extraordinary shapes. We tumbled along in our 7 dollar rattletrap – neither of the doors w^d. shut & Hermans ship chair fell down upon the horse – The only thing that I noticed along the road w^h. was a seedy sort of boulevard was that all the women & children wore top boots.

It was perhaps not the most auspicious of arrivals, but no worse than the experience of many who disembarked at New York, and far better than that of the majority emerging from steerage.

Their first visitors in New York were the ageing Baxters, who still mourned Sally. There was something sad about this family group, their best times now behind them, constantly thinking back to the years of prosperity when Thackeray had known them well. But at last the Baxters were meeting one of the daughters about whom they had heard so much, and Minny felt the presence of ghosts in this place of vanished friendships, where the charming Sally had captured her father's foolish heart. Perhaps she recalled her childish jealousy of Sally, whom Thackeray had described in the letters he sent to Paris. Now they would never meet. Lucy Baxter in some ways was emblematic of what her sister would have become, but it is a little disconcerting to read the comparison Minny then draws with Julia Jackson – actually Julia Duckworth by now.[33]

> They all talk so about Papa & of their bright days when he was there – for they are all half ruined & sad now – and Lucy – Lucy is an angel. She is most beautiful – what must Sally have been & Lucy is like a dark & pensive Julia Jackson – She has just the same line of eyes & nose but is very thin – but oh so interesting & beautiful – I shall try hard to get her to come back with us, her cousin Libbie has begged me to, & says that she thinks it would set her up in life again – that for the last 6 or 7 years she has had nothing but sorrow & unhappiness & no sort of pleasure.... It is like walking into a dream – & it makes me so sad to think that their sunshine & bright days are over – They seem quite to live in the old ones – Also I cant help feeling afraid of disappointing them – I did so long to have seen Sally, today, for Lucy seemed to me almost divinely beautiful.[34]

The first few days were spent planning their itinerary. New Yorkers encouraged them to think of heading for Newport, Rhode Island – whither Herman Charles Merivale had departed soon after arrival – but Leslie and Minny tended to favour Lake George and a possible walking trip up into the Adirondacks. This offered something to each of them, for also spending the summer at Lake George was Minny's old friend and Herman's sister, Ella Merivale, now married to the Washington diplomat Peere Freeman. The Stephens later regretted this expedition, because Minny's illness required them to abandon the Adirondacks. Before setting out, Minny had her first taste of American political sensitivities. With Mrs Baxter's sister she tried to play safe 'by saying that Lez was fond of negroes & all that – but the old lady said, he would soon change his mind about them when he saw them so I couldnt quite make out her politics'. After this, she tried a different strategy. 'Almost every one I have seen here takes one aside & gives one all their political views; it is very easy to agree with them because they always take it for granted that you do or that they have converted you on the spot & as they never give you a chance of contradicting them, one is likely to get on pretty smoothly.'

She began to register New York ways. Finding the women's fashions 'dowdy in the extreme', she was quick to understand the cosmopolitan flavour of a city built upon immigration. 'Cooking is

Sketch by Thackeray

quite french so are rooms but New York is every thing you come on a bit of Paris Oxford Street the Hague Bagneres Bigorre.' But her most striking impressions were of seediness, high costs, and of a shortage of good domestic servants. The novelty of seeing black people prompted the racial stereotyping which we (and presumably she) read in her father's letters, but like his, her prejudices became refined by empirical observation.

> The rich people here are not comfortable because they can get no servants & the middleclass people I mean people about as rich as we are must be miserably uncomfortable, for everything is so frightfully dear. A pair of gloves costs 10^s & a bottle of common wine about the same. Then there are no cabs – & the fly that brought us to this hotel cost us over a pound. Everyone goes about here in enormous omnibuses on rails that are pretty comfortable & hold about 20 people but they take in any number & today there were at least 40 people in one that we took. All stand together packed like herrings, and occasionally a black herring, I thought I should have disliked them very much but find that they dont smell like Nankeen w^h. was what I expected – & indeed the few Negroes that I have seen in New York have been among the smartest people there.[35]

They took one of the large steamboats up the Hudson to Saratoga Springs, the first leg of the journey to Lake George, whereupon the bronchial symptoms which then plagued Minny for weeks became evident. At Saratoga they were assigned a room in an annexe to the Congress Hall hotel, and were attended by 'a nice gentle negro man'. Complaints about American food begin to surface, misgivings which remained for most of their three months away, for Minny was often hungry. 'It does very well for fairies, but I wonder at men finding it enough, & I am afraid of Leslie growing thinner.' They must have yearned nostalgically for the gross excesses of their honeymoon meals. Some American informalities were disconcerting to Minny, though not unappealing, such as 'quite respectable' parents carrying their own children and not relying upon nurses. And yet she had expected to be more challenged by new experiences than she was, so she resorted instead to imagining how people like themselves organised their domestic arrangements.

> It is not so strange as the Continent when one comes to think of it, for after all it is a great enormous half grown place & theres lots of vacuity about.... I have not yet seen any society to speak of & have only looked at all the Jews & Germans & blacks & Irish & Yankees who live in the streets & the cars – I have asked everybody I saw if there was any opening for Governesses & servants they say theres none for governesses but plenty for servants – but I dont think our servants w^d. like it at all. people about like us, such as the Bellows & Baxters would only keep 2 servants – & the cook

w^d. wash all the house linen & the chamber maid all the rest of the things – so of course they only get inferior servants to do such a deal of work.'[36]

From Saratoga they travelled by rail and then by horse-drawn wagon to the shores of Lake George, 'pretty much like the Italian lakes', where they saw a steamboat approaching to take them the final few miles down the lake to Bolton. On board were Ella Freeman and her sister Agnes Merivale, come to greet them. At Bolton they all stayed in the small boarding house next to the 'ridiculous little pier', where fellow guests included a handful of Europeans and Americans. Their Alpine experiences meant that the Stephens were not strangers to rough living, but this was not the Alps, and Minny feared that to humour her Leslie was missing out.

There were authentic touches of traditional backwoods' life. The overwhelming smell of a skunk permeated the boarding house, and unusual food, 'green corn that all the people eat with butter dripping from it', which Minny didn't like, and egg plant, which she did. Annie's long-awaited first letter arrived, carrying news of children and of Leslie's much-missed dog. 'Poor Lez walks about here mechanically picking up sticks for Troy – I am afraid he is rather bored here.'[37] Realising that Minny's cold made the Adirondacks trip impossible, without a second thought Leslie gave up the one thing which would have made this leg of their tour interesting to him. After six days she could tolerate the draught and discomfort of Bolton no longer – it suggested to her Mrs Todgers' establishment in *Martin Chuzzlewit*, 'what with the squalor & dancing & a young man called Sham, who said, Oh my, how lovely Miss Agnes does look tonight' – and they left at once for the nearest passable hotel.

They would meet Ella and Peere Freeman again in Washington at the end of their trip, but for now Boston was their goal. One of Leslie's reasons for visiting America was to witness the Presidential election campaign, but this created its own set of problems, for in Albany they found themselves entangled with a large democratic convention in their hotel, so that even securing a room proved difficult. 'The Convention is a quantity of rather seedy looking men who continually stand in the passage & liquor up & whose martial cry seems to be "not for Joseph" w^h. a band outside plays.'[38] Minny asked Annie to send out a warm shawl and a single jar of Liebig, a recently patented concentrated beef extract taken as an energy supplement, and towards the end of their trip she was highly amused by the arrival in New York of multiple jars, 'enough I am sure to feed a whole herd of Australian oxen',[39] which she offloaded with largesse to her American acquaintances. She was looking forward to Boston and Cambridge, perhaps more for Leslie's sake than for her own, for he would have friends like Holmes and the poet and future diplomat James Russell Lowell to talk to. They would spend six weeks there.

A bridge fire halted the overnight train to Boston, requiring everyone to disembark at two in the morning and walk to another train, 'poor Lez staggering along with the great bag, & bundle of cloaks, & I plodding on behind him trying to keep my scattered garments together'. Leslie met up with Holmes in Boston, and then on the same day crossed the river to Cambridge where Lowell insisted that the travellers should stay with him. By the next morning, they were comfortably installed in his house, Elmwood, and at last Minny could nurse what had become a persistent cough. She enjoyed the companionship of Lowell's daughter Mabel, 'a dear little gentle booky creature like a countrified Edith Story' – or as she later described her to Annie, 'one of your young women, so pretty & gentle & simple'. Upon her twenty-first birthday, which was celebrated a few days after their arrival, Lowell presented his daughter with a set of Thackeray's works. His second wife, Mabel's former governess, was elusive and shy, spending most of her time tending her tomatoes and supervising the kitchen. Minny was struck by the modesty of their lives, openness and kindness balanced by simplicity and rigour. 'Mr Lowell was telling us of the astonishment of a young Englishman who came in to see them at dinner time & found them sitting round 1 mackerel. I said I supposed that they had a bit of meat, & he said no nothing except some blackberries.'[40] Leslie added a note to Annie, which whilst intending to reassure does hint at his own concern. 'I am so glad to have got my darling here in comfort; for to say the truth, the travelling hitherto has been much too rough for her, & the cold has hung about longer than it might. That infernal railway was the climax of our misfortunes, & I hope will be the end. I mean to stay here quietly till Min is perfectly free from every vestige of a cold & then we shall go I hope to some other friends. The Lowells were so anxious & so kind that they quite touched me.'

Oliver Wendell Holmes senior, the writer and former medical practitioner who had known Thackeray, came out from Boston to dinner. Minny was charmed, but felt ashamed at being so distracted by his ancient dress suit. He talked non-stop for four hours until she slipped away to rest, 'but not before the old D^r. had prescribed a sort of Elixir for me which prevented me from coughing & made me sleep all night, so that I think him more charming than ever dress clothes &

all'.⁴¹ She presented Holmes with Annie's special gift of a paperknife, a singular triumph. 'I wish you could have seen the funny little D^rs unbounded delight & astonishment over your paper cutter, he held it out in front of him & weighed it & walked round it, & said it was the most beautiful thing he had ever seen, & that it would be the most cherished object in his library – The only fears I have about it are that he will never be able to wield it for it seems to me quite as tall as he is.'⁴² He had retired from medical practice, but as her cough still lingered a week later he arranged for a university colleague to examine Minny. Writing to thank Annie for the paperknife, he reassured her about her sister's health.

> A week ago when I first saw her she seemed quite poorly and I ventured on the strength of my former medical skill to give her a simple prescription. I was both pleased and proud to find that it comforted her, but as she still coughed I wished her to see one of our best practising physicians. I therefore went out to Cambridge, to Mr. Lowell's where, as you know, she is staying, and introduced my friend and colleague in the University, Dr Edward Clarke, who had a good medical talk with her and left her I think greatly encouraged. He thinks a few quiet days under a very slight and very mild treatment will be all that is necessary....
>
> And now, my dear Miss Thackeray, let me thank you once more in laboured words, for your kind and memorable gift, bringing with it more associations than I dare to recall in words. I hope I shall soon cut the leaves of another story of yours with it as delightful as 'The Village on the Cliff.'⁴³

Without question, Minny's illness coloured her views of the country, which fluctuated wildly according to mood and appetite. At one moment she longs for English pork pies and Freshwater potted lobsters, having condemned popped corn for tasting like burnt quill pens – 'I expect I shall soon be nibbling at my boots & Leslie asked me for a pair of gloves this morning in a very suspicious manner' – or rages at people for being 'so beastly virtuous & abstemious', declaring America to be 'a great big hideous overrated place.... Im sure it must be changed since Papa came here, only he didnt like Boston much did he.' But then, two lines later, 'I have had some lunch I am better – I think America is not such a bad place on the whole'. She was startled by Leslie's professed sympathy for what he called 'a good sleepy sensible cheap existence.... Min blows me up for saying so, but I sometimes rather envy this way of life.'⁴⁴ But Leslie also knew its limitations

– 'in my dreams there is always a London in the background – to say nothing of an Anny in the foreground – so that there is no danger of my taking root here or turning my dreams into reality'.

When Minny tried to analyse her responses more rationally, she concluded that her sister would have judged Boston more fairly. 'I sometimes feel inclined to ask them how such nice intelligent people can go on living in this great bare unkempt country & why they dont all come & live in London, but somehow they have the bad taste to prefer their own country.'[45]

James Lowell was very happy to have Leslie's company, and they had long smoky discussions about literature and politics, but he paid special attention to Minny's comforts too, bringing her peaches and pears from the garden, and when she unguardedly asked about American novels he rushed off to find books, keeping her supplied for the rest of their time in Cambridge. The reading matter was hard-going. 'All the ladies are called Humility & the gentlemen Kejasariah & other scripture names, & they spend their whole days in the Kitchen cooking & singing hymns, & on Sundays they go to church & die without marrying anyone – They draw a fearful picture w^h I believe to be true.'[46] Certainly Minny had found New England thus far to be distressingly dull, mainly because her health confined her to her room, as even a little conversation made her cough.

On one of her rare trips out, she enjoyed seeing the beautifully designed Mount Auburn cemetery, appreciating a seeming matter-of-factness about death which was less cloying than the English manner. 'There is rather a pretty chapel all adorned with pine branches & with painted windows & in it there is the Statue of Judge Story that I remember seeing at Rome – & there were also statues of people that I thought were Shakespear & Robespierre, but they turned out to be Winthrope & somebody else.'[47] She particularly liked meeting the 'Boston swell' Mrs Ticknor – not least for a confusing conversation at the end of which Minny realised that Mrs Ticknor thought she had been talking to Annie – for the old lady was another of the large band who had known Thackeray on his American visits, and she amused Minny with her cryptic observation of how her father 'had suffered a great deal of discomfort in America. I said he had never complained of any – she said I mean in the way of attentions.'[48]

They had spent nearly a fortnight with the Lowells, lingering a day or two in the hope of meeting Ralph Waldo Emerson, the much respected and influential transcendentalist thinker. Lowell himself remained something of a puzzle for Minny, and she was curious at the apparent quietness of his life, while accepting that her illness had only allowed her a very partial view of people and places. 'I am always wishing that things here were a little more as they are in London for the men here seem to me to lead such poor sort of lives, but I suppose they like it. I cant help continually making up my mind about everything here, without really having seen anything.'

The Weston sisters, all strong New England abolitionists, called at the Lowells to urge the English visitors to stay in their Weymouth house near Boston, leaving Minny with the feeling of having being visited by family members, so affectionate and genuine was their welcome. And at Weymouth her bronchial condition at last improved, an efficient heating system being complemented by fresh air from the open windows, so that Leslie with evident relief reported that 'for the last day or two [she] has fairly been at the top of the hill'.[49] Minny was stronger, the company was highly congenial, and the conversation flowed easily. There were three unmarried Weston sisters, Dora, Anne and Caroline, an ancient bed-bound mother, as well as a married brother and his children staying with them. The sisters revered Jane Austen, so Leslie and Minny found themselves re-reading her, leading him to offer Annie the kind of unsolicited advice more in Fitzy's line, only to withdraw as he recognised his own inclination to preach. For all of Jane Austen's virtues, he was not inclined to bow down and worship. 'However she is good reading for you, because her merits are such as you might study to advantage – specially the careful way in wh. the stories are worked out but I will not give you a lecture about it now. Nor at any time, as far as that goes, for a critic is after all a contemptible thing.'

Minny learned more of Lowell's history, including her father's affection for the first Mrs Lowell.

> The Miss W^s told me last night that Mr Lowell was first married to a most beautiful & clever & charming Mrs Lowell & that Papa liked her very much, & that it was a sort of poetic marriage only she was consumptive & died & 2 or 3 children died & he was left with only Mabel & then to everybodys surprise & rather horror he married Mabels governess who is the present Mrs Lowell. I am sorry to say that he seemed extremely fond of her altho she is not at all poetic or intellectual but she is a kind goodnatured little woman, only I do dislike people to marry for company anybody who turns up after having had delightful wives, dont you? If I was an intellectual wife in heaven, I should be disgusted, but I dont think I should mind near so much if my successor was up to me.[50]

She now began to regret her somewhat unguarded earlier criticisms. 'I can only go on imploring you not to tell any one anything abusive that I say of America for I am beginning really to like it very much indeed, now that I am quite well again – and getting over homesickness w^h. is quite a material thing whatever people may say.'[51] Her fondness for the Westons was tempered only by their political dogmatism. She found it hard to understand how after the loss of so many sons, brothers and husbands in the War, people could still hold such entrenched positions.

> I dont mean to say that abolition is not very right & proper, but it seems to me to make people as warlike & ferocious as Cherokees, & I can no more sympathise with people for hacking at each other & blowing out each others brains for 4 years than I can sympathise with Queen Marys religious frolics – I am quite sure that wars must go out with civilization, it is too horrid & when you come to a country like this where people have not yet recovered from killing their neighbours & being killed, you see how brutal it is....
> It is bad enough here & in the South it must be a hundred times more horrible.

The couple were also introduced by the Westons to a woman anxious to learn everything she could about Annie, *The Story of Elizabeth* and *The Village on the Cliff* having already won her an American following as Thackeray's daughter. '[S]he said now my dear make haste make haste & tell me everything that you can think of about Lizabeth (meaning you).... The Miss Westons put in a few words here & there, & the old lady went off with, looks like you, taller, great talker, fond of society, sympathetic, sweet voice, &c &c, checking it off on her fingers.'

In Boston they took rooms in 'Mrs Putnam's fashionable boarding house' in Pemberton Square. There was nothing of the Mrs Todgers about Mrs Putnam. 'She ruins herself every year by giving good dinners to her boarders & has written a cookery book – & is very fat, but a melancholy sort of fat.'[52] Minny provides a colourful description of the old Boston neighbourhood in which they were staying, conjuring up the kind of scenes that Annie would know well from home. 'Some of the places here are just like queer old fashioned dreams. The place we live in is just like Rock gardens or the old Steyne, with bright red brick bow window houses, & red tiled pavements like the pantiles in Tunbridge Wells.'[53] Leslie was now able to see more of Oliver Wendell Holmes, father and especially son, and also met Emerson 'who is a very good specimen of the Yankee. His face is exactly of the Yankee type, that is, only with a milder more benevolent look than common.... He came up & talked to me most civilly & promised to call; so I hope Min will see him.'[54] Emerson did not manage the visit, but sent them invitations to his lecture-series instead. 'I take the liberty to enclose cards for my lectures if you should be at liberty on any Monday evening to try such risks.'[55]

Suddenly, Minny had a social life again, with visits and people calling, and everyone talking about Longfellows, Nortons, Storys and the rest of the Brahmins. They saw a lot of the Eldredges, the brother and family of William Wetmore Story's wife, Emelyn, who lived at Roxbury. 'They are quite the people I have taken most to.' It was enjoyable company, but Minny had the measure of it. 'It was exactly like an Edinburgh party only not so dowdy. All the gentlemen were professors, all the ladies had much soul, but they were all so kind, & made such a deal of me & Lez – & talked about you darling as if you was [sic] an angel. I have taken to soul here, & have got to do it quite nicely. Its much easier to me than talking literature especially when its something I havent read.... Mr Barnard gave me a lovely little Emersons Poems, w^h. will help me to get on with my soul.'[56]

She was wise to keep her silence in the presence of confidently articulated unionism, but in writing to Annie her frustrations at the routine expressions of liberal Boston opinion sometimes provoked an established Old World prejudice. She and Leslie visited the son and daughter of the noted abolitionist Josiah Quincy, but despite their kindness she did not take to them at all. 'Mr Quincy is a fine handsome looking man but Miss Q is just like a negro, I thought she was one at first, that is a yellow girl. Perhaps it was because the parents thought so much about it.'[57] She felt more relaxed in the company of the older generation, not least Mrs Ticknor whose memories of Thackeray diverted her.

> She had got a beautiful pen and ink sketch of Werther & Charlotte that Papa made for her, he had been a great deal with them, & she told me that one New Years eve he sat there till the clock struck 12 & then she gave him a glass of wine & he said, heres to my daughters God bless them – She said he was dreadfully bored in America. Isnt it curious how very little he ever said about the roughness & discomfort, & it must have been very bad when he was here 10 years ago, & travelling south & west.

Another of Thackeray's friends was the former Massachusetts senator and radical abolitionist Charles Sumner, who recalled Annie as a child from his earlier days in England '& praised you very much & I praised you still more, he knew Papa before I was born & wanted to know what he thought ab^t. American politics, but said that he didnt think Papa took much interest in them. I told him that I thought he cared much more for the people here than the politics.'[58]

The Eldredges had recently built a new house in Beacon Street, close to Boston Common, and Minny was delighted to be taken over it. Its combination of high-quality wood fittings with the latest technology fascinated her, and reinforced her interest in domestic interior design.

> You have no idea of the comfort & beauty of a well-fitted American house – This is a house with about the same n° of rooms as ours but the whole of it filled up with real wood all the doors & shutters & panels & staircases are made of this beautiful dark wood. Then there are bath rooms & wash rooms & cupboards without number, a great cedar wood closet to make anything smell nice that they put there then there are lifts & speaking trumpets & every possible thing. I believe a house of that sort costs £5 or £6000, but altho it is small there are such houses in London.[59]

It helped in the formation of her ideas for specifications and decor when their own new Southwell Gardens house was being built in the early 1870s. Upon returning to New York she gathered together some house plans to bring back, and it led her to think more broadly of women's social roles. 'I should so like to become a house builder & dont see why I shouldnt. See Mrs Fawcetts article on female emancipation – What an odd thing it is about Radicals. Leslie & Mr Godkin were talking about it last night & they said that they couldnt bear Ladies to be anything but Conservatives, meaning I suppose that ladies ought to have charming weaknesses, but I told them what was right for men to believe, must be right for women if it was only true.'[60]

Herman Merivale rejoined them in Boston, and they went to *Hamlet* to see Edwin Booth, brother of Abraham Lincoln's assassin (also an actor), and a couple of days later saw the comic actor William Warren. Minny thought that Booth was striking looking – resembling William Brookfield to her eyes – but that his famed Hamlet lacked depth – 'he is a figetty [*sic*] actor & made Hamlet nothing but a ferocious madman, & not an interesting young man'. As for Warren, 'he is a dear fat old man but doesnt act very well'. They got to Emerson's lecture at last, but Minny was already rather weary of his reputation. 'M^r. Emerson is absolutely worshipped in this little literary circle – & the other day at dinner Mr Sumner actually spoke of him as equal to Shakespear – I felt much disposed to throw my soup plate at his head, but in this country a person like myself is obliged to hide all her feelings & be painfully civil.'[61] In New York she picked up an amusing Emerson anecdote from Mrs Baxter, and reflected at some length on the difference between those who are wise and those who are simply good.

> I heard a funny story about Mr. Emerson & Margaret Fuller today from Mrs Baxter. They went together to see Miss Fanny Ellsler a great opera dancer, and were captivated by her a la transcendental. She gave one kick that quite upset Mr Emerson, who said – Oh Margaret this is poetry. She then gave another kick still higher upon w{h}. Margaret said – Oh Ralph <u>this</u> is religion – I am afraid that you think it horrid of me to laugh at Mr Emerson. He really is a dear old boy very like Mr Spedding [*Thackeray's friend from Cambridge days*] & you know Papa thought Mr Spedding one of the wisest men in the world, but I dont think Papa thought very very much of Mr Emerson did he? & I am sure I should never have found out that Mr Spedding was one of the wisest men in the world.... I think it comes more naturally to you than to me to admire those qualities very much, where they havent got cleverness too, but I am sure that one ought to & that I only belong to an older Magdalene Brookfield type, only of course it is more difficult for us who have had all our lives the pure goodness & the other thing as well in Papa.

They returned to New York on 14 October, though their rooms at the Clarendon were not so fine as before. Leslie enjoyed the prospect of the approaching election, but was sad to leave Boston whose values and assumptions he appreciated as much as Minny doubted them. He was particularly despondent to leave Lowell, in whom he perceived a vein of melancholy – 'he gives one rather the impression of a man who has retreated from the world with something of a spite. However, I like him far better than any one here & better than most people in England.... I left him after he had walked with me to a certain corner of the road at wh. we had parted last time & felt quite sentimental.'[62] Leslie thought of New England as America's spiritual backbone. Boston's provincialism appealed to him, whereas New York was sprawling and ugly, its streets filthy, its cabmen dishonest, and everything worth seeing difficult to get to. Minny saw the contrasts in rather different terms. New York suggested to her something of what it holds for modern visitors, a lively and brash metropolis, 'a jolly reckless sort of place' defined by its mixed peoples, whereas she perceived an arrogance in Boston's intellectual elite. 'When you are at Boston, you think that Boston governs America they are certainly very clever people & quite desperate about having their own way. When you are at New York you seem to see the size of America much more, it expands into a great sort of ungovernable ocean w^h. every day has ships from all nations poured into it.'[63]

New Yorkers who had left the city for the humid summer months were returning, and the more fashionable streets were beginning to fill. 'I quite now understand what Papa felt when he said walking up Broadway was like a glass of Champagne. It is [a] bounding sort of goahead air, & so shockingly managed, with such a lot of cheating & bribery that nobody ever crams its excellence down your throat like New England, & in fact one feels quite at home here.'[64] At West Point on the Hudson River they visited the Pells, more of Thackeray's former acquaintances, and Mr Pell regaled Minny with anti-semitic anecdotes (standard for the time) to pass on to Annie. 'One is that he & Papa were walking one day up Bowery w^h. is a sort of Brompton Road full of Jews at NY, & Papa said American Jews looked different to ours & that in another generation Americans would have unhooked all their noses.'

After booking their passage for 25 November, there was a tangible sense of things drawing to a close. Having previously found little to praise or to be curious about, Minny now began talking of returning in two years when the railway linking east and west coasts might be completed, eager to show Annie around – 'I shall know it well enough to be able to arrange everything & not make mistakes as we have this time.'[65] Just as Leslie began to tire of America and even felt rather homesick, Minny was suddenly ready to visit new places. 'I feel so well & jolly now that I cant help enjoying myself, & I also want to travel a little before we come home for we have been so very unadventuresome. I have heard of a southern university near Richmond that I hope we shall go to besides Philadelphia & Baltimore in the meantime I like New York very much indeed & enjoy all the Theatres extremely.' She was getting about within the city quite freely now, though she would have preferred not having to negotiate the public transport system. Visiting the Baxters beyond the city limits was particularly trying. 'People often have to stand in the street cars all jammed together & smelling most horrid.'[66]

She went to dinner at the sumptuous Fifth Avenue Hotel, where a black maid who greeted her as 'Miss Minny' turned out to have known

Thackeray, 'so that I felt quite fond of her'.[67] More than once between now and their return home she considers the possibility of bringing back a negro servant. Presumably this is a rather laboured joke, but one cannot be entirely certain, and the frequency with which she returns to the topic suggests the same patronising, dehumanising attitude typical of her father's generation. 'We sometimes think of bringing home a black boy as we have taken a great fancy to them, they are excellent waiters & look very nice & funny in their white costumes. I think it would be exceedingly stupid of us if we did, for he would be a regular slave & entirely on our shoulders. I dont fancy the black females there is something creepy about them, but the black boys are very nice; M[rs] Field knows a very nice family of black children – he would bring you your cups of tea & sleep on a mat with Troy outside your door.'[68]

A letter from Annie announcing that she was planning to spend the winter with the Storys in Rome provoked a frantic response. Seeing Minny's distress, Leslie weighed in and urged that Annie should delay going, trying to deflect some of the responsibility for this extended separation upon Annie's own shoulders. 'Surely it is bad enough that you shd be separated from us four months on end without immediately deserting us again for a couple more. I dont like to feel that I shall be the cause of separating you & Min for 6 months in one year.'[69] Minny felt miserable about it. 'If you must go couldnt you go about March, in the east winds when we should have been at home for 3 months.'[70] Annie gave way and arranged to spend Easter in Rome. Most of Leslie's share of the letter described the election of the great Civil War hero, Ulysses S. Grant as President, both the poll itself and the gatherings of the opposing camps.

> When you see a long row of shabby Irish labourers dropping in & deciding by their votes what is to be the policy of a big country in all kinds of difficult questions, it must be admitted that it seems rather queer. The most remarkable experience was at Tammany Hall where the democrats collect – There was a huge crowd of the roughs of New York, packed as tight as herrings in a barrel – I was one of the herrings & the others smelt decidedly strong.... Then I went to the Republican meeting, wh was Yankee instead of Irish & far more washed & decent. They were very enthusiastic & cheered & sang till the atmosphere became too much for me & I went & eat oysters at the Century.

They went fresh from the election result to Washington, their furthest destination south, where Ella Freeman had booked rooms for them. They saw little of Washington the night they arrived, but the next day toured with Ella and were startled by its bleakness, a mixture of scattered public buildings and the occasional private house, with swarms of mosquitoes to be fought off – 'it is more like a horrid dream than anything else I can think of. It is full of immensely broad streets with nothing at all in them. The few homes in the place seem to have been stuck as far apart as possible to make them look like more.'[71] They visited Mount Vernon on the Potomac. 'I dont suppose that it has been touched since Washington died & there is his little old garden just as it was with the box hedges sprouting out everywhere, & the old rose trees. I never saw a place so like a little old person.'

What most interested Minny was their visit to the medical museum within the Smithsonian Institution, built upon the site of the theatre where Lincoln had been assassinated. Their guide was the Smithsonian's first secretary, Professor Joseph Henry, and Minny was surprised to find that false eyes, fractured bones, and enlarged photographs of boils could hold her attention. 'It was a sort of record of the war.'[72] Henry accompanied them to the White House, having arranged introductions to the out-going President Andrew Johnson and to the new incumbent. She did not take to Ulysses S. Grant – his politics were against him – whereas she was touched by the shy and slightly awkward manner of the exhausted Johnson – 'my heart melted to the poor man in one instant, he looked so so tired & fagged, & it is perfectly astounding for a tailor but he had very dignified manners quite different to little Fritz Grant. When we were going away he went to the chimney piece & took a nosegay of flowers out of a china pot, & said to me with the air of a melancholy prince – will you allow me to give you some of our flowers – I have nothing better to offer you – & I concluded by think[ing] him a most illused man.' Leslie added to Minny's letter a more measured political judgment, but it is she who gets closer to the man.

After Washington, they stayed a couple of days in Baltimore, judged by Minny the most comfortable town they had seen, and Philadelphia took up several days on the final return leg to New York. She was interested to find evidence of the Quaker origins of this 'City of brotherly love', which perhaps was what made the people less self-assured than Bostonians, for in other ways she thought the two places similar. But the theatre life was quite different – even Leslie lamented the contrast. 'Puritanical Boston has got its beautiful theatres – each better than any in London; but this cavalier city has only one wretched place into wh. I was crammed with Min & the Freemans & made to sit amongst a tobacco-chewing apple-eating nutcracking with their teeth kind of audience.'[73] Minny had picked up the fact that among the Quaker community there was considerable wealth, but an absence of personal extravagance. 'I am told that many of them are enormously rich & that they spend fortunes upon Stereoscopes, w^h. are the only artistic luxuries that they allow themselves.'[74]

There was just time for one last visit before returning to New York and packing up. Thackeray had been intimate with the Kemble family, including the actress Fanny, sister to Adelaide Sartoris, and his daughters had come to know both Kemble sisters. Fanny had married a southern planter, Pierce Butler, and lived on a Georgia plantation for a few years. After the collapse of her marriage in 1849, she had returned to the stage and her one-woman shows, and was currently touring in the west which made it impossible for Minny to see her, but her daughters Sarah Wister and Fanny Butler lived in Philadelphia and they and the Stephens met several times. Minny was much taken with them. They also had dinner with Sarah's sister-in-law, whose company Thackeray had enjoyed and who had sung Scottish ballads to him. In the last of her surviving American letters to Annie, written late at night in Butler Place, the home of Mrs Kemble's daughter, Fanny, she contemplates the sadness of the failed marriage to Butler, the father whom the daughters still loved. Thankful for her own security, it leads her to reflect again on the difficulty of being separated from those one loves, her thoughts now given over to the prospect of the return voyage.

> My own dearest darling darling darling, I never never will go away from you again like this – The week after next, we shall be at home.... Good night my blessing I must go to bed. Lez is already asleep & I feel a little afraid of ghosts. Oh what a mercy it is that we are not Mrs Kemble & Mr Butler poor things – Poor little Fanny has quite affected me by talking of her father of whom both she & Sarah were very fond, altho no-one else was. Oh what a blessing it is to be fond of one another, isnt it darling. It has only one disadvantage, that its so disagreeable to be away from them – we will not again.[75]

Ten

THE SHABBY TIDE OF PROGRESS
(1869-1873)

The best thing I ever did in my life was marrying Min; for you and she have made the last seven years a time of happier relations between us all than any years before.

Leslie to Annie
3 June 1874

Minny brought to her marriage love, pragmatism, goodhumour and the intuitive skills of an effective home-maker. She also brought Annie, whose own affection for Leslie, unalike though they were in so many ways, ended only with his death in 1904. During his long final illness, Annie was the one person who could always cheer him. The enduring tie was sealed by a common grief after Minny died, and then took on a momentum of its own. They were also bound by the child of the marriage, Laura Makepeace Stephen, not least because of the difficulties that would touch the life of this fragile survivor.

From the very outset, the household dynamics had their moments of tension. Annie was hopeless over money, a tendency not improved by philanthropic gestures which she could ill afford, whilst Leslie's morbid fears of impending penury would lead eventually to terrible confrontations with the children of his second marriage. But Annie's love and loyalty conquered him, and he saw in her the spark of authentic Thackeray genius which set her apart. His daughter, Virginia Woolf, would similarly detect this touch of 'a writer of genius' in all of Annie's books, but Leslie had believed in her from the beginning.

> She is still, she was, I think, still more obviously when I first knew her, the most sympathetic person I ever knew. By 'sympathetic' I mean able to sympathize quickly with the feelings of all manner of people, to throw herself into

their interests and thoughts and even for a time adopt their opinions. I have never observed such readiness, such accessibility to appeals from others, in any human being.... She resembled [Thackeray] in so far as this, that she had a decided sense of humour, a distinct perception of the weak side of people even whom she loved, and – though absolutely without bitterness – could see the seamy side of things too clearly to be quite carried away by sentimentalism.[1]

In March 1869, Annie made her delayed journey to Rome, travelling via Bordighera (briefly visiting Mrs Fanshawe and daughter Rosa who had settled there), and Florence. Here she enjoyed the view from the Duomo – 'a country rippling at my feet & glittering with imperial mountains'[2] – and saw the Medici tombs. About five days later she travelled overnight to Rome and was welcomed to the Palazzo Barberini by her expatriate American hosts, the Wetmore Storys.

The pace of life at Onslow Gardens was quiet without her. 'Lez says – the house (this is dictated) is like a deaf & dumb asylum, ever since you went, a horrible silence broods over the establishment.... The one good result of your leaving is that I havent missed a pencil or a book lately & I am thinking of having an investigation upstairs for stolen property.'[3] Their Kensington dinner parties were lively occasions when Annie was herself of the company, but she was away for Henry James's first invitation. James and Annie were close in later years, and she always was likely to have found him more sympathetic than did Minny, whose dislike of Boston did not act in his favour. 'Yesterday we had a rather dull young Bostonian called Mr James to spend the day – Lez took him & Jane Norton to the Zoo.'[4] In fact, the New York-born James had only limited associations with Boston. He recorded the occasion more generously, their earlier meeting in that city not having been especially auspicious. 'On Saturday I received a visit from Mr. Leslie Stephen (blessed man) who came unsolicited and with the utmost civility in the world invited me to dine with him (early) the next day. This I did in company with Miss Jane Norton. His wife made me very welcome and they both appear to much better effect on their own premises than they did in America.'[5]

The Stephens enjoyed entertaining Jane Norton, sister of Leslie's friend, the American scholar and critic Charles Eliot Norton, and a few Sundays later Minny took her to the Kensington studios of Leighton, Watts and Val Prinsep, which were open for public viewing.

> She is so nice and intelligent & says such pretty nice things to the painters. I dont know how to pay them compliments.

Yesterday was the friends day, and today an open day. Val & Mʳ. Leighton were crowded with carriages specially Val. the Signor [*Watts*] not so much, but he has painted a lovely lovely picture of the moon kissing Endymion, & also a Scripture picture, old sinner, the dove returning to the Arc [*sic*] across thousands of miles of waves. It is a touching picture, one feels so sorry for the poor little brave tired dove – It is rather like the O[xford] & C[ambridge] Boatrace – The old Signor was very kind, & liked Jane Norton.⁶

On behalf of Frederick Greenwood, editor of the *Pall Mall Gazette*, 'who would very much like a description of the Pope & all his foolery from you', Leslie asked for a couple of Holy Week pieces from Annie.⁷ Rome was full of Easter penitents and the traditional elaborate ceremonies, giving her ample material. 'Its a great deal bigger grander <u>Romer</u> than we remember it even – Every doorway & window & arch is noble & seems glad to see me & to say how is Minny.'⁸ There was plenty of convivial company at the Palazzo Barberini, always open to passing visitors, though Story's iconoclasm disconcerted her. He 'railed at philanthropy & observances & said that as for a sense of duty it was only an imaginary thing & really meant doing as one really liked best. I never know what to think when I see people like him & Leslie who speak the truth & work hard & keep faith to their neighbours talking in this sort of way.'⁹ In fact Story regarded Thackeray's daughter with great affection, revealing that one of the poems in his 1868 collection, *Graffiti D'Italia*, was inscribed to her.¹⁰

Each day she and Edith Story might visit a gallery or a church, then call at Story's studio where he worked at his sculptures. She was alert to the customs of an ancient culture surviving into the modern age, such as in the observation of the rites carried out for the dead. At San Lorenzo 'there were some gilt tressells & a cloth where the coffin had been all night & some candles & flowers & 2 old men pottering about clearing away & a blear eyed young man whose business it was to sleep by the corpses. It seemed so queer & melancholy & flowery coming in from the rolling street all chattering & twinkling & flowering too.' But current gossip was equally rewarding, and she eagerly swallowed (and then passed on) a rumour concerning Robert Browning's romantic interest in Blanche Ritchie before her marriage. 'The Storys were telling me something interesting about Mʳ Browning which was that he was immensely attracted by Blanchie & that Mʳ Cornish went to him & begged him not to go down to Henbury till after he had been, & that after a short consideration he had consented to this.' When Browning learned of Annie's role in helping to circulate the story, it made for an awkwardness in relations lasting a couple of years, ending only when he dedicated *Red Cotton Nightcap Country* to her.

She could have done without the arrival of Herman Charles Merivale, who had worked himself into a hopeless passion for Edith Story since declaring himself at Oatlands in August 1868. Merivale would suffer various nervous illnesses through his life – his later memoir of Thackeray had to be completed by someone else because of a breakdown – and aspects of his erratic character were already evident in behaviour which was both comic and pathetic. 'Wasnt it rash of him to propose to Edith at Oatlands – she said something one day & I said <u>what</u> did he actually propose, & she said I thought he had told you. But dont tell anyone for I promised her I would keep the secret – & so I have not even let Herman guess I know.'[11]

Leslie went on feeling Annie's absence acutely, pleading that she should resist the blandishments of the Storys who wanted her to extend her visit, for 'however kind they are, they dont want you more than we do – nor so much'.[12] Yet there was certainly much to divert her. On 18 April Browning and Longfellow were fellow lunch guests at the Storys, and a couple of days later she took a walk with the revered American poet. 'People saluting him as we went along. His simpleness & sweetness.'[13] The Palazzo Barberini itself held her enthralled. Her story 'Bluebeard's Keys', composed in 1871, has its origins here, as cryptically suggested in her journal – 'My fright on the staircase – see Bluebeards keys.' The Bluebeard myth was almost certainly brought to her attention by Story himself, who in *Graffiti D'Italia* had included a long poem called 'Blue Beard's Cabinets'. Her own reworking of this disturbing tale of sexual predation is set in Rome in the 'Palazzo Barbi' and features the Travers sisters: the elder is called Anne, and the bold younger sister is Fanny, who falls for the Bluebeard figure of the Marquis Barbi. The sisters' relationship is a curious gloss on that of Minny and Annie – '"Oh, Fanny, don't," Anne said, very faintly; for Anne, with all her sweetness, was human, and curious too.'[14]

At the Vatican, Annie now found herself appreciating the statues which had done little for her years earlier. 'It is like scales fallen from my eyes – Do you remember how we did not care for them. Now quite naturally as I look I love, without any one, except papa somehow, to say a word to. It isn't sham makeup, its like a new delightful sense come to me which I didn't know I had got, & I am sure you would feel just the same.' But sometimes the frozen beauty of the monuments filled her with a sense of absence and something close to disappointment. 'One of the odd effects of Rome is to set one longing – I dont know for what exactly – The beautiful things & sights excite one, & it is not warm enough to soothe one at the same time. I keep wondering where all the great men & women can be gone to, & whether the Huxleys & Spencers are really the statues & conquerors of these days.'[15]

Annie did not manage to track down George Eliot who was also then in Rome – participating in scenes which would be reworked in *Middlemarch* – but nor would she have attempted to avoid her in the prudish way that Minny thought justified for someone whose behaviour left much to be desired.

> Darling I dont at all see why you should go out of your way to make friends with George Eliot & I am very glad you didnt find her. If a person chooses to sin against the laws of society, I dont see why she is to be forgiven because she is clever when no one would think of touching her less talented & weaker brethren with tongs. I suppose if one admired her talents immensely one couldnt help it, but then I dont, & of course I do not look upon the breakage of laws as really and hopelessly wicked. Only it would be extremely inconvenient & disagreeable if they werent kept to & above all by people who make themselves teachers of their neighbours.[16]

Minny often expressed strongly-held views of this kind to Annie, where perhaps with Leslie she would have been more circumspect. She was angered at the time by some of Dickens's remarks in a Liverpool speech, only to be consoled by the generosity of William Brookfield's praise for Thackeray's writing.

> What irritated me in his speech was his patronage of Literature – saying that by it he would stand or fall as if it had never existed before he was created & as if it hadnt put £100,000 in his pocket. Mr Brookfield paid me a long visit the other day he *is* so kind & quite touched me by the way he indirectly talked of Papa. I was saying that I thought Copperfield the most dramatic of Mr Dickens books, & Mr Brookfield said he believed that this was because Papa was just making his success at that time & that Mr Dickens was put on his mettle & determined to try & write a book in good English, & that it was the book he had taken most pains with – & the last good thing he had ever written.[17]

That summer Annie accompanied Leslie and Minny to St Moritz, Santa Catarina, the Dolomites and finally to Venice, returning through Germany, and early ideas were forming for what would be her most ambitious work, the novel *Old Kensington*, serialised from April 1872. Back in London they heard of the engagement of Gussie, the oldest of their Ritchie cousins, to Douglas Freshfield, heir to the family legal firm and, like Leslie, an expert Alpinist. It had been a swift romance, though not a particularly passionate one on her part, as Gussie hinted to her sister Blanche. 'I let myself be persuaded into saying yes. I have been perfectly happy ever since.'[18] Marriage to Freshfield and the money it brought gave Gussie a place in society, and she invested much energy into running her salon, but there was always something a little reserved at the heart of the relationship. Where Minny's wedding was subdued, Gussie's was necessarily carried out in style, and amidst much excitement which thrilled Annie. 'Min & I fluttered up & down stairs not quite liking to go into your room till Pinkie took us & we found the phalanx all assembled. I think your Russian going away dress was perfectly beautiful & so were our shot silk feelings as Blanchie said.'[19] It made Minny hope that similar happiness might still be possible for her own sister, but Fitzjames Stephen cautioned her against willing Annie into a sudden marriage in which her spirit, he feared, might be broken in dutiful devotion.

> I think that that beautiful mixture of genius & innocent simple goodness & kindness which belongs to her, makes her into a jewel, which ought to be properly set, & I cannot endure to think of her throwing herself away upon any man who is unworthy of her, or unsuited to her, either from a fanciful notion about marriage in general being better than unmarried life, or for some small collateral reason, like caring for a man's children. I know what would happen if she did make such a marriage. She is as good as she is charming, & she would do her duty to her husband, till she broke her heart under it.... I dont think she need wait for a man of genius. One genius is enough in a family perhaps.... I [should] ten times rather never know her under any other name than that she should not change it wisely.[20]

In November, Fitzy had set out for India where as a member of the Legal Council he would spend the next two years. Minny wrote to him regularly, offering an intelligent and sympathetic support during his long months away. Mary Stephen based herself in England with the children, but made two long visits to India during his posting there. On board the *Golconda* during the outward journey he wrote from the Red Sea, imagining himself once more sampling the Onslow Gardens winter, '& the dearest & kindest hearts in all the world to warm & light it up', and this passage to India brought Thackeray to mind. 'I think that I always liked the Waterloo scenes best of all the scenes in Vanity Fair, & better on the whole than almost anything that the author of Vanity Fair ever wrote & the particular thing about them which I liked so specially was the way in which the most commonplace people are drawn – talking & laughing & flirting, & having all of them absurd little jealousies & vulgarities, & how in the midst of it all, they blaze up, all of a sudden, & go out & help to win one of the greatest battles of modern times.'[21]

At the year end, several of Annie's shorter pieces were republished by Smith, Elder as *To Esther and Other Sketches*, which Fitzy read in India. In a long critique he mixes praise with advice, and draws parallels with her father ('you remind me of him at every turn'), urging her to undertake next a more ambitious work. She had not heeded his previous suggestions about a regime of reading which might best assist her; this time, he chimed well with her own instincts, with embryonic ideas for *Old Kensington* already surfacing. 'I have no sort of right to dictate or even to suggest', he wrote, 'but I should so like you to take rather a larger canvass, to try to construct a story with a really striking incident for its centre, and to put in vigorous characters acting on rather a large scale. I think in that way you might write novels which would be a great possession for us all, & would influence people in a thousand subtle ways – I am quite sure you could do it if you pleased and if you took trouble enough.'[22]

Plotting her ideas as she worked with that 'larger canvass' proved more difficult than anything Annie had attempted before. During the early months of 1870 she was 'chopping & changing Old Kensington & writing occasional articles & not in a satisfactory swing'. It was a full two years before the serious writing got under way. A challenging distraction came when Edward Thackeray's decision to remarry appeared to mean that young Margie and Anny would permanently rejoin their father's new establishment. As things turned out, the girls continued to spend extended periods in Onslow Gardens as Edward pursued his peripatetic Indian army career. Minny at times found him infuriatingly unreliable so far as his own daughters' welfare was concerned, whereas Annie was just pathetically grateful to see as much of them as possible. She went as usual to Freshwater in the spring, sat as one of Julia Margaret Cameron's photographic subjects, and with Pinkie Ritchie became inveigled into Mrs Cameron's stratagems to charm Alfred Tennyson into compliance. 'Cammy wanted Annie and me to persuade Tennyson to be photographed with us but that was more than could be expected and she is furious with him.'[23] Tennyson's close Freshwater friend Sir John Simeon died in May, and

Annie assured the grieving daughter that one's memories of the dead keep them close. 'It is seven years nearly since I heard Papas voice & yet it seems to me as if it was but a moment since he left the room.'[24]

In the early summer Minny became pregnant again, and soon her health was causing concern; she was confined to sofas and submitted herself to being carried around. Annie later admitted that 'she was so seriously ill as to frighten us very much'. They escaped the oppressive heat of London by taking a house with a riverside garden in Kingston upon Thames, in which Millais's mother had lived; 'some strange grotesque early works of his were hanging up'. They began their stay the day following the death of Dickens, the news of which was telegraphed to Fitzjames. His thoughts were for Kate Collins, and for Thackeray's daughters also. 'It will have given you & Minnie a great shock, & have stirred up sad recollections.'[25]

Unwell herself, Minny nonetheless insisted that Leslie should have some time in the Alps, for she feared the risks of him over-working. He had become a prolific and wide-ranging writer of periodical articles and journalism, for *Fraser's Magazine,* the *Cornhill,* and the *Saturday Review* in particular, and in 1871 would embark upon the closely-researched critical work which underpinned his *History of English Thought in the Eighteenth Century* (completed in 1876). Shortly before they left Kingston for Lady Stephen's summer cottage at Bramley, near Guildford, she gave indications of her own returning strength. 'I am to be allowed to walk about a little in a few days which will be a great luxury after my 3 months of sofa – & yesterday I took my first drive through cornfields to Wimbledon, it was quite heavenly.'[26] Leslie left for the Alps, seeing evidence of the Franco-Prussian hostilities as he passed through Paris. Writing from Grindewald he pictured Minny at Bramley 'in your little nest in that vast bed', and looked ahead a year to when they might take an Alpine chalet for the summer, '& my Min shall get to look quite fat & strong'.[27]

Minny was still sending regular letters out to Fitzy. She touched on matters of faith, his strict Anglicanism contrasting with Leslie's agnosticism and her own and Annie's freethinking. The distance of several thousand miles made her able to be entirely frank about issues to which Fitzy attached great weight.

> Anny & I have qualms of conscience as to whether it is right or wrong of us to go to Church. Anny believes enough of it to satisfy anyone – but she says that it always happens on a Sunday morning that she has something that she can do that will be of use to other people, or else she gets a fit of work upon

> her wh she thinks is also more useful than going to church
> – altho she positively enjoys the service & believes a great deal
> of it. My case is different. I enjoy going to church because I
> like the 2 hours quiet... but on the whole, I dont believe that it
> can be right for me to go & repose myself, while really I appear
> to be joining in a service, in which I do not believe.[28]

She discussed family matters with him, acknowledging that Leslie's fear of speech-making ruled out a political career. 'I am almost reconciled to Leslies never getting into Parliament for I believe his nervousness over speaking would make him quite ill.'[29] She was stronger by the autumn, so Annie felt able to visit Scotland and Yorkshire, partly as research for the northern scenes in *Old Kensington*. She was delighted to meet her old nurse Brodie, 'sweet & eighty & tender', and stayed with her Low cousins at Clatto, by which time she was virtually voiceless with laryngitis. She was away a month, and as she set off for home again was seen into the railway carriage at Edinburgh by Dr John Brown, who presented her with a basket of fruit to sustain her. Even in her weakened state, she relished the irony of a meeting with two fellow passengers who had been visiting Edinburgh and who engaged her in conversation. 'Well we have seen everything we wanted except D^r. John Brown. I said Why that was D^r. John Brown – wont you have some of his fruit. To my dismay they took the beautiful Peach in the centre of the basket leaving me only the humbler plums. So much for affability.'[30]

It took a week of Minny's gentle nursing for Annie to feel restored, whereupon she resumed her London life, seeing much of Margie and Anny, the 'darling children so dear'. She rejoiced in the birth of Gerald Duckworth, Julia's son, involved herself in fund-raising activity for the embattled French, and worked at the novel. And on 6 December, she returned after dining out to find that Minny had gone into early labour. Laura Makepeace Stephen was born at 3 am, a premature baby, as Thackeray had been, but apparently a healthy 'six months child.' Leslie doted on the infant Laura, proudly announcing her arrival to Oliver Wendell Holmes. 'Her head is indicative of remarkable intelligence; her hands are obviously framed to grasp the pen & her feet show that she will be a firstrate mountaineer.'[31] His infatuation lasted throughout her early years, and when Laura was eighteenth months old Annie regularly noted that when he returned from the Cornhill offices, 'tired, dusty, overworked, I hear the clump clump of footsteps running to the nursery'.[32] This early affection contrasts sadly with his eventual treatment of the adolescent Laura, for he was unable to come to terms with her subsequent mental impairment, and she was

Ten: The Shabby Tide of Progress

Minny with Laura and Leslie's dog, Troy

placed in secure institutional care for the rest of her life. But for the time he was enchanted by the newly-arrived baby.

The time remaining to Minny after Laura's birth were years of very great happiness. Her natural affection for children at last was fulfilled. Leslie claimed never to have known anyone 'whose manner to children was so perfect'.[33] He opened up a little more to Holmes. 'As for a mother & child in the attitude of a Madonna, I can only say that the sight goes some way to reconcile me to papists.' From his great distance in Calcutta, Fitzy was still able to summarise the feelings occasioned by the arrival of a first child. 'The change from anxiety

& illness, to a sort of renewal of youth, & the new interest & ties, are wonderful pleasures, which I have no doubt you are both enjoying to the very utmost.'[34] Laura's name was taken from *Pendennis* (in which the worthy and watchful Laura Bell is not unlike the saintly Agnes in *David Copperfield*), about which Fitzy had minor reservations. 'I don't think your father much meant one to like her. I always thought he meant her as a sort of penitential character whose mission it was to be always absolving Pendennis from his sins, & sanctifying him & his children by her general moral & religious superiority.'[35]

Annie rejoiced in the parents' happiness. 'All goes well thank God in our small household & the Emperor of all the Germanys isn't so important to us as that little mite on Minny's knee. The mite keeps her Mama wide awake & her Papa hard at work & her aunts hoverescent.'[36] Because Laura was premature she was also tiny, but despite being described by Leslie a long time later as 'a very delicate child', she appears not to have been especially troubled by infant illnesses. He chiefly remembered that Laura 'was carried through her infantile troubles by her mother's intense tenderness and unremitting care'.[37] A further change in the Stephens' lives had come when in January Leslie accepted George Smith's offer of the editorship of the *Cornhill*, at an annual salary of £500. This was a particular pleasure for Thackeray's daughters, even if for Minny it took time for this additional happiness to sink in. 'I am still so elated about having her, that perhaps I am hardly sufficiently pleased ab^t. the Cornhill, but I am sure that Leslie has been well to take it in preference to Fraser w^h. the Longmans were rather tardy in offering.'[38] He worked at the *Cornhill* for the next eleven years, his relationship with the Smith, Elder enterprise continuing when he transferred to oversee the immense editorial enterprise represented by George Smith's commitment to the publication of a *Dictionary of National Biography*.

Meanwhile, other anniversaries were also occurring. Thomas Carlyle was seventy-five on 4 December, and it was Annie's idea to gather together his female admirers for some kind of formal presentation. Blanche Airlie suggested that they give a clock, and Annie collected the necessary sum from subscribers who included Emily Tennyson, Margaret Oliphant, Mary Stephen (wife of Fitzy) and Minny, Annie underwriting the cost by making up the balance. In one of her later *Chapters from Some Memoirs* she described the perhaps predictably dour occasion.

> Somewhat chilled and depressed, we all assembled in Lady Stanley's great drawing-room in Dover Street, where the fog had also penetrated, and presently from the further end of

the room, advancing through the darkness, came Carlyle.... Lady Stanley went to meet him. 'Here is a little birthday present we want you to accept from us all, Mr. Carlyle,' said she, quickly pushing up before him a small table upon which stood the clock ticking all ready for his acceptance. Then came another silence, broken by a knell, sadly sounding in her ears. 'Eh, what have I to do with Time any more?' he said. It was a melancholy moment.[39]

In mid-March, Annie crossed the channel to visit her father's cousin, Charlotte Ritchie, who stayed all through the worst of the Franco-Prussian conflict to support the Parisian poor. The scenes of ruin and deprivation struck her forcibly, the stored-up memories being used later in *Mrs Dymond*. That summer they all went to the Alps again, to St Gervais and Chamonix. It seems remarkable that they could contemplate taking a baby of only seven months on such a journey, but Minny was undaunted and of course had a nursemaid to assist her. In sweltering heat they passed through a Paris reeling from fresh conflicts. 'Many parts of it were utterly in ruins & it seemed to me that none of the principal streets were without many marks & holes & burns' – but at St Gervais they relaxed in idyllic surroundings. In letters to Lady Stephen, Minny described the hotel 'high up in a beautiful wide valley with a great snow mountain behind us.... We have been sitting on the hill behind the house this morning Laura rolling about on a blanket in rather a precarious fashion – but she does enjoy it so. She coos & crows & flings her dear little arms about – & kicks her little legs up in the air, & Leslie smiles at her so & seems so happy at having her surrounded by his mountains.' The nursemaid was clearly an asset, intrepidly carrying Laura up and down hillsides, but Minny also found her time taken up with the baby, and her attempts at sketching were curtailed. 'I only have 2 or 3 hours together in the afternoon & then I like to take a walk... so I hope to come home a little less stout.' Laura adjusted well to the local milk; one beast particularly suited her and they were able to ask for it to be milked whenever fresh supplies were needed. Minny worried about the child's smallness, yet other than the side effects occasioned by her cutting some teeth she was healthy – 'she does not seem to grow in size, but in firmness & weight I dont think I am more anxious about her than any common mother, I mean, than the mother of any common child'. A year later Annie summed up these early anxieties – 'she was the tinyest mite that ever was born & for months we never dared to believe in her'.[40] At Chamonix, where from her bed Minny watched the sun rising over

Mont Blanc, she was reminded of the time five years before when she had insisted that their party should leave for Zermatt in the expectation of encountering Leslie. 'I only hope that our sweet Laura may have as delightful a lovemaking as we had, but it will be a painful time for L. & me. I dont think she is a sentimental child & she is not at all shy, but there is a great dignity about her – it is so nice that she should be a child that everybody seems to like.'[41]

The year ended with the death of their Shawe grandmother, the woman whose behaviour in the face of her daughter's illness had so shocked Thackeray in 1840. Her passing is recorded without emotion by Annie, who probably had not seen this grandmother for many years, but she felt for her aunt Jane and went to Clifton, near Bristol, to support her. It was a 'horrid time', and it proved difficult to settle Jane Shawe and to return to London. Things were not made easier by the performance of her uncle, Arthur Shawe, who got 'rather tipsy'. The petty quarrels which accompanied the settling of her grandmother's affairs, and in later years those of aunt Jane, were an on-going concern for Annie, who always sought a fair outcome. The foolish pettiness that had characterised Mrs Shawe in life survived her in death, as her Shawe relatives squabbled over her estate.

The new year brought another death, and one which Annie felt much more acutely. Just eighteen months earlier she had attended the wedding of their friend Agnes Merivale, the sister of Herman and of Ella Freeman who had been with them at Lake George when Minny and Leslie travelled there from New York. Annie now heard that Agnes was dangerously ill in the late stages of pregnancy, and she hurried to the house but 'all was over'. With Minny and Leslie she attended the rather prosaic Methodist funeral on 11 January, an occasion made worse by the rain. Marriages, births and deaths – Onslow Gardens seemed to have been preoccupied with little else for some time. Thanking Hallam Tennyson for 'a little delicious whiff of primroses & Freshwater & the beloved Island', she responded to news of another engagement with the gentlest of swipes at Leslie and a slightly more risqué hint that the schoolboy Hallam might consider Margie as a future bride. 'When people marry they marry so many people besides their wives – Im sure in my own case when my sister married I got a dear grim brother whom I love dearly – will you wait for Margy & be my stepson in law? – but she is engaged to Richmond & Im afraid Anny is too young.'[42] There was always a certain innocence about Annie, but nothing in the least prudish.

During the early 1870s, Annie and Minny became close to both of Tennyson's sons, Hallam and Lionel. They saw much of them at Freshwater until they went away to school, Hallam to Marlborough,

Lionel to Eton. As Emily Tennyson became increasingly confined to her sofa, Hallam took on more of the supporting secretarial role to his father, eventually surrendering his chance of a Cambridge degree in order to return to Farringford. Annie enjoyed the company of these boys. They were of the same generation as Richmond Ritchie who now increasingly features in her correspondence, and in his own letters there is the faint hint of an adolescent infatuation with his older, charming, and increasingly celebrated Thackeray cousin. The spring of 1872 was a happy time for them all at Freshwater, with a ball at Farringford and the Ritchies renting a cottage nearby. Annie remembered a 'full moon walk across the downs. M\\r. Bryce, Minny, Richmond.'[43] *Old Kensington* had at last started its serial run in the *Cornhill*.

By the end of May, the Stephens and Annie had resolved to take one of the new houses being built in Southwell Gardens, South Kensington, larger and more convenient than Onslow Gardens. It is easy to overlook the extent of the speculative building to the west of London in the last third of the century. The 'shabby tide of progress' talked of in the first line of *Old Kensington* transformed the ancient borough's farms and pastures into the modern city suburb. Until they eventually moved in March 1873, Minny was choosing furnishings and fittings, a task she undertook with considerable flair.

Perhaps daily life was as idyllic as it sounds, with Annie's success as a novelist now secure and her sister contentedly married with her own child at last. Yet Annie felt the need to record her self-doubts at the end of May. 'Fresh Resolutions to avoid all unreasonable agitations, to be good & settle down calmly to my every day living my heaven upon earth as far as I can and paying debts of time & debts of friendship & gratitude to god Amen.' On reaching thirty-five, was she facing up to the realities of spinsterhood, and accepting that this might be as good as life was to be? There is courage in her passing remark which suggests that, providing her health was good, she entertained no other expectations for herself. 'I find middle age perfectly suitable & comfortable & not nearly so old as I used to think it when I was a girl, for one thing I am stronger now than I ever was before & am not always sick & miserable as I was at one time.'[44] Yet even now the seeds of a different future were being sown, of which the outcome was an unforeseen happiness that would rescue her from the second great trial of her life. At the end of June, in terms which are perhaps a little too self-assured even for this clever Eton schoolboy, Richmond Ritchie describes to his older sister a day on the river with Annie, Magdalene Brookfield (herself soon to marry into the Ritchies) and young Margie. 'We drove to Marlow through corn-fields and poppies, with a delicious baking sun, and then through rippling woods, flowing down a hill side; with here and there the British Summer House appearing. Margaret came & behaved like an angel. At Marlow we found a particularly odious Regatta just a going to begin; so we took a boat, and rowed up to Henley; where we basked amidst flowers and roses and red-brick.' And when Annie visited him at Eton early the following year, he wrote of her gift for brightening the day. 'She of course changed the grindy gloom into pure happiness; and left a cheerful little stock of sunshine to go on with.'[45] In June 1872 Richmond was not yet eighteen, but seemed unusually grown-up. Five years later Annie, then aged forty, would marry him.

Minny spent from July to October in a cottage near Falmouth in Cornwall, the property of the Sterlings, whose larger house stood nearby. Leslie was with her at first, and then Annie joined them, but during August Minny was alone with Laura whilst sister and husband went their separate ways, Annie to Normandy and Leslie to the Alps. The plan was for Annie to rejoin her with Margie and Anny after returning from France, but when the girls succumbed to whooping cough it seemed unwise to risk infecting Laura, so they all stayed away. It was a curious arrangement for Minny to be solitary and so far from London, and not to have accompanied Leslie abroad. It was hard to hide her loneliness once Leslie had left, and she invited people to visit. 'I must say that I do feel it most kind & extraordinary that people should come all this way – with only me at the end of it. It has very much cheered me up for of course there were moments in w^h. I felt very low yesterday – blow blow thou summer wind.'[46] But the place was enchanting, and she lost herself in its Celtic magic. Annie recalled the cottage fondly. 'How well I remember coming there after travelling all night, & Minnie coming along the green starry avenue to meet me, the blue sea like silent depths of cool verdure, the pretty iron gates, the old house & the stone hall which Minny had made into a drawingroom. Lauras little foster brother the donkey trolling in.'[47] Minny was painting tiles for Southwell Gardens, working first on the room which Leslie would use as his study – 'I am doing such a dear little tile of Laura & Troy'[48] – and was kept busy right through to October when Annie did eventually return.

Laura's baby chatter provided the name which Leslie and Minny habitually used for her, 'Meme' or 'Meemee', or sometimes just 'Mee'. There was an early indication in Cornwall of a wilful tendency when she wandered off alone and only returned after four hours. 'I sent Leslie & the farmer to scour the country for her & at last she appeared quite dry in her little waterproof & laughing. She had stayed in a cottage to tea, but I was much upset.'[49] As she approached her second birthday,

Ten: The Shabby Tide of Progress

Minny remained concerned about Laura's immaturity, and Lady Stephen wrote reassuringly. 'Everyone is quite right in saying that she is a most engaging child – it is not your fancy only & I am quite sure that no one can tell yet "what high capacious powers lie folded up in her" & that we shall see a great deal of progress which is invisible to you who are watching her every hour.'[50] Annie similarly insisted that Minny should not worry, although her argument seems shaky. 'I am so rejoiced to hear of her dear little tooth; as for her being a little backward that is all the better. You were a backward child & I should think Leslie must have been.'[51] She was staying with their cousin Blanche and her children at Lyon-sur-Mer on the Normandy coast, a visit during which the former misunderstanding with Browning was eased when he walked over to see her and Blanche, the object of his supposed former admiration. 'A solemn reconciliation with Mr Browning who had been vexed with me. He wrote his book [*Red Cotton Nightcap Country*] & dedicated it to me.'

When Annie was in France, Julia Margaret Cameron wrote to Pinkie Ritchie about one of her Freshwater cottages, having undertaken a number of improvements.

> I have a lovely little home here sixty guineas a year <u>furnished</u> 4 bed rooms and 2 sitting rooms. Which of you will invest in it? In the season you may let it for 4 gns a week. In the winter for 2 gns a week. It is the very house that I prevented our darling Annie Thackeray from <u>taking</u> saying it was stuffed in at the back and could give no air – whereas I as Henry Taylor says <u>happened to it</u>.
>
> I discovered in the W.C. (a W.C. that had never been used) a peephole that <u>betrayed</u> a view of the mighty ocean. Then I saw that the fortune of the House was made.
>
> I tore away all trace of W.C., moved it outside the House – and made a long window with a large view of the great ocean and added this to one bed room. To the other bed room I put a window where there was a dead wall and got fresh air and full view of the Afton fields. Then I placed two Balconies outside this House, furnished it exquisitely and finally christened it <u>The Porch!!!!!</u> Will you inhabit the Porch – will you send this history on to Annie. It is mine for 21 years if I choose. I could not bestow my creative genius on it for nothing and oh! I have done such wonderful Photographs lately. Watts writes under them 'I wish I could paint such a picture as this'....[52]

Although she did not decide immediately, Annie would eventually rent The Porch from Mrs Cameron, and it was where she died nearly fifty years later. It became integral to her fresh plan for maintaining some independence, for amongst a number of resolutions made on 3 September 1873 the most concrete was 'to live with M. but to keep a cottage to go to'. That same day she wrote 'to engage the Porch at F.W.'

William Ritchie, the oldest of the brothers, became engaged to Magdalene Brookfield early in 1873, creating a final tie between the Brookfield and Thackeray/Ritchie clans. The announcement created great happiness. Willie was Hallam Tennyson's contemporary at Cambridge, and Emily Tennyson's letter of congratulation went via Annie, appropriately registering her ranking in the complex of cousinly relationships.

> From what I know of your love for Magdalene & from what I have heard of her & him from others who know them better than I do it does seem an exceeding happy thing for both – One seldom sees a marriage that appears so fitting, one in which 'The two-cell'd heart beating with one full stroke Life' is more apparent. So I hope you are very happy about them & that we may congratulate you for I look upon you as a kind of sister Guardian cousin all in one to the whole family of Ritchies you know & much the same to Magdalene.[53]

Annie duly passed this note on to Pinkie, who herself replied gratefully to Mrs Tennyson. 'I can still hardly believe it, for you know how fond we are of Magdalene and she seems of late to have belonged more & more to us.'[54]

In March occurred the move from Onslow Gardens to 8 Southwell Gardens, an occasion later recalled in Annie's journal. 'Goodbye dear old house. You have sheltered warmed & comforted us. We were having a tea party I remember when the Vans came to move us & our cups were carried right away out of the drawingroom.'[55] Scarcely had they begun to settle in before Minny and Annie were off to spend Easter at Freshwater. However much she tried to rationalise it, Minny was still fretting about Laura's smallness, as her anxious comments to Lady Stephen reveal. 'Laura is most satisfactory with 2 cheeks like apples & brimming over with fun & happiness – She has not more teeth & does not say many more words but I have quite made up my mind to be rather glad that she is backward for I am sure it is better for her little brain to rest while it will.'[56] She sounded more desperate to Annie during the summer – 'I cant bear to think that she is nearly 3. she looks

Ten: The Shabby Tide of Progress

to me so much more like nearly 2 – I cant think why she doesnt pick up more – for I am sure she was a very healthy little tiny baby – she is very funny though.'[57] And it is poignant to see Annie dedicating the book publication of *Old Kensington* to her 'new friends', the children of Blanche Cornish, Julia Duckworth, Gussie Freshfield and to 'our Laura' who 'measures the present with her soft little fingers as she beats time upon her mother's hand to her own vague music'. It was sadly prescient.

That summer, the Stephens and Annie returned once more to the Alps, to Chamonix. There were times during this holiday when Annie felt a little apart from the happy family group. She felt strangely awkward, probably regretting having come this time, and it influenced her decision to take The Porch. A portion of original diary pasted into her later journal is starkly honest. 'Still depressed but going to try & write. I wont come abroad again without a companion to distract me f^m morbidness for Leslie naturally wants Minny. Wrote a little cried g^t. deal. Very angry with myself.'[58] She was back in London in time for the wedding of Willie and Magdalene on 2 September, a 'happy day with a song in it'.

Later in September Annie and Minny were in Brighton, and Richmond visited them there. Delighted in his company, Annie told Pinkie of taking him around the places she knew so well. 'I enjoy having Richmond very much as I needn't tell you & I insist upon going on rather crazy expeditions & showing him Brighton.'[59] Their friendship was assuming a new dimension during these late months of 1873, gaining a significance which probably neither of them could easily define but which left her excited and alive. Magdalene noticed it and felt that she needed to caution Annie – 'she says I'm too gushing about the boys'.[60] The 'boys' were Richmond, Hallam and Lionel, and perhaps others of their Cambridge friends. She was easy and natural in their company, tending to treat them as her equals in age, which of course they were not, though both Richmond and Hallam seemed immensely grown-up. With someone like Hallam, to whom she felt linked through the former friendship of their illustrious fathers, Annie talked freely and seriously about ideas, as she would to any intelligent person irrespective of age. Unsympathetic to new developments in the arts, she shared her thoughts with him after writing a piece for the *Pall Mall Gazette*.

> I finished in a little thrill thinking of the day I first read the Idylls, O such a lovely spring day & this which is that people may say what they like about modern thought (& I know there

is a[n] utterly astounding & complicated Something gathering which is quite too strong & great for people like me who were brought up in narrower times), but what I do feel is that neither the awful truth of science nor the melodies & raptures & roses of [William] Morris nor the vivisoulections [*sic*] of Contemporaries & Fortnightlies need put away the dear old clear clanging of King Arthurs spurs or Colonel Newcomes old cavalry sword & those Excaliburs I thank God our Fathers have always held & this is only the sentence I didnt write in my article but I cant help finishing it off to you.[61]

The boys rather enjoyed these flattering attentions, though Annie's own generation undoubtedly felt a little awkward at her unconventionality. All too soon they would be overtaken by an event of such piercing sadness that Annie might well have assumed that she had been robbed for ever of the possibility of happiness.

Eleven

THE INSCRUTABLE DESIGN
(1873-1875)

No death – no loss anywhere that I could have imagined <u>could</u> have been more terrible, for I know how most precious she was to you both – how all your happiness was staked on her life.

Meta Gaskell to Annie
1 December 1875

Old Kensington completed its *Cornhill* run in April 1873 and then immediately appeared in book form. Although somewhat episodic, it is probably Annie's most thoughtfully plotted piece of fiction, and the work with which she is most characteristically identified. It is autobiographical to the extent that it is situated in the places which Annie knew best – in the Kensington houses of her childhood (with scenes also in Paris) – whilst drawing also on her more recent awareness of the masculine worlds of Eton and Cambridge. It is richer in its characterisations than her previous works, and Winifred Gérin is right to suggest that it embraces a larger social canvas than before, and that the subtlety with which the figure of Frank Raban is drawn may partly be explained by her growing closeness to Richmond Ritchie.[1] Gordon Ray and others have drawn on the novel as a usefully nostalgic record of the environs of Young Street in the 1840s, before the major building works seen during the lifetimes of Thackeray's daughters. *Old Kensington* went through several immediate reprints, achieving sales which were more than respectable – 2,750 copies were printed in the first year.[2] Her expanding reputation allowed Annie to secure much better terms than she had previously enjoyed. As he always had done with her father, George Smith acted generously, all of the financial risk falling upon himself. 'Perhaps it will meet your wishes if I say that you may reckon on receiving not less than a thousand pounds for the right of printing your novel in the "Cornhill Magazine," and of our publishing it afterwards on the terms of your receiving half the profits derived from the separate publication. And you may draw the above sum at any time or in any manner that will suit your convenience.'[3]

These were exceptional terms for a writer whose previous sales had been modest enough, but Smith's belief in her was justified, much to his pride and delight. Publishing was only part of his business interests, and when he became involved in a shipping firm he insisted that one of the fleet should be named the Old Kensington. Minny was all for investing in him – 'by the way in Mr Smiths ships, you get a very high per cent & they are insured. I think we had much better take shares in Old K.'[4] It would be nice to think that he may also have been the owner of a horse called Anne Thackeray which ran almost daily at racecourses during the early 1870s.

The success of the book was probably the stimulus for Smith, Elder's eight-volume collected edition, and it was chosen to launch 'The Works of Miss Thackeray', which Julia Margaret Cameron spotted her fellow passengers reading when she was bound for Ceylon in November 1875. 'I find your name beloved Annie like a household word in this ship each one knowing about you and many a one carrying your book in their hand.'[5] By the start of 1874 Annie was entitled to think of herself as successful, and for her next subject she turned to the life of the eighteenth-century painter, Angelica Kaufmann, leading to a freely-imagined *roman à clef*. *Miss Angel* became her main work for the year.

Having taken The Porch at Freshwater, Annie subsequently bought some land at Colwell Bay with a view to build, benefitting from Hallam Tennyson's local expertise and the legal advice of Jeanie Senior's brother, Hastings Hughes. Leslie urged caution, for although at the time he was in favour of leaving London, perhaps for Slough which was on a good train route to the capital, he had no wish to move to the Island. 'If you snap at things you are sure to be done; and moreover I am very unwilling that you should fix yourself whilst our plans of life are unsettled. If we wanted to leave London in a year or two, we should be rather hampered by your being tied to Freshwater. And, seriously, I am growing anxious to change as my ties here grow weak. I think it would be good for Laura to be in the country &, in short, there is much to be said about it.'[6] Annie never did build on the land, which was eventually resold.

Lady Stephen's health was failing, and though she lived on until February 1875 her decline led Leslie to share his thoughts with Annie on his own changed fortunes. 'The best thing I ever did in my life was marrying Min; for you and she have made the last seven years a time

Eleven: The Inscrutable Design

of happier relations between us all than any years before. I wont say any more of that.' He was perfectly aware of the seriousness of his mother's condition, despite Minny's attempts to hide some of the more distressing symptoms of infirmity. 'I do rather try & keep all the little melancholy details of her illness from him, at any rate in the morning, so that he may get through his work.'[7] It was time to say farewell to other old friends too. The elder Herman Merivale died in February, and William Brookfield, that sometimes unsettling link with Thackeray's past, early in July. Annie spent much time with Jane Brookfield during these sad weeks.

Minny and Leslie left London for the summer and took a cottage at Englefield Green, near Egham, Leslie travelling up by train as required. This peripatetic existence fuelled his desire for a country life of the kind enjoyed by Lowell in New England, even so far as wanting to keep some farm animals. It was hopelessly impractical, of course, and Minny's thoughts led in a different direction. She got into negotiations for a house in Hereford Square, concluding that the ideal would be to divide their time between 'a nice house & garden in the easy suburbs – Switzerland for August & Sep. & Paris for a month or so in the winter... only dont say anything more ab^t. it before Leslie, or he will disagree again, he cant bear people to think about doing anything they w^d like'. Then she considered Brighton. Nothing came of any of it, but she enjoyed the planning and the thrill of the chase. Content to stay in the shadows of a now celebrated sister and an increasingly influential husband, it is clear that Minny was no fool. She was intelligent, well-read and opinionated, combining intuition with more measured judgments. In the quiet times at Englefield Green she read George Sand ('which made me laugh but I think it is rather shocking'), Maurice de Guérin and Alfred de Musset ('horrible, ugly & dull'), and was quietly triumphant in identifying a novel under consideration for the *Cornhill* as being by Mrs Henry Wood. 'Leslie is very much put out when I say so, he thought he had discovered a promising new author.'[8]

Once Leslie had left for his normal Alpine break, Minny decided that it was time to deal with Laura's increasing wilfulness. 'I want to cure her of her bad habits while you are away. Today she began throwing about the things as usual so I said Laura will you be good. No. & so I said you must either be good here or go upstairs.'[9] She was a child of nearly four, no longer a baby. Meanwhile, Annie divided her summer between time at Freshwater and with Blanche and Frank at Lynton in Devon, where she put the finishing touches to a collection of stories, *Bluebeard's Keys and Other Tales*, republished from the *Cornhill*. For this reissue she arranged for Richmond, Hallam, Julian

Sturgis and Frank Warre Cornish to provide poems in hexameters before each of the four stories. Her formal thanks to the poets mixes an arch archaism with the prosaic.

A DEDICATION TO THE WRITERS OF FAIRY-TALE HEXAMETERS F.W.C., H.T., J.R.S. AND R.T.R.

> It is time I leave my proofs and my fairy-follies and despatch them to the printer in London, far away; these pages in my own, and in the familiar handwritings, that have brought me (not without some protest) the stories as I asked for them, told once more, in a certain cadence.
>
> The original tunes had seemed to me lost somehow, in my experiments and variations, and these kind musicians and another, not refusing to please me, have played them once more to the measure I asked for.
>
> To friend H.T. and to kinsman R. I must write my thankyou here; to F. I can say it as he stands smoking his pipe upon the terrace-walk.

A week or so later she wrote gratefully to Hallam, acknowledging also his father's help, he being the hidden 'another' of the dedication. 'How shall I ever thank you enough dear for the delightful Hexameters dearest AT dearest HT.'[10] Their friendship had emerged safely from an awkward patch, as for some time she had been doing her best to manoeuvre Hallam's affection for Pinkie Ritchie into a marriage proposal. When Annie confronted him and suggested that he had been leading Pinkie on, she saw to her intense embarrassment that she had entirely misread the situation. 'He was never in earnest ab^t P. except as a friend.'[11] Pinkie would remain Hallam's loyal supporter throughout his two marriages, perhaps never quite forgetting the quiet hopes that she had once entertained for herself.

A restlessness in Annie's character meant that she always seemed to be in the process of leaving one place for somewhere else. At Freshwater with Minny she made plans to leave for Italy, in search of background material for *Miss Angel*. And this time Italy would mean Richmond; he would be there with some of his sisters, his mother, and their aunt Charlotte Ritchie who would accompany Annie from Paris. Minny was still trying to plot out a future for them all which involved her sister building on the Colwell Bay land where she could live modestly and secure her capital, together with their collective disposal of the Southwell Gardens house. She set out her plans to Leslie.

> It is worth our while to put a good price on Southwell G. even

if we are more than a year in selling it, but whatever happens you <u>must</u> give up the Saturday [Review]. If you thought it possible for us to leave London, we could not do better than take the Slough house, but I dont think you will – & now for Anny – all next year she will not have the children so that she will have a whole year to build a cottage. She will have the money from her book & if she doesnt spend it on something solid it will all slip away.... It is not the faintest use telling her to invest the money – she will not do so – & even a useless cottage is better than no money. There is no doubt ab^t. it that the land will rise & that she will be able to make a profit upon the whole thing if she wants to sell after the railway comes near the Island.[12]

She also told Leslie about an entertainment in which the eccentric personalities who peopled Freshwater were about to be portrayed. 'The children are going to act a charade today in which Mee is to join. The word is Freshwater & all the FW characters are to be brought in' – thus anticipating by five decades Virginia Woolf's knowing play *Freshwater*.[13] Virginia might have been surprised to learn that Laura Stephen, the half-sister for whom she would show such little concern and felt scant sympathy, had been capable of playing her part in a similar if wholly innocent joke so many years before.

Annie paused in Milan and stayed a couple of nights in Verona before meeting the Ritchies in Venice on 21 September. The Hôtel de la Ville in Milan triggered memories, to be shared with her sister to whom she wrote constantly. 'We are in the gorgeous saloon we had last time we came with Papa – I think its the same with yellow velvet chairs & a blue & embroidered ceiling.'[14] Charlotte Ritchie was venerated by the family for her sweetness and good works, but there was a toughness of character too which had got her through the Franco-Prussian war. Her growing impatience regarding Annie's friendship with Richmond sometimes bubbled to the surface, such as when she vetoed his offer to come to Verona merely to escort them to Venice. 'I blew up Charlotte poor dear, who has to be blown up to know what a tender old Darling she is. It was all about a note from R^d who said he w^d. come and meet me at Verona if I liked to go on w^h. needless to say she wouldnt hear of.' Venice was everything Annie expected it to be. 'We came in a dark gondola last night. Richmond met us – It is so nice to see him again & Pinnie & Nelly & Mrs Ritchie is so kind & quite as economical as Charlotte to whom Im afraid Ive been rather cross. But one cant be perfect.'[15]

For reasons of economy Charlotte had proposed sharing a hotel room with Annie, but she insisted on independence in order to write. Minny knew that Annie's letters could quickly turn into rhapsodic impressions of paintings, which in her Freshwater isolation she did not need. 'When you write to me dont describe the Tintorets nor the tints, for I know exactly what it is like & I like descriptions of people best & I can place them in Venice. I feel that from this beastly solitood I have a right to demand the sorts of letters I want but I am not at all unhappy or lonely & I enjoy the quiet.'[16] Annie attempted a protest. 'How can I write without Tints darling.' Paintings to her were as much about the personal histories of the models whose modern counterparts she saw praying in the churches and shopping in the markets of Venice. They gave a contemporary life to the timeless canvasses.

> Fancy all the pictures out of all the churches sitting & busying & laughing, your Virgins carrying their infants, S^t. Peter with the fish, S^t. Mark with the scales, Judas with a long nose making a low bow to a fat old monk who steps into his fusty mysterious gondola with two fat bare dirty white legs – there was a most mysterious little dark cabin inside into w^h. the old monk crept all lined with pens & inks & books & then Judas & Maccabaeus pushed off the gondola first carefully closing the door.[17]

For Minny, missing both Annie and Leslie, and longing for Venice – 'dear sweet stinking gorgeous golden Venice' – their absence was to some degree mollified by the presence of Hallam and Lionel Tennyson, who in taking time to divert her were 'very affect^{ate} & kind'.[18] She proudly copied out Laura's improvised poem in separate letters to them both – 'Dorothy is a flower / Meemee is the sea / Dorothy will swim swim swim / Dorothy will swim in the sea.'[19]

After a week in Venice the party transferred to Florence, where the Freshfields joined them. Douglas and Richmond took responsibility for seeking out the best sights. The debonair Douglas was 'a most capital escorter', but the less worldly if self-confident Richmond also earned his spurs. 'Richmond is the most devoted & delightful of cicerones. It is wonderful how he manages for everyone. I thought it sounded so delightful when he exclaimed with joy at picture no. 6247, & said think of 6246 more all to come.'[20] But her delight in his presence was all too transparent it seems for Charlotte. Everyone chimed in, leaving Annie 'rather seedy' on the sofa in the Freshfields' luxurious rooms. 'I was also made rather rabid by poor dear Chattie who begged me not to accaparate Richmond at w^h. everybody from different points of

Eleven: The Inscrutable Design

view took it up & altogether it was most irritating & as I was far from well I felt most furious.' Perugia was like a 'fairy town' and revived her, whilst in Genoa memories of the time with Minny and their father came flooding back, and yet she was willing to recognise that things could be even better now. The upset about Richmond had shown her that there was something important about the nature of their friendship, even if she could not yet quite understand what it was.

> Oh! darling the garden was <u>tumbling</u> with sweetness & shaking sun into flowers & insects & the bay looked as blue as it used to look when we were little girls & a steamer slipped & slipped away & I thought <u>we</u> were on board & Papa – & yet – It is not ungrateful to say that those days weren't so complete as now, when we seem to have him still & all the other things beside – Even for me darling – Laura Leslie & Anny & Margy seem to repeat him over & over again, & tho Im afraid it will never be quite the same with my dear little Richmond he too will always be one of the people in my heart. I daresay I shall soon forget all about it but the fuss was a bore & makes one feel all uncomfortable. Please dont say anything about it to anyone.

After her return to London, Annie went with Minny to the first night of Henry Irving's *Hamlet* at the Lyceum Theatre. They made their way backstage during the curtain calls, met Irving 'looking very handsome & pale & quite natural as a man must be whose just been being anything so real',[21] and watched as he took the applause. A few weeks later Annie and Irving happened to be on the same train going down to Brighton, where Minny hoped that the sea air would improve Laura's cough. 'All the ticket porters knew him, flew for his luggage to which he pointed as if it had been the grave of Ophelia.... Irving was very melancholy & talked mysterious allusions to his wife. He says he envies painters so who can see the works of those who went before while poor actors can only look at each other.'[22]

Annie worked hard at *Miss Angel* until the end of the year, incorporating her Venetian material and checking historical details. Whilst she had been in Italy, Leslie had asked her to plug the gap in the *Cornhill* once Thomas Hardy's novel *Far From the Madding Crowd* ended in December. He assumed that *Miss Angel* would not be ready in time, but in fact Annie now made good progress and it began its *Cornhill* run in January. Earlier in the year they had entertained Hardy to dinner, not the most successful of occasions according to Minny's account.

> Darling your letters & proceedings are so entirely insane that I can make no comment upon them – They are about as muddled as our dinner of yesterday which was a wild wild chaos – I tried to drown my cares in drink but it only affected my <u>feet</u> & not my head. Mr Hardy is a very damp young man & dampness I abominate.... The Ice too was warm. The only cool things were the soup & the hot viands – I had an expensive dish of peas which came up like so many hard blue pills & about as digestible & this what comes of trying to have a dinner without extraneous help – I will never do it again.[23]

Leslie viewed Annie's closeness to Richmond and the Tennyson boys with some distaste, believing that she had a tendency to expend much energy in needless fuss. 'Anny was low this morning & talked a good deal about her soul. I could not persuade her that it did not matter whether she had a soul or not. However she has now brightened up & is gone off to Eton to gush over her beloved Richmond & the young Tennysons & the whole lot.'[24] And yet she and Richmond seemed close to putting a stop to things. Just a day or two later she was with Minny at Brighton. 'Tuesday [1 December] a letter f^m. R perhaps the last.'[25] A resolution that they should refrain from seeing each other, whilst continuing to write, did not last very long, and in March she was delighted when Richmond unexpectedly appeared at a family party at Southwell Gardens, 'for I thought we were to meet no more. I <u>very very</u> happy.'[26]

Annie had at least one marriage proposal in the spring of 1875. She may have been momentarily flattered, even touched, but it also flustered her and was an unwelcome distraction. Hastings Hughes, who was advising on her Colwell Bay land, had become increasingly interested in developing a friendship during recent months, but it was scarcely a romantic attachment. He was a lonely widower in search of a mother for his children. Jeanie Senior probably put the idea in her brother's mind; she certainly did all she could to facilitate a match and urged Annie to accept the proposal when it came. Hastings paid more than one visit to Southwell Gardens shortly before she left for Paris on 8 April, 'glad to escape from all this sentiment'.[27] But Annie immediately ran up against another admirer, for Gabriel Loppé, the painter and Leslie's fellow Alpinist, presented himself just at this moment and 'talked sentiment'. She resolutely ignored his attentions. As for Hastings, he did not brim with confidence about his own chances.

Eleven: The Inscrutable Design

> It is a very great pleasure to write to you, almost as good as talking, and has this great advantage over the latter. One cannot possibly bore you because you needn't either read or answer, whereas when one is talking to you with your abominable good nature you listen or pretend to listen, and answer, and one goes away quite pleased with oneself & without a suspicion that one has bored you to death. You won't mind my going now & then to Southwell Gardens to hear how you are? But I shall not go till I hear from you – or if you write a line from time to time to Jeanie I shall hear of you from her.[28]

Yet he would soon send a formal proposal to Paris, probably at his sister's instigation. Jeanie's role in the business was crucial. She wrote to Annie on 19 April, urging her to think about marriage to 'some man of your own standing'. Perhaps unwisely, Annie had confided in Jeanie as to the nature of her feelings for Richmond, and Jeanie worked this to her own advantage, fired by her own disapproval of the mismatch in ages and stations in life. It was a rearguard action in advance of what was meant to be her brother's telling strike.

> Don't think me impertinent my Annie for speaking so coolly of what you ought to do. You gave me your confidence about poor Richmond, & of course I have thought a great deal about it ever since. – You said in a vague way that you sh^d. not think it well to marry because of this complication in your life. But do you really <u>mean</u> this? Surely it w^d. be better for him & for yourself that you should marry some man of suitable age? The love you have for R. w^d. not stand in the way of your being happy in marriage, if your husband was willing that your old influence over the boy sh^d. continue – And no man who deserved you would be such a fool as to be jealous of your love for R. & his for you; – You & R. c^d. be the dearest friends still, & if you were married, a certain calmness w^d. come to you both, w^h. it is very difficult to ensure now. –
>
> My Annie I don't want you to sacrifice all the rest of your life to <u>an idea</u>, a chimera, w^h. tortures you on the present footing. You are calculated to make a man so very happy, & to be so very happy yourself, & I can't bear that you should be fretted, or look on y^r. affection for R – & his for you in a morbid way, w^h. might stand in the way of your marrying some man of your own standing who w^d. make your life

> blessed & happy – & in whose protection & love you w^d. find rest of body & soul & mind. –
>
> ... The best help you c^d. give R – in getting rid of the side of his love that torments him & you too, w^d. be to let him see you calm & happy in a suitable marriage. – He would not <u>lose</u> you – you w^d not lose him – You both w^d. be gainers; & he w^d. have a chance of setting that side of his heart on a woman of a suitable age.[29]

Jeanie's advice was anything but neutral, but Annie was strong enough to resist it. Neither of them mention Hastings, but he is an unspoken presence, and Annie's carefully crafted reply was perhaps meant to forewarn against any coming approach. She claimed to have put the idea of marriage behind her altogether.

> I got into a foolish exaggerated phase about Richmond , w^h. is quite over, & was always more a fancy of my own than anything else. but Im thankful I told you for I know I can trust you, & <u>you</u> were the sunshine & the light let in.
>
> It is nothing concerning him dearest which makes me now feel that I have not got it in me to marry anybody. I have not the instinct towards anyone without which it would be not honest love but impossible and mere calculation. Yesterday half a dozen old '<u>failures</u>' (without even votes) came to see me & filled me with an odd prescience of a possible future, but it is better to be an honest dreary old maid than to go against my deliberate conscience & instinct which is the only thing I have to go by, & the one help one has in life. I know no one I could marry tho' it does not prevent my feeling very grateful & touched to think that anyone should ever have thought of marrying me.[30]

Hastings would not be so easily deflected, perhaps because Jeanie chose to believe that Annie simply needed to be persuaded of the merits of the right man. On 23 April, Annie gave his written proposal serious consideration, though she was never strongly inclined to accept. She kept her thoughts for her journal. 'Should I be justified? You do nothing for a Real life and nothing for a comfortable one. One of my usual revolutions of feeling.' Only the previous day she had written to Hastings, and also prepared a letter to Richmond, which she then tore up.

As an intelligent counterweight to Jeanie's far from disinterested urgings, Annie could have done with hearing Fitzjames's remarkable

Eleven: The Inscrutable Design

insight into her character – offered six years earlier to Minny, when he had feared just such a moment as this – that from a perverse sense of duty she might marry a man unworthy of her 'till she broke her heart under it'. She sent Minny the draft of a reply to Hastings, presumably her refusal of his formal proposal. Minny's comment was reassuring, written from the lofty position of a married woman to her spinster sister. 'That letter to Hastings H. will do perfectly. I am sure you neednt write any more – In these cases it is absolutely necessary to be decisive – because if you let a man dangle on he is sure to think you have illused him.'[31]

Hastings was nothing if not resilient, now attempting to use the irritated Minny as a go-between. 'I am so glad you left Hastings' letter unopened for it was such an absurd one, I was quite angry when I first read it. He sent me the draft of it I dont know why, but he is not worth being angry with poor fellow, it is only want of tact & stupidity, & Leslie recommended me not to answer the letter & if it pleases him to think that your heart is being broken by this, atrocious male flirt – let him think it.'[32] Hastings appears to have made some kind of open-ended offer, but at the end of May Leslie too had received a letter, which he relayed to Minny. 'He says that I am not to tell you all what he tells me but am to give you & Anny to understand that he does not mean to make any more offers. I have replied that he is quite right – so I suppose there is an end of that.'[33] One detects Leslie's despair at the triviality of it all. Loppé had also renewed his attentions in Paris, appearing shortly before Annie was due to come home. But she was now decided that she needed a better reason for marrying than merely as a strategy for avoiding staying single, and on 10 May had no difficulty in deflecting him. 'Woke up in my right mind & greatly bored. Shall try & be as useful as I can & as happy as I can & will not marry to simplify confusions. Enter M Loppé – who proposes – L'homme propose. Dieu dispose. He drinks some soda water & goes away.'

Complex as her feelings for Richmond were, there was no other man with whom she could be so open. Before the Parisian episode, she had told him about visiting George Eliot and, in talking of her feelings, receiving good advice in return. It may have helped arm her for the battle of wills with Jeanie over which she would expend considerable nervous energy before emerging confident that her decision was the right one.

> Scene a cup of tea. George Eliot in a beautiful black satin dressinggown by the fire snow outside & German paper books on the table a green lamp & a paper cutter. The shrine was so serene & kind that this authoress felt like a wretch for having refused to worship there before.

> She looked very noble with two steady little eyes & the sweetest stateliest expression – You must go & see her I am sure she will be a friend just as I felt her yesterday – not a personal friend exactly, but a sort of good impulse trying to see truly not be afraid & do good to other people.
>
> She said it was much better in life to face the very worst & build ones cottage in a valley so as not to fall away & that the very worst was this – that people are living with a power of work & of help in them w^h. they scarcely estimate. That we know by ourselves how very much other people influence our happiness & feelings & that we ought to remember that we have the same effect upon them. That we can remember in our own lives how different they might have been if others even good people had conducted themselves differently (This part Im glad to say I couldnt follow, nor could she remember a single instance of any single person's misconduct). She said we ought to learn to be satisfied with immediate consequences, & respect our work. It is all nonsense about not meeting every five minutes if we feel inclined, but it is certainly aggravating to know you just within reach & not to see you. But that is only a fancy & not real affection. And a future of trust & confidence is after all better than almost anything and I have quite cheered up again now & feel as if you had too.[34]

Annie must have felt that everyone had an opinion about how she should behave. When Leslie wrote, at least he kept off that topic, instead becoming expansive on the theme of her poor financial judgment. In a way, she had provoked the reprimand, having told him that she needed to write to raise money. Leslie claimed to be shocked by such a sentiment, and proceeded to attack on two fronts. First, she kept no record of her spending, so that her money was 'simply muddled away'. Secondly, her writing would suffer by being driven by the cheque book. 'You are making yourself into a pump instead of a spring, & if you will go on at this rate you must end by pumping yourself out. I cant bear to think of it.' His tone is one of affectionate bullying, born out of a genuine respect for her ability, for 'there are not half a dozen people who have your genius in England'.[35]

Leslie's pathological anxiety about money is well recorded, but here he is not primarily prompted by any selfish motives, even though any shortfall in Annie's finances would be a liability upon the household

Eleven: The Inscrutable Design 265

as a whole, which in practice meant upon him. He feared that she undervalued her capacity to do good work through her writing, rather than through charitable giving, the same point that his brother had previously made from India.

> You fancy that your novels do not do more good than your charity. You are wrong. Good literature has an immense influence. George Eliot has influenced people more than if she had given away millions, & you can do the same if you like.
> ... Minny & Meemee & I can live for £1,000 or £1,200 a year, for millions of people do it. I wont make more. As for you, I will tell you what I think. Make up your mind to do two things; always to pay ready money & to live for a moderate sum. Make yourself an allowance & then you cant exceed it. You will have to cut off some of your habitual indulgences, charitable & otherwise, for a time; but you will find life is quite as agreeable & at any rate much more usefully employed.

It was good advice, and Annie was not offended by it, for she knew the generosity of spirit in which it was given. But she was temperamentally incapable of following it, breaking her regular resolutions to cut back on spending even more easily than they were made. Minny had taught Leslie how to show affection; unfortunately he was less successful in instructing her sister in financial prudence.

It was a source of great amusement to Minny when the page proofs for the Australian publication of *Miss Angel* all got muddled, and as Annie was in Paris, Leslie and the *Cornhill* staff were left trying to work out the thread of the narrative to get things back in order. 'I cant help laughing when I think of Leslie & Mr Payn sitting in the office & spelling out the sentiment & not knowing which was meant for sense. However you can of course alter it for the Cornhill. The chief objection seems to be that she seems to be unmarried at the end.'[36] Leslie would cite this incident as an example of how Annie's inability to organise her life spilled over into her work. 'G. Smith and I used to entreat for a little more orderly arrangement of her plots, the relationship of her characters and so forth; but I saw in time that such criticism only bothered her and did no good.'[37]

Leslie, Minny and Laura spent a week at Cambridge in May, staying at the University Arms Hotel and visiting various of Leslie's friends. Minny also hunted out 'our three young men', Lionel Tennyson, Richmond and his elder brother, Gerald Ritchie. 'My Lionel & your

Richmond are both looking brown & beautiful.'[38] Howard (Howie) Sturgis was a fellow undergraduate, and much attached to Richmond. Early indications of Sturgis's aestheticism were already present, as Minny knowingly remarked. 'Howard seems to adore Richmond & is really a dear little fellow. It is so funny to see them in all their little establishments. Howard had borrowed a cake of Richmonds & was in a yellow flowery lodging with a great many antimacassars & luxuries.'[39] For her, a week was long enough. Cambridge talk was unremittingly earnest and the comforts few – 'to me it is a terrible want in a place having no theatrical or musical interest'. Leslie discovered her starting to wilt in an intense conversation with the classicist Richard Jebb. 'I was sitting with M^r J, on the sofa & talking about eternity & a few other trifling subjects of the sort. I am sorry to say I said one of those things to him that makes one shudder in bed – but is too long to tell you now.'[40] She found Henry Sidgwick the easiest don to talk to, and was grateful for his ability to shift quickly between subjects.

Early in the summer Minny found that she was pregnant, and once again the early months were difficult for her. On their doctor's advice they set out for the curative benefits of the Alps, Annie having agreed to join them later. Inevitably, the long train journey between Brussels and Bâle was tiring, though Leslie eased things by booking places in the 'boudoir car', and Minny urged Annie to follow by the same route. They rested for a few days before moving on to Thun, Mürren and Interlaken. Minny put a brave face on things, but clearly she was not well. 'I have had little or no neuralgia since I left & my horrid salivation is better today & is never very bad except at night.'[41] She kept to her hotel room, only going down once a day to dinner, whilst Leslie ate at the table d'hôte. She was concerned that Laura was not eating well, for she disliked the local bread and they would not get good milk until they were higher in the Alps. Minny knew that she was holding Leslie back, for he yearned to get into the mountains, but they were managing only about three hours travelling each day, 'for now that the terrific struggle is over I feel less inclined than ever to move'. At Mürren she still felt very low. 'We have got very nice rooms – & the place is perfection for Leslie but I am afraid it will be too cold for me who of course cannot walk to help myself.... In my half distracted state I dont know how to get things done ... & I cant bear to suggest to Leslie that we should go anywhere else.... I dont know when you are coming – but I hope it will not be very long.' About a week before Annie started from London for Interlaken, Minny wrote from there, recording Laura's touching little query about her two grandfathers. 'Laura said the other day, Mama when yous Papa saw Papas Papa in even what did he say to im.'[42]

Annie's arrival was cheering, and she became a companion for Leslie who took her for walks while Minny rested in the hotel and gradually regained her strength. She wrote to Richmond, her 'dearest tonic', without delay, for their correspondence was again becoming increasingly important to her, their agreement to calm things down having fast retreated.

> I feel as if all was full of hope & gratefulness still & if I still blame myself for my want of self control, it only makes me feel again & again how far kinder life is than I can realise, & how dear dear people are, & you wont always feel old dear because you have helped me: but I know you will like me to tell you how I have felt it & I have even put away my old bits of self reproach & been happy once more & feeling as if you were a blessing indeed w^h. I may count upon, w^h. couldnt be if I thought you were bothered by my faults, but still worse than anything w^d. it be if you <u>didnt</u> tell me – whenever you felt inclined – exactly, – even disagreeable things – & the truth abt yourself.

They encountered the novelist Margaret Oliphant and her children at Grindewald, sealing a friendship which lasted until Mrs Oliphant's death in 1897. Annie wrote confidently to Magdalene Ritchie on 5 August about Minny's recovery, describing her as 'delightfully well' and commending the doctor as 'a good genius for having sent her here to escape her miserableness'.[43] She and Minny stayed on at Interlaken for some weeks after Leslie had gone back temporarily to London, and Minny rejoiced in being fully restored. 'What a clever thing it was to come here.'[44] But now Richmond's health began to be a source for some concern, for he was reading hard for his Cambridge exams and Annie feared for his nerves – 'a young man cannot live by work alone but must be well & fulfil his life & my dearest young man I think takes things too <u>hard</u> somehow mentally. You always tell me to take things easy & mind you do & follow my advice, & that of all who love you.'[45]

During the autumn the business over Hastings Hughes appeared to resolve itself when he became engaged to someone else, although he only finally remarried in 1887. Annie had no doubts about her own decision in refusing Hastings in April. She took much trouble composing a letter of congratulations, for it was important to get her thoughts clear as much for herself as for him.

> Dear Hastings how thankful I am all has turned out as it has done. If I had, as I was very near doing at one time married you for the sake of ease & quiet peace, only with the thought of being taken care of & useful to you perhaps, this best blessing would have been wanting to us both. I think you ought to have perhaps told me something – you would have spared me many & many a troubled hour if you had done so, – & yet I understand the feeling w^h. prevented you only I was so afraid of being ungrateful & you know how I love our saint [*Jeanie*] – she as usual made things seem clear to me again.[46]

News also came through that Lionel Tennyson was engaged to Eleanor Locker, although they did not marry until 1877, and earlier in the summer, Robert Browning had told Annie that Edith Story was to marry an Italian nobleman, Simone Peruzzi. It must have seemed that all of her friends were settling down, an opportunity which had been available to her too but from which she had chosen to turn away. It took courage to live with her conviction of what was right, especially as she felt so confused about her feelings for Richmond. She must have talked to Minny about him, hard though it was to articulate even for herself quite what this relationship meant. She may not have been seeking advice, but Minny provided some, which Annie tried to persuade herself she understood and accepted. 'Says Minnie. You are not behaving Rightly; you ought to make a little joke of things instead of taking them so seriously, even if it is disagreeable to you you ought to do so. There is no reason why you & Richmond shouldnt go on as usual only without all this emotion. M is quite right. If Heaven gives each of us the blessing of real friendship & a real interest, how good it will be of Heaven & how grateful I shall feel.'[47] A veneer of calmness might well have made things easier for the reluctant witnesses to this strange romance, but it did little to simplify the feelings of the principal protagonists. Nevertheless, Annie felt Richmond's mother deserved an explanation, and they spoke towards the end of October. Whatever was said, she was 'glad to have it out'.

Minny's pregnancy meant that the Southwell Gardens establishment was scheduled to grow, and not for the first time Annie thought about having her own base in London. At the end of October 1875 she obtained the details of a new apartment block, Queen Anne's Mansions in St James's Park. These were high quality flats, with central services included in the rental – 'Lift, coal, wine & plate cellars, Kitchen & Office, servants quarters, Public Dining Room & a Private Dining Room – both served by a lift from the Kitchen' – as well as a scheme for shared servants 'under a superior housekeeper'.[48] It was an unsettling time, for she was also saying her farewells to Henry and Julia Margaret Cameron, Mr Cameron having decided that he wished to return to Ceylon and to spend his final years there. She crossed to Freshwater to help them prepare for the long sea voyage. 'The Porch was one large packing case with more men & things stowed away than anyone cd have thought possibly possible. M^r. Cameron went off quite brisk & young again at 82. M^{rs}. Camme said goodbye very wistfully & sent a dear God bless you flying after me from the ship. I shall miss her horribly when I go to the Island.... Mr Tennyson came to Yarmouth & Dear M^{rs}. Tennyson lay on her sofa & cried – I cant think what she will do without M^{rs}. Camme.'[49]

In mid-November Minny became ill whilst staying with the Huths at Wykehurst Park, Sussex, experiencing persistent nausea which she thought was aggravated by their vegetable-free diet. She wrote cheerfully enough to Leslie, though one detects a nagging anxiety. '[I]f I am not better tonight I think I shall come home tomorrow ... because I think I had better try & stop this sickness that I have had every night. I think it has had to do with the food & having no vegetables – which dont appear to grow here, but if I am better tonight I will stay as I am sure M^{rs} H would like me to.... F Gibbs & Mr H. Spencer cant come. The Lord be praised for the latter not coming I mean he w^d quite have finished me off.'[50]

Leslie would later annotate this letter, noting that he went to Wykehurst on the Sunday and returned with her the next day, 22 November, 'and then we were together till the end'. Annie stayed overnight with Mrs Oliphant at Windsor on the following Saturday, something which normally she would not have considered had Minny been more than ordinarily out of sorts. Nevertheless, when compiling her journal years later Annie wrote of her own 'strange sort of fright two days before Minny died' – that is to say, on the 26th, Friday, and Mrs Oliphant herself, writing to Blackwood's daughter on 2 December, was aware that Annie 'had made up her mind with some doubt to be absent from her for one evening to come to see me'.[51] As had happened at other moments of trauma, most notably after the death of her father, Annie recalled her experience of the time leading up to Minny's death in language suggestive of a dreamlike state, so that it is not clear whether these are real events or imagined ones. During these final days the cool-headed Minny was able to provide calming words and simple explanations. But the memory stayed with Annie, a '<u>certitude</u> that wherever I went sorrow w^d. follow. It was horrible. I went to Mr Chopes church [*St Augustine's, South Kensington*] hunted by this feeling then I went to an empty house. They w^d. not let me in; then I went to the old [Valentine] Smiths they could not see me & I came home & looked at myself in the glass & the terrors left me. Then came Minny who laughed when I told her my confused story. I didnt tell her I did not see the V. Smiths – she said "you went there because you thought them so old & so ill – nothing would much matter". And this was true.'

Leslie and Minny sat quietly at home on the Saturday evening, 'in perfect happiness and security'.[52] Julia Duckworth called in but left early, sensing that her widowhood jarred in the presence of such content. Feeling some slight discomfort, Minny decided to sleep that night in a room where Annie's maid, Maryanne, could be close at hand. During the night Maryanne woke Leslie, for Minny had gone into premature labour and convulsions, and then seems quickly to have sunk into unconsciousness. A doctor was called, and a telegraph sent to Annie in the morning. She hurried from Windsor and was met at the station by Fitzjames, but Minny had died at about midday and Annie was too late for those last moments, just as she had been denied being with her father who had died alone. Minny's death was far from serene, and Leslie felt unable to describe anything of those last hours. 'I remember all too well the details of what followed; but I will not set them down.' Annie fixes an elegiac quality to her account – 'when I got home my darling child was lying in ineffable peace far away from pain from the anguish of life & parting & my yearning heart' – but it was a cruel and painful end, and the horror never left her.

There was Laura to be coped with, and here Annie could do good. With great tenderness she devoted herself to Minny's vulnerable child over the next days and weeks. Indeed, during the nearly forty-five years which remained to Annie, nobody provided Laura with more affection. In these first hours of sorrow, she ensured that the five-year-old child made her own farewell to Minny. 'I took Laura in my arms & made her say goodnight to her Mommie.' The shattered Leslie was also in need of support. It was his birthday, 28 November, a day from which in future he removed all personal celebrations. Again Annie was selfless, though desolate in her loneliness. That night she sat with Leslie by the fire in her room, probably saying little, but each taking comfort in the presence of the other. She experienced something like a benediction during the silent hours of the night, for 'it seemed to me as if Papa was in all the house'.[53]

When people heard the news, the letters of consolation flooded in. Those who were close to Leslie wondered how he would cope, for Minny had transformed him and given joy to this shy and emotionally reserved man. Blanche Warre Cornish articulated this simply – 'we always felt how happy you were when Minny was in the room'.[54] In

Eleven: The Inscrutable Design

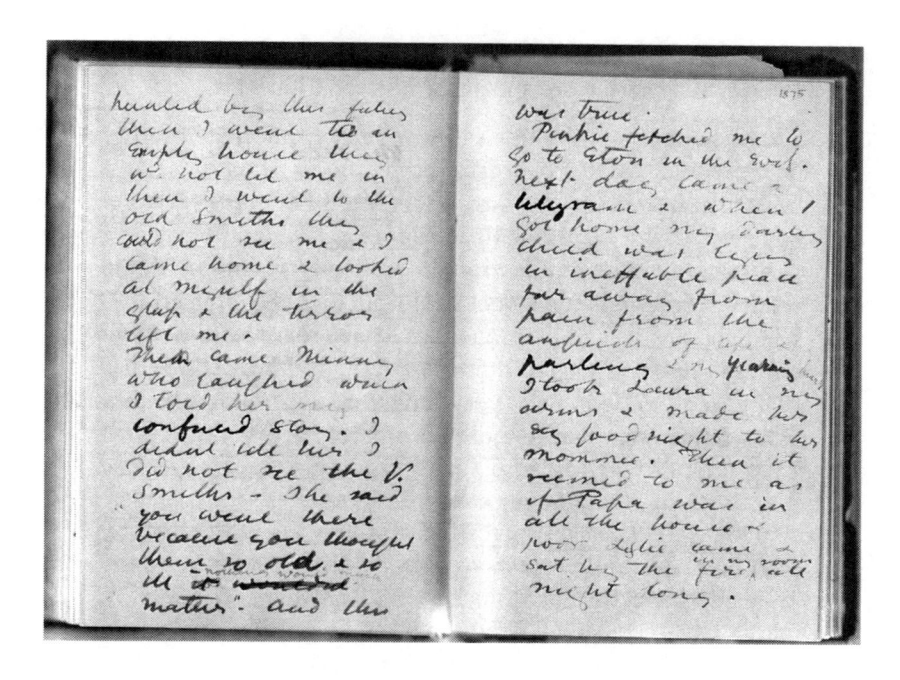

Pages from Annie's journal, describing Minnie's death in 1875

writing of the event to Hallam Tennyson, Richard Jebb expressed the anxiety which his academic associates were feeling, and was remarkably astute in estimating the effect upon Annie. 'He has a great power of doing without human sympathy, but, just for that reason, he clings to it where he finds it as if it were part of his life, & I dread the effect of this on him, when I think of it. To Miss Thackeray it will be as sharp a trial now, but not in the years to come.'[55] After the funeral, Annie and Leslie went together to Brighton and stayed with Julia Duckworth whose sensitive care was a balm. Jane Brookfield, 'a sort of mother-angel', also visited them there and offered kind support, reminiscing about earlier days in a way that 'brought back all our early life to try & cheer me dear soul & she tells us about Papa so patiently'.[56] Annie sent Jeanie Senior the briefest of notes. 'I cant write much but I want to tell you that it is & has been a comfort to think of you. We are all very quiet & scared & waiting for better times when she will be with us in a less sorrowful house – I only mean here – There in time we shall know – God bless you all. JOB is such a comfort. Meme & Leslie are making paper animals & the sun is coming out.'[57]

Annie exchanged many letters with her Ritchie cousins, especially with Pinkie, and there were special words for Charlotte.

> I was going to write for I know how your dear mother heart would yearn towards us all. This is Thursday the 2 of December & for the first night in all her life my sweet has slept away from her little Meme.... Darling Chattie, I would not change at this moment with <u>any</u> person in all the world. Her love is too sweet & simple to give <u>bitter</u> grief & what she has left so precious that I only fear to die without having the happiness of doing the things I know she would like done. Leslie is very very tender & our hearts are very full – Mine seems quite quiet & almost hard at times but I keep it quiet when I can. Even sympathy makes me realise it all w^h. I dont want ever ever quite to do.
>
> Dont grieve for us dearest dearest, but yes a little for my own one who did her task so sweetly & who was so happy & would have shrunk from leaving her Meme & Leslie & me had she not been spared the knowledge. She & I talked it all over the other day & settled that even if we all 3 died there were still many many people to love little Meme & take care of her. Your children have been so dear. Leslie says their sympathy does help him & JOB & Julia – We are going to Brighton for a week or two to look about darling Chattie. Leslie says he & I must always keep together now, & we must always mustn't we.[58]

Minny had touched so many lives. Browning's sister tried to tell Annie something of how they had been affected. 'Robert and I feel your grief and share it – The horror has haunted us night and day ever since. I have dreamt of it night after night. He has not got the courage to write – He told me, that the day he called he hardly had courage to ring the bell.'[59] There were notes from Tennyson, Trollope, Morley, Millais, Mrs Oliphant, John Addington Symonds, and many others. Richard Doyle (illustrator of *The Newcomes*) recalled 'the charm of her look the union of a certain strength with a singular youthfulness, a brow so like her Fathers and the rest of the face in its pretty form and expression so childlike'.[60] When the news reached America, Mrs Baxter wrote recalling Thackeray's death at that Christmas season twelve years before. She would never meet Annie, but Minny of course she had got to know well during the 1868 visit. 'I am so glad that I saw your Minnie, that I can think of her as one I knew, and loved for her own sweet sake, and

Eleven: The Inscrutable Design 273

for the dear kind interest she manifested for her father's friends.' It was with lines from Thackeray's poem 'The End of the Play' in *Dr Birch and his Young Friends* that Mrs Baxter now contemplated this new sadness.

> Who knows the inscrutable design?
> Blessed be he who took and gave!
> We bow to Heaven that willed it so
> That darkly rules the fate of all,
> That sends the respite or the blow,
> That's free to give, or to recall
>
> What can I say more or better to you – Do you know how green & fresh is your dear father's memory in America – The young come to me for anything I can tell of him, & his volumes make always a part of the bridal gifts to our young friends.[61]

After Annie and Leslie had gone to Brighton, Mrs Ritchie wrote to her two married daughters, Gussie and Blanche. She touched on some difficult issues about Minny's problem pregnancies and cast her mind back over the Thackeray family history.

> Although so very rare I have known two instances of similar cases to dearest Minnie's and singularly enough both this year.... Here they called it meningitis or cerebral disease provoked by pregnancy. Darling Minnie used to make us very anxious as a child for her poor Mother's illness came on before her birth or while nursing her and evidently there was something peculiar about her as this is the third time of her being enceinte and unable to go on the whole time. You know dear William Thackeray was born at 7 months and the Doctors told M^rs. Smyth it was happy for her he was as otherwise she might have died. All this rather explains this awful event.... Oh my darlings I fear so for Leslie can derive but little comfort from his mysterious creed. I trust he does not reject immortality for then life must be simply unbearable in such terrible losses. [62]

The funeral on 1 December was at Kensal Green cemetery, and Minny was buried on the edge of the Stephen family plot, which earlier that year had received the body of Leslie's mother. In due course Fitzjames and Mary and their children would be buried there too. Minny's grave is to the left of the others, and in the following May Annie and Leslie arranged for her tombstone to feature some of her

Minny's grave at Kensal Green, part of the Stephen family plot

favourite mountain flowers, 'specially the cyclamen w^h. grew wild in the Dolomites'.⁶³ The plot is pleasantly sited and shaded by horse chestnuts, and nearly thirty years later, when she visited Kensal Green in 1903, Annie would note that 'a chestnut had fallen on my Minnies grave'. There is something rather solitary about Minny's location, alongside yet not quite one of the principal family group, which makes her seem a little stranded. But not too far off is Thackeray's grave, close to that of Jane, the sister whom Minny never knew. Somehow, that seems fitting.

NOTES

Chapter One:
SCENES OF ALL SORTS *(1798-1839)*

1. *RJ.*
2. *Adversity*, 42-3.
3. *Adversity*, 44.
4. *Adversity*, 54.
5. AC to AI and HM, 1847, *E.*
6. WMT to AP, 14-6-1849, *Harden.*
7. *Ray*, I, cxiii.
8. RT to his mother, ?1803-4, *JM.*
9. For the mores of Anglo-Indian society see Dennis Kincaid, *British Social Life in India 1608-1937*, London: Routledge & Kegan Paul, 2nd edn., 1973, 107. 'There were in Calcutta few unmarried [English]men without a mistress.... But if these youths had to overcome a colour-prejudice, they often ended by becoming genuinely attached to their dark mistresses.'
10. Annie's description of her father's eyes on the day before he died. *Shankman*, 126.
11. *Ray*, I, cxiv.
12. WMT to AC, 30-8-1849, *Ray.*
13. WMT to AC, 30-12-1845, *Ray.*
14. *Adversity*, 70.
15. WMT to AC, 11-6-1818, *Ray.*
16. AC to Mrs Butler, 10-7-1820, in *Adversity*, 75.
17. Cited *Adversity*, 95.
18. WMT to AC, 20-1-1823, *Ray.*
19. Whitwell Elwin, *Some XVIII Century Men of Letters*, 2 vols, London: 1902, I, 17.
20. WMT to AC, 21-8-1829, *Ray.*
21. *Adversity*, 125.
22. WMT to AC, 20-10-1830, *Ray.*
23. WMT to AC, 17-11-1830, *Ray.*
24. WMT to AC, 3-12-1830, *Ray.*
25. WMT to AC, 31-12-1830, *Ray.*
26. *Adversity*, 149.

27. John Everett Millais to AI, 25-8-1893, *E.*
28. *Adversity,* 76.
29. *Biographical,* I, xvi.
30. WMT diary entry, 1/2-11-1834, *Ray.*
31. WMT to Frank Stone, 17-4-1835, *Harden.*
32. WMT to AC, 6-9-1833 and 22-10-1833, *Ray.*
33. WMT to William Ritchie, 9-1835, *Harden.*
34. WMT to IT, 14-4-1836, *Ray.*
35. WMT to IT, 25-4-1836, *Ray.*
36. WMT to IT, 3-7-1836, *Ray.*
37. WMT to IT, 7-1836, *Ray.*
38. WMT to GS, 9-7-1861, *Harden.*
39. WMT to AC, 9-1836, *Ray.*
40. WMT to John Macrone, 1-1837, *Ray.*
41. I to AC, two letters probably 12-1836, *Harden.*
42. WMT to AC, 13-12-1836, *Harden.*
43. Journal 1864-1865, *Shankman,* 124.
44. AC to A, ?6-1852, *E.*
45. IT to Mrs Isabella Shawe, 23-7-1838, *Ray.*
46. WMT to Mrs Isabella Shawe, 12-7-1838, *Ray.*
47. WMT to IT, 11-3-1838, *Ray.*
48. WMT to AC, 3-1839, *Ray.*
49. IT to AC, 25/27-3-1839, *Harden.*

Chapter Two:
NOT YET ACTORS IN THE PLAY *(1839-1846)*

1. *Biographical,* IV, xiii.
2. WMT to AC, 16-12-1839, *Ray.*
3. WMT to AC, 15-2-1840, *Ray.*
4. IT to AC, 23-5-1839, *Harden.*
5. *Shankman,* 129-30.
6. WMT to AC, 18-1-1840, *Ray.*
7. *Biographical,* IV, xxiii.
8. WMT to AC, 1/2-12-1839, *Ray.*
9. WMT to AC, 19-12-1839 and 23-12-1839, *Ray.*
10. WMT to AC, 2/3-3-1840, *Harden.*
11. WMT to AC, 3-1840, *Ray.*
12. WMT to AC, 5-1840, *Ray.*
13. WMT to AC, 1-6-1840, *Ray.*
14. *Shankman,* 197.
15. IT to AC, ?28/29-6-1840, *Ray.*
16. IT to AC, 4-8-1840, *Ray.*
17. IT to AC, 11-12-1839, *Harden.*
18. WMT to AC, 20/21-8-1840, *Ray.*
19. WMT to AC, 1-9-1840, *Ray.*

20. *Shankman*, 132.
21. WMT to Isabella Shawe, 10-9-1840, *Ray*.
22. WMT to Mrs Charlotte Ritchie, 10-9-1840, *Ray*.
23. WMT to Chapman and Hall, 8-9-1840, *Ray*.
24. WMT to AC, 17-9-1840, *Ray*.
25. WMT to AC, 4/5-10-1840, *Ray*.
26. WMT to AC, 21/23-9-1840, *Ray*.
27. WMT to AC, 19/20-9-1840, *Ray*.
28. *Shankman*, 197.
29. WMT to AC, 21/23-9-1840, *Ray*.
30. WMT to AC, 10-9-1840, *Ray*.
31. WMT to AC, 11-10-1840, *Ray*.
32. *Shankman*, 130.
33. *Biographical*, IV, xxx-xxxii.
34. *Shankman*, 130.
35. WMT to EF, 10-1-1841, *Ray*.
36. *Chapters*, 29-30.
37. *Chapters*, 34-35.
38. WMT to Mary Carmichael-Smyth, 15-3-1841, *Harden*.
39. *Biographical*, V, xiii-xiv.
40. WMT to AC, 27-2-1841, *Ray*.
41. WMT to AP, 5-4-1841, *Harden*.
42. WMT to AC, 4-1841, *Ray*.
43. WMT to AP, 28-5-1841, *Ray*.
44. WMT to Henry Carmichael-Smyth, 25-4-1841, *Ray*.
45. WMT to Mrs Charlotte Ritchie, 19-8-1841, *Ray*.
46. WMT to EF, 9/10-1841, *Ray*.
47. WMT to Mrs Spencer, 10-2-1842, *Ray*.
48. *Biographical*, V, xiii.
49. Henrietta Garnett, *Anny. A Life of Anne Isabella Thackeray Ritchie*, London: Chatto & Windus, 2004, 16-18.
50. *Shankman*, 200.
51. *Chapters*, 15-16.
52. WMT to JOB, 12-1-1851, *Ray*.
53. *Chapters*, 22.
54. *Chapters*, 14.
55. *Chapters*, 26-7.
56. Ruth Jordan, *Nocturne: a Life of Chopin*, London: Constable, 1978, 213.
57. WMT to AI, summer 1842, *Harden*.
58. WMT to AI, 3-1843, *Ray*.
59. WMT to AC, 12/14-8-1842, *Ray*.
60. *Shankman*, 197-8.
61. WMT to AC, 31-8/1-9-1842, *Ray*.
62. WMT to AC, 26-9-1843, *Ray*.
63. *Shankman*, 198.
64. *Biographical*, V, xxxiv-xxxv.
65. WMT to AC, 31-8-1844, *Ray*.

66. WMT to IT, 17-9-1844, *Ray*.
67. WMT to CR, 23-10-1844, *Ray*.
68. WMT 1844 diary, *Ray*.
69. *Shankman*, 199.
70. WMT to CR, 9-6-1845, *Ray*.
71. *Shankman*, 200-1.
72. WMT to AC, 28-11-1845, *Ray*.
73. WMT to AI, 30-12-1845, *Ray*.
74. WMT to Jane Shawe, 7-1846, *Ray*.
75. WMT to AC, 2-7-1846, *Ray*.
76. Diary 11/18-8-1846, *Ray*.
77. *Shankman*, 201.
78. WMT to AC, 4-12-1846, *Ray*.
79. *Biographical*, I, xxviii.

Chapter Three:
OUR STREET *(1847-1852)*

1. AI to AC, 14-1-1847, *Shankman*
2. Added to letter, AI to AC, 26-2-1847, *Shankman*.
3. WMT to AC, 16-3-1847, *Ray*.
4. WMT to Bess Hamerton, 16-3-1847, *Ray*.
5. Thackeray did not forget Bess's good nature, once sending her £10 when she was ill. 'I remember always what a kind friend she was to me and to my children, and pray her to let me bring her a little ease.' WMT to Maria Hamerton, 5-11-1849, *Ray*.
6. *Shankman*, 201.
7. *Shankman*, 203.
8. *Chapters*, 84. As Annie said in this later record, 'I sometimes hear from my old friend, and I hope he may not be pained by reading of these childish jealousies long past.'
9. AC to AI and HM, 5-12-1846, *E*.
10. WMT to AC, 16-3-1847, *Ray*.
11. AC to AI and HM, 29-3-1847, *Ray*.
12. AI to AC, 4-1847, *Shankman*.
13. WMT to AC, 3-1846, *Ray*.
14. WMT to AC, 15-4-1847, *Ray*.
15. *Chapters*, 73-5.
16. WMT to AC, 2-7-1847, *Ray*.
17. AI to AC, 26-2-1847, *Shankman*.
18. AC to AI, 6-3-1847, *Ray*.
19. AC to AI and HM, ?2-1847, *E*.
20. *Adversity*, 285.
21. WMT to JOB, 4-5-1849, *Ray*.
22. WMT to William Brookfield, ?4-5-1849, *Ray*.
23. CD to WMT, 30-3-1848 and 9-1-1848, *Ray*.

24. *Shankman*, 201.
25. *Biographical*, VI, xxvi.
26. AC to AI and HM, ?2-1847, *E*.
27. WMT to AC, 2-7-1847, *Ray*.
28. AC to AI and HM, ?2-1847, *E*.
29. He also borrowed the name of Jane Brookfield's maid, but Jane thought that it would 'pass as a mere coincidence' (JOB to WMT, 1-7-1848, *Ray*).
30. AC to AI and HM, 6-1848, *E*.
31. WMT to AC, 2-11-1847, *Ray*.
32. AC to AI and HM, 12-1847, *E*.
33. AC to AI and HM, 1-1848, *E*.
34. AC to AI and HM, 1-2-1848, *E*.
35. *Shankman*, 204.
36. WMT to JOB, 26/28-7-1848, *Ray*.
37. WMT to AC, 7-1-1848, *Ray*.
38. WMT to AC, 14-4-1848, *Ray*.
39. WMT to Mrs Bayne, ?5-1849, *Ray*.
40. *Chapters*, 83.
41. *Chapters*, 88.
42. *Chapters*, 80.
43. AI to AC, 14-1-1847, *Shankman*; AC to AI and HM, 21-1-1847, *E*.
44. *Chapters*, 88.
45. WMT to AC, 15-5-1848, *Ray*.
46. *Wisdom*, 73.
47. WMT to AC, 5-6-1848, *Ray*.
48. WMT to JOB, 7-1848, *Ray*.
49. WMT to AP, 13-9-1848, *Harden*.
50. WMT to Jane Shawe, 19-9-1848, *Ray*.
51. WMT to JOB, 7/9-10-1848, *Ray*.
52. *Wisdom*, 69.
53. WMT to JOB, 11-1848. French original in *Harden*, whose translation this is.
54. WMT to JOB, 15/16-7-1849, *Harden*.
55. WMT to AC, 18-7-1849, *Ray*.
56. JOB to WB, *Wisdom*, 87.
57. *Biographical*, II, xxxvii.
58. *Shankman*, 205.
59. WMT to Mrs Charlotte Ritchie, 19-11-1849, *Ray*.
60. AC to AI and HM, 13-12-1850, *E*. The dedication reads: 'And as you would take no other fee but thanks, let me record them here in behalf of me and mine.'
61. *Biographical*, II, xxxv.
62. WB to WMT, 26-2-1850, *Ray*.
63. WMT to Magdalene Brookfield, 26-2-1850, *Ray*.
64. WMT to JOB, 1/2-3-1850, *Ray*.
65. JOB to WMT, 9-3-1850, *Harden*.
66. WMT to KP, 9-1851, *Harden*.
67. WMT to JOB, 8-6-1849, *Ray*.
68. WMT to JOB, 26-7-1850, *Ray*.

69. JOB to WMT, 21-12-1850, *Harden.*
70. WMT to A, ?22-5-1850, *Ray.*
71. M to AC, ?1848, *E.*
72. *Shankman,* 205.
73. AC to AI, 8-6-1850, *E.*
74. AC to AI and HM, ?late summer 1850, *E.*
75. WMT to JOB, 27-11-1850, *Ray.*
76. AC to AI and HM, 13-12-1850, *E.*
77. WMT to JOB, 12-1-1851, *Ray.*
78. AC to AI and HM, 1-5-1851, *E.*
79. AC to AI and HM, 21-5-1851, *E.*
80. WMT to JB, 21-9-1851, *Ray.*
81. *Shankman,* 205.
82. WMT to JOB, 13/15-7-1851, *Ray.*
83. *Shankman,* 206.
84. AC to AI and HM, 13-8-1851, *E.*
85. WMT to Mrs Elliot and KP, 26-9-1851, *Harden.*
86. WMT to AI, 29-10-1851, *Ray.*
87. WMT to AC, 10-11-1851, *Ray.*
88. WMT to AC, ?17/18-11-1851, *Ray.*
89. *Biographical,* VII, xix.
90. AC to AI and HM, 4-11-1851, *E.*
91. WMT to AC, 15-3-1852, *Ray.*
92. AC to AI and HM, 20-2-1852, 31-3-1852 and 18-4-1852, *E.*
93. WMT to AC, 26-2-1852, *Ray.*
94. WMT to MH, 25-2-1852, *Ray.*
95. WMT to AC, 26-2-1852, *Ray.*
96. AC to AI and HM, ?5-1852, *E.*
97. AC to AI and HM, 18-4-1852, *E.*
98. Ibid.
99. AC to AI, 23-4-1852. *E.*
100. *Freeman's Journal and Daily Commercial Advertiser,* 18-1-1876.
101. WMT to AC, 17/19-4-1852, *Ray.*
102. *Chapters,* 75.
103. *Shankman,* 206.
104. *Chapters,* 76.
105. *Shankman,* 212.
106. *Chapters,* 145.
107. WMT to Mrs Elliot and KP, 21-6-1852, *Ray.*
108. AC to WMT, 18-7-1852, *E.*
109. WMT to AI, 21-9-1852, *Ray.*
110. WMT to Lady Stanley, 29-9-1852, *Ray.*
111. EF to WMT, 4-1852, *Ray.*
112. WMT to EF, 27-10-1852, *Ray.*
113. WMT to AI and HM, 29/30-10-1852, *Ray.*

Chapter Four:
A LITTLE RAIN OF DOLLARS *(1852-1855)*

1. *Chapters*, 146-7.
2. *Chapters*, 150.
3. AC to WMT, 26-9-1852, posted 20-1-1853, *Ray.*
4. WMT to AI, 10-1852, *Ray.*
5. HM to WMT, 11-1852, *JM.*
6. AI to WMT, 30-11-1852, *Ray.*
7. AI to Laetitia Cole, 2-12-1852, *Shankman.*
8. AI to WMT, 5-12-1852, *Ray.*
9. *Chapters*, 151-2.
10. *Shankman*, 207-8.
11. WMT to AC, 4-1-1853, *Ray.*
12. AC to WMT, 19-1-1853, *E.*
13. AC to WMT, 9-6-1853, *JM.*
14. WMT to AI and HM, 11-11-1852, *Ray.*
15. WMT to AI and HM, 7-12-1852, *Ray.*
16. WMT to Mrs Elliot and KP, 28-11-1852, *Ray.*
17. WMT to JOB, 23-11-1852, to Mrs Elliot and KP, 28-11-1852, to Lady Stanley, 21-1-1853, *Ray.*
18. WMT to HM, 17-1-1853, *Ray.*
19. WMT to AC, 26-1-1853, *Ray.*
20. WMT to AC, 13-2-1853, *Ray.*
21. WMT to HM, 11-3-1853, *Ray.*
22. WMT to AC, 25/28-3-1853, *Ray.*
23. WMT to AC, 20-12-1852, *Ray.*
24. HM to WMT, 12-1-1853, *Shankman.*
25. WMT to Mrs Baxter, 30-12-1852, *Ray.*
26. WMT to JOB, 21/23-1-1853, *Ray.*
27. WMT to GS, 14-1-1853, *Harden.*
28. *Ray,* I, lxxxviii.
29. WMT to Mrs Elliot and KP, 3-3-1853, *Harden.*
30. WMT to LB, 26-2-1853, *Ray.*
31. WMT to AC, 25/28-3-1853, *Ray.*
32. WMT to AP, 4-4-1853, *Harden.*
33. WMT to AC, 26-1-1853, *Ray.*
34. WMT to AI and HM, 14-3-1853, *Ray.*
35. WMT to George B. Jones, 20-4-1853, *Ray.*
36. WMT to George Baxter, 20-4-1853, *Ray.*
37. WMT to Mrs Baxter, 3-5-1853, *Ray.*
38. *Shankman*, 210.
39. Mrs Baxter to WMT, 17-5-1853, *Harden.*
40. WMT to Mrs Baxter, 18-5-1853, *Ray.*
41. AC to Mrs Baxter, 25-5-1853, *Ray.*
42. WMT to AI, 9-6-1853, *Ray.*

43. WMT to SB, 4/5-7-1853, *Ray*.
44. Mrs Baxter to WMT, 5-12-1853, *Harden*.
45. WMT to AC, 18-7-1853, *Ray*.
46. WMT to Mrs Elliot and KP, 13-7-1853, *Harden*.
47. WMT to SB, 26-7-1853, *Harden*.
48. *Biographical*, VIII, xxii.
49. WMT to Mrs Elliot and KP, 31-7-1853, *Harden*.
50. WMT to AC, 1-9-1853, *Ray*.
51. WMT to William Brookfield, 24-9-1853, *Harden*.
52. WMT to Libby Strong and LB, 18-10-1853, *Ray*.
53. *Chapters*, 173.
54. *Biographical*, VIII, xxviii.
55. HM to AC, 30-11-1853, *Ray*.
56. *Chapters*, 180-1.
57. *Chapters*, 183.
58. WMT to AC, 5-12-1853, *Ray*.
59. *Chapters*, 190-1.
60. WMT to Mrs Baxter and SB, 17-12-1853, *Ray*.
61. *Records*, 40.
62. WMT to AC, 31-12-1853, *Ray*.
63. Emelyn Story, quoted in Henry James, *William Wetmore Story and his Friends*, 2 vols, Edinburgh and London: Blackwood, 1903, I, 367-8.
64. Ibid, 286.
65. The page probably dates from the 1920s, after Annie's death. *BNB*.
66. WMT to Mrs Elliot and KP, 1-12-1852, *Ray*.
67. WMT to AP, 1-1854, *Harden*.
68. WMT to AC, 7-2-1854, *Ray*.
69. WMT to AC, 7-3-1854, *Ray*.
70. WMT to GS, 22-4-1854, *Harden*.
71. *Biographical*, VIII, xxxv.
72. WMT to ?, 5-1854, *Ray*.
73. WMT to AC, 10-5-1854, *Ray*.
74. *Shankman*, 138.
75. AC to AI and HM, 22-6-1854, *E*.
76. AC to AI and HM, 29-9-1854, *E*.
77. WMT to Mrs Baxter, 3-11-1853, *Ray*.
78. WMT to ACR, 27-9-1854, *Harden*.
79. AC to AI and HM, 29-11-1854, *E*.
80. AC to AI and HM, 6-10-1854, *E*.
81. AC to AI and HM, 13-10-1854, *E*.
82. WMT to AC, 8-11-1854, *Ray*.
83. WMT to Revered John Allen, 7-2-1855, *Ray*.
84. WMT to the English minister at the Hague, 10-2-1855, *Ray*.
85. AI to Susan Scott, 18-2-1855, *Shankman*.
86. WMT to AC, 22-4-1855, *Ray*.
87. WMT to Mrs Elliot and KP, 2-7-1855, *Ray*.
88. AI to Mrs Fanshawe, May-early June 1855, *Shankman*.

Notes 283

89. WMT to Mrs Baxter, 3-8-1855, *Ray*.
90. WMT to AC, 13-10-1855, *Ray*.
91. *Shankman*, 209.

Chapter Five:
TOWARDS THE UNKNOWN OCEAN *(1855-1862)*

1. WMT to AI and HM, 23-2-1856, *Ray*.
2. WMT to Henry Beecher, 5-1-1856, *Ray*.
3. WMT to his family, 30-10-1855, *Ray*.
4. WMT to Mrs Elliot and KP, 20-11-1855, *Harden*.
5. WMT to Mrs Baxter and SB, 11-12-1855, *Ray*.
6. WMT to AI, 18-12-1855, *Ray*.
7. WMT to Mrs Hampton, 12/13-7-1856, *Ray*.
8. WMT to AI and HM, 6-1-1856, *Ray*.
9. WMT to AC, 15-1-1856, *Ray*.
10. WMT to AP, 15-3-1856, *Ray*.
11. WMT to Mrs Elliot and KP, 7-2-1856, *Ray*.
12. WMT to AI and HM, 10-3-1856, *Ray*.
13. WMT to Mrs Elliot, 24/26-3-1856, *Ray*.
14. WMT to AI and HM, and to Story, both 27-11-1855, *Ray*.
15. WMT to Mrs Baxter, 7-5-1856, *Ray*.
16. WMT to Mrs Elliot and KP, 10-9-1856, *Ray*.
17. AI to ACR, 22-8-1856, *Shankman*.
18. HM to ACR, 22-8-1856, *E*.
19. WMT to Mrs Baxter, 2-11-1856, *Ray*.
20. WMT to AI and HM, 11-11-1856, *Ray*.
21. AI to ACR, 28-11-1856, *Shankman*.
22. WMT to AI and HM, 3-12-1856, *Ray*.
23. WMT to ACR, ?11-1856, *Harden*.
24. WMT to CR and Jane Ritchie, 5-12-1856, *Ray*.
25. AC to AI and HM, 16-1-1857, *E*.
26. WMT to AP, 26-11-1856, *Harden*.
27. WMT to AC, 9-1-1857, *Ray*.
28. WMT to William Reed, 14-5-1857, *Ray*.
29. WMT to the Baxters, 31-10-1857, *Ray*.
30. Julian Sturgis, *From Books and Papers of Russell Sturgis*, Oxford: OUP, 1893, 260.
31. WMT to AC, 25-12-1857, *Ray*.
32. WMT to AC, 2-4-1858, *Ray*.
33. WMT to John Reuben Thompson, 25-2-1858, *Ray*.
34. Frederick Cozzens (citing Irving) to WMT, 21-3-1858, *Ray*.
35. WMT to AC, 5-1858, *Ray*.
36. Cited *Wisdom*, 279.
37. WMT to the Baxters, 25-8-1858, *Ray*.
38. WMT to Lady Stanley, 23-9-1858, *Ray*.

39. WMT to JB, 4-11-1858, *Harden.*
40. AI to JB, 26-1-1859, *Ray.*
41. WMT to AC, after 19-2-1859, *Ray.*
42. AI to ACR, 12-1858, *Shankman.*
43. AI to W.W.F. Synge, 6-3-1859, *Shankman.*
44. George Smith, 'Our birth and parentage', *Cornhill*, January 1901, reprinted in *George Smith, a Memoir with some pages of Autobiography* (London: printed privately), 1902.
45. *JM.*
46. 'Our birth and parentage'.
47. WMT to Mrs Baxter, 21-9-1859, *Harden.*
48. Henry James, *Notes of a Son and Brother* (1914), in Frederick W. Dupee (ed) *Henry James Autobiography*, Princeton: Princeton University Press, 1983, 251.
49. *Biographical*, XI, xxviii.
50. WMT to GS, 10-1859, *Harden.*
51. WMT to Thomas Carlyle, 16-10-1859, *Harden.*
52. WMT to GS, 17-11-1859, *Harden.*
53. GS to WMT, 9-12-1859, *JM*; WMT to GS, 12-1859, *Harden.*
54. 'Our birth and parentage'.
55. GS to WMT, 15-11-1860, 28-12-1860 and 12-3-1861, *JM.*
56. Anne Ritchie,' The First Editor: and the Founder', *Cornhill*, January 1910, 2.
57. GS to WMT, 15-5-1860, *JM.*
58. GS to WMT, 28-4-1860, *JM.*
59. GS to WMT, 31-1-1860, *JM.*
60. WMT to GS, 9-11-1860, draft, *JM.*
61. GS to WMT, 9-11-1860, *JM.*
62. WMT to GS, probably early November 1860, *Harden.*
63. GS to WMT, 21-11-1860, *JM.*
64. WMT letters *Harden*; GS letters *JM.*
65. *Great Expectations* began on 1 December in *Once a Week*
66. GS to WMT, 26-4-1861, *JM.*
67. WMT to GS, late April 1861, *Harden.*
68. WMT to GS, 7-1861, *Harden.*
69. GS to WMT, 28-9-1861, *JM.*
70. Draft, *JM.* The shortened version which he posted is in *Harden.*
71. WMT to GS, ?21-1-1862, *Harden.*
72. WMT to GS, 23-1-1862, *Harden.*
73. GS to WMT, 7-3-1862, *JM.*
74. 18-3-1862, *Ray.*

Chapter Six:
HERE IS NIGHT AND REST *(1860-1863)*

1. WMT to William Duer Robinson, 28-9-1860, *Ray.*
2. AI to AC, 16-9-1859, *Shankman.*
3. WMT to Mrs Baxter, 21-9-1859, *Harden.*

4. WMT to GS, 29-9-1859, *Harden*.
5. *J*, 9-1862.
6. AI to GS, ?autumn 1900, *JMA NLS*.
7. WMT to GS, 9-4-1860, *Harden*.
8. GS to WMT, 9-4-1860, *JM*.
9. WMT to Sir Henry Davison, 4-5-1860, *Ray*.
10. WMT to GS, ?6-1860, *Ray*.
11. Thomas Carlyle to WMT, 26-5-1860, *Ray*.
12. HM to AC, 9-1860, *E*.
13. WMT to GS, 8-1860, *Harden*.
14. WMT to the Baxters, 25-12-1860, *Harden*. The joke was Charles Carmichael's, his wife's simmering jealousy of Thackeray the stimulus.
15. AI to Mrs Corkran, 21-1-1861, *P*.
16. WMT to Thomas Elliot, and to KP, 11-1-1861, *Harden*.
17. WMT to the Baxters, 25-12-1860, *Harden*.
18. *J*, 19-2-1861.
19. AI to Mrs Baxter, 25-4-1861, *Ray*.
20. Elizabeth Barrett Browning to WMT, 21-4-1861, *Ray*.
21. WMT, 1861 diary, *Ray*.
22. WMT to John Boyes, 1-10-1861, *Ray*.
23. *Shankman*, 212, and *J* 12-9-1861.
24. WMT to Mrs Baxter, 24-5-1861, *Ray*.
25. GS to WMT, 21-9-1861, *JM*.
26. WMT to GS, 2-10-1861, *Harden*.
27. WMT to GS, 9-10-1861, *Harden*.
28. *J*, 2-10-1861.
29. WMT to GS, 6-12-1861, *Harden*.
30. GS to WMT, 7-12-1861, *JM*.
31. *HL* and *JM*.
32. HM to Elizabeth Smith, 2-1862, *NLS*.
33. M.C.M. Simpson [Minny Senior], *Many Memories of Many People*, London: Edward Arnold, 1898, 107-8.
34. Blanche Warre Cornish, *Some Family Letters of W.M. Thackeray together with Recollections by his Kinswoman*, London: Smith, Elder, 1911, 57-8. Sunny it may have been, but the hair was the same age as its owner, twenty-one at this time.
35. WMT to GS, 2-1862, *Harden*.
36. *Centenary*, XXVI.
37. *Shankman*, 211.
38. SB to WMT, 5-4-1862, *Harden*.
39. WMT to AI and HM, 21-4-1862, *Ray*.
40. WMT to the Baxters, 9-5-1862, *Ray*.
41. *Shankman*, 212.
42. AC to AI, 8-6-1862, *E*.
43. WMT to GS, 1-7-1862, *Harden*.
44. WMT to AC, 5-7-1862, *Harden*
45. AC to AI and HM, 20-7-1862, *E*.

46. AI to JS, 11-1862, *Y.*
47. HM to AI, 11-1862, *JM.*
48. WMT to the Baxters, 25-12-1862, *Harden.*
49. AI to Jane Shawe, c. 6-1863, *E.*
50. *Shankman*, 126.
51. WMT to GS, 14-1-1863, *Harden.*
52. AC to AI and HM, 16-8-1863, *E.*
53. HM to AI, 9-1863, *E.*
54. WMT to JB, 23-9-1863, *Harden.*
55. HM to AI, 27-9-1863, *E.*
56. HM to AI, 4-10-1863, *E.*
57. *Shankman*, 122-3.
58. WMT to GS, 17-12-1863, *Harden.*
59. John Jones Merriman, 'Kensington Worthies, III, W.M. Thackeray', *St Mary Abbots Parish Magazine*, 1889, 226.
60. Merriman described this view as '"Our Street" Thackeray – & Surgery 1868'. The photographs are contained within his copy of Thomas Faulkner's *History and Antiquities of Kensington*, held in the Local Studies archive of the Kensington and Chelsea Public Library.
61. Annie's account of these days come from *Shankman.*
62. *Cornhill*, IX, 129.
63. *Shankman*, 124-8.
64. 'Kensington Worthies', 226.
65. *Wisdom*, 416, from various secondary accounts.
66. Lucinda Hawksley, *Katie*, London: Doubleday, 2006, 200.
67. 'Kensington Worthies', 226.

Chapter Seven:
ALL THIS ENDLESS YEAR *(1863-1865)*

1. Mrs Harriet Collins to Wilkie Collins, 30-12-1863, *HL (HEW 8.6.2).*
2. *Shankman*, 126.
3. John Guille Millais, *The Life and Letters of Sir John Everett Millais*, 2 vols, London: Methuen, 1899, I, 375.
4. Hallam Tennyson (ed), *Tennyson and his Friends*, London: Macmillan, 1911, 153-4.
5. *J*, 17-2-1864.
6. AI to Minny Senior, 2-1864, *E.*
7. AI to Marian Cole, 2/3-1864, *Shankman.*
8. AI to Mrs Baxter, 20-4 to 1-5-1864, *Ray.*
9. AC to AI, ?4-1864, *E.*
10. GS to AI, 17-3-1864, *JM.*
11. GS to AI, 23-4-1864, *JM.*
12. GS to AI, 4-5-1864, *JM.*
13. AI to GS, 5-1864, *JMA.*

14. *J*, 8-6-1864.
15. AI to Mrs Baxter, 30-4-1864, *Ray*.
16. AI to JS, ?5-1864, *Y*.
17. AC to AI and HM, ?5/6-1864, *E*.
18. AC to AI and HM, 23-5-1864 and 5/6-1864, *E*.
19. GS to AI, 7-7-1864, *JM*. On 1 December, the *Times* reported the Abbey authorities' approval of a monumental bust, which was commissioned from Baron Marochetti, 'who had the advantage of being [Thackeray's] intimate friend'. The projected cost was £600, to be met by public subscription.
20. AI to GS, ?9-7-1864, *JMA*.
21. AI to Mrs Baxter, 24-10-1864, *Ray*.
22. 20-8-1864, *NLS*.
23. *J*, 10-8-1864.
24. *J*, 6-9-1864.
25. AC to AI and HM, 28-9-1864, *E*.
26. *Shankman*, 138.
27. AI to Mrs Baxter, 24-10-1864, *Ray*
28. AI to Miss Boyle, 2-11-1864, *HU (HM 15293)*.
29. AC to AI and HM, 6-11-1864, *E*.
30. *J*, 16-12-1864.
31. *Shankman*, 138-9.
32. AI to Mrs Synge, 28-12-1864, *Shankman*.
33. *Shankman* , 138-9.

Chapter Eight:
A WOMAN'S CARES AND JOYS *(1865-1867)*

1. Caroline Emilia Stephen (Milly or Carrie), became a Quaker. She was known by the children of Stephen's second marriage as 'the Nun'.
2. AI to Walter Senior, 10-4-1865, *Y*.
3. FS to AI, 15-4-1865, *E. Essays by a Barrister*, London: Smith, Elder, 1862.
4. *Mausoleum*, 9-10.
5. *Mausoleum*, 12.
6. *Mausoleum*, 33.
7. FS to AI, 17-1-1871, *E*.
8. *Mausoleum*, 9.
9. *Mausoleum*, 10.
10. *J*, 9-6-1866.
11. *Mausoleum*, 31.
12. *Mausoleum*, 33.
13. CR to AI and HM, May 1864, *E*.
14. *J*, 24-8-1865.
15. HM to CR, 9-12-1865, *D*.
16. *Mausoleum*, 10.
17. *J*, 7-1866.

18. *Mausoleum*, 10-11.
19. *Mausoleum*, 12.
20. *Mausoleum*, 11.
21. *J*, 4-12-1866.
22. HM to AI, ?8-12-1866, *E*. Leslie was shy at 'being cast into a vortex of comparative strangers, to whom I am perfectly sensible that I must be an object of curiosity though also of hospitality'. LS to AI, 6-12-1866, *Bicknell*.
23. AI to Lady Houghton, 12-1886, *TCC*.
24. Charlotte Williams-Wynn to AI, 22-12-1866, *E*.
25. HM to LS, 24-12-1866, *D*.
26. LS to HM, 24/25-12-1866, *Bicknell*.
27. *J*, 25-112-1866.
28. HM to JJ, 25-12-1866, *D*.
29. HM to LS, 26-12-1866, *D*.
30. LS to HM, 26-12-1866, *D*.
31. HM to LS, 27-12-1866, *D*.
32. HM to LS, 28-12-1866, *D*.
33. LS to HM, 30-12-1866, *D*.
34. *J* 31-12-1866. This original diary entry is stuck in.
35. This would have been an advance copy of the book publication, which was published by Smith, Elder on 25 February.
36. Julia Sterling to AI, 2-1-1867, *E*.
37. GW to HM, ?1-1867, *E*.
38. LS to AI, 1-1867, *E*.
39. LS to OH, 9-6-1867, *Bicknell*.
40. *Mausoleum*, 20.
41. Elizabeth Bonython and Anthony Burton, *The Great Exhibitor: The Life and Work of Henry Cole*, London: V&A Publications, 2003, 227.
42. HM to AI, 19-6-1867, *E*.
43. AI to HM, 20-6-1867, *E*.
44. AI to MM, 21-6-1867, *E*.
45. Lady Stephen to HM and LS, 21-6-1867, *D*.
46. AI to HM, 21-6-1867, *E*.

Chapter Nine:
A GREAT ENORMOUS HALF GROWN PLACE
(1867-1868)

1. HM to AI, 21/22-6-1867, *E*.
2. LS to AI, 20-7-1867, *E*.
3. HM to AI, 236-6-1867, *E*.
4. J A Froude to AI, 24-2-?1867, *E*.
5. AI to HM, 6-7-1867, *E*.
6. AI to HM, ?5-7-1867, *E*.
7. LS to AI, 9-7-1867, *E*.

8. HM to AI, 13-7-1867, *E.*
9. AI to GS, 7-1867, *JMA.*
10. HM and LS to AI, 17-7-1867, *E.*
11. HM to BC, 19-7-1867, *D.*
12. HM to AI, 19-7-1867, *E.*
13. LS to AI, 20-7-1867, *E.*
14. HM to AI, 29-7-1867, *E.*
15. HM to AI, 21-7-1867, *E.*
16. HM to CS, 24-7-1867, *D.*
17. HM to AI, 26-7-1867, *E.*
18. HM to CS, 24-7-1867, *D.*
19. AI to GS, ?late summer 1867, *JMA.*
20. Frederic Leighton to AI, 13-10-1867, *E.*
21. LS to OH, 18-8-1867, *Bicknell.*
22. LS to AI, ?8-1867, *E.*
23. LS to OH, 22-12-1867, *Bicknell.*
24. *J*, 22-2-1868.
25. AI to AF, ?3-1868, *E.*
26. LS to OH, 25-6-1868, *Bicknell.*
27. LS to OH, 25-3-1867, *Bicknell.*
28. AI to Mrs Baxter, 8-1868, *Shankman.*
29. *J.*
30. AI to JF, 26-8-1867, *HU (F1 3739).*
31. HM to AI, 9-8-1868, *E.*
32. HM to AI, 10/18-8-1868, *E.*
33. Julia married Herbert Duckworth in 5-1867, a month before Leslie and Minny married.
34. HM to AI, 20-8-1868, *E.*
35. HM to CS and Lady Stephen, 2-8-1868, *D.*
36. HM to AI, 23-8-1868, *E.*
37. HM to AI, 25/26-8-1868, *E.*
38. HM to AI, 2-9-1868, *E.*
39. HM to AI, 29-10-1868, *E.*
40. HM to AI, 4-9-1868, *E.*
41. HM to Lady Stephen, 6-9-1868, *D.*
42. HM to AI, 7-9-1868, *E.*
43. OH (Sr.) to AI, 12-9-1868, *E.*
44. LS to AI, ?10-9-1868, *E.*
45. HM to AI, 13-9-1868, *E.*
46. HM to CS and Lady Stephen, 13-9-1868, *E.*
47. HM to AI, 15-9-1868, *E.*
48. HM to AI, ?16-9-1868, *E.*
49. LS to AI, 17-9-1868, *E.*
50. HM to AI, 18-9-1868, *E.*
51. HM to AI, 24-9-1868, *E.*
52. HM to AI, 3-10-1868, *E. Mrs. Putnam's Receipt Book and Young Housekeeper's Assistant* was first published in 1849 in Boston by Ticknor, Reed & Fields and

went through eight further editions before appearing in an enlarged New York edition in 1860, published by Phinney, Blakeman & Mason.
53. HM to AI, 26-9-1868, *E*.
54. LS to AI, 26-9-1868, *E*.
55. Ralph Waldo Emerson to LS, 4-10-1868, Eleanor M. Tilton (ed), *Letters of Ralph Waldo Emerson, Vol IX, 1860-1869*, New York: Columbia University Press, 1994.
56. HM to AI, 2-10-1868, *E*.
57. HM to AI, 3-10-1868, *E*.
58. HM to AI, 5-10-1868, *E*.
59. HM to AI, ?8-10-1868, *E*.
60. HM to AI, 1-11-1868, *E*.
61. HM to AI, 12-10-1868, *E*.
62. LS to AI, 16-10-1868, *E*.
63. HM to AI, 17-10-1868, *E*.
64. HM to AI, 1-11-1868, *E*.
65. HM to AI, 29-10-1868, *E*.
66. HM to AI, 27-10-1868, *E*.
67. HM to CS and Lady Stephen, 26-10-1868, *D*.
68. HM to CS and Lady Stephen, and to AI, 1-11-1868 and 15-11-1868, *E*.
69. LS to AI, 4-11-1868, *E*.
70. HM to AI, 5-11-1868, *E*.
71. HM to AI, 6-11-1868, *E*.
72. HM to AI, 11-11-1868, *E*.
73. LS to AI, 15-11-1868, *E*.
74. HM to CS and Lady Stephen, 15-11-1868, *E*.
75. HM to AI, 19-11-1868, *E*.

Chapter Ten:
THE SHABBY TIDE OF PROGRESS *(1869-1873)*

1. *Mausoleum*, 12-15.
2. AI to HM, ?16-3-1869, *E*.
3. HM and LS to AI, 4-3-1869, *E*.
4. HM to AI, 8-3-1869, *E*.
5. HJ to Alice James, 10-3-1869, in Leon Edel (ed), *Henry James Letters*, vol *1. 1843-75*, London: Macmillan, 1974.
6. HM to AI, 5-4-1869, *E*.
7. LS to AI, 12-3-1869, *E*. They appeared in the *Pall Mall Gazette* for 6 and 7 April.
8. AI to HM, 22-3-1869, *E*.
9. AI to HM, 23-3-1869, *E*.
10. 'Under the Ilexes', which is 'Dedicated to A.I.T.' has as its last lines: 'No more! the shadows shrink; the prying sun / Hath found me out. The morning's gone – how soon! / The far cathedral bell is striking noon. / This sketch, dear Annie, is for you – half done.'
11. AI to HM, 7-4-1869, *E*.

12. LS to AI, 28-3-1869, *E*.
13. *J*, 20-4-1869.
14. 'Bluebeard's Keys', *Cornhill* (February and June 1871). Nathaniel Hawthorne's 1858 notebook reveals Story's long-term interest in the myth. 'On [25 March] we went to breakfast at William Story's in the Palazzo Barberini…. He spoke of an expansion of the story of "Blue Beard," which he himself had either written or thought of writing, in which the contents of the several chambers which Fatima opened, before arriving at the fatal one, were to be described.' Nathaniel Hawthorne, *Passages from the French and Italian Note-Books*, London: Kegan Paul, Trench, Trübner, 1893, 133-4.
15. AI to HM, 6-4-1869 and 7-4-1869, *E*.
16. HM to AI, 10-4-1869, *E*.
17. HM to AI, 24-4-1869, *E*. Brookfield was probably recalling what WMT once written to him about the possible influence of his own style upon Dickens's writing. See above, Chapter 3, 67-8.
18. AF to BC, summer 1869, cited Hervey Fisher, *From a Tramp's Wallet. A Life of Douglas William Freshfield*, Banham: The Erskine Press, 2001, 103.
19. AI to AF, 29-11-1869, *BNB*.
20. FS to HM, 19-12-1869, transcribed MS, *CUL*.
21. FS to AI, 25-11-1869, transcribed MS, *CUL*.
22. FS to AI, 5-3-1870, *E*.
23. ER to ?BC, 4-1870, Helmut Gernsheim, *Julia Margaret Cameron Her Life and Photographic Work*, London: Gordon Fraser, 1975.
24. AI to Louisa Simeon, ?25-5-1870, *MM*.
25. FS to AI, 6-1870, transcribed MS, *CUL*.
26. HM to FS, 4-8-1870, *D*.
27. LS to HM, 13-8-1870 and 27-8-1870, *D*.
28. HM to FS, 11-11-1870, *D*.
29. HM to FS, 18-11-1870, *D*.
30. *J*, 1-10-1870.
31. LS to OH, 4-1-1871, *Bicknell*.
32. AI to ?, 6-1872, *E*.
33. *Mausoleum*, 16.
34. FS to HM, 15-1-1871, transcribed MS, *CUL*.
35. FS to AI, 17-1-1871, transcribed MS, *CUL*.
36. AI to FS, 20-1-1871, *E*.
37. *Mausoleum*, 21.
38. HM to FS, 16-1-1871, *D*.
39. *Chapters*, 138-9.
40. AI to ?, 6-1872, *E*.
41. HM to Lady Stephen, 15-7-1871, 22-7-1871, 12-8-1871 and 20-8-1871, *D*.
42. AI to HT, 11-3-1872, *E*.
43. *J*, 12-4-1872.
44. AI to ?, 6-1872, *E*.
45. RR to AF, 25-6-1872 and ?10 February 1873, *E*.
46. HM to AI, 10-8-1872, *E*.
47. *J*, 30-7-1872.

48. HM to AI, ?10-1872, *E.*
49. HM to AI, 7-8-1872, *E.*
50. Lady Stephen to HM, 14-8-1872, *D.*
51. AI to HM, 2-9-1872, *E.*
52. JC to AI, 17-9-1872, Gernsheim.
53. ET to AI, 2-2-1873, *E.*
54. ER to ET, 4-2-1873, *TRC.*
55. *J*, 8-3-1873.
56. HM to Lady Stephen, 28-4-1873, *D.*
57. HM to AI, ?8-1873, *E.*
58. *J*, 26-7-1873.
59. AI to ER, ?9-1873, *E.*
60. *J*, 27-11-1873.
61. AI to HT, ?1873, *E.*

Chapter Eleven:
THE INSCRUTABLE DESIGN *(1863-1865)*

1. Winifred Gérin, *Anne Thackeray Ritchie*, Oxford: OUP, 1981, 173.
2. Copy of Smith, Elder account statements, *E.* After its first printing in March 1873, the book was reprinted in April, June and September.
3. GS to AI, 21-2-1872, *JMA.*
4. HM to AI, ?11-1874, *E.*
5. JC to AI, 10-11-1875, *HRC.*
6. LS to AI, 3-6-1874, *E.*
7. HM to AI, about June 1874, *E.*
8. HM to AI, 7/8-1874, *E.*
9. HM to LS, 1-9-1874, *D.*
10. AI to HT, 17-8-1874, *TRC.*
11. *J*, 13-6-1874.
12. HM to LS, 12-9-1874, *D.*
13. Virginia's *Freshwater, a Comedy in Three Acts* was first conceived in about 1923. Its targets were easy and long dead, but it greatly amused Bloomsbury at its sole performance in 1935 in Vanessa Bell's studio.
14. AI to HM, ?19-9-1874, *E.*
15. AI to HM, 22-9-1874, *E.*
16. HM to AI, 9-1874, *E.*
17. AI to HM, 9-1874, *E.*
18. HM to LS, 19-9-1874, *D.*
19. HM to AI, 19-9-1874, *E.*
20. AI to HM, 10-1874, *E.*
21. AI to HT, 11-1874, *E.*
22. AI to ER, ?30-11-1874, *E.*
23. HM to A, 1874, *E.*
24. LS to HM, 28-11-1874, *D.*
25. *J.*

26. *J*, 18-3-1875.
27. *J.*
28. HH to AI, ?7-4-1874, *E.*
29. JS to AI, 19-4-1875, *E.*
30. AI to JS, ?22-4-1875, *Y.*
31. HM to AI, 4-1875, *E.*
32. HM to AI, ?27-4-1875, *E.*
33. LS to HM, 26-5-1875, *D.*
34. AI to RR, 2-3-1875, *E.*
35. LS to AI, 29-4-1875, *Bicknell.*
36. HM to AI, 4-1875, *E.*
37. *Mausoleum*, 14.
38. HM to AI, 3-5-1875, *E.*
39. HM to AI, 9-5-1875, *E.*
40. HM to AI, 7-5-1875, *E.*
41. HM to AI, 7-1875, *E.*
42. HM to AI, 7-1875, *D.*
43. AI to Magdalene Ritchie, 8-1875, *E.*
44. HM to LS, 14-8-1875, *D.*
45. AI to RR, ?14-8-1875, *E.*
46. AI to HH, autumn 1875, *Y.* In 1887 he married Sarah Forbes.
47. *J.*
48. Henry Hankey to AI, 28-10-1875, *E.*
49. AI to CR, 10-1875, *E.*
50. HM to LS, 18-11-1875, *D.*
51. MO, *Autobiography.*
52. *Mausoleum*, 22. Details of these last hours are derived from Leslie's account.
53. *J.*
54. BC to LS, 1-12-1875, *D.*
55. R.C. Jebb to HT, 4-12-1875, *E.*
56. AI to ER, 12-1875, *E.*
57. AI to JS, 6-12-1875, *Y.*
58. AI to CR, 2-12-1875, *BNB.*
59. SA to AI, 6-12-1875, *E.*
60. Richard Doyle to AI, 2-3-1876, *E.*
61. Mrs Baxter to AI, 'Christmas 1875', *E.*
62. Mrs Ritchie to AF and BC, 5-12-1875, *E.*
63. *J*, 23-5-1876.

THACKERAY AND RITCHIE FAMILY TREE

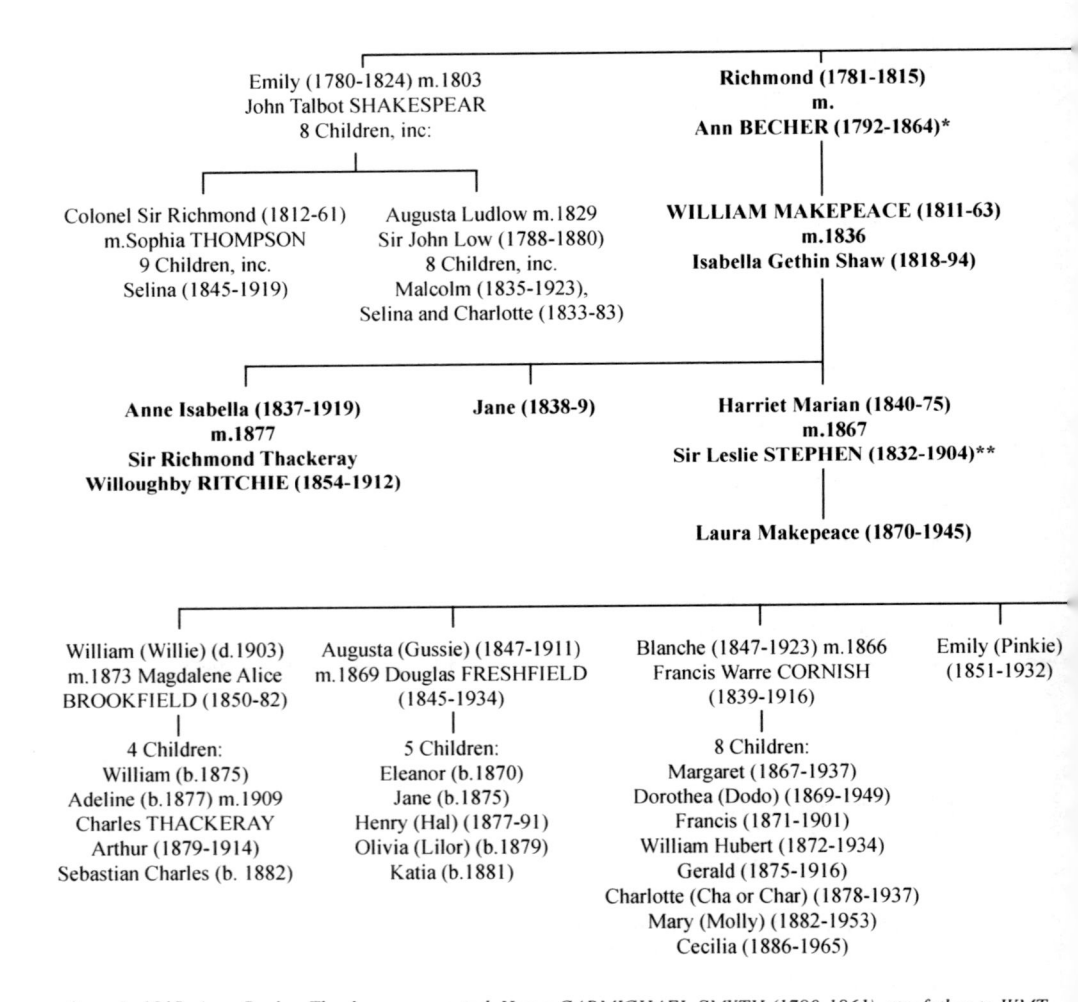

Emily (1780-1824) m.1803
John Talbot SHAKESPEAR
8 Children, inc:

Richmond (1781-1815)
m.
Ann BECHER (1792-1864)*

Colonel Sir Richmond (1812-61)
m.Sophia THOMPSON
9 Children, inc.
Selina (1845-1919)

Augusta Ludlow m.1829
Sir John Low (1788-1880)
8 Children, inc.
Malcolm (1835-1923),
Selina and Charlotte (1833-83)

WILLIAM MAKEPEACE (1811-63)
m.1836
Isabella Gethin Shaw (1818-94)

Anne Isabella (1837-1919)
m.1877
Sir Richmond Thackeray
Willoughby RITCHIE (1854-1912)

Jane (1838-9)

Harriet Marian (1840-75)
m.1867
Sir Leslie STEPHEN (1832-1904)**

Laura Makepeace (1870-1945)

William (Willie) (d.1903)
m.1873 Magdalene Alice
BROOKFIELD (1850-82)

4 Children:
William (b.1875)
Adeline (b.1877) m.1909
Charles THACKERAY
Arthur (1879-1914)
Sebastian Charles (b. 1882)

Augusta (Gussie) (1847-1911)
m.1869 Douglas FRESHFIELD
(1845-1934)

5 Children:
Eleanor (b.1870)
Jane (b.1875)
Henry (Hal) (1877-91)
Olivia (Lilor) (b.1879)
Katia (b.1881)

Blanche (1847-1923) m.1866
Francis Warre CORNISH
(1839-1916)

8 Children:
Margaret (1867-1937)
Dorothea (Dodo) (1869-1949)
Francis (1871-1901)
William Hubert (1872-1934)
Gerald (1875-1916)
Charlotte (Cha or Char) (1878-1937)
Mary (Molly) (1882-1953)
Cecilia (1886-1965)

Emily (Pinkie)
(1851-1932)

*   In 1817, Anne Becher Thackeray remarried, Henry CARMICHAEL-SMYTH (1780-1861), stepfather to WMT

**   In 1878, Leslie Stephen remarried, Julia Jackson DUCKWORTH,
       becoming stepfather to the children of her first marriage:
       George, Stella and Gerald de L'Etang. The children of this marriage were
       Vanessa (1879-1961), m. Clive BELL
       Thoby (1880-1906)
       Virginia (1882-1941) m. Leonard WOOLF
       Adrian (1883-1948) m. Karin COSTELLOE

*** Edward Talbot Thackeray remarried, Elizabeth PLEYDELL
       Four children, inc. Charles THACKERAY, m. Adeline RITCHIE

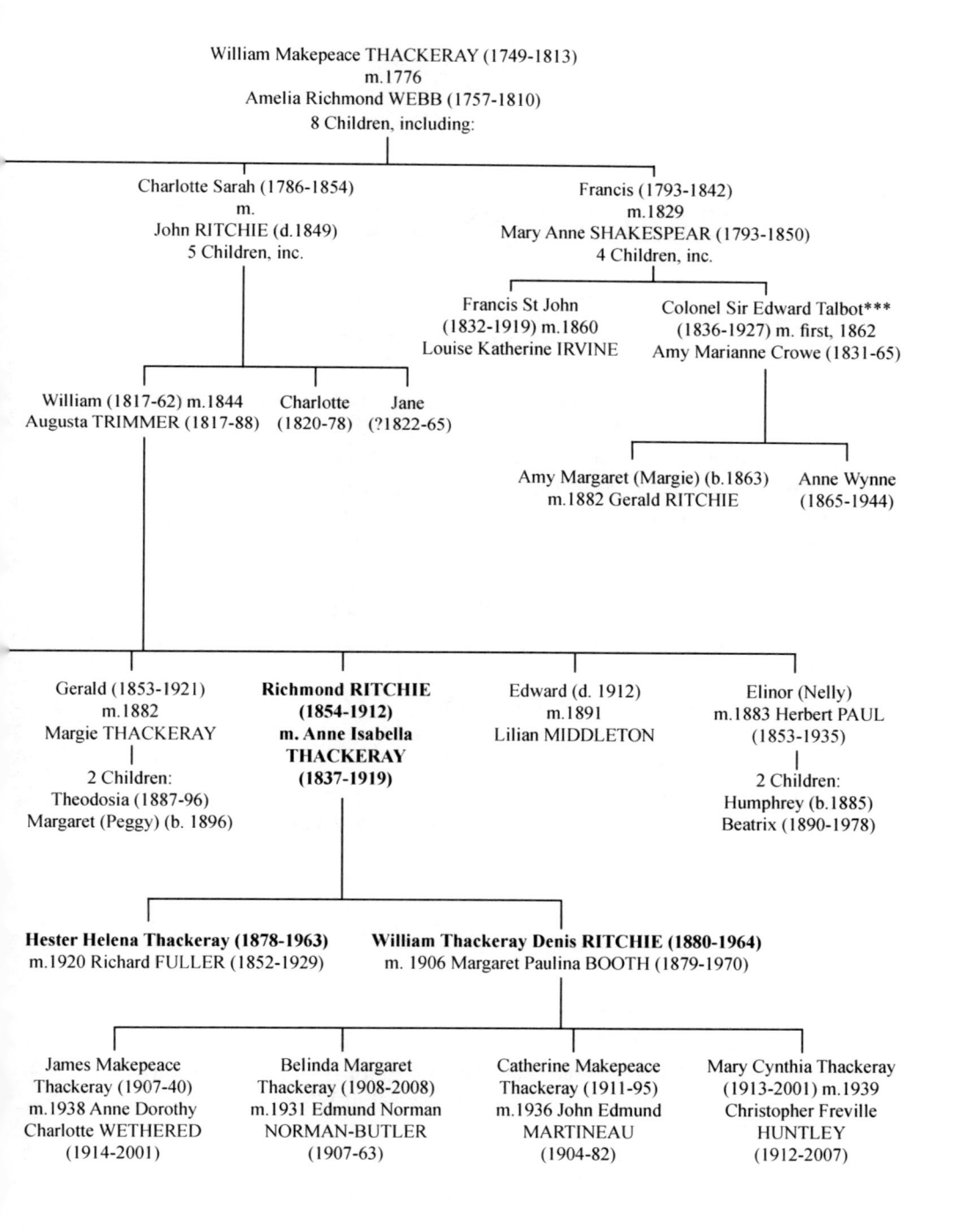

William Makepeace THACKERAY (1749-1813)
m.1776
Amelia Richmond WEBB (1757-1810)
8 Children, including:

Charlotte Sarah (1786-1854)
m.
John RITCHIE (d.1849)
5 Children, inc.

Francis (1793-1842)
m.1829
Mary Anne SHAKESPEAR (1793-1850)
4 Children, inc.

Francis St John (1832-1919) m.1860
Louise Katherine IRVINE

Colonel Sir Edward Talbot*** (1836-1927) m. first, 1862
Amy Marianne Crowe (1831-65)

William (1817-62) m.1844
Augusta TRIMMER (1817-88)

Charlotte (1820-78)

Jane (?1822-65)

Amy Margaret (Margie) (b.1863)
m.1882 Gerald RITCHIE

Anne Wynne (1865-1944)

Gerald (1853-1921)
m.1882
Margie THACKERAY

2 Children:
Theodosia (1887-96)
Margaret (Peggy) (b. 1896)

Richmond RITCHIE (1854-1912)
m. Anne Isabella THACKERAY (1837-1919)

Edward (d. 1912)
m.1891
Lilian MIDDLETON

Elinor (Nelly)
m.1883 Herbert PAUL (1853-1935)

2 Children:
Humphrey (b.1885)
Beatrix (1890-1978)

Hester Helena Thackeray (1878-1963)
m.1920 Richard FULLER (1852-1929)

William Thackeray Denis RITCHIE (1880-1964)
m. 1906 Margaret Paulina BOOTH (1879-1970)

James Makepeace Thackeray (1907-40)
m.1938 Anne Dorothy Charlotte WETHERED (1914-2001)

Belinda Margaret Thackeray (1908-2008)
m.1931 Edmund Norman NORMAN-BUTLER (1907-63)

Catherine Makepeace Thackeray (1911-95)
m.1936 John Edmund MARTINEAU (1904-82)

Mary Cynthia Thackeray (1913-2001) m.1939
Christopher Freville HUNTLEY (1912-2007)

ABBREVIATIONS AND SOURCES

1. Names of Correspondents

AI	Anne Isabella Thackeray (Annie), Anne Isabella Ritchie after her marriage in 1877 (elder daughter of WMT)
AC	Anne Carmichael-Smyth (mother of WMT)
ACR	Amy Crowe (Amy Thackeray after her marriage)
AF	Augusta (Gussie) Ritchie (Gussie Freshfield after her marriage)
AP	Anne Procter
AT	Alfred Tennyson
BC	Blanche Ritchie (Blanche Warre Cornish after her marriage)
CD	Charles Dickens
CN	Charles Eliot Norton
CR	Charlotte Ritchie (cousin of WMT)
CS	Caroline Stephen
EF	Edward FitzGerald
EL	Eliza Field
EP	Elinor (Nelly) Ritchie (Elinor Paul after her marriage)
ER	Emily (Pinkie) Ritchie
ET	Emily Tennyson
FS	James Fitzjames Stephen
GW	George Frederic Watts
GS	George Smith
HH	Hastings Hughes
HJ	Henry James
HM	Harriet Marian Thackeray (Minny), Harriet Marian Stephen after her marriage in 1867 (younger daughter of WMT)
HR	Hester Ritchie
HT	Hallam Tennyson
IT	Isabella Shawe, Isabella Thackeray after her marriage in 1836 (wife of WMT)

Abbreviations and Sources 297

JB	John Brown
JC	Julia Margaret Cameron
JF	James Fields
JJ	Julia Jackson (later Julia Duckworth and finally Julia Stephen)
JO	John Field
JOB	Jane Octavia Brookfield
JS	Jeanie Nassau Senior
KD	Kate Dickens (later Kate Collins and finally Kate Perugini)
KP	Kate Perry
LB	Lucy Baxter
LS	Leslie Stephen
MH	Mary Holmes
MO	Margaret Oliphant
MS	Mary Stephen
MT	Margie Thackeray (Margie Ritchie after her marriage)
OH	Oliver Wendell Holmes (Jr., unless noted)
RR	Richmond Ritchie
RT	Richmond Thackeray (father of WMT)
SA	Sarianna Browning
SB	Sally Baxter (Sally Hampton after her marriage)
WMT	William Makepeace Thackeray
WS	Walter Senior

2. Sources and Locations

PUBLISHED

Adversity	Gordon Ray, *The Uses of Adversity 1811-1846*, London: OUP, 1955
Autobiography	Margaret Oliphant, *Autobiography and Letters*, 1899
Bicknell	John Bicknell (ed), *Selected Letters of Leslie Stephen*, 2 vols., Columbus, OH: Ohio State University Press, 1996
Biographical	*The Biographical Edition of the Works of William Makepeace Thackeray, with Biographical Introductions by his Daughter, Anne Ritchie,* 13 vols., London: Smith, Elder, 1898-99
Chapters	Anne Isabella Ritchie, *Chapters from Some Memoirs*, London: Macmillan, 1894
Centenary	Anne Isabella Ritchie, *Centenary Biographical Edition of the Works of William Makepeace Thackeray, with Biographical Introductions by his Daughter, Lady Ritchie,* 26 vols., London: Smith, Elder, 1910-11

Daughter	Hester Fuller and Violet Hammersley, *Thackeray's Daughter*, Dublin: Euphorion Books, 1951
Harden	Edgar Harden, *The Letters and Private Papers of William Makepeace Thackeray* (supplement to *Ray*) 2 vols, New York and London: Garland Press, 1994
Letters	Hester Ritchie, *Letters of Anne Thackeray Ritchie*, London: John Murray, 1924
Mausoleum	Alan Bell (ed), *Sir Leslie Stephen's Mausoleum Book*, Oxford: Clarendon Press, 1977
Ray	Gordon Ray, *The Letters and Private Papers of William Makepeace Thackeray*, 4 vols, Cambridge, MA: Harvard University Press, 1946
Records	Anne Isabella Ritchie, *Records of Tennyson, Ruskin, Browning*, London: Macmillan, 1892
Shankman	Lilian Shankman, *Anne Thackeray Ritchie Journals and Letters*, Columbus, OH: Ohio State University Press, 1994
Wisdom	Gordon Ray, *The Age of Wisdom 1847-1863*, London: OUP, 1958

MANUSCRIPT

BNB	Belinda Norman-Butler (private collection deposited at *E*)
CUL	Cambridge University Library
D	Duke University
DCM	Dorset County Museum, Dorchester
DI	Annie's year diaries (*BNB*)
E	Eton College Library
HL	Houghton Library, Harvard University
HRC	Harry Ransom Center, University of Texas at Austin
HU	Huntington Library, San Marino, California
J	Annie's Journal (*BNB*)
JM	Juliet Murray (private collection)
JMA	John Murray Archive, National Library of Scotland
MM	Michael Millgate (private collection)
NLS	National Library of Scotland
P	Princeton University Library
RJ	Richmond Thackeray's journal (*JM*)
TCC	Trinity College Cambridge
TRC	Tennyson Research Centre, Lincolnshire County Council
Y	Beinecke Library, Yale University

SELECT BIBLIOGRAPHY

Books described in the list of principal sources are not repeated here.

Blainey, Ann, *Fanny and Adelaide. The Lives of the Remarkable Kemble Sisters*, Chicago, IL: Ivan R. Dee, 2001
Bobbitt, Mary Reed, *With Dearest Love to All. The Life and Letters of Lady Jebb*, London: Faber & Faber, 1960
Boynthon, *Elizabeth and Anthony Burton, The Great Exhibitor. The Life and Work of Henry Cole*, London: V&A Publications, 2003
Collins, Philip (ed.), *Thackeray Interviews and Recollections*, 2 vols, London: Macmillan, 1983
Cornish, Blanche Warre, *Some Family Letters of W. M. Thackeray together with Recollections by his Kinswoman*, London: Smith, Elder, 1911
Dakers, Caroline, *The Holland Park Circle. Artists and Victorian Society*, London: Yale University Press, 1999
Edel, Leon (editor), *Henry James Letters*, 4 vols, London: Macmillan, 1974-84
Elwin, Whitwell, *Some XVIII Century Men of Letters*, 2 vols, London: 1902
Fisher, Hervey, *From a Tramp's Wallet. A Life of Douglas William Freshfield*, Banham: The Erskine Press, 2001
Garnett, Henrietta, *Anny. A Life of Anne Isabella Thackeray Ritchie*, London: Chatto & Windus, 2004
Gérin, Winifred, *Anne Thackeray Ritchie*, Oxford: Oxford University Press, 1981
Gernsheim, Helmut, *Julia Margaret Cameron Her Life and Photographic Work*, London: Gordon Fraser, 1975
Glyn, Jenifer, *Prince of Publishers. A Biography of George Smith*, London: Allison & Brisby, 1986
Harden, Edgar, *Thackeray the Writer. 1: From Journalism to 'Vanity Fair'*, Basingstoke: Macmillan, 1998
———, *Thackeray the Writer. 2: From 'Pendennis' to 'Denis Duval'*, Basingstoke: Macmillan, 2000
Hawksley, Lucinda, *Katie*, London: Doubleday, 2006

Hawthorne, Nathaniel, *Passages from the French and Italian Note-Books*, London: Kegan Paul, Trench, Trübner, 1893

Higginson, Thomas Wentworth, *Cheerful Yesterdays*, Boston and New York: Houghton, Mifflin, 1898

James, Henry, *William Wetmore Story and his Friends*, 2 vols, Edinburgh and London: Blackwood, 1903

Kincaid, Dennis, *British Social Life in India 1608-1937*, London: Routledge & Kegan Paul, 2nd edn., 1973

Knoepflmacher, U.C., *Ventures into Childland. Victorians, Fairy Tales, and Femininity*, Chicago, IL: University of Chicago Press, 1998

Merriman, John Jones, 'Kensington Worthies, III, W. M. Thackeray', *St Mary Abbots Parish Magazine*, 1889

Millais, John Guille, *The Life and Letters of Sir John Everett Millais*, 2 vols, London: Methuen, 1899

Monsarrat, Ann, *An Uneasy Victorian. Thackeray the Man*, London: Cassell, 1980

Newman, Hilary, *Laura Stephen: A Memoir*, London: Cecil Woolf, 2006

Olsen, Victoria, *Julia Margaret Cameron and Victorian Photography*, London: Aurum Press, 2003

Ray, Gordon, *The Buried Life*, London: Oxford University Press, 1952

Shillingsburg, Peter, *Pegasus in Harness. Victorian Publishing and W. M. Thackeray*, Charlottesville, VI and London: University Press of Virginia, 1992

———, *William Makepeace Thackeray: a Literary Life*, Basingstoke: Palgrave, 2001

Simpson, M.C.M., *Many Memories of Many People*, London: Edward Arnold, 1898

Smith, George, 'Our birth and parentage', *Cornhill*, January 1901

Sturgis, Julian, *From Books and Papers of Russell Sturgis*, Oxford: Oxford University Press, 1893

Smith, K.J.M., *James Fitzjames Stephen. Portrait of a Victorian Rationalist*, Cambridge: Cambridge University Press, 2002

Taylor, D.J., *Thackeray*, London: Chatto & Windus, 1999

Tennyson, Hallam (ed.), *Tennyson and his Friends*, London: Macmillan, 1911

Tilton, Eleanor M. (ed.), *The Letters of Ralph Waldo Emerson, Vol IX, 1860-1869*, New York: Columbia University Press, 1994

INDEX

Airlie, Blanche, 244
Alexander, Miss (governess), 70
American Civil War, 148-9, 154, 213
American Presidential Election (1868), 221, 231
Andersen, Hans Christian, 86
Appleton, Thomas Gold, 214, 216
Ashburton, William Bingham Barham (second Baron Ashburton) and Lady Ashburton (formerly Louisa Stewart-Mackenzie), 84
Austen, Jane, 225

Bakewell, Mrs (Isabella Thackeray's carer), 59
Baxter, George, 100, 102; offered money by WMT, 155
Baxter, Mrs George, 100-4, 123, 143, 146, 148-9, 172-3, 214, 217-8, 229, 272-3
Baxter, Lucy, 100, 101, 218
Baxter, Sally, 100-1, 104, 146, 154, 158, 217-8; engagement and marriage, 120-1
Becher, Anne (mother of WMT – *see* Anne Carmichael-Smyth)
Becher, Miss Anne (great-aunt of WMT), 7
Becher, John Harman (maternal grandfather of WMT), 6
Becher, Maria (aunt of WMT), 23
Becket, Gilbert à, 63
Berry, Miss, 85
Blechynden, James, 8

Booth, Edwin, in *Hamlet*, 228
Bradbury and Evans, 63, 84, 126
British East India Company, 1
Brodie, Jessie (childhood nurse of Annie and Minny), 35, 38, 41, 46, 242
Brookfield, Jane Octavia [JOB], 57, 65, 69-70, 72-3, 76-81, 83-4, 101, 104, 120-1, 146, 164, 169, 171, 208, 255, 271
Brookfield, Magdalene (later Magdalene Ritchie), 229, 247, 267; birth, 77-8; engagement and marriage, 250-1
Brookfield, William, 57, 68, 69, 73, 76, 77-9, 83-4, 106, 157, 238; death, 255
Brontë, Charlotte, on *Esmond*, 85
Brotherton, Mary, 108
Brown, Dr John, 129, 161, 242
Browning, Elizabeth Barrett, 86, 109-10; death, 149
Browning, Robert, 86, 108, 109, 168, 194, 236-7, 249, 268, 272; *Red Cotton Nightcap Country*, 237, 249
Browning, Robert Wiedeman Barrett (Pen), 86
Browning, Sarianna, 272
Bryce, James, 192, 247
Bullock, Henry (captain of the *Thetis*), 2, 5
Butler, Edward, 7
Butler, Fanny, 233

Butler, Harriet (maternal grandmother of WMT), 6-7, 23, 45, 46, 60
Butler, Pierce, 233

Cameron, Hardinge Hay, 169
Cameron, Henry, 269
Cameron, Julia Margaret, 157, 169, 172, 185, 240, 249-50, 254, 269; photographs Annie, 240
Carlyle, Thomas, 133, 145, 244-5
Carmichael, Charles (Cheri), 112; birth, 55
Carmichael, Mary (cousin of WMT), 44; engaged to Charles Carmichael-Smyth, 46; jealousy of WMT, 112
Carmichael-Smyth, Anne (née Becher; married firstly Richmond Thackeray, married secondly Henry Carmichael-Smyth; mother of WMT), birth and early years, 6-8; character, 15-16, 49-50; concerns over Minny's health, 177; correspondence with granddaughters, 65-6; death, 182-3; Henry Carmichael-Smyth: death, 149-50 / first meeting, 7-8 / meets in Calcutta, 10-11; illness, 123; model for 'Helen Pendennis', 76; on modern women, 69, 86-7; on WMT and high society, 85; on WMT visiting America, 88-9; possible pension rights, 150; religious views: differences with WMT, 21, 92-6, 115-6 / discussions with granddaughters, 169 / late change of mind, 182; relationship with granddaughters after WMT's death, 169 and *passim*; Richmond Thackeray: marriage, 8 / remembered, 180, 182; supporter of homeopathy, 27, 31, 49; viewed by WMT, 85-6
Carmichael-Smyth, Charles (later Charles Carmichael, brother of Henry Carmichael-Smyth), 46, 112
Carmichael-Smyth, Henry (GP; stepfather of WMT), 7-8, 10-11; benefits from magnetism, 113, 116; death, 149-50; debts, 60; grandfatherly role, 49; launches *The Constitutional and Public Ledger*, 25; model for 'Colonel Newcome', 91, 103-4; participates in water-cure, 47-8
Carmichael-Smyths (Anne and Henry): English community in Paris, 50; final return from India, 15-16; settle in Brompton, 132
Cayley, Charles, 164
Chapman and Hall, 40
Charterhouse School, 13
Chartist uprisings, 70
Chinnery, George, portrait of WMT and parents, 9-10, 11
Chope, Rev Richard, 269
Chopin, Frédéric, 51-2
Christie, Charles, 6
Clarke, Dr Edward, 223
Clevedon Court, 73, 76
Clough, Arthur Hugh, 76
Cole, Alan, 187, 203
Cole, Sir Henry, 79, 168, 172, 173, 202, 206
Cole, Henrietta, 151
Cole, Laetitia, 93
Cole, Marian, 169, 171
Collins, Charles, 164-5, 167, 168, 169
Collins, Kate (*see* Dickens, Kate)
Collins, Wilkie, 167
Colmache, Laura, 51, 59
Colmache, Pauline, 51
Colvile, Lady (formerly Elinor Grant), 162
The Constitutional and Public Ledger, 25, 27, 30-1
Corkran, Alice, 51
Corkran, Henriette, 51
Corkran, Mrs, 146-7
The Cornhill Magazine, 111, 126, 141-5, 150-1, 174-5, 176, 191, 253-4, 259, 265; dinners for contributors, 135; inaugural issue, 132-3; Leslie Stephen appointed

Index 303

editor, 244; relationship between WMT and George Smith, 132-41; WMT appointed editor, 131-2; WMT resigns editorship, 139-41
Cornish, Blanche Warre (née Ritchie), 152-3, 160, 193-4, 204, 210, 236, 239, 249, 251, 255, 271, 273
Cornish, Frank Warre, 193-4, 204, 236, 255-6
Cowper, Harriet (maternal grandmother of WMT – *see* Harriet Butler)
Creyke, Mr, 121
Crimean War, 116-7
Crowe, Amy (later Amy Thackeray), 24, 123-4, 149, 156-7, 170, 189; companion and housekeeper to Thackerays, 113-6; marries Edward Thackeray, 158
Crowe, Eyre, 24, 113, secretary-companion to WMT on first American trip, 89-90
Crowe, Eyre Evans, 24
Curtis, Ariana, 109

Davison, Sir Henry, 71
Dickens, Catherine, 67, 113
Dickens, Charles, 67-8, 77, 97, 104, 108, 120, 127-8, 129-30, 164, 167, 168, 238, 241; children's parties, 71-2; Garrick Club Affair, 128, 129-30; on *Vanity Fair*, 68; writing admired by WMT, 67-8, 104; *American Notes*, 97; *David Copperfield*, 67-8, 238; 244; *Dombey and Son*, 67, 68; *Little Dorrit*, 120, 124; *Martin Chuzzlewit*, 221
Dickens, Charley, 130
Dickens, Kate (later Kate Collins, then Kate Perugini), 71, 164, 165, 167, 168, 241
Disraeli, Benjamin, 108
Doyle, Richard, 63, 272
Drury, Miss (governess), 66, 69
Duckworth, George, 242

Edgeworth, Maria, 36
Eldredge family, 227, 228
Eliot, George (Mary Anne [Marian] Evans), 203-4, 263-4, 265; *Middlemarch*, 238
Elliotson, Dr John, dedicatee of *Pendennis*, 77; fictional portrayal in *Philip*, 77
Elliot, Jane, 88, 146-7
Elton, Charles, 73
Emerson, Ralph Waldo, 224, 226-7, 229
Esquirol, Jean, 45

Fanshawe, Mrs ('Aunt Fan'), 79, 118, 235
Fanshawe, Rosa, 79, 235
Fawcett, Henry, 195, 197
Fawcett, Millicent Garrett, 228
Fields, James, 135, 215
FitzGerald, Edward, 17, 22, 23, 29, 45, 48, 63, 89-90, 106; legacy to WMT's daughters, 89
Forster, John, 77
Franco-Prussian War, 241, 245
Fraser's Magazine, 32, 241, 244
Freshfield, Douglas, 239, 258
Freshfield, Gussie (née Ritchie), 155, 160, 203, 204, 213, 239, 251, 273
Freshwater (Isle of Wight), 157, 169, 171-2, 185, 240-1, 250, 254, 255, 256-7
Froude, James, 206
Fuller, Margaret, 229

Garrick Club Affair, 128, 129-30
Gaskell, Elizabeth, 187-8
Gérin, Winifred, 253
Gibbs, Frederick, 207, 269
Godkin, Edwin, 228
Goethe, Johann Wolfgang von, 18-19
Goldsworthy, John (servant), 35-6
The Gownsman (Cambridge student newspaper), 18
Graham, Mary (*see* Mary Carmichael)
Grant, Ulysses S., 231, 232
Great Coram Street, 31-2
Greenwood, Frederick, 172, 236
Guérin, Maurice de, 255

Hamerton, Bess (governess), 65-6
Hampsthwaite (ancestral birthplace of

Thackerays), 160
Hardy, Thomas, 259-60; *Far from the Madding Crowd*, 259
Henry, Professor Joseph, 232
Holmes, Mary, 85-6
Holmes, Oliver Wendell, Jr, 200-1, 212-3, 222, 226, 242-3
Holmes, Oliver Wendell Sr, 222-3, 226
Hood, Thomas, 134
Houghton, Lady (formerly the Hon. Annabella Crewe), 194-5
Houghton, Lord (first Baron Houghton, formerly Richard Monckton Milnes), 160
Hughes, Hastings, 254, 267-8; proposes marriage to Annie, 260-3
Hughes, Thomas, 131, 152
Hunt, William Holman, 195
Huth, Augusta, 171, 191, 199, 269
Huth, Henry, 171, 269
Huxley, Thomas, 238

Irving, Henry, in *Hamlet*, 259
Irving, Washington, praises *The Virginians*, 127

Jackson, Julia (later Julia Duckworth and finally Julia Stephen), 157, 187, 188, 195-6, 218, 242, 251, 270, 271, 272; Leslie Stephen first becomes aware of, 188
James, Henry, 132-3, 235
James, Samuel (servant), 65
Jebb, Richard, 266, 271
Jerrold, Douglas, 63
Joachim, Joseph, 158
Johnson, Andrew, 232
Jowett, Benjamin, 185
Judd, Charlotte (Anglo-Indian mistress of Richmond Thackeray), 8
Judd, Sarah (half-sister of WMT), 8

Keble, John, 182
Kemble, Fanny, 233
Kensal Green Cemetery, 32, 169, 183, 273-4

Landseer, Edwin, 135
Leech, John, 63, 181, 196

Leighton, Frederic, 135, 188, 211-2, 235-6
Lemon, Mark, 63
Lewes, George, 169, 203-4
Locker, Eleanor, 268
Lockhart, John, 108
London Exhibition (1862), 155
Longfellow, Henry Wadsworth, 227, 237
Loppé, Gabriel, possible marriage proposal to Annie, 260, 263
Low family of Cupar (cousins of WMT), 161, 242
Lowell, Frances Dunlap, 222, 225
Lowell, James Russell, 222-5, 229, 255
Lowell, Mabel, 222, 225
Lowell, Maria, liked by WMT, 225
Lytton, Bulwer, 108

Macaulay, Thomas, 82
MacBean, Alexander, 108
McKay, Charles, 139
Macrone, John, 30
Maryanne (maid), 270
Mayhew, Henry, 63
Merivale, Agnes (later Agnes Trench), 221, 246
Merivale, Ella (later Ella Williams-Freeman), 158, 218, 221, 231-2
Merivale, Herman, 135, 139-40, 164, 169, 173, 180, 255
Merivale, Herman Charles, 152, 162, 187, 213, 216, 217, 218, 228, 237
Merriman, Dr John Jones, 77, 162-4, 166-7
Millais, John Everett, 22, 168, 241, 272
Milnes, Richard Monckton (*see* Lord Houghton)
Monod, Adolphe, 93-6
Morley, John (later Viscount Morley of Blackburn), 272
Morris, William, 252
Musset, Alfred de, 255
Mussy, Dr Henri de, 177

Norton, Charles Eliot, 235
Norton family, 227
Norton, Jane, 235-6
The National Standard, 21

Index

Oliphant, Margaret, 244, 267, 269, 272
Onslow Gardens, Brompton, 172-3, 180-2, 193, 195, 201-2, 211, 247, 250
Osborne, George, 68-9

The Pall Mall Gazette, 185-6, 236, 251
Pappenheim, Jenny von, 20
Paris Universal Exhibition (1867), 206, 211
Paul, Charles Kegan, 194
Paul, Margaret (née Colvile), 194
Payn, James, 265
Pearman, Charles (servant), 103, 121
Pell, Alfred, 230
Perry, Kate, 88, 146-7
Peruzzi, Simone, 268
Pollock, Juliet (née Creed), 139
Prinsep, Val, 188, 235-6
Procter, Anne Benson, 122, 125, 177
Procter, Bryan ('Barry Cornwall'), 177
Putnam's, Mrs (Boston boardinghouse), 226
Puzin, Dr, 48

Quincy, Josiah, 227

Ray, Gordon, 101, 253
Ritchie, Augusta (née Trimmer, widow of William Ritchie), 155, 169, 257, 268, 273
Ritchie, Blanche (*see* Blanche Warre Cornish)
Ritchie, Charlotte (cousin of WMT), 57, 123, 151, 154, 177, 178, 189, 206, 245, 256, 257-8, 272; criticises Annie and Richmond's intimacy, 258-9
Ritchie, Elinor (later Elinor Paul), 257
Ritchie, Emily [Pinkie], 169, 206, 240, 249, 250, 257, 272; affection for Hallam Tennyson, 256
Ritchie, Gerald, 265
Ritchie, Gussie (*see* Gussie Freshfield)
Ritchie, Jane (cousin of WMT), 151, 183, 189-90, 191
Ritchie, John (uncle of WMT), 23-4
Ritchie, Richmond (later marries Anne Isabella Thackeray), 246-8, 251; ch. 11 *passim*
Ritchie, William (cousin of WMT and father of the eight Ritchie children), 24, 25, 151, 154-5
Ritchie, Willie (eldest son of William Ritchie), 151, 250, 251
Rothschild family, 213
Rothschild, Sir Anthony de, 149
Russell, Dr John, 13

Sand, George, 255
Sartoris, Adelaide, 108, 160, 169-70, 188, 233
Scott, Alexander, 131
Scott, Walter, 108
Senior, Jeanie (née Hughes), 152, 188, 254, 260, 261-3, 268; advises Annie on marriage, 261-2
Senior, Minnie, 152
Shakespear, John (uncle of WMT), 8
Shakespear, Richmond (cousin of WMT), 11
Shakespear, Selina, 178
Shawe, Arthur (brother-in-law of WMT), 246
Shawe family, 24
Shawe, Henry (brother-in-law of WMT), 117
Shawe, Isabella Creagh (mother-in-law of WMT), 25, 40-3, 48, 112, 117; death, 246; objects to daughter marrying WMT, 27-9
Shawe, Isabella Gethin (wife of WMT; *see* Isabella Thackeray)
Shawe, Jane (sister-in-law of WMT), 73, 159-60
Sidgwick, Henry, 187, 266
Simeon, Sir John, 240-1
Smith, Elizabeth, 152, 182
Smith, George Murray, 29, 84, 85, 101, 130-41, 143, 144-5, 147, 150, 151, 152, 168, 172, 173-6, 178-80, 182, 187, 208, 211, 253-4; business relationship with WMT, 130-41; hires WMT as *Cornhill* editor, 131-2; purchases WMT copyrights, 173-4, 179-80

Smith, Valentine, 270
Smithsonian Institution, 232
The Saturday Review, 257
The Snob (Cambridge student newspaper), 18
Southwell Gardens, South Kensington, 228, 247, 248, 250, 256-7
Spedding, James, 64, 229
Spencer, Herbert, 238, 269
Spiegel, Melanie von, 19-20
Stephen, Caroline, 185, 193, 195, 203, 204, 211
Stephen, Fitzjames, 169, 185-6, 239-40, 241-2, 243-4, 262-3, 270; admiration for WMT, 240, 244; advises Annie on her reading, 186; correspondence with Minny, 241-2
Stephen, Lady (formerly Jane Venn), 185, 195, 204, 211, 241, 249, 250, 273 final illness, 254-5
Stephen, Laura Makepeace (daughter of Leslie and Minny), 234, 242-4, 245-6, 248-9, 250-1, 255, 257, 258, 259, 265, 266, 270, 272; behavioural problems, 248-9, 255; birth, 242; slow physical development, 245, 249, 250-1
Stephen, Leslie, 171; admires *Vanity Fair*, 185; American trip (1868), 215-29; Annie: admires her 'genius', 234-5, 264 / affection for, 193, 234 / assessment of abilities 264-5 / chaotic organisation, 265 / critical of spending, 265 / part of Onslow Gardens household, 201; appointed editor of *Cornhill*, 244; compared with WMT, 188-9; early affection for Laura, 242-3; first aware of Julia Jackson, 188; first meets Thackeray sisters 184; Minny: engaged, 193 / health concerns, 210 / honeymoon, 202-3, 205-11 / transformed by her love, 197 / marries, 202
Stephen, Mary (née Cunningham), 187, 239, 244
Sterling family, 248

Sterling, Julia, 198
Story, Edith (later Edith Peruzzi), 109, 110, 222, 236-7, 268
Story, Emelyn Eldredge, 109, 213-4, 227, 231, 235, 236
Story, William Wetmore, 109, 123, 213-4, 224, 227, 231, 235, 236-7; at Oatlands Park, Walton-on-Thames, 213-4; at Palazzo Barberini (Rome), 235, 237; *Graffiti D'Italia*, 237
Sturgis, Julian, 127, 255-6
Sturgis, Howard, 266
Sturgis, Russell, 127, 173
Sumner, Charles, 228, 229
Symonds, John Addington, 153, 272
Synge, Henrietta (née Wainwright), 183

Tennyson, Alfred, 64, 70, 108, 133, 143, 157, 169, 185, 193, 240, 250, 252, 256, 269, 272; *Cornhill* contributor, 133; *Idylls of the King*, 252; 'The Lady of Shalott', 143; 'Tithonus', 133
Tennyson, Emily, 157, 244, 247, 250, 269
Tennyson, Hallam, 70, 246-7, 251-2, 254, 255-6, 258, 260
Tennyson, Lionel, 246-7, 251, 258, 260, 265-6, 268
Ternan, Ellen, 127-8
Thackerays (WMT and daughters), at Onslow Square, Brompton, 106, 111-2, 113, 147, 151; at Palace Green, Kensington, 143, 154 / performance of *The Wolves and the Lamb*, 150-1, 152-3 / sold after death of WMT, 169, 171; at Young Street, Kensington, 60-2, ch. 3, *passim*, 162-4, 167
Thackeray, Anne Isabella [Annie], (later Anne Thackeray Ritchie, eldest daughter of WMT), affection for Leslie Stephen, 234-5; amanuensis to WMT, 104-5; as narrator of family history, 34-6; bad behaviour as child, 54-5, 59-

60, 65; birth, 31; collected edition, 254; *Denis Duval*: her 'Note' in the *Cornhill*, 174-7; disorganised, 265; dreams and dreamlike states, 159-60, 165, 168, 169-70, 207, 269-70; earliest memories of WMT, 34-5; feelings of guilt, 160, 165, 167; Henley cottage, 201, 204, 208-9, 211, 212-13; impractical with money, 37, 264-5; jealously possessive of WMT, 65; journal, 142-3; loneliness, 251; memories of mother, 34-5; Minny: courted by Leslie, 188, 191, 193 / death, 270-4 / reaction to engagement, 193, 194-5, 199 / reaction to wedding, 202-4; model for WMT sketches, 68; neuralgia, 157; Parisian childhood, 49-55, 59-60; The Porch, Freshwater, 249-50; possible powers of clairvoyance and automatic writing, 109-10; refuses marriage proposals, 260-3; Richmond Ritchie: affection grows, 215, ch. 11, *passim*; scarlet fever, 110-11; uncertainties about her future, 118, 159-60; views about religion, 93-6; writing success, 253-4 WORKS 'Bluebeard's Keys', 237; *Bluebeard's Keys and Other Tales*, 255-6; *Chapters from Some Memoirs*, 244-5; 'How I Quitted Naples', 147; 'Little Scholars', 144-5; *Miss Angel*, 254, 256, 259, 265; *Mrs Dymond*, 245; *Old Kensington*, 162, 238-9, 240, 242, 247, 251, 253-4; *The Story of Elizabeth*, 96, 154, 191, 226; *To Esther and other Sketches*, 240; 'Toilers and Spinsters', 147-8; *The Village on the Cliff*, 92, 191, 193, 198, 199-200, 208, 223

Thackeray, Anny (younger daughter of Edward Thackeray and Amy Crowe), 189-91, 215, 240, 246, 248, 259

Thackeray, Augusta (later twice married, aunt of WMT), 8; death, 11

Thackeray, Charlotte (later Charlotte Ritchie, aunt of WMT), 23-4

Thackeray, Edward (later Colonel Sir Edward Thackeray, cousin of WMT), 115, 156-7, 158, 189-90, 240

Thackeray, Emily (later Emily Shakespear, aunt of WMT), 8

Thackeray, Harriet Marian [Minny], (later Harriet Marian Stephen, younger daughter of WMT); acting and love of theatre, 87, 152-3; amanuensis and copyist to WMT, 139, 151-2; American trip (1868): 215-33 / abolitionists, 218, 225-6 / illness, 215, 216, 221-4 / on America generally, 220-1, 223, 228/ opinion of Boston, 229-30 / opinion of New York, 218-20, 229-30 / racial stereotyping, 218-20, 230-1 / slavery, 226 / sympathy for Southern states, 213 / visits Mount Auburn Cemetery, Cambridge, Mass., 224; anxiety about Laura's progress, 245, 249, 250-1; appetite, 210, 223; birth, 37-8; character, 60, 87; childhood recalled by Annie, 54-5, 87; craves WMT's affection, 161; critical of George Eliot, 238; disadvantaged after Isabella's illness, 53; dry humour, 161-2; early jealousy of Annie, 83; female emancipation, 228; final illness and death, 269-70; grave in Kensal Green cemetery, 273-4; health concerns, 177, 210, 213, 215, 216, 221-4, 266; honeymoon trip to Alps, 205-11; jealousy of Sally Baxter, 101; Leslie Stephen: early relationship, 186-93 / engaged, 193, 198-200 / marries, 202-3; letter-writer, 205; love of animals, 87; model for WMT sketches, 68;

motherhood, 243-4; paints tiles for Southwell Gardens house, 248; Parisian childhood, 49-51, 53-5; pregnancies, 213, 241, 266; recalls visits with WMT, 205; Richmond Ritchie and Annie, 268; scarlet fever, 110-1; talent for design, 87, 228; views on marriage, 206; writes 'The Fox and the Cat", 153-4

Thackeray, Isabella (wife of WMT), 24-33, 34-48, 55-7, 58-9, 73, 102, 117, 124, 164, 273; alternative therapies, 44-8; attempts suicide, 41; general health before marriage, 27; mental health, 32-3, 37, 39-40; placed in care in London, 58-9; puerperal psychosis, 39-40; pregnancy, 31, 37; relationship with mother, 26-8, 42-3; relationship with WMT's mother, 30, 32-3, 39, 40; WMT wishes to marry, 25-9

Thackeray, Jane (daughter of WMT), 102, 274; birth, 31; death, 32-3

Thackeray, Louisa (wife of St John Thackeray), 202

Thackeray, Margie (later Margie Ritchie, elder daughter of Edward Thackeray and Amy Crowe), 189-91, 194, 203-4, 215, 240, 246, 248, 259

Thackeray, Richmond (father of WMT), career in East India Company, 8, 10; caricaturist, 3-4; character, 23; death, 11; Charlotte Judd, 8; Sarah Judd, 8; journal, 1-6; marriage, 8; remembered by ACS, 180, 182; voyage to Calcutta (1798) 1-6

Thackeray, St John (cousin of WMT), 202, 203

Thackeray, William (uncle of WMT), 1, 5-6

Thackeray, William Makepeace (paternal grandfather of WMT), 1-2

Thackeray, William Makepeace [WMT], American trips: 82, 84, 88-90, 97-102, 117, 118-9, 120-3 / earnings from lecturing, 97, 120 / flirtation with Sally Baxter, 100-1, 120-1 / general impressions, 97-8 / views on slavery, 98-100, 122; anti-Semitism, 230; 'Arthur Pendennis' as alter ego, 72; artistic ambitions and training in Paris, 21-3; avoidance of formal farewells, 12, 87-8; birth, 8-9; Charterhouse, 13; contemplates surgery for stricture, 129, 150, 162; copyrights, 173-4, 179-80; courtship of Isabella, 24-9; dangerously ill when writing *Pendennis*, 76-7; early journalism, 21, 25, 30, 32; early law training, 21; editorship of *Cornhill*, 125-6, 131-41; estate, 170; 'The Fat Contributor', 63; fears of inherited mental disease, 124; final illness and death, 162-7; funeral, 168; gambling, 16, 18; generosity, 155; governess appointments, 64, 66, 69-71, 79, 85, 103; Great Coram Street, 31-2; health, 36, 105-7, 108, 111, 117, 123, 129, 138, 149, 150, 162-3, 165; illustrations for *Pendennis*, 80-1; importance of his children to him, 101-2, 103; India, 8-12,, 189; inherits father's legacy, 21; Ireland, 41-3, 48, 52-3; Isabella Thackeray (wife), 29, ch. 2 *passim*; leaves India for schooling in England, 11-12; lecturer, 82, 84-5, 89, 97, 120, 125-6; marriage prospects of daughters, 121-2, 128, 147-8; marries, 29; memorial bust in Westminster Abbey, 178; 'Michael Angelo Titmarsh', 38, 72; Middle East trip, 55-7; objects to possible romantic attachment for Annie, 121-2; Paris, 17-18, 23-30, 43-8; *Punch*, 63; 1, relationship with

Jane Brookfield, 72-3, 76-9, 80, 83-4, 101; relationship with mother, 12, 25; relationship with mother-in-law, 27-8, 42-3, 48; relationship with George Smith, 130-41; religious beliefs, 92-6; resemblances to father, 23; schooling, 12-13; sexual experience, 17-18; special constable, 70; student journalism, 18; sympathy for mundane lives of schoolboys, 13; Trinity College, Cambridge, 16-18; unafraid of death, 125, 129; unsuccessful Parliamentary campaign, 126; unsympathetic to mother's illness, 123-4; view of Annie as a writer, 122, 144; view of medical practitioners, 77; visits Weimar (1830), 18-21; Young Street, Kensington, 60-2, ch. 3 *passim* WORKS *A Shabby Genteel Story*, 32; *The Book of Snobs*, 63; 'The Cane-bottomed Chair' (ballad), 164; *Catherine*, 32; *Denis Duval*, 160, 162, 174-7; *Dr Birch and his Young Friends*, 273; *The English Humourists*, 82; *Esmond*, 58, 84, 85, 87-8, 89-90, 100, 127, 128; *The Four Georges*, 111, 118, 123-4, 125-6, 128, 136; *Irish Sketch Book*, 40, 48, 52-3; *The Kickelburys on the Rhine*, 80, 84; *Lovel the Widower*, 135, 136 151; *The Newcomes*, 13, 84, 91, 103-4, 110, 111, 113, 117-8, 126, 252; *Notes of a Journey from Cornhill to Grand Cairo*, 55; *Our Street*, 70, 164; *Paris Sketch Book*, 30, 38; *Pendennis*, 16, 60, 68, 72-7, 80-1, 112, 127, 244; *Philip*, 29, 77, 111, 127, 133, 136-9, 147, 149-50, 152, 155; *The Rose and the Ring*, 109, 110, 113; *Roundabout Papers*: 111, 135 / 'On a Lazy Idle Boy', 135 / 'On Screens in Dining Rooms', 145 / 'On Ribbons', 137, 152 / 'On Some Late Great Victories', 136; *The Second Funeral of Napoleon*, 45; *Vanity Fair*, 60, 63, 65, 66-9, 70, 72, 73, 146, 164; *The Virginians*, 84, 98, 111, 126-7, 129, 132, 143, 145; *The Wolves and the Lamb*, 150-1, 152-3; *The Yellowplush Papers*, 32, 65

Thompson, Dr Henry, 129, 162
Ticknor, Mrs, recalls WMT in America, 224, 227
Tintoretto, 258
Titmarsh, Michael Angelo (WMT alias), 38, 72
Town Talk, 128
Trollope, Anthony, 84, 168, 272; *Cornhill* contributor, 133; *Framley Parsonage*, 133, 139
Trulock, Alice (governess), 79, 85
Tupper, Martin, 13

Venables, George, 13
Vulpius, Christiane (mistress and later wife of Goethe), 20

Warren, William, 228
Washington, George, 232
Watts, George Frederic, 157, 235-6; portrait of Annie, 198
Webb, Amelia Richmond (paternal grandmother of WMT), 1-2, 3-4
Weston sisters (Anne, Caroline and Dora), 225-6

Williams-Freeman, William Peere, 158, 218, 220
Williams-Wynn, Charlotte, 195
Wister, Sarah Butler, 233
Wood, Mrs Henry, 255
Woolf, Virginia (née Virginia Stephen), 235, 257; *Freshwater*, 257

Yates, Edmund, 145, 165; Garrick dispute with WMT, 128, 129-30

Lightning Source UK Ltd.
Milton Keynes UK
07 October 2010

160908UK00001B/14/P